T0161267

Autobiography of Mark Twain

Autobiography of Mark Twain

Mark Twain

MINT EDITIONS

Autobiography of Mark Twain was first published in 1906.

This edition published by Mint Editions 2021.

ISBN 9781513282077 | E-ISBN 9781513287096

Published by Mint Editions®

 MINT
EDITIONS

minteditionbooks.com

Publishing Director: Jennifer Newens
Design & Production: Rachel Lopez Metzger
Project Manager: Micaela Clark
Typesetting: Westchester Publishing Services

Contents

Introduction

M ark Twain had been a celebrity for a good many years before he could be persuaded to regard himself as anything more than an accident, a news-writer to whom distinction had come as a matter of good fortune rather than as a tribute to genius. Sooner or later his "vein" would be worked out, when he would of necessity embark in other pursuits.

He had already owned a newspaper, and experimented more or less casually—and unfortunately—with a variety of other enterprises, when in 1884 he capitalized a publishing concern, primarily to produce his own works, but not without a view to the establishment of something more dependable than authorship. It probably never occurred to him during those years that he had achieved anything like a permanent place in literary history; if the idea of an autobiography had intruded itself now and then, it had not seriously troubled him.[1]

But a year later, when the publication by his firm of the Memoirs of Gen. U. S. Grant brought him into daily association with the dying conqueror, the thought came that the story of this episode might be worthy of preservation. It was not, for the present, at least, to be an autobiography, but no more than a few chapters, built around a great historic figure. General Grant's own difficulties in setting down his memories suggested prompt action. Mark Twain's former lecture agent, James Redpath, was visiting him at this time, and with a knowledge of shorthand became his amanuensis. The work they did together was considerable, covering in detail the story of the Grant publishing venture. Clemens may have planned other chapters of a personal sort, but, unaccustomed to dictation, he found the work tedious, with a result, as it seemed to him, unsatisfactory.

A number of important things happened to Mark Twain during the next dozen years, among them his business failure, which left him with a load of debt, dependent entirely upon authorship and the lecture platform for rehabilitation and support. The story of his splendid

---

1. Most of Mark Twain's work up to this time, Roughing It, Tom Sawyer, Life on the Mississippi, etc., had been of an autobiographical nature. Also, as early as 1870 he had jotted down an occasional reminiscent chapter, for possible publication, though apparently with no idea of a continuous narrative. Such of these chapters as have survived are included in Vol. I of the present work.—A. B. P.

victory, the payment to the last dollar of his indebtedness, has been widely told. He was in Vienna when he completed this triumph, and, whatever he had been before, he was now unquestionably a world figure with a recognized place in history. Realization of this may have prompted him to begin, during those busy Vienna winters (1897 to 1899), something in the nature of an autobiography, recollections of his Missouri childhood, a picture as primitive and far removed from to-day as anything of the Colonial period. These chapters were handwritten, his memory was fresh and eager, and in none of his work is there greater charm.

As he proceeded he did not confine himself to his earlier years, but traveled back and forth, setting down whatever was in his mind at the moment. He worked incidentally at this record for two or three years, eventually laying it aside for more immediate things. Five years later, in Florence, where he had taken Mrs. Clemens for her health, he again applied himself to what he now definitely termed his "Autobiography." As in that earlier day, he dictated, and this time found it quite to his liking. He completed some random memories of more or less importance, and might have carried the work further but for his wife's rapidly failing health. Her death and his return to America followed, and there was an interval of another two years before the autobiographical chapters were again resumed.

It was in January, 1906, that the present writer became associated with Mark Twain as his biographer. Elsewhere I have told of that arrangement and may omit most of the story here. It had been agreed that I should bring a stenographer, to whom he would dictate notes for my use, but a subsequent inspiration prompted him to suggest that he might in this way continue his autobiography, from which I would be at liberty to draw material for my own undertaking. We began with this understanding, and during two hours of the forenoon, on several days of each week, he talked pretty steadily to a select audience of two, wandering up and down the years as inclination led him, relating in his inimitable way incidents, episodes, conclusions, whatever the moment presented to his fancy.

It was his custom to stay in bed until noon, and he remained there during most of the earlier dictations, clad in a handsome dressing-gown, propped against great snowy pillows. He loved this loose luxury and ease and found it conducive to thought. On a little table beside him, where lay his cigars, papers, pipes, and various knickknacks, shone a reading lamp, making more brilliant his rich coloring and the gleam of his shining hair. There was daylight, too, but it was north light and the winter days were dull, the walls of the room a deep, unreflecting red. His bed was a vast carved antique affair, its outlines blending into the luxuriant background. The whole, focusing to the striking central figure, made a picture of classic value.

His talk was absorbingly interesting—it never failed to be that, even when it left something to be desired as history. Mark Twain's memory had become capricious and his vivid imagination did not always supply his story with details of crystal accuracy. But always it was a delightful story, amusing, tragic, or instructive, and it was likely to be one of these things at one instant and another at the next. Often he did not know until the moment of beginning what was to be his subject for the day; then he was likely to go drifting among his memories in a quite irresponsible fashion, the fashion of table conversation, as he said, the methodless method of the human mind. He had concluded that this was the proper way to write autobiography, or, as he best conveys it in his own introductory note:

Start at no particular time of your life; wander at your free will all over your life; talk only about the things which interest you for the moment; drop it the moment its interest threatens to pale, and turn your talk upon the new and more interesting thing that has intruded itself into your mind meantime.

Certainly there is something to be said in favor of his plan, and I often thought it the best plan for his kind of autobiography, which was really not autobiography at all, in the meaning generally conveyed by that term, but a series of entertaining stories and opinions—dinner-table talks, in fact, such as he had always delivered in his own home and elsewhere, and with about the same latitude and elaboration.

I do not wish to convey that his narrative is in any sense a mere fairy tale. Many of the chapters, especially the earlier ones, are vividly true in their presentation; the things he told of Mrs. Clemens and Susy are marvelously and beautifully true in spirit and aspect, and the story as a whole is amazingly faithful in the character picture it presents of the man himself. It was only when he relied upon his memory for details of general history, or when his imagination responded to old prejudice, or when life-long habit prompted a "good story" that he went wandering into fields of elaboration and gathered there such flowers and thorns as his fancy or feelings seemed to require. Mark Twain's soul was built of the very fabric of truth, so far as moral intent was concerned, but memory often betrayed him, even when he tried most to be accurate. He realized this himself, and once said, plaintively:

"When I was younger I could remember anything, whether it happened or not; but I am getting old and soon I shall remember only the latter."

And at another time, paraphrasing Josh Billings:

"It isn't so astonishing the things that I can remember, as the number of things I can remember that aren't so."

Perhaps it is proper to assure the reader that positive mistakes of date and occurrence have been corrected, while, for the rest, the matter of mere detail, is of less importance than that the charm of the telling should remain undisturbed.

Our work, begun in the New York house at 21 Fifth Avenue, continued with considerable regularity during a period of about two years, and intermittently during another two. When the first spring came it was transferred to the Upton House, on the slopes of Monadnock, near Dublin, New Hampshire, a perfect setting for the dictations. He no longer remained in bed, but, clad in creamy-white flannels and loose morocco slippers, bareheaded, he paced up and down the long veranda against a background of far-lying forest and distant hill. As I think of that time, now, I can still hear the ceaseless slippered, shuffling walk, and see the white figure, with its rocking, rolling movement, that preternaturally beautiful landscape behind it, and hear his deliberate speech—always deliberate except at rare intervals; always impressive, whatever the subject might be. In September we returned to the New York house and the work was continued there, that winter and the next. It reached its conclusion at Stormfield, the new home which he had built at Redding, Connecticut, and it was here that he died, April 21, 1910.

In the beginning it was Mark Twain's frequently expressed command that the "Autobiography" was not to be published until he had been dead at least a hundred years. But as the months passed he modified this idea, and himself selected a number of chapters for use in the North American Review. Discussing the matter later, he expressed a willingness that any portions of the work not dealing too savagely with living persons or their immediate descendants should be published sooner, either serially or in book form.

The manuscript in time became very large and very inclusive. He even incorporated in it articles and stories which he had written and laid aside, among them "Captain Stormfield's Visit to Heaven." "Is Shakespeare Dead?" was originally a part of the "Autobiography," but he published it separately in a small volume. "The Death of Jean," written (not dictated) immediately following that tragic event, was to be the closing chapter, and such in time it will become. He wished, however, that it should have separate publication and it is for the present included in another volume. It was his last complete writing of any sort, and in all his work from beginning to end there is nothing more perfect—nothing more beautiful.

Albert Bigelow Paine

Preface

As from the Grave

In this Autobiography I shall keep in mind the fact that I am speaking from the grave. I am literally speaking from the grave, because I shall be dead when the book issues from the press.

I speak from the grave rather than with my living tongue, for a good reason: I can speak thence freely. When a man is writing a book dealing with the privacies of his life—a book which is to be read while he is still alive—he shrinks from speaking his whole frank mind; all his attempts to do it fail, he recognizes that he is trying to do a thing which is wholly impossible to a human being. The frankest and freest and privatest product of the human mind and heart is a love letter; the writer gets his limitless freedom of statement and expression from his sense that no stranger is going to see what he is writing. Sometimes there is a breach-of-promise case by and by; and when he sees his letter in print it makes him cruelly uncomfortable and he perceives that he never would have unbosomed himself to that large and honest degree if he had known that he was writing for the public. He cannot find anything in the letter that was not true, honest, and respect-worthy; but no matter, he would have been very much more reserved if he had known he was writing for print.

It has seemed to me that I could be as frank and free and unembarrassed as a love letter if I knew that what I was writing would be exposed to no eye until I was dead, and unaware, and indifferent.

Mark Twain

EARLY FRAGMENTS

1870–1877

Note.—The various divisions and chapters of this work, in
accordance with the author's wish, are arranged in the order in
which they were written, regardless of the chronology of events.

I will construct a text:

What a wee little part of a person's life are his acts and his words! His
real life is led in his head, and is known to none but himself. All day long,
and every day, the mill of his brain is grinding, and his thoughts, not
those other things, are his history. His acts and his words are merely
the visible, thin crust of his world, with its scattered snow summits and
its vacant wastes of water—and they are so trifling a part of his bulk! a
mere skin enveloping it. The mass of him is hidden—it and its volcanic
fires that toss and boil, and never rest, night nor day. These are his life,
and they are not written, and cannot be written. Every day would make
a whole book of eighty thousand words—three hundred and sixty-five
books a year. Biographies are but the clothes and buttons of the man—
the biography of the man himself cannot be written.

M. T.

VOLUME 1

The Tennessee Land[1]

The monster tract of land which our family own in Tennessee was purchased by my father a little over forty years ago. He bought the enormous area of seventy-five thousand acres at one purchase. The entire lot must have cost him somewhere in the neighborhood of four hundred dollars. That was a good deal of money to pass over at one payment in those days—at least it was considered so away up there in the pineries and the "Knobs" of the Cumberland Mountains of Fentress County, East Tennessee. When my father paid down that great sum, and turned and stood in the courthouse door of Jamestown, and looked abroad over his vast possessions, he said, "Whatever befalls me, my heirs are secure; I shall not live to see these acres turn to silver and gold, but my children will." Thus with the very kindest intentions in the world toward us, he laid the heavy curse of prospective wealth upon our shoulders. He went to his grave in the full belief that he had done us a kindness. It was a woeful mistake, but, fortunately, he never knew it.

He further said: "Iron ore is abundant in this tract, and there are other minerals; there are thousands of acres of the finest yellow-pine timber in America, and it can be rafted down Obeds River to the Cumberland, down the Cumberland to the Ohio, down the Ohio to the Mississippi, and down the Mississippi to any community that wants it. There is no end to the tar, pitch, and turpentine which these vast pineries will yield. This is a natural wine district, too; there are no vines elsewhere in America, cultivated or otherwise, that yield such grapes as grow wild here. There are grazing lands, corn lands, wheat lands, potato lands, there are all species of timber—there is everything in and on this great tract of land that can make land valuable. The United States contain fourteen millions of inhabitants; the population has increased eleven millions in forty years, and will henceforth increase faster than ever; my children will see the day that immigration will push its way to Fentress County, Tennessee, and then, with 75,000 acres of excellent land in their hands, they will become fabulously wealthy."

---

1. The Tennessee Land is an important feature in a novel by Mark Twain and Charles Dudley Warner, The Gilded Age.

Everything my father said about the capabilities of the land was perfectly true—and he could have added, with like truth, that there were inexhaustible mines of coal on the land, but the chances are that he knew very little about the article, for the innocent Tennesseeans were not accustomed to digging in the earth for their fuel. And my father might have added to the list of eligibilities, that the land was only a hundred miles from Knoxville, and right where some future line of railway leading south from Cincinnati could not help but pass through it. But he never had seen a railway, and it is barely possible that he had not even heard of such a thing. Curious as it may seem, as late as eight years ago there were people living close to Jamestown who never had heard of a railroad and could not be brought to believe in steamboats. They do not vote for Jackson in Fentress County; they vote for Washington.

My eldest brother was four or five years old when the great purchase was made, and my eldest sister was an infant in arms. The rest of us—and we formed the great bulk of the family—came afterward, and were born along from time to time during the next ten years. Four years after the purchase came the great financial crash of '34, and in that storm my father's fortunes were wrecked. From being honored and envied as the most opulent citizen of Fentress County—for outside of his great landed possessions he was considered to be worth not less than three thousand five hundred dollars—he suddenly woke up and found himself reduced to less than one-fourth of that amount. He was a proud man, a silent, austere man, and not a person likely to abide among the scenes of his vanished grandeur and be the target for public commiseration. He gathered together his household and journeyed many tedious days through wilderness solitudes, toward what was then the "Far West," and at last pitched his tent in the little town of Florida, Monroe County, Missouri. He "kept store" there several years, but had no luck, except that I was born to him. He presently removed to Hannibal, and prospered somewhat; rose to the dignity of justice of the peace and had been elected to the clerkship of the Surrogate Court, when the summons came which no man may disregard. He had been doing tolerably well, for that age of the world, during the first years of his residence in Hannibal, but ill fortune tripped him once more. He did the friendly office of "going security" for Ira—, and Ira walked off and deliberately took the benefit of the new bankrupt law—a deed which enabled him to live easily and comfortably along till death called for him, but a deed which ruined my father, sent him poor to his grave, and condemned his heirs to a long and discouraging struggle with the world for a livelihood. But my father would brighten up and gather heart, even upon his death-bed, when he thought of the Tennessee land. He said that it would soon make us all rich and happy. And so believing, he died.

We straightway turned our waiting eyes upon Tennessee. Through all our wanderings and all our ups and downs for thirty years they have still gazed thitherward, over intervening continents and seas, and at this very day they are yet looking toward the same fixed point, with the hope of old habit and a faith that rises and falls, but never dies.

After my father's death we reorganized the domestic establishment, but on a temporary basis, intending to arrange it permanently after the land was sold. My brother borrowed five hundred dollars and bought a worthless weekly newspaper, believing, as we all did, that it was not worth while to go at anything in serious earnest until the land was disposed of and we could embark intelligently in something. We rented a large house to live in, at first, but we were disappointed in a sale we had expected to make (the man wanted only a part of the land and we talked it over and decided to sell all or none) and we were obliged to move to a less expensive one.

Written in 1877

Early Years in Florida, Missouri

I was born the 30th of November, 1835, in the almost invisible village of Florida, Monroe County, Missouri. I suppose Florida had less than three hundred inhabitants. It had two streets, each a couple of hundred yards long; the rest of the avenues mere lanes, with rail fences and cornfields on either side. Both the streets and the lanes were paved with the same material—tough black mud in wet times, deep dust in dry.

Most of the houses were of logs—all of them, indeed, except three or four; these latter were frame ones. There were none of brick, and none of stone. There was a log church, with a puncheon floor and slab benches. A puncheon floor is made of logs whose upper surfaces have been chipped flat with the adz. The cracks between the logs were not filled; there was no carpet; consequently, if you dropped anything smaller than a peach, it was likely to go through. The church was perched upon short sections of logs, which elevated it two or three feet from the ground. Hogs slept under there, and whenever the dogs got after them during services, the minister had to wait till the disturbance was over. In winter there was always a refreshing breeze up through the puncheon floor; in summer there were fleas enough for all.

A slab bench is made of the outside cut of a saw-log, with the bark side down; it is supported on four sticks driven into auger holes at the ends; it has no back and no cushions. The church was twilighted with yellow tallow candles in tin sconces hung against the walls. Week days, the church was a schoolhouse.

There were two stores in the village. My uncle, John A. Quarles, was proprietor of one of them. It was a very small establishment, with a few rolls of "bit" calicoes on half a dozen shelves; a few barrels of salt mackerel, coffee, and New Orleans sugar behind the counter; stacks of brooms, shovels, axes, hoes, rakes, and such things here and there; a lot of cheap hats, bonnets, and tinware strung on strings and suspended from the walls; and at the other end of the room was another counter with bags of shot on it, a cheese or two, and a keg of powder; in front of it a row of nail kegs and a few pigs of lead, and behind it a barrel or two of New Orleans molasses and native corn whisky on tap. If a boy bought five or ten cents' worth of anything, he was entitled to half a handful of sugar from the barrel; if a woman bought a few yards of calico she was entitled to a spool of thread in addition to the usual gratis "trimmin's"; if a man bought a trifle, he was at liberty to draw and swallow as big a drink of whisky as he wanted.

Everything was cheap: apples, peaches, sweet potatoes, Irish potatoes, and corn, ten cents a bushel; chickens, ten cents apiece; butter, six cents a pound; eggs, three cents a dozen; coffee and sugar, five cents a pound; whisky, ten cents a gallon. I do not know how prices are out there in interior Missouri now, but I know what they are here in Hartford, Connecticut. To wit: apples, three dollars a bushel; peaches, five dollars; Irish potatoes (choice Bermudas), five dollars; chickens, a dollar to a dollar and a half apiece, according to weight; butter, forty-five to sixty cents a pound; eggs, fifty to sixty cents a dozen; coffee, forty-five cents a pound; native whisky, four or five dollars a gallon, I believe, but I can only be certain concerning the sort which I use myself, which is Scotch and costs ten dollars a gallon when you take two gallons—more when you take less.

Thirty to forty years ago, out yonder in Missouri, the ordinary cigar cost thirty cents a hundred, but most people did not try to afford them, since smoking a pipe cost nothing in that tobacco-growing country. Connecticut is also given up to tobacco raising, today, yet we pay ten dollars a hundred for Connecticut cigars and fifteen to twenty-five dollars a hundred for the imported article.

At first my father owned slaves, but by and by he sold them and hired others by the year from the farmers. For a girl of fifteen he paid twelve dollars a year and gave her two linsey-wolsey frocks and a pair of "stogy" shoes—cost, a modification of nothing; for a negro woman of twenty-five, as general house servant, he paid twenty-five dollars a year and gave her shoes and the aforementioned linsey-wolsey frocks; for a strong negro woman of forty, as cook, washer, etc., he paid forty dollars a year and the customary two suits of clothes; and for an able-bodied man he paid from seventy-five to a hundred dollars a year and gave him two suits of jeans and two pairs of "stogy" shoes—an outfit that cost about three dollars. But times have changed. We pay our German nursemaid $155 a year; Irish housemaid, $150; Irish laundress, $150; negro woman, a cook, $240; young negro man, to wait on door and table, $360; Irish coachman, $600 a year, with gas, hot and cold water, and dwelling consisting of parlor, kitchen, and two bedrooms, connected with the stable, free.[1]

---

1. These prices of 1877 are as interesting to-day as those of forty years earlier.

THE GRANT DICTATIONS

——1885——

The Chicago G. A. R. Festival

The first time I ever saw General Grant was in the fall or winter of 1866 at one of the receptions at Washington, when he was general of the army. I merely saw and shook hands with him along with the crowd, but had no conversation. It was there, also, that I first saw General Sheridan.

I next saw General Grant during his first term as President. Senator Bill Stewart, of Nevada, proposed to take me in and see the President. We found him in his working costume, with an old, short, linen duster on, and it was well spattered with ink. I had acquired some trifle of notoriety through some letters which I had written, in the New York Tribune, during my trip round about the world in the Quaker City expedition. I shook hands, and then there was a pause and silence. I couldn't think of anything to say. So I merely looked into the general's grim, immovable countenance a moment or two, in silence, and then I said: "Mr. President, I am embarrassed. Are you?" He smiled a smile which would have done no discredit to a cast-iron image, and I got away under the smoke of my volley.

I did not see him again for some ten years. In the meantime I had become very thoroughly notorious.

Then, in 1879, the general had just returned from his journey through the European and Asiatic world, and his progress from San Francisco eastward had been one continuous ovation; and now he was to be feasted in Chicago by the veterans of the Army of the Tennessee—the first army over which he had had command. The preparations for this occasion were in keeping with the importance of it. The toast committee telegraphed me and asked me if I would be present and respond at the grand banquet to the toast to the ladies. I telegraphed back that the toast was worn out. Everything had been said about the ladies that could be said at a banquet, but there was one class of the community that had always been overlooked upon such occasions and if they would allow me I would take that class for a toast—The Babies. They were willing, so I prepared my toast and went out to Chicago.

There was to be a prodigious procession. General Grant was to review it from a rostrum which had been built out for the purpose from the second-story window of the Palmer House. The rostrum was carpeted and otherwise glorified with flags and so on.

The best place of all to see the procession was, of course, from this rostrum, so I sauntered upon that rostrum, while as yet it was empty, in the hope that I might be permitted to sit there. It was rather a conspicuous place, since upon it the public gaze was fixed and there was a countless multitude below. Presently two gentlemen came upon that platform from the window of the hotel and stepped forward to the front. A prodigious shout went up from the vast multitude below, and I recognized in one of these two gentlemen General Grant; the other was Carter Harrison, the Mayor of Chicago, with whom I was acquainted. He saw me, stepped over to me, and said wouldn't I like to be introduced to the general? I said I should. So he walked over with me and said, "General, let me introduce Mr. Clemens." We shook hands. There was the usual momentary pause, and then the general said: "I am not embarrassed. Are you?"

It showed that he had a good memory for trifles as well as for serious things.

That banquet was by all odds the most notable one I was ever present at. There were six hundred persons present, mainly veterans of the Army of the Tennessee, and that in itself would have made it a most notable occasion of the kind in my experience, but there were other things which contributed. General Sherman, and in fact nearly all of the surviving great generals of the war, sat in a body on a dais round about General Grant.

The speakers were of a rare celebrity and ability.

That night I heard for the first time a slang expression which had already come into considerable vogue, but I had not myself heard it before.

When the speaking began about ten o'clock, I left my place at the table and went away over to the front side of the great dining room, where I could take in the whole spectacle at one glance. Among others, Colonel Vilas was to respond to a toast, and also Colonel Ingersoll, the silver-tongued infidel, who had begun life in Illinois and was exceedingly popular there. Vilas was from Wisconsin and was very famous as an orator. He had prepared himself superbly for this occasion.

He was about the first speaker on the list of fifteen toasts, and Bob Ingersoll was the ninth.

I had taken a position upon the steps in front of the brass band, which lifted me up and gave me a good general view. Presently I noticed, leaning against the wall near me, a simple-looking young man wearing the uniform of a private and the badge of the Army of the Tennessee. He seemed to be nervous and ill at ease about something; presently, while the second speaker was talking, this young man said, "Do you know Colonel Vilas?" I said I had been introduced to him. He sat silent awhile and then said, "They say he is hell when he gets started!"

I said: "In what way? What do you mean?"

"Speaking! Speaking! They say he is lightning!"

"Yes," I said, "I have heard that he is a great speaker."

The young man shifted about uneasily for a while, and then he said, "Do you reckon he can get away with Bob Ingersoll?"

I said, "I don't know."

Another pause. Occasionally he and I would join in the applause when a speaker was on his legs, but this young man seemed to applaud unconsciously.

Presently he said, "Here, in Illinois, we think there can't nobody get away with Bob Ingersoll."

I said, "Is that so?"

He said, "Yes; we don't think anybody can lay over Bob Ingersoll." Then he added sadly, "But they do say that Vilas is pretty nearly hell."

At last Vilas rose to speak, and this young man pulled himself together and put on all his anxiety. Vilas began to warm up and the people began to applaud. He delivered himself of one especially fine passage and there was a general shout: "Get up on the table! Get up on the table! Stand up on the table! We can't see you!" So a lot of men standing there picked Vilas up and stood him on the table in full view of the whole great audience, and he went on with his speech. The young man applauded with the rest, and I could hear the young fellow mutter without being able to make out what he said. But presently, when Vilas thundered out something especially fine, there was a tremendous outburst from the whole house, and then this young man said, in a sort of despairing way:

"It ain't no use. Bob can't climb up to that!"

During the next hour he held his position against the wall in a sort of dazed abstraction, apparently unconscious of place or anything else, and at last, when Ingersoll mounted the supper table, his worshiper merely straightened up to an attitude of attention, but without manifesting any hope.

Ingersoll, with his fair and fresh complexion, handsome figure, and graceful carriage, was beautiful to look at.

He was to respond to the toast of "The Volunteers," and his first sentence or two showed his quality. As his third sentence fell from his lips the house let go with a crash and my private looked pleased and for the first time hopeful, but he had been too much frightened to join in the applause. Presently, when Ingersoll came to the passage in which he said that these volunteers had shed their blood and periled their lives in order that a mother might own her own child, the language was so fine, whatever it was (for I have forgotten), and the delivery was so superb that the vast multitude rose as one man and stood on their feet, shouting, stamping, and filling all the place with such a waving of napkins that it was like a snowstorm. This prodigious outburst continued for a minute or two, Ingersoll standing and waiting. And now I happened to notice my private. He was stamping, clapping, shouting, gesticulating like a man who had gone truly mad. At last, when quiet was restored once more, he glanced up at me with the tears in his eyes and said:

"Egod! He didn't get left!"

MY OWN SPEECH WAS GRANTED the perilous distinction of the place of honor. It was the last speech on the list, an honor which no person, probably, has ever sought. It was not reached until two o'clock in the morning. But when I got on my feet I knew that there was at any rate one point in my favor: the text was bound to have the sympathy of nine-tenths of the men present, and of every woman, married or single, of the crowds of the sex who stood huddled in the various doorways.

I expected the speech to go off well—and it did.

In it I had a drive at General Sheridan's comparatively new twins and various other things calculated to make it go. There was only one thing in it that I had fears about, and that one thing stood where it could not be removed in case of disaster.

It was the last sentence in the speech.

I had been picturing the America of fifty years hence, with a population of two hundred million souls, and was saying that the future President, admiral, and so forth, of that great coming time were now lying in their various cradles, scattered abroad over the vast expanse of this country, and then said "and now in his cradle somewhere under the flag the future illustrious commander-in-chief of the American armies is so little burdened with his approaching grandeur and responsibilities as to be giving his whole strategic mind at this moment to trying to find some way to get his big toe into his mouth—something, meaning no disrespect to the illustrious guest of this evening, which he turned his entire attention to some fifty-six years ago—"

And here, as I had expected, the laughter ceased and a sort of shuddering silence took its place—for this was apparently carrying the matter too far.

I waited a moment or two to let this silence sink well home, then, turning toward the general, I added:

"And if the child is but the father of the man there are mighty few who will doubt that he succeeded."

Which relieved the house, for when they saw the general break up in good-sized pieces they followed suit with great enthusiasm.

Dictated in 1885

GRANT AND THE CHINESE

Early in 1884, or late in 1883, if my memory serves me, I called on General Grant with Yung Wing, late Chinese minister at Washington, to introduce Wing and let him lay before General Grant a proposition. Li Hung-Chang, one of the greatest and most progressive men in China since the death of Prince Kung, had been trying to persuade the imperial government to build a system of military railroads in China, and had so far succeeded in his persuasions that a majority of the government were willing to consider the matter—provided that money could be obtained for that purpose outside of China, this money to be raised upon the customs of the country and by bonding the railway, or in some such manner. Yung Wing believed that if General Grant would take charge of the matter here and create the syndicate, the money would be easily forthcoming. He also knew that General Grant was better and more favorably known in China than any other foreigner in the world, and was aware that if his name were associated with the enterprise—the syndicate—it would inspire the Chinese government and people and give them the greatest possible sense of security. We found the general cooped up in his room with a severe rheumatism, resulting from a fall on the ice which he had got some months before. He would not undertake a syndicate, because times were so hard here that people would be loath to invest money so far away; of course Yung Wing's proposal included a liberal compensation for General Grant for his trouble, but that was a thing that the general would not listen to for a moment. He said that easier times would come by and by, and that the money could then be raised, no doubt, and that he would enter into it cheerfully and with zeal and carry it through to the very best of his ability, but he must do it without compensation. In no case would he consent to take any money for it. Here, again, he manifested the very strongest interest in China, an interest which I had seen him evince on previous occasions. He said he had urged a system of railways on Li Hung-Chang when he was in China, and he now felt so sure that such a system would be a great salvation for the country, and also the beginning of the country's liberation from the Tartar rule and thralldom, that he would be quite willing at a favorable time to do everything he could toward carrying out that project, without other compensation than the pleasure he would derive from being useful to China.

This reminds me of one other circumstance.

About 1879 or 1880 the Chinese pupils in Hartford and other New England towns had been ordered home by the Chinese government. There were two parties in the Chinese government—one headed by Li Hung-Chang, the progressive party, which was striving to introduce Western arts and education into China; the other was opposed to all progressive measures. Li Hung-Chang and the progressive party kept the upper hand for some time, and during this period the government had sent one hundred or more of the country's choicest youth over here to be educated. But now the other party had got the upper hand and had ordered these young people home. At this time an old Chinaman named Quong, non-progressionist, was the chief China minister at Washington, and Yung Wing was his assistant. The order disbanding the schools was a great blow to Yung Wing, who had spent many years in working for their establishment. This order came upon him with the suddenness of a thunderclap. He did not know which way to turn.

First, he got a petition signed by the presidents of various American colleges, setting forth the great progress that the Chinese pupils had made and offering arguments to show why the pupils should be allowed to remain to finish their education. This paper was to be conveyed to the Chinese government through the minister at Peking. But Yung Wing felt the need of a more powerful voice in the matter, and General Grant occurred to him. He thought that if he could get General Grant's great name added to that petition, that alone would outweigh the signatures of a thousand college professors. So the Rev. Mr. Twichell and I went down to New York to see the general. I introduced Mr. Twichell, who had come with a careful speech for the occasion, in which he intended to load the general with information concerning the Chinese pupils and the Chinese question generally. But he never got the chance to deliver it. The general took the word out of his mouth and talked straight ahead, and easily revealed to Twichell the fact that the general was master of the whole matter and needed no information from anybody, and also the fact that he was brimful of interest in the matter. Now, as always, the general was not only ready to do what we asked of him, but a hundred times more. He said, yes, he would sign that paper, if desired, but he would do better than that: he would write a personal letter to Li Hung-Chang, and do it immediately. So Twichell and I went downstairs into the lobby of the Fifth Avenue Hotel, a crowd of waiting and anxious visitors sitting in the anteroom, and in the course of half an hour he sent for us again and put into our hands his letter to Li Hung-Chang, to be sent directly and without the intervention of the American minister, or anyone else. It was a clear, compact, and admirably written statement of the case of the Chinese pupils, with some equally clear arguments to show that the breaking up of the schools would be a mistake. We shipped the letter and prepared to wait a couple of months to see what the result would be.

But we had not to wait so long. The moment the general's letter reached China a telegram came back from the Chinese government, which was almost a copy, in detail, of General Grant's letter, and the cablegram ended with the peremptory command to old Minister Wong to continue the Chinese schools.

It was a marvelous exhibition of the influence of a private citizen of one country over the counsels of an Empire situated on the other side of the globe.

Such an influence could have been wielded by no other citizen in the world outside of that Empire; in fact, the policy of the imperial government had been reversed from Room 45, Fifth Avenue Hotel, New York, by a private citizen of the United States.

Dictated in 1885

A Call With W. D. Howells on General Grant

Howells wrote me that his old father, who was well along in the seventies, was in great distress about his poor little consulate up in Quebec. Somebody, not being satisfied with the degree of poverty already conferred upon him by a thoughtful and beneficent Providence, was anxious to add to it by acquiring the Quebec consulate. So Howells thought if we could get General Grant to say a word to President Arthur it might have the effect of stopping this effort to oust old Mr. Howells from his position. Therefore, at my suggestion Howells came down, and we went to New York to lay the matter before the general. We found him at No. 2 Wall Street, in the principal office of Grant & Ward, brokers.

I stated the case and asked him if he wouldn't write a word on a card which Howells could carry to Washington and hand to the President.

But, as usual, General Grant was his natural self—that is to say, ready and also determined to do a great deal more for you than you could possibly have the effrontery to ask him to do. Apparently he never meets anybody halfway; he comes nine-tenths of the way himself voluntarily. "No," he said, he would do better than that, and cheerfully; he was going to Washington in a couple of days to dine with the President and he would speak to him and make it a personal matter. Now, as General Grant not only never forgets a promise, but never even the shadow of a promise, he did as he said he would do, and within a week came a letter from the Secretary of State, Mr. Frelinghuysen, to say that in no case would old Mr. Howells be disturbed. And he wasn't. He resigned a couple of years later.

But to go back to the interview with General Grant, he was in a humor to talk—in fact, he was always in a humor to talk when no strangers were present—and he resisted all our efforts to leave him.

He forced us to stay and take luncheon in a private room and continued to talk all the time. (It was bacon and beans. Nevertheless, "How he sits and towers"—Howells, quoting from Dante.)

He remembered "Squibob" Derby at West Point very well. He said that Derby was forever drawing caricatures of the professors and playing jokes of all kinds on everybody. He also told of one thing, which I had heard before but which I have never seen in print. At West Point, the professor was instructing and questioning a class concerning certain particulars of a possible siege, and he said this, as nearly as I can remember. I cannot quote General Grant's words:

Given: that a thousand men are besieging a fortress whose equipment of men, provisions, etc., are so and so—it is a military axiom that at the end of forty-five days the fort will surrender. Now, young men, if any of you were in command of such a fortress, how would you proceed?

Derby held up his hand in token that he had an answer for that question. He said, "I would march out, let the enemy in, and at the end of forty-five days I would change places with him."

I TRIED VERY HARD TO get General Grant to write his personal memoirs for publication, but he would not listen to the suggestion. His inborn diffidence made him shrink from voluntarily coming forward before the public and placing himself under criticism as an author. He had no confidence in his ability to write well, whereas everybody else in the world, excepting himself, is aware that he possesses an admirable literary gift and style. He was also sure that the book would have no sale, and of course that would be a humiliation, too. He instanced the fact that General Badeau's military history of General Grant had had but a trifling sale, and that John Russell Young's account of General Grant's trip around the globe had hardly any sale at all. But I said that these were not instances in point; that what another man might tell about General Grant was nothing, while what General Grant should tell about himself, with his own pen, was a totally different thing. I said that the book would have an enormous sale; that it should be in two volumes, sold, in cash, at $3.50 apiece, and that the sale in two volumes would certainly reach half a million sets. I said that, from my experience, I could save him from making unwise contracts with publishers, and could also suggest the best plan of publication—the subscription plan— and find for him the best men in that line of business.

I had in my mind at that time the American Publishing Company, of Hartford, and, while I suspected that they had been swindling me for ten years, I was well aware that I could arrange the contract in such a way that they could not swindle General Grant. But the general said that he had no necessity for any addition to his income. I knew that he meant by that that his investments, through the firm in which his sons were partners, were paying him all the money he needed. So I was not able to persuade him to write a book. He said that some day he would make very full notes and leave them behind him; and then, if his children chose to make them into a book, that would answer.

Dictated in 1883

ABOUT GENERAL GRANT'S "MEMOIRS"

I want to set down somewhat of a history of General Grant's Memoirs.

By way of preface I will make a remark or two indirectly connected therewith.

During the Garfield campaign Grant threw the whole weight of his influence and endeavor toward the triumph of the Republican party. He made a progress through many of the states, chiefly the doubtful ones, and this progress was a daily and nightly ovation as long as it lasted. He was received everywhere by prodigious multitudes of enthusiastic people, and, to strain the facts a little, one might almost tell what part of the country the general was in, for the moment, by the red reflections on the sky caused by the torch processions and fireworks.

He was to visit Hartford, from Boston, and I was one of the committee sent to Boston to bring him down here. I was also appointed to introduce him to the Hartford people when the population and the soldiers should pass in review before him. On our way from Boston in the palace car I fell to talking with Grant's eldest son, Col. Fred Grant, whom I knew very well, and it gradually came out that the general, so far from being a rich man, as was commonly supposed, had not even income enough to enable him to live as respectably as a third-rate physician.

Colonel Grant told me that the general left the White House, at the end of his second term, a poor man, and I think he said he was in debt, but I am not positively sure (I know he was in debt $45,000, at the end of one of his terms). Friends had given the general a couple of dwelling houses, but he was not able to keep them or live in either of them. This was all so shameful and such a reproach to Congress that I proposed to take the general's straitened circumstances as my text in introducing him to the people of Hartford.

I knew that if this nation, which was rising up daily to do its chief citizen unparalleled honor, had it in its power, by its vote, to decide the matter, it would turn his poverty into immeasurable wealth in an instant. Therefore the reproach lay not with the people, but with their political representatives in Congress, and my speech could be no insult to the people.

I clove to my plan, and in introducing the general I referred to the dignities and emoluments lavished upon the Duke of Wellington by England and contrasted with that conduct our far finer and higher method toward the savior of our country—to wit, the simple carrying him in our hearts without burdening him with anything to live on.

In his reply the general, of course, said that this country had more than sufficiently rewarded him and that he was well satisfied.

He could not have said anything else, necessarily.

A few months later I could not have made such a speech, for by that time certain wealthy citizens had privately made up a purse of a quarter of a million dollars for the general, and had invested it in such a way that he could not be deprived of it either by his own want of wisdom or the rascality of other people.

Later still, the firm of Grant & Ward, brokers and stock dealers, was established at No. 2 Wall Street, New York City.

This firm consisted of General Grant's sons and a brisk young man by the name of Ferdinand Ward. The general was also, in some way, a partner, but did not take any active part in the business of the house.

In a little time the business had grown to such proportions that it was apparently not only profitable, but it was prodigiously so.

The truth was, however, that Ward was robbing all the Grants and everybody else that he could get his hands on, and the firm was not making a penny.

The general was unsuspicious and supposed that he was making a vast deal of money, whereas, indeed, he was simply losing such as he had, for Ward was getting it.

About the 5th of May, I think it was, 1884, the crash came and the several Grant families found themselves absolutely penniless.

Ward had even captured the interest due on the quarter of a million dollars of the Grant fund, which interest had fallen due only a day or two before the failure.

General Grant told me that that month, for the first time in his life, he had paid his domestic bills with checks. They came back upon his hands dishonored. He told me that Ward had spared no one connected with the Grant name, however remote—that he had taken all that the general could scrape together and $45,000 that the general had borrowed on his wife's dwelling house in New York; that he had taken $65,000, the sum for which Mrs. Grant had sold, recently, one of the houses which had been presented to the general; that he had taken $7,000, which some poverty-stricken nieces of his in the West had recently received by bequest, and which was all the money they had in the world—that, in a word, Ward had utterly stripped everybody connected with the Grant family.

It was necessary that something be immediately done toward getting bread.

The bill to restore to General Grant the title and emoluments of a full general in the army, on the retired list, had been lagging for a long time in Congress—in the characteristic, contemptible, and stingy congressional fashion. No relief was to be looked for from that source, mainly because Congress chose to avenge on General Grant the veto of the Fitz-John Porter bill by President Arthur.

The editors of the Century Magazine, some months before, conceived the excellent idea of getting the surviving heroes of the late Civil War, on both sides, to write out their personal reminiscences of the war and publish them, now, in the magazine. But the happy project had come to grief, for the reason that some of these heroes were quite willing to write out these things only under one condition, that they insisted was essential: they refused to write a line unless the leading actor of the war should also write.[1] All persuasions and arguments failed on General Grant; he would not write. So the scheme fell through.

Now, however, the complexion of things had changed and General Grant was without bread, not figuratively, but actually.

The Century people went to him once more, and now he assented eagerly. A great series of war articles was immediately advertised by the Century publishers.

I knew nothing of all this, although I had been a number of times to the general's house, to pass half an hour, talking and smoking a cigar.

However, I was reading one night, in Chickering Hall, early in November, 1884, and as my wife and I were leaving the building we stumbled over Mr. Gilder, the editor of the Century, and went home with him to a late supper at his house. We were there an hour or two, and in the course of the conversation Gilder said that General Grant had written three war articles for the Century and was going to write a fourth. I pricked up my ears.[2] Gilder went on to describe how eagerly General Grant had entertained the proposition to write when it had last been put to him, and how poor he evidently was, and how eager to make some trifle of bread-and-butter money, and how the handing him a check for five hundred dollars for the first article had manifestly gladdened his heart and lifted from it a mighty burden.

The thing which astounded me was that, admirable man as Gilder certainly is, and with a heart which is in the right place, it had never seemed to occur to him that to offer General Grant five hundred dollars

1. August, 1885. They deny this now, but I go bail I got that statement from Gilder himself.—S. L. C.
2. In a statement made somewhat later, Mr. Clemens said that he had first heard Gilder mention this fact as they were leaving Chickering Hall.

for a magazine article was not only the monumental injustice of the nineteenth century, but of all centuries. He ought to have known that if he had given General Grant a check for ten thousand dollars, the sum would still have been trivial; that if he had paid him twenty thousand dollars for a single article, the sum would still have been inadequate; that if he had paid him thirty thousand dollars for a single magazine war article, it still could not be called paid for; that if he had given him forty thousand dollars for a single magazine article, he would still be in General Grant's debt. Gilder went on to say that it had been impossible, months before, to get General Grant to write a single line, but that, now that he had once got started, it was going to be as impossible to stop him again; that, in fact, General Grant had set out deliberately to write his memoirs in full, and to publish them in book form.

I went straight to General Grant's house next morning and told him what I had heard. He said it was all true.

I said I had foreseen a fortune in such a book when I had tried, as early as 1881, to get him to write it; that the fortune was just as sure to fall now. I asked him who was to publish the book, and he said doubtless the Century Company.

I asked him if the contract had been drawn and signed.

He said it had been drawn in the rough, but not signed yet.

I said I had had a long and painful experience in book making and publishing, and that if there would be no impropriety in his showing me the rough contract, I believed I might be useful to him.

He said there was no objection whatever to my seeing the contract, since it had proceeded no further than a mere consideration of its details, without promises given or received on either side. He added that he supposed that the Century offer was fair and right and that he had been expecting to accept it and conclude the bargain or contract. He read the rough draft aloud, and I didn't know whether to cry or laugh.

Whenever a publisher in the "trade" thinks enough of the chances of an unknown author's book to print it and put it on the market, he is willing to risk paying the man 10-per-cent royalty, and that is what he does pay him. He can well venture that much of a royalty, but he cannot well venture any more. If that book shall sell 3,000 or 4,000 copies there is no loss on any ordinary book, and both parties have made something; but whenever the sale shall reach 10,000 copies the publisher is getting the lion's share of the profits and would continue to get the lion's share as long thereafter as the book should continue to sell.

When such a book is sure to sell 35,000 copies an author ought to get 15 per cent—that is to say, one-half of the net profit; when a book is sure to sell 80,000 or more, he ought to get 20-per-cent royalty—that is, two-thirds of the total profits.

Now, here was a book that was morally bound to sell several hundred thousand copies in the first year of its publication, and yet the Century people had had the hardihood to offer General Grant the very same 10-per-cent royalty which they would have offered to any unknown Comanche Indian whose book they had reason to believe might sell 3,000 or 4,000 or 5,000 copies.

If I had not been acquainted with the Century people I should have said that this was a deliberate attempt to take advantage of a man's ignorance and trusting nature to rob him; but I do know the Century people, and therefore I know that they had no such base intentions as these, but were simply making their offer out of their boundless resources of ignorance. They were anxious to do book publishing as well as magazine publishing, and had tried one book already, but, owing to their inexperience, had made a failure of it. So I suppose they were anxious, and had made an offer which in the general's instance commended itself as reasonable and safe, showing that they were lamentably ignorant and that they utterly failed to rise to the size of the occasion. This was sufficiently shown in the remark of the head of that firm to me a few months later, a remark which I shall refer to and quote in its proper place.

I told General Grant that the Century offer was simply absurd and should not be considered for an instant.

I forgot to mention that the rough draft made two propositions—one at 10-per-cent royalty, and the other the offer of half the profits on the book, after subtracting every sort of expense connected with it, including office rent, clerk hire, advertising, and everything else, a most complicated arrangement and one which no business-like author would accept in preference to a 10-per-cent royalty. They manifestly regarded 10-per-cent and half profits as the same thing—which shows that these innocent geese expected the book to sell only 12,000 or 15,000 copies.

I told the general that I could tell him exactly what he ought to receive; that, if he accepted a royalty, it ought to be 20 per cent on the retail price of the book, or, if he preferred the partnership policy, then he ought to have 70 per cent of the profits on each volume, over and above the mere cost of making that volume. I said that if he would place these terms before the Century people they would accept them, but if they were afraid to accept them he would simply need to offer them to any great publishing house in the country, and not one would decline them. If any should decline them, let me have the book. I was publishing my own book, under the business name of Charles L. Webster & Co., I being the company, and Webster being my business man, on a salary, with a one-tenth interest, and I had what I believed to be much the best equipped subscription establishment in the country.

I wanted the general's book, and I wanted it very much, but I had very little expectation of getting it. I supposed that he would lay these new propositions before the Century people, that they would accept immediately, and that there the matter would end; for the general evidently felt under great obligations to the Century people for saving him from the grip of poverty by paying him $1,500 for three magazine articles which were well worth $100,000, and he seemed wholly unable to free himself from this sense of obligation; whereas, to my mind, he ought rather to have considered the Century people under very high obligations to him, not only for making them a present of $100,000, but for procuring for them a great and desirable series of war articles from the other heroes of the war, which, according to Gilder, they could never have got their hands on if he had declined to write.

I now went away on a long Western tour on the platform, but Webster continued to call at the general's house and watch the progress of events.

Col. Fred Grant was strongly opposed to letting the Century people have the book, and was, at the same time, as strongly in favor of my having it.

The general's first magazine article had immediately added 50,000 names to their list of subscribers and thereby established the fact that the Century people would still have been the gainers if they had paid General Grant $50,000 for the articles—for the reason that they could expect to keep the most of these subscribers for several years, and, consequently, get a profit out of them in the end of $100,000 at least.

Besides this increased circulation, the number of the Century's advertising pages at once doubled, a huge addition to the magazine's cash income in itself—(an addition of $25,000 a month, as I estimate it from what I have paid them for one-fifth of a page for six months—$1,800).

The Century people had eventually added to the original check of $1,500 a check for a thousand dollars, after perceiving that they were going to make a fortune out of the first of the three articles.

This seemed a fine liberality to General Grant, who was the most simple-hearted of all men; but, to me, it seemed merely another exhibition of incomparable nonsense, as the added check ought to have been for $30,000 instead of $1,000. Col. Fred Grant looked upon the matter just as I did, and had determined to keep the book out of the Century people's hands if possible. This action merely confirmed and hardened him in his purpose.

While I was in the West, propositions from publishers came to General Grant daily, and these propositions had a common form—to wit: "only tell us what your best offer is and we stand ready to make a better one."

These things had their effect. The general began to perceive, from these various views, that he had narrowly escaped making a very bad bargain for his book; and now he began to incline toward me, for the reason, no doubt, that I had been the accidental cause of stopping that bad bargain.

He called in George W. Childs of Philadelphia and laid the whole matter before him and asked his advice. Mr. Childs said to me afterward that it was plain to be seen that the general, on the score of friendship, was so distinctly inclined toward me that the advice which would please him best would be advice to turn the book over to me.

He counseled the general to send competent people to examine into my capacity to properly publish the book and into the capacity of the other competitors for the book, and (this was done at my own suggestion—Fred Grant being present) if they found that my house was as well equipped in all ways as the others, that he give the book to me.

The general sent persons selected by a couple of great law firms (Clarence Seward's was one) to make examinations, and Col. Fred Grant made similar examinations for himself personally.

The verdict in these several cases was that my establishment was as competent to make a success of the book as was that of any of the firms competing.

The result was that the contract was drawn and the book was placed in my hands.

In the course of one of my business talks with General Grant he asked me if I felt sure I could sell 25,000 copies of his book, and he asked the question in such a way that I suspected that the Century people had intimated that that was about the number of the books that they thought ought to sell.[1]

I replied that the best way for a man to express an opinion in such a case was to put it in money—therefore, I would make this offer: if he would give me the book I would advance him the sum of $25,000 on each volume the moment the manuscript was placed in my hands, adding that I would draw the first check immediately. If I never got the $50,000 back again, out of the future copyrights due, I would never ask him to return any part of the money to me.

The suggestion seemed to distress him. He said he could not think of taking in advance any sum of money large or small which the publisher would not be absolutely sure of getting back again. Some time afterward, when the contract was being drawn and the question was whether it should be 20-percent royalty or 70 per cent of the profits, he inquired which of the two propositions would be the best all round. I sent Webster to tell him that the 20-per-cent royalty would be the best for him, for the reason that it was the surest, the simplest, the easiest to keep track of, and, better still, would pay him a trifle more, no doubt, than with the other plan.

He thought the matter over and then said in substance that by the 20-per-cent plan he would be sure to make, while the publisher might possibly lose; therefore, he would not have the royalty plan, but the 70-per-cent-profit plan, since, if there were profits, he could not then get them all, but the publisher would be sure to get 30 per cent of it.

This was just like General Grant. It was absolutely impossible for him to entertain for a moment any proposition which might prosper him at the risk of any other man.

After the contract had been drawn and signed, I remembered I had offered to advance the general some money and that he had said he might possibly need $10,000 before the book issued. The circumstance had been forgotten and was not in the contract, but I had the luck to remember it before leaving town; so I went back and told Col. Fred Grant to draw upon Webster for the $10,000 whenever it should be wanted.

---

1. This had occurred during their first interview.

That was the only thing forgotten in the contract, and it was now rectified and everything was smooth.

And now I come to a circumstance which I have never spoken of and which cannot be known for many years to come, for this paragraph must not be published until the mention of so private a matter cannot offend any living person.

The contract was drawn by the great law firm of Alexander & Green, on my part, and Clarence Seward, son of Mr. Lincoln's Secretary of State, on the part of General Grant.

Appended to the contract was a transfer of the book to General Grant's wife, and the transfer from her to my firm for the consideration of $1,000 in hand paid.

This was to prevent the general's creditors from seizing the proceeds of the book.

Webster had said, "Yes," when the sum named was a thousand dollars, and, after he had signed the contract and was leaving the law office, he mentioned, incidentally, that the thousand dollars was of course a mere formality in such a paper, and meant nothing. But Mr. Seward took him privately aside and said, "No, it means just what it says—for the general's family have not a penny in the house and they are waiting at this moment with lively anxiety for that small sum of money."

Webster was astonished. He drew a check at once and Mr. Seward gave it to a messenger boy and told him to take it swiftly—by the speediest route—to General Grant's house, and not let the grass grow under his feet.

It was a shameful thing that the man who had saved this country and its government from destruction should still be in a position where so small a sum—so trivial an amount—as $1,000 could be looked upon as a godsend. Everybody knew that the general was in reduced circumstances, but what a storm would have gone up all over the land if the people could have known that his poverty had reached such a point as this.

The newspapers all over the land had been lauding the princely generosity of the Century people in paying General Grant the goodly sum of $1,500 for three magazine articles, whereas, if they had paid him the amount which was his just due for them, he would still have been able to keep his carriage and not have been worrying about $1,000. Neither the newspapers nor the public were probably aware that fifty-five years earlier the publishers of an annual in London had offered little Tom Moore twice $1,500 for two articles and had told him to make them long or short and to write about whatever he pleased. The difference between the financial value of any article written by Tom Moore in his best day and a war article written by General Grant in these days was about as one to fifty.

To go back awhile. After being a month or two in the West, during the winter of 1884-85, I returned to the East, reaching New York about the 20th of February.

No agreement had at that time been reached as to the contract, but I called at General Grant's house simply to inquire after his health, for I had seen reports in the newspapers that he had been sick and confined to his house for some time.

The last time I had been at his house he told me that he had stopped smoking because of the trouble in his throat, which the physicians had said would be quickest cured in that way. But while I was in the West the newspapers had reported that this throat affection was believed to be in the nature of a cancer. However, on the morning of my arrival in New York the newspapers had reported that the physicians had said that the general was a great deal better than he had been and was getting along very comfortably. So, when I called at the house, I went up to the general's room and shook hands and said I was very glad he was so much better and so well along on the road to perfect health again.

He smiled and said, "If it were only true."

Of course I was both surprised and discomfited, and asked his physician, Doctor Douglas, if the general were in truth not progressing as well as I had supposed. He intimated that the reports were rather rose colored and that this affection was no doubt a cancer.

I am an excessive smoker, and I said to the general that some of the rest of us must take warning by his case, but Doctor Douglas spoke up and said that this result must not be attributed altogether to smoking. He said it was probable that it had its origin in excessive smoking; but that was not the certain reason of its manifesting itself at this time; that more than likely the real reason was the general's distress of mind and year-long depression of spirit, arising from the failure of the Grant & Ward firm.

This remark started the general at once to talking; and I found then and afterward that, when he did not care to talk about any other subject, he was always ready and willing to talk about that one.

He told what I have before related about the robberies perpetrated upon him and upon all the Grant connection, by this man Ward whom he had so thoroughly trusted, but he never uttered a phrase concerning Ward which an outraged adult might not have uttered concerning an offending child. He spoke as a man speaks who has been deeply wronged and humiliated and betrayed; but he never used a venomous expression or one of a vengeful nature.

As for myself, I was inwardly boiling all the time; I was scalping Ward, flaying him alive, breaking him on the wheel, pounding him to jelly, and cursing him with all the profanity known to the one language that I am acquainted with, and helping it out, in times of difficulty and distress, with odds and ends of profanity drawn from the two other languages of which I have a limited knowledge.

He told his story with deep feeling in his voice, but with no betrayal upon his countenance of what was going on in his heart. He could depend upon that countenance of his in all emergencies. It always stood by him. It never betrayed him.

(July 1st or 2d, at Mount McGregor, 1885, about three weeks before the general's death, Buck Grant and I sat talking an hour to each other across the general's lap, just to keep him company—he had only to listen. The news had just come that that Marine Bank man (Ward's pal—what was that scoundrel's name?) had been sent up for ten years. Buck Grant said the bitterest things about him he could frame his tongue to; I was about as bitter myself. The general listened for some time, then reached for his pad and pencil and wrote, "He was not as bad as the other"—meaning Ward. It was his only comment. Even his writing looked gentle.)

While he was talking, Colonel Grant said, "Father is letting you see that the Grant family are a pack of fools, Mr. Clemens!"

The general combated that statement. He said, in substance, that facts could be produced which would show that when Ward laid siege to a man, that man would turn out to be a fool, too—as much of a fool as any Grant; that all men were fools if the being successfully beguiled by Ward was proof, by itself, that the man was a fool. He began to present instances. He said (in effect) that nobody would call the president of the Erie Railroad a fool, yet Ward beguiled him to the extent of $800,000, robbed him of every cent of it. He mentioned another man who could not be called a fool; yet Ward had beguiled that man out of more than half a million dollars and had given him nothing in return for it. He instanced a man with a name something like Fisher, though that was not the name, whom he said nobody could call a fool; on the contrary a man who had made himself very rich by being sharper and smarter than other people and who always prided himself upon his smartness and upon the fact that he could not be fooled, he could not be deceived by anybody; but what did Ward do in his case? He fooled him into buying a portion of a mine belonging to ex-Senator Chaffee—a property which was not for sale, which Ward could produce no authority for selling—yet he got out of that man $300,000 in cash, without the passage of a single piece of paper or a line of writing to show that the sale had been made. This man came to the office of Grant & Ward every day for a good while, and talked with Ward about the prospects of that rich mine (and it was very rich), and these two would pass directly by Mr. Chaffee and go into the next room and talk. You would think that a man of his reputation for shrewdness would at some time or other have concluded to ask Mr. Chaffee a question or two; but, no, Ward had told this man that Chaffee did not want to be known in the transaction at all, that he must seem to be at Grant & Ward's office on other business, and that he must not venture to speak to Chaffee or the whole business would be spoiled.

There was a man who prided himself on being a smart business man, and yet Ward robbed him of $300,000 without giving him a scrap of anything to show that the transaction had taken place, and to-day that man is not among the prosecutors of Ward at all, for the reason, perhaps, that he would rather lose all of that money than to have the fact get out that he was deceived in so childish a way.

General Grant mentioned another man who was very wealthy, whom no one would venture to call a fool, either businesswise or otherwise, yet this man came into the office one day and said: "Ward, here is my check for $50,000. I have no use for it at present; I am going to make a flying trip to Europe. Turn it over for me; see what you can do with it." Some time afterward I was in the office when this gentleman returned from his trip and presented himself. He asked Ward if he had accomplished anything with that money? Ward said, "Just wait a moment," went to his books, turned over a page, mumbled to himself a few moments, drew a check for $250,000, handed it to this man with the air of a person who had really accomplished nothing worth talking of! The man stared at the check a moment, handed it back to Ward, and said, "That is plenty good enough for me; set that hen again," and he went out of the place. It was the last he ever saw of any of that money.

I had been discovering fools all along when the general was talking, but this instance brought me to my senses. I put myself in this fellow's place and confessed that if I had been in that fellow's clothes it was a hundred to one that I would have done the very thing that he had done, and I was thoroughly well aware that, at any rate, there was not a preacher or a widow in Christendom who would not have done it; for these people are always seeking investments that pay illegitimately large sums; and they never, or seldom, stop to inquire into the nature of the business.

When I was ready to go, Col. Fred Grant went downstairs with me, and stunned me by telling me, confidentially, that the physicians were trying to keep his father's real condition from him, but that in fact they considered him to be under sentence of death and that he would not be likely to live more than a fortnight or three weeks longer.

This was about the 21st of February, 1885.

After the 21st of February, General Grant busied himself, daily, as much as his strength would allow, in revising the manuscript of his book. It was read to him by Colonel Grant, very carefully, and he made the corrections as he went along. He was losing valuable time because only one-half or two-thirds of the second and last volume was as yet written. However, he was more anxious that what was written should be absolutely correct than that he should finish the book in an incorrect form, and then find himself unable to correct it. His memory was superb, and nearly any other man with such a memory would have been satisfied to trust it. Not so the general. No matter how sure he was of the fact or the date, he would never let it go until he had verified it with the official records. This constant and painstaking searching of the records cost a great deal of time, but it was not wasted. Everything stated as a fact in General Grant's book may be accepted with entire confidence as being thoroughly trustworthy.

Speaking of his memory, what a wonderful machine it was! He told me one day that he never made a report of the battles of the Wilderness until they were all over and he was back in Washington. Then he sat down and made a full report from memory, and, when it was finished, examined the reports of his subordinates, and found that he had made hardly an error. To be exact, he said he had made two errors.

The general lost some more time in one other way. Three Century articles had been written and paid for, but he had during the summer before promised to write a fourth one. He had written it in a rough draft, but it had remained unfinished.

The Century people had advertised these articles and were now fearful that the general would never be able to complete them. By this time news of the general's failing health had got abroad and the newspapers were full of reports about his perilous condition. The Century people called several times to get the fourth article, and this hurt and offended Col. Fred Grant, because he knew that they were aware, as was all the world, that his father was considered to be in a dying condition. Colonel Grant thought that they ought to show more consideration—more humanity. By fits and starts, the general worked at that article whenever his failing strength would permit him, and was determined to finish it, if possible, because his promise had been given and he would in no way depart from it while any slight possibility remained of fulfilling it. I asked if there was no contract or no understanding as to what was to be paid by the Century people for the article. He said there was not. "Then," I said, "charge them $20,000 for it. It is well worth it—worth double the money. Charge them this sum for it in its unfinished condition and let them have it, and tell them that it will be worth still more in case the general shall be able to complete it. This may modify their ardor somewhat and bring you a rest." He was not willing to put so large a price upon it, but thought that if he gave it to them he might require them to pay $5,000. It was plain that the modesty of the family in money matters was indestructible.

Just about this time I was talking to General Badeau there one day. when I saw a pile of typewriter manuscript on the table and picked up the first page and began to read it. I saw that it was an account of the siege of Vicksburg. I counted a page and there were about three hundred words on the page; 18,000 or 20,000 words altogether.

General Badeau said it was one of the three articles written by General Grant for the Century.

I said, "Then they have no sort of right to require the fourth article, for there is matter enough in this one to make two or three ordinary magazine articles." The copy of this and the other two articles were at this moment in the Century's safe; the fourth-article agreement was therefore most amply fulfilled already, without an additional article; yet the Century people considered that the contract would not be fulfilled without the fourth article, and so insisted upon having it. At the ordinary price paid me for Century articles, this Vicksbury article, if I had written it, would have been worth about $700. Therefore, the Century people had paid General Grant no more than they would have paid me; and this including the $1,000 gratuity which they had given him.

If the Century people knew anything at all, they knew that a single page of General Grant's manuscript was worth more than a hundred of mine. They were honest, honorable, and good-hearted people according to their lights, and if anybody could have made them see differently they would have rectified the wrong. But all the eloquence that I was able to pour out upon them, went for nothing, utterly nothing. They still thought that they had been quite generous to the general and were not able to see the matter in any other light.

AFTERWARD, AT MOUNT McGREGOR, THEY consented to give up half of the Vicksburg article; and they did; they gave up more than half of it—cut it from twenty-two galleys down to nine, and only the nine will appear in the magazine, and they added $2,500 to the $2,500 already paid. Those people could learn to be as fair and liberal as anybody if they had the right schooling.

Some time after the contract for General Grant's book was completed, I found that nothing but a verbal understanding existed between General Grant and the Century Company giving General Grant permission to use his Century articles in his book. There is a law of custom which gives an author the privilege of using his magazine articles in any way he pleases, after it shall have appeared in the magazine; and this law of custom is so well established that an author never expects to have any difficulty about getting a magazine copyright transferred to him, whenever he shall ask for it, with the purpose in view of putting the article in a book. But in the present case I was afraid that the Century Company might fall back upon their legal rights and ignore the law of custom, in which case we should be debarred from using General Grant's Century articles in his book—an awkward state of things, because he was now too sick a man to rewrite them. It was necessary that something should be done in this matter, and done at once.

Mr. Seward, General Grant's lawyer, was a good deal disturbed when he found that there was no writing. But I was not. I believed that the Century people could be relied upon to carry out any verbal agreement which they had made. The only thing I feared was that their idea of the verbal agreement, and General Grant's idea of it, might not coincide. So I went back to the general's house and got Col. Fred Grant to write down what he understood the verbal agreement to be, and this piece of writing he read to General Grant, who said it was correct, and then signed it with his own hand, a feeble and trembling signature, but recognizable as his.

Then I sent for Webster and our lawyer, and we three went to the Century office, where we found Roswell Smith (the head man of the company) and several of the editors. I stated my case plainly and simply and found that their understanding and General Grant's were identical; so the difficulty was at an end at once and we proceeded to draw a writing to cover the thing.

When the business was finished, or perhaps in the course of it, I made another interesting discovery.

I was already aware that the Century people were going to bring out all their war articles in book form, eventually, General Grant's among the number; but, as I knew what a small price had been paid to the general for his articles, I had a vague notion that he would receive a further payment for the use of them in their book—a remuneration which an author customarily receives, in our day, by another unwritten law of custom. But when I spoke of this, to my astonishment they told me that they had bought and paid for every one of these war articles with the distinct understanding that that first payment was the last. In confirmation of this amazing circumstance, they brought out a receipt which General Grant had signed, and therein it distinctly appeared that each $500 not only paid for the use of the article printed in the magazine, but also in the subsequent book!

One thing was quite clear to me: if we consider the value of those articles to that book, we must grant that the general was paid very much less than nothing at all for their issue in the magazine.

The Century people didn't blush, and, therefore, it is plain that they considered the transaction fair and legitimate; and I believe myself that they had no idea that they were doing an unfair thing. It was easily demonstrable that they were buying ten-dollar gold pieces from General Grant at twenty-five cents apiece, and I think it was as easily demonstrable that they did not know that there was anything unfair about it.

Roswell Smith said to me, with the glad air of a man who has stuck a nail in his foot, "I'm glad you've got the general's book, Mr. Clemens, and glad there was somebody with courage enough to take it, under the circumstances. What do you think the general wanted to require of me?"

"What?"

"He wanted me to insure a sale of twenty-five thousand sets of his book! I wouldn't risk such a guaranty on any book that ever was published."[1]

I DID NOT SAY ANYTHING, but I thought a good deal. This was one more evidence that the Century people had no more just idea of the value of the book than as many children might be expected to have. At this present writing (May 25, 1885) we have not advertised General Grant's book in any way; we have not spent a dollar in advertising of any kind; we have not even given notice by circular or otherwise that we are ready to receive applications from book agents; and yet, to-day, we have bona fide orders for 100,000 sets of the book—that is to say, 200,000 single volumes; and these orders are from men who have bonded themselves to take and pay for them, and who have also laid before us the most trustworthy evidence that they are financially able to carry out their contracts. The territory which these men have taken is only about one-fourth of the area of the Northern states. We have also under consideration applications for 50,000 sets more; and although we have confidence in the energy and ability of the men who have made these applications, we have not closed with them because, as yet, we are not sufficiently satisfied as to their financial strength.

When it became known that the general's book had fallen into my hands, the New York World and a Boston paper (I think the Herald) came out at once with the news; and in both instances the position was taken that, by some sort of superior underhanded smartness, I had taken an unfair advantage of the confiding simplicity of the Century people and got the book away from them—a book which they had the right to consider their property, inasmuch as the terms of its publication had been mutually agreed upon and the contract

---

1. This is the remark I have already several times referred to. I've got Smith's exact language (from my notebook); it proves that they thought 10-per-cent royalty would actually represent half profits on General Grant's book!

Note added Sept. 10, 1885, 250,000 sets—500,000 single copies—have been sold to date—and only half the ground canvassed.

covering it was on the point of being signed by General Grant when I put in my meddling appearance.

None of the statements of these two papers was correct, but the Boston paper's account was considered to be necessarily correct, for the reason that it was furnished by the sister of Mr. Gilder, editor of the Century, so there was considerable newspaper talk about my improper methods; but nobody seemed to have wit enough to discover that if one gouger had captured the general's book, here was evidence that he had only prevented another gouger from getting it, since the Century's terms were distinctly mentioned in the Boston paper's account as being 10-per-cent royalty. No party observed that, and nobody commented upon it. It was taken for granted all round that General Grant would have signed that 10-per-cent contract without being grossly cheated. It is my settled policy to allow newspapers to make as many misstatements about me or my affairs as they like; therefore I had no mind to contradict either of these newspapers or explain my side of the case in any way. But a reporter came to our house at Hartford (from one of the editors of the Courant) to ask me for my side of the matter for use in the Associated Press dispatches. I dictated a short paragraph in which I said that the statement made in the World, that there was a coolness between the Century Company and General Grant, and that, in consequence of it, the Century would not publish any more articles by General Grant, notwithstanding the fact that they had advertised them far and wide, was not true. I said there was no coolness and no ground for coolness; that the contract for the book had been open for all competitors; that I had put in my application and had asked the general to state its terms to the other applicants in order that he might thereby be enabled to get the best terms possible; that I had got the book, eventually, but by no underhand or unfair method. The statement I made was concise and brief and contained nothing offensive. It was sent over the wires to the Associated Press headquarters in New York, but it was not issued by that concern. It did not appear in print. I inquired why, and was told that, although it was a piece of news of quite universal interest, it was also more or less of an advertisement for the book—a thing I had not thought of before. I was also told that if I had had a friend round about the Associated Press office, I could have had that thing published all over the country for a reasonable bribe. I wondered if that were true. I wondered if so great and important a concern dealt in that sort of thing.

GERHARDT[1] AND THE GRANT BUST

I will make a diversion here, and get back upon my track again later.

While I was away with G. W. Cable, giving public readings in the theaters, lecture halls, skating rinks, jails, and churches of the country, the travel was necessarily fatiguing, and, therefore, I ceased from writing letters excepting to my wife and children. This foretaste of heaven, this relief from the fret of letter-answering, was delightful; but it finally left me in the dark concerning things which I ought to have been acquainted with at the moment.

Among these the affairs of Karl Gerhardt, the young artist, should be mentioned.

I had started out on this reading pilgrimage the day after the presidential election; that is to say, I had started on the 5th of November, and had visited my home only once between that time and the 2d of March following.

During all these four months, Gerhardt had been waiting for a verdict of a dilatory committee, concerning a Nathan Hale statue, and had taken it out in waiting; that is to say, he had sat still and done nothing to earn his bread. He had been tirelessly diligent in asking for work in the line of his art, and had used all possible means in that direction; he had written letters to every man he could hear of who was likely to need a mortuary monument for himself, or his friends, or acquaintances, and had also applied for the chance of a competition for a soldiers' monument—for all things of this sort—but always without success; the natural result, as his name was not known. He had no reputation.

Once, J. Q. A. Ward, in speaking of his early struggles to get a status as a sculptor, had told me that he had made his beginning by hanging around the studios of sculptors of repute and picking up odd jobs of journey work in them, for the sake of the bread he could gain in that way.

I may as well say here, and be done with it, that my connection with Gerhardt had very little sentiment in it, from my side of the house; and

1. Karl Gerhardt, a young sculptor sent by Mr. and Mrs. Clemens to Paris to perfect himself in his art.

no romance. I took hold of his case, in the first place, solely because I had become convinced that he had it in him to become a very capable sculptor. I was not adopting a child, I was not adding a member to the family, I was merely taking upon myself a common duty—the duty of helping a man who was not able to help himself. I never expected him to be grateful, I never expected him to be thankful—my experience of men had long ago taught me that one of the surest ways of begetting an enemy was to do some stranger an act of kindness which should lay upon him the irritating sense of an obligation. Therefore my connection with Gerhardt had nothing sentimental or romantic about it. I told him in the first place that if the time should ever come when he could pay back to me the money expended upon him, and pay it without inconvenience to himself, I should expect it at his hands, and that, when it was paid, I should consider the account entirely requited—sentiment and all; that that act would leave him free from any obligation to me. It was well, all round, that things had taken that shape in the beginning, and had kept it, for if the foundation had been sentiment that sentiment might have grown sour.

One evening Gerhardt appeared in the library and I hoped he had come to say he was getting along very well and was contented; so I was disappointed when he said he had come to show me a small bust he had been making, in clay, of General Grant, from a photograph. I was the more irritated for the reason that I had never seen a portrait of General Grant—in oil, water-colors, crayon, steel, wood, photograph, plaster, marble, or any other material—that was to me at all satisfactory; and, therefore, I could not expect that a person who had never even seen the general could accomplish anything worth considering in the way of a likeness of him.

However, when he uncovered the bust my prejudices vanished at once.

The thing was not correct in its details, yet it seemed to me to be a closer approach to a good likeness of General Grant than any one which I had ever seen before. Before uncovering it, Gerhardt had said he had brought it in the hope that I would show it to some member of the general's family and get that member to point out its chief defects, for correction; but I had replied that I could not venture to do that, for there was a plenty of people to pester these folks without me adding myself to the number. But a glance at the bust had changed all that in an instant. I said I would go to New York in the morning and ask the family to look at the bust, and that he must come along to be within call in case they took enough interest in the matter to point out the defects.

We reached the general's house at one o'clock the next afternoon, and I left Gerhardt and the bust below and went upstairs to see the family.

And now, for the first time, the thought came into my mind that perhaps I was doing a foolish thing; that the family must of necessity have been pestered with such matters as this so many times that the very mention of such a thing must be nauseating to them. However, I had started, and so I might as well finish. Therefore, I said I had a young artist downstairs who had been making a small bust of the general from a photograph, and I wished they would look at it, if they were willing to do me that kindness.

Jesse Grant's wife spoke up with eagerness and said, "Is it the artist who made the bust of you that is in Huckleberry Finn?" I said, "Yes." She said, with great animation, "How good it was of you, Mr. Clemens, to think of that!" She expressed this lively gratitude to me in various ways until I began to feel somehow a great sense of merit in having originated this noble idea of having a bust of General Grant made by so excellent an artist. I will not do my sagacity the discredit of saying that I did anything to remove or modify this impression that I had originated the idea and carried it out to its present state through my own ingenuity and diligence.

Mrs. Jesse Grant added, "How strange it is; only two nights ago I dreamed that I was looking at your bust in Huckleberry Finn and thinking how nearly perfect it was, and then I thought that I conceived the idea of going to you and asking you if you could not hunt up that artist and get him to make a bust of father!"

Things were going on very handsomely!

The persons present were Col. Fred Grant, Mrs. Jesse Grant, and Doctor Douglas.

I went down for Gerhardt and he brought up the bust and uncovered it. All of the family present exclaimed over the excellence of the likeness, and Mrs. Jesse Grant expended some more unearned gratitude upon me.

The family began to discuss the details, and then checked themselves and begged Gerhardt's pardon for criticizing. Of course, he said that their criticisms were exactly what he wanted and begged them to go on. The general's wife said that in that case they would be glad to point out what seemed to them inaccuracies, but that he must not take their speeches as being criticisms upon his art at all. They found two inaccuracies; in the shape of the nose and the shape of the forehead. All were agreed that the forehead was wrong, but there was a lively dispute about the nose. Some of those present contended that the nose was nearly right—the others contended that it was distinctly wrong. The general's wife knelt on the ottoman to get a clearer view of the bust, and the others stood about her—all talking at once. Finally, the general's wife said, hesitatingly, with the mien of one who is afraid he is taking a liberty and asking too much, "If Mr. Gerhardt could see the general's nose and forehead, himself, that would dispose of this dispute at once." Finally, "The general is in the next room. Would Mr. Gerhardt mind going in there and making the correction himself?"

Things were indeed progressing handsomely!

Of course, Mr. Gerhardt lost no time in expressing his willingness.

While the controversy was going on concerning the nose and the forehead, Mrs. Fred Grant joined the group, and then, presently, each of the three ladies, in turn, disappeared for a few minutes, and came back with a handful of photographs and hand-painted miniatures of the general.

These pictures had been made in every quarter of the world. One of them had been painted in Japan. But, good as many of these pictures were, they were worthless as evidence, for the reason that they contradicted one another in every detail.

The photograph apparatus had lied as distinctly and as persistently as had the hands of the miniature-artists. No two noses were alike and no two foreheads were alike.

We stepped into the general's room—all but General Badeau and Doctor Douglas.

The general was stretched out in a reclining chair with his feet supported upon an ordinary chair. He was muffled up in dressing gowns and afghans, with his black woolen skull-cap on his head.

The ladies took the skull-cap off and began to discuss his nose and his forehead, and they made him turn this way and that way and the other way, to get different views and profiles of his features. He took it all patiently and made no complaint. He allowed them to pull and haul him about, in their own affectionate fashion, without a murmur.

Mrs. Fred Grant, who is very beautiful and of the most gentle and loving character, was very active in this service, and very deft, with her graceful hands, in arranging and rearranging the general's head for inspection, and repeatedly called attention to the handsome shape of his head—a thing which reminds me that Gerhardt had picked up an old plug hat of the general's downstairs, and had remarked upon the perfect oval shape of the inside of it, this oval being so uniform that the wearer of the hat could never be able to know, by the feel of it, whether he had it right end in front or wrong end in front; whereas the average man's head is broad at one end and narrow at the other.

The general's wife placed him in various positions, none of which satisfied her, and finally she went to him and said: "Ulyss! Ulyss! Can't you put your feet to the floor?" He did so at once and straightened himself up.

During all this time the general's face wore a pleasant, contented, and I should say benignant, aspect, but he never opened his lips once. As had often been the case before, so now his silence gave ample room to guess at what was passing in his mind—and to take it out in guessing. I will remark, in passing, that the general's hands were very thin, and they showed, far more than did his face, how his long siege of confinement and illness and insufficient food had wasted him. He was at this time suffering great and increasing pain from the cancer at the root of his tongue, but there was nothing ever discoverable in the expression of his face to betray this fact, as long as he was awake. When asleep, his face would take advantage of him and make revelations.

At the end of fifteen minutes, Gerhardt said he believed he could correct the defects now. So we went back to the other room.

Gerhardt went to work on the clay image, everybody standing round, observing and discussing with the greatest interest.

Presently the general astonished us by appearing there, clad in his wraps and supporting himself in a somewhat unsure way upon a cane. He sat down on the sofa and said he could sit there if it would be for the advantage of the artist.

But his wife would not allow that. She said that he might catch cold. She was for hurrying him back at once to his invalid chair. He succumbed and started back, but at the door he turned and said:

"Then can't Mr. Gerhardt bring the clay in here and work?"

This was several hundred times better fortune than Gerhardt could have dreamed of. He removed his work to the general's room at once. The general stretched himself out in his chair, but said that if that position would not do, he would sit up. Gerhardt said it would do very well indeed, especially if it were more comfortable to the sitter than any other would be.

The general watched Gerhardt's swift and noiseless fingers for some time with manifest interest in his face, and no doubt this novelty was a valuable thing to one who had spent so many weeks that were tedious with sameness and unemphasized with change or diversion. By and by, one eyelid began to droop occasionally; then everybody stepped out of the room, excepting Gerhardt and myself, and I moved to the rear, where I would be out of sight and not be a disturbing element.

Harrison, the general's old colored body servant, came in presently, and remained awhile, watching Gerhardt, and then broke out, with great zeal and decision:

"That's the general! Yes, sir, that's the general! Mind! I tell you that's the general!"

Then he went away and the place became absolutely silent.

Within a few minutes afterward the general was sleeping, and for two hours he continued to sleep tranquilly, the serenity of his face disturbed only at intervals by a passing wave of pain. It was the first sleep he had had for several weeks uninduced by narcotics.

To my mind this bust, completed at this sitting, has in it more of General Grant than can be found in any other likeness of him that has ever been made since he was a famous man. I think it may rightly be called the best portrait of General Grant that is in existence. It has also a feature which must always be a remembrancer to this nation of what the general was passing through during the long weeks of that spring. For into the clay image went the pain which he was enduring, but which did not appear in his face when he was awake. Consequently, the bust has about it a suggestion of patient and brave and manly suffering which is infinitely touching.

At the end of two hours General Badeau entered abruptly and spoke to the general, and this woke him up. But for this interruption he might have slept as much longer, possibly.

Gerhardt worked on as long as it was light enough to work, and then he went away. He was to come again, and did come the following day; but at the last moment Col. Fred Grant would not permit another sitting. He said that the face was so nearly perfect that he was afraid to allow it to be touched again, lest some of the excellence might be refined out of it, instead of adding more excellence to it. He called attention to an oil painting on the wall downstairs and asked if we knew that man.

We couldn't name him—had never seen his face before. "Well," said Colonel Grant, "that was a perfect portrait of my father once. It was given up by all the family to be the best that had ever been made of him. We were entirely satisfied with it, but the artist, unhappily, was not; he wanted 'to do a stroke or two to make it absolutely perfect' and he insisted on taking it back with him. After he had made those finishing touches it didn't resemble my father or anyone else. We took it, and have always kept it as a curiosity. But with that lesson behind us we will save this bust from a similar fate."

He allowed Gerhardt to work at the hair, however; he said he might expend as much of his talent on that as he pleased, but must stop there.

Gerhardt finished the hair to his satisfaction, but never touched the face again. Colonel Grant required Gerhardt to promise that he would take every pains with the clay bust, and then return it to him, to keep, as soon as he had taken a mold from it. This was done.

Gerhardt prepared the clay as well as he could for permanent preservation and gave it to Colonel Grant.

Up to the present day, May 22, 1885, no later likeness of General Grant, of any kind, has been made from life, and if it shall chance to remain the last ever made of him from life, coming generations can properly be grateful that one so nearly perfect of him was made after the world learned his name.

Dictated 1885

The Reverend Doctor N—Visits General Grant

July 4, 1885.—General Grant is still living this morning. Many a person between the two oceans lay hours awake last night listening for the booming of the fire bells which should speak to a nation in simultaneous voice and tell it its calamity. The bell strokes are to be thirty seconds apart and there will be sixty-three—the general's age. They will be striking in every town in the United States at the same moment—the first time in the world's history that the bells of a nation have tolled in unison— beginning at the same moment and ending at the same moment.

More than once, during two weeks, the nation stood watching with bated breath, expecting the news of General Grant's death.

The family, in their distress, desired spiritual help, and one Reverend

Doctor N—was sent for to furnish it. N—had lately gone to California, where he had got a ten-thousand-dollar job to preach a funeral sermon over the son of an ex-governor, a millionaire; and a most remarkable sermon it was—and worth the money. If N—got the facts right, neither he nor anybody else—any ordinary human being—was worthy to preach that youth's funeral sermon, and it was manifest that one of the disciples ought to have been imported into California for the occasion. N—came on from California at once and began his ministration at the general's bedside; and, if one might trust his daily reports, the general had conceived a new and perfect interest in spiritual things. It is fair to presume that the most of N—'s daily reports originated in his own imagination.

Col. Fred Grant told me that his father was, in this matter, what he was in all matters and at all times—that is to say, perfectly willing to have family prayers going on, or anything else that could be satisfactory to anybody, or increase anybody's comfort in any way; but he also said that, while his father was a good man, and indeed as good as any man, Christian or otherwise, he was not a praying man.

Some of the speeches put into General Grant's mouth were to the last degree incredible to people who knew the general, since they were such gaudy and flowering misrepresentations of that plain-spoken man's utterances.

About the 14th or 15th of April, Reverend Mr. N—reported that upon visiting the general in his sick chamber, the general pressed his hand and delivered himself of this astounding remark:

"Thrice have I been in the shadow of the Valley of Death and thrice have I come out again."

General Grant never used flowers of speech, and, dead or alive, he never could have uttered anything like that, either as a quotation or otherwise.[1]

Written in the closing days of 1890

The Machine Episode

This episode has now spread itself over more than one-fifth of my life—a considerable stretch of time, as I am now fifty-five years old.

---

1. The Grant dictations ended here. General Grant died July 25, 1885. More than 300,000 sets, of two vols. each, of his Memoirs were sold.

Ten or eleven years ago, Dwight Buell, a jeweler, called at our house and was shown up to the billiard room—which was my study; and the game got more study than the other sciences. He wanted me to take some stock in a type-setting machine. He said it was at the Colt arms factory, and was about finished. I took $2,000 of the stock. I was always taking little chances like that—and almost always losing by it, too—a thing which I did not greatly mind, because I was always careful to risk only such amounts as I could easily afford to lose. Some time afterward I was invited to go down to the factory and see the machine, I went, promising myself nothing, for I knew all about type-setting by practical experience, and held the settled and solidified opinion that a successful type-setting machine was an impossibility, for the reason that a machine cannot be made to think, and the thing that sets movable type must think or retire defeated. So the performance I witnessed did most thoroughly amaze me. Here was a machine that was really setting type, and doing it with swiftness and accuracy, too. Moreover, it was distributing its case at the same time. The distribution was automatic. The machine fed itself from a galley of dead matter, and without human help or suggestion; for it began its work of its own accord when the type channels needed filling, and stopped of its own accord when they were full enough. The machine was almost a complete compositor; it lacked but one feature—it did not "justify" the lines; this was done by the operator's assistant.

I saw the operator set at the rate of 3,000 ems an hour, which, counting distribution, was but little short of four case-men's work.

Mr. H—was there. I had known him long; I thought I knew him well. I had great respect for him and full confidence in him. He said he was already a considerable owner and was now going to take as much more of the stock as he could afford. Wherefore I set down my name for an additional $3,000. It is here that the music begins.[1]

Before very long H—called on me and asked me what I would charge to raise a capital of $500,000 for the manufacture of the machine. I said I would undertake it for $100,000. He said, "Raise $600,000, then, and take $100,000." I agreed. I sent for my partner, Webster. He came up from New York and went back with the project. There was some correspondence. H—wrote Webster a letter.

---

1. This was the Farnam machine—so called.

I will remark here that James W. Paige, the little bright-eyed, alert, smartly dressed inventor of the machine is a most extraordinary compound of business thrift and commercial insanity; of cold calculation and jejune sentimentality; of veracity and falsehood; of fidelity and treachery; of nobility and baseness; of pluck and cowardice; of wasteful liberality and pitiful stinginess; of solid sense and weltering moonshine; of towering genius and trivial ambitions; of merciful bowels and a petrified heart; of colossal vanity and—But there the opposites stop. His vanity stands alone, sky-piercing, as sharp of outline as an Egyptian monolith. It is the only unpleasant feature in him that is not modified, softened, compensated by some converse characteristic. There is another point or two worth mentioning. He can persuade anybody, he can convince nobody. He has a crystal-clear mind as regards the grasping and concreting of an idea which has been lost and smothered under a chaos of baffling legal language; and yet it can always be depended upon to take the simplest half dozen facts and draw from them a conclusion that will astonish the idiots in the asylum. It is because he is a dreamer, a visionary. His imagination runs utterly away with him. He is a poet, a most great and genuine poet, whose sublime creations are written in steel. He is the Shakespeare of mechanical invention. In all the ages he has no peer. Indeed, there is none that even approaches him. Whoever is qualified to fully comprehend his marvelous machine will grant that its place is upon the loftiest summit of human invention, with no kindred between it and the far foothills below.

But I must explain these strange contradictions above listed or the man will be misunderstood and wronged. His business thrift is remarkable, and it is also of a peculiar cut. He has worked at his expensive machine for more than twenty years, but always at somebody else's cost. He spent hundreds and thousands of other folks' money, yet always kept his machine and its possible patents in his own possession, unencumbered by an embarrassing lien of any kind—except once, which will be referred to by and by. He could never be beguiled into putting a penny of his own into his work. Once he had a brilliant idea in the way of a wonderfully valuable application of electricity. To test it, he said, would cost but twenty-five dollars. I was paying him a salary of nearly $600 a month and was spending $1,200 on the machine, besides. Yet he asked me to risk the twenty-five dollars and take half of the result. I declined, and he dropped the matter. Another time he was sure he was on the track of a splendid thing in electricity. It would cost only a trifle—possibly $200—to try some experiments; I was asked to furnish the money and take half of the result. I furnished money until the sum had grown to about a thousand dollars, and everything was pronounced ready for the grand exposition. The electric current was turned on—the thing declined to go. Two years later the same thing was successfully worked out and patented by a man in the State of New York and was at once sold for a huge sum of money and a royalty reserve besides. The drawings in the electrical journal showing the stages by which that inventor had approached the consummation of his idea, proving his way step by step as he went, were almost the twins of Paige's drawings of two years before. It was almost as if the same hand had drawn both sets. Paige said we had had it, and we should have known it if we had only tried an alternating current after failing with the direct current; said he had felt sure, at the time, that at cost of a hundred dollars he could apply the alternating test and come out triumphant. Then he added, in tones absolutely sodden with self-sacrifice and just barely touched with reproach:

"But you had already spent so much money on the thing that I hadn't the heart to ask you to spend any more."

If I had asked him why he didn't draw on his own pocket, he would not have understood me. He could not have grasped so strange an idea as that. He would have thought there was something the matter with my mind. I am speaking honestly; he could not have understood it. A cancer of old habit and long experience could as easily understand the suggestion that it board itself awhile.

In drawing contracts he is always able to take care of himself; and in every instance he will work into the contracts injuries to the other party and advantages to himself which were never considered or mentioned in the preceding verbal agreement. In one contract he got me to assign to him several hundred thousand dollars' worth of property for a certain valuable consideration—said valuable consideration being the regiving to me of another piece of property which was not his to give, but already belonged to me! I quite understand that I am confessing myself a fool; but that is no matter, the reader would find it out anyway as I go along. H—was our joint lawyer, and I had every confidence in his wisdom and cleanliness.

Once when I was lending money to Paige during a few months, I presently found that he was giving receipts to my representative instead of notes! But that man never lived who could catch Paige so nearly asleep as to palm off on him a piece of paper which apparently satisfied a debt when it ought to acknowledge a loan.

I must throw in a parenthesis here or I shall do H—an injustice. Here and there I have seemed to cast little reflections upon him. Pay no attention to them. I have no feeling about him; I have no harsh words to say about him. He is a great, fat, good-natured, kind-hearted, chicken-livered slave; with no more pride than a tramp, no more sand than a rabbit, no more moral sense than a wax figure, and no more sex than a tapeworm. He sincerely thinks he is honest, he sincerely thinks he is honorable. It is my daily prayer to God that he be permitted to live and die in those superstitions. I gave him a twentieth of my American holding, at Paige's request; I gave him a twentieth of my foreign holding, at his own supplication; I advanced nearly forty thousand dollars in five years to keep these interests sound and valid for him. In return, he drafted every contract which I made with Paige in all that time—clear up to September, 1890—and pronounced them good and fair; and then I signed.

Yes, it is as I have said: Paige is an extraordinary compound of business thrift and commercial insanity. Instances of his commercial insanity are simply innumerable. Here are some examples. When I took hold of the machine, February 6, 1886, its faults had been corrected and a setter and a justifier could turn out about 3,500 ems an hour on it, possibly 4,000. There was no machine that could pretend rivalry to it. Business sanity would have said, put it on the market as it was, secure the field, and add improvements later. Paige's business insanity said, add the improvements first and risk losing the field. And that is what he set out to do. To add a justifying mechanism to that machine would take a few months and cost $9,000 by his estimate, or $12,000 by Pratt and Whitney's. I agreed to add said justifier to that machine. There could be no sense in building a new machine, yet in total violation of the agreement, Paige went immediately to work to build a new machine, although aware, by recent experience, that the cost could not fall below $150,000 and that the time consumed would be years instead of months. Well, when four years had been spent and the new machine was able to exhibit a marvelous capacity, we appointed the 12th of January for Senator Jones of Nevada to come and make an inspection. He was not promised a perfect machine, but a machine which could be perfected. He had agreed to invest one or two hundred thousand dollars in its fortunes, and had also said that if the exhibition was particularly favorable he might take entire charge of the elephant. At the last moment Paige concluded to add an air blast (afterward found to be unnecessary); wherefore, Jones had to be turned back from New York to wait a couple of months and lose his interest in the thing. A year ago Paige made what he regarded as a vast and magnanimous concession, and said I might sell the English patent for $10,000,000! A little later a man came along who thought he could bring some Englishmen who would buy that patent, and he was sent off to fetch them. He was gone so long that Paige's confidence began to diminish, and with it his price. He finally got down to what he said was his very last and bottom price for that patent—$50,000! This was the only time in five years that I ever saw Paige in his right mind. I could furnish other examples of Paige's business insanity—enough of them to fill six or eight volumes, perhaps, but I am not writing his history, I am merely sketching his portrait.

I WENT ON FOOTING THE bills and got the machine really perfected at last, at a full cost of about $150,000, instead of the original $30,000.

W. tells me that Paige tried his best to cheat me out of my royalties when making a contract with the Connecticut Company.

Also that he tried to cheat out of all share Mr. North (inventor of the justifying mechanism), but that North frightened him with a lawsuit threat and is to get a royalty until the aggregate is $2,000,000.

Paige and I always meet on effusively affectionate terms, and yet he knows perfectly well that if I had him in a steel trap I would shut out all human succor and watch that trap till he died.[1]

---

1. The machine in the end proved a complete failure, being too complicated, too difficult to keep in order. It cost Mark Twain a total of about $190,000.—A. B. P.

MARK TWAIN

CHAPTERS BEGUN IN VIENNA

Early Days

... So much for the earlier days, and the New England branch of the Clemenses.[1] The other brother settled in the South and is remotely responsible for me. He has collected his reward generations ago, whatever it was. He went South with his particular friend Fairfax, and settled in Maryland with him, but afterward went further and made his home in Virginia. This is the Fairfax whose descendants were to enjoy a curious distinction—that of being American-born English earls. The founder of the house was the Lord General Fairfax of the Parliamentary arm, in Cromwell's time. The earldom, which is of recent date, came to the American Fairfaxes through the failure of male heirs in England. Old residents of San Francisco will remember "Charley," the American earl of the mid-'sixties—tenth Lord Fairfax according to Burke's Peerage, and holder of a modest public office of some sort or other in the new mining town of Virginia City, Nevada. He was never out of America. I knew him, but not intimately. He had a golden character, and that was all his fortune. He laid his title aside, and gave it a holiday until his circumstances should improve to a degree consonant with its dignity; but that time never came, I think. He was a manly man and had fine generosities in his make-up. A prominent and pestilent creature named Ferguson, who was always picking quarrels with better men than himself, picked one with him one day, and Fairfax knocked him down. Ferguson gathered himself up and went off, mumbling threats. Fairfax carried no arms, and refused to carry any now, though his friends warned him that Ferguson was of a treacherous disposition and would be sure to take revenge by base means, sooner or later. Nothing happened for several days; then Ferguson took the earl by surprise and snapped a revolver at his breast. Fairfax wrenched the pistol from him and was going to shoot him, but the man fell on his knees and begged, and said: "Don't kill me. I have a wife and children." Fairfax was in a towering passion, but the appeal reached his heart, and he said, "They have done me no harm," and he let the rascal go.

---

1. Mr. Clemens evidently intended to precede this paragraph with some data concerning his New England ancestry, but he never did so.—A. B. P.

Back of the Virginian Clemenses is a dim procession of ancestors stretching back to Noah's time. According to tradition, some of them were pirates and slavers in Elizabeth's time. But this is no discredit to them, for so were Drake and Hawkins and the others. It was a respectable trade then, and monarchs were partners in it. In my time I have had desires to be a pirate myself. The reader, if he will look deep down in his secret heart, will find—but never mind what he will find there. I am not writing his autobiography, but mine. Later, according to tradition, one of the procession was ambassador to Spain in the time of James I, or of Charles I, and married there and sent down a strain of Spanish blood to warm us up. Also, according to tradition, this one or another—Geoffrey Clement, by name—helped to sentence Charles to death. I have not examined into these traditions myself, partly because I was indolent and partly because I was so busy polishing up this end of the line and trying to make it showy; but the other Clemenses claim that they have made the examination and that it stood the test. Therefore I have always taken for granted that I did help Charles out of his troubles, by ancestral proxy. My instincts have persuaded me, too. Whenever we have a strong and persistent and ineradicable instinct, we may be sure that it is not original with us, but inherited—inherited from away back, and hardened and perfected by the petrifying influence of time. Now I have been always and unchangingly bitter against Charles, and I am quite certain that this feeling trickled down to me through the veins of my forebears from the heart of that judge; for it is not my disposition to be bitter against people on my own personal account. I am not bitter against Jeffreys. I ought to be, but I am not. It indicates that my ancestors of James II's time were indifferent to him; I do not know why; I never could make it out; but that is what it indicates. And I have always felt friendly toward Satan. Of course that is ancestral; it must be in the blood, for I could not have originated it.

. . . And so, by the testimony of instinct, backed by the assertions of Clemenses, who said they had examined the records, I have always been obliged to believe that Geoffrey Clement, the martyr maker, was an ancestor of mine, and to regard him with favor, and in fact, pride. This has not had a good effect upon me, for it has made me vain, and that is a fault. It has made me set myself above people who were less fortunate in their ancestry than I, and has moved me to take them down a peg, upon occasion, and say things to them which hurt them before company.

A case of the kind happened in Berlin several years ago. William

Walter Phelps was our minister at the Emperor's court then, and one evening he had me to dinner to meet Count S——, a Cabinet Minister. This nobleman was of long and illustrious descent. Of course I wanted to let out the fact that I had some ancestors, too; but I did not want to pull them out of their graves by the ears, and I never could seem to get the chance to work them in in a way that would look sufficiently casual. I suppose Phelps was in the same difficulty. In fact, he looked distraught now and then—just as a person looks who wants to uncover an ancestor purely by accident and cannot think of a way that will seem accidental enough. But at last, after dinner, he made a try. He took us about his drawing-room, showing us the pictures, and finally stopped before a rude and ancient engraving. It was a picture of the court that tried Charles I. There was a pyramid of judges in Puritan slouch hats, and below them three bareheaded secretaries seated at a table. Mr. Phelps put his finger upon one of the three and said, with exulting indifference:

"An ancestor of mine."

I put my finger on a judge, and retorted with scathing languidness:

"Ancestor of mine. But it is a small matter. I have others."

It was not noble in me to do it. I have always regretted it since. But it landed him. I wonder how he felt! However, it made no difference in our friendship; which shows that he was fine and high, notwithstanding the humbleness of his origin. And it was also creditable in me, too, that I could overlook it. I made no change in my bearing toward him, but always treated him as an equal.

But it was a hard night for me in one way. Mr. Phelps thought I was the guest of honor, and so did Count S——, but I didn't, for there was nothing in my invitation to indicate it. It was just a friendly offhand note, on a card. By the time dinner was announced Phelps was himself in a state of doubt. Something had to be done, and it was not a handy time for explanations. He tried to get me to go out with him, but I held back; then he tried S——, and he also declined. There was another guest, but there was no trouble about him. We finally went out in a pile. There was a decorous plunge for seats and I got the one at Mr. Phelps's left, the count captured the one facing Phelps, and the other guest had to take the place of honor, since he could not help himself. We returned to the drawing-room in the original disorder. I had new shoes on and they were tight. At eleven I was privately crying; I couldn't help it, the pain was so cruel. Conversation had been dead for an hour. S——had been due at the bedside of a dying official ever since half past nine. At last we all rose by one blessed impulse and went down to the street door without explanations—in a pile, and no precedence; and so parted.

The evening had its defects; still, I got my ancestor in, and was satisfied.

Among the Virginian Clemenses were Jere and Sherrard. Jere Clemens had a wide reputation as a good pistol-shot, and once it enabled him to get on the friendly side of some drummers when they wouldn't have paid any attention to mere smooth words and arguments. He was out stumping the state at the time. The drummers were grouped in front of the stand and had been hired by the opposition to drum while he made his speech. When he was ready to begin he got out his revolver and laid it before him and said, in his soft, silky way:

"I do not wish to hurt anybody and shall try not to, but I have got just a bullet apiece for those six drums, and if you should want to play on them don't stand behind them."

Sherrard Clemens was a republican Congressman from West Virginia in the war days, and then went out to St. Louis, where the James Clemens branch lived and still lives, and there he became a warm rebel. This was after the war. At the time that he was a Republican I was a rebel; but by the time he had become a rebel I was become (temporarily) a Republican. The Clemenses have always done the best they could to keep the political balances level, no matter how much it might inconvenience them. I did not know what had become of Sherrard Clemens; but once I introduced Senator Hawley to a Republican mass meeting in New England, and then I got a bitter letter from Sherrard from St. Louis. He said that the Republicans of the North—no, the "mudsills of the North"—had swept away the old aristocracy of the South with fire and sword, and it ill became me, an aristocrat by blood, to train with that kind of swine. Did I forget that I was a Lambton?

That was a reference to my mother's side of the house. My mother was a Lambton—Lambton with a p, for some of the American Lamptons could not spell very well in early times, and so the name suffered at their hands. She was a native of Kentucky, and married my father in Lexington in 1823, when she was twenty years old and he twenty-four. Neither of them had an overplus of property. She brought him two or three negroes, but nothing else, I think. They removed to the remote and secluded village of Jamestown, in the mountain solitudes of east Tennessee. There their first crop of children was born, but as I was of a later vintage, I do not remember anything about it.

I was postponed—postponed to Missouri. Missouri was an unknown new state and needed attractions.

I think that my eldest brother, Orion, my sisters Pamela and Margaret, and my brother Benjamin were born in Jamestown. There may have been others, but as to that I am not sure. It was a great lift for that little village to have my parents come there. It was hoped that they would stay, so that it would become a city. It was supposed that they would stay. And so there was a boom; but by and by they went away, and prices went down, and it was many years before Jamestown got another start. I have written about Jamestown in the Gilded Age, a book of mine, but it was from hearsay, not from personal knowledge. My father left a fine estate behind him in the region roundabout Jamestown—75,000 acres.[1] When he died in 1847 he had owned it about twenty years. The taxes were almost nothing (five dollars a year for the whole), and he had always paid them regularly and kept his title perfect. He had always said that the land would not become valuable in his time, but that it would be a commodious provision for his children some day. It contained coal, copper, iron, and timber, and he said that in the course of time railways would pierce to that region and then the property would be property in fact as well as in name. It also produced a wild grape of a promising sort. He had sent some samples to Nicholas Longworth of Cincinnati to get his judgment upon them, and Mr. Longworth had said that they would make as good wine as his Catawbas. The land contained all these riches; and also oil, but my father did not know that, and of course in those early days he would have cared nothing about it if he had known it. The oil was not discovered until about 1895. I wish I owned a couple of acres of the land now, in which case I would not be writing autobiographies for a living. My father's dying charge was, "Cling to the land and wait; let nothing beguile it away from you." My mother's favorite cousin, James Lampton, who figures in the Gilded Age as Colonel Sellers, always said of that land—and said it with blazing enthusiasm, too—"There's millions in it—millions!" It is true that he always said that about everything—and was always mistaken, too, but this time he was right; which shows that a man who goes around with a prophecy-gun ought never to get discouraged. If he will keep up his heart and fire at everything he sees, he is bound to hit something by and by.

---

1. Correction (1906)—it was above 100,000, it appears.

Many persons regarded Colonel Sellers as a fiction, an invention, an extravagant impossibility, and did me the honor to call him a "creation"; but they were mistaken. I merely put him on paper as he was; he was not a person who could be exaggerated. The incidents which looked most extravagant, both in the book and on the stage, were not inventions of mine, but were facts of his life; and I was present when they were developed. John T. Raymond's audiences used to come near to dying with laughter over the turnip-eating scene; but, extravagant as the scene was, it was faithful to the facts, in all its absurd details. The thing happened in Lampton's own house, and I was present. In fact, I was myself the guest who ate the turnips. In the hands of a great actor that piteous scene would have dimmed any manly spectator's eyes with tears, and racked his ribs apart with laughter at the same time. But Raymond was great in humorous portrayal only. In that he was superb, he was wonderful—in a word, great; in all things else he was a pygmy of pygmies. The real Colonel Sellers, as I knew him in James Lampton, was a pathetic and beautiful spirit, a manly man, a straight and honorable man, a man with a big, foolish, unselfish heart in his bosom, a man born to be loved; and he was loved by all his friends, and by his family worshiped. It is the right word. To them he was but little less than a god. The real Colonel Sellers was never on the stage. Only half of him was there. Raymond could not play the other half of him; it was above his level. There was only one man who could have played the whole of Colonel Sellers, and that was Frank Mayo.[1]

It is a world of surprises. They fall, too, where one is least expecting them. When I introduced Sellers into the book, Charles Dudley Warner, who was writing the story with me, proposed a change of Sellers's Christian name. Ten years before, in a remote corner of the West, he had come across a man named Eschol Sellers, and he thought that Eschol was just the right and fitting name for our Sellers, since it was odd and quaint and all that. I liked the idea, but I said that that man might turn up and object. But Warner said it couldn't happen; that he was doubtless dead by this time and, be he dead or alive, we must have the name; it was exactly the right one and we couldn't do without it. So the change was made. Warner's man was a farmer in a cheap and humble way. When the book had been out a week,

---

1. Raymond was playing Colonel Sellers in 1876 and along there. About twenty years later Mayo dramatized Pudd'nhead Wilson and played the title role delightfully.

a college-bred gentleman of courtly manners and ducal upholstery arrived in Hartford in a sultry state of mind and with a libel suit in his eye, and his name was Eschol Sellers! He had never heard of the other one and had never been within a thousand miles of him. This damaged aristocrat's program was quite definite and business-like: the American Publishing Company must suppress the edition as far as printed and change the name in the plates, or stand a suit for $10,000. He carried away the company's promise and many apologies, and we changed the name back to Colonel Mulberry Sellers in the plates. Apparently there is nothing that cannot happen. Even the existence of two unrelated men wearing the impossible name of Eschol Sellers is a possible thing.

James Lampton floated, all his days, in a tinted mist of magnificent dreams, and died at last without seeing one of them realized. I saw him last in 1884, when it had been twenty-six years since I ate the basin of raw turnips and washed them down with a bucket of water in his house. He was become old and white-headed, but he entered to me in the same old breezy way of his earlier life, and he was all there yet—not a detail wanting; the happy light in his eye, the abounding hope in his heart, the persuasive tongue, the miracle-breeding imagination—they were all there; and before I could turn around he was polishing up his Aladdin's lamp and flashing the secret riches of the world before me. I said to myself: "I did not overdraw him by a shade, I set him down as he was; and he is the same man to-day. Cable will recognize him." I asked him to excuse me a moment and ran into the next room, which was Cable's. Cable and I were stumping the Union on a reading tour. I said:

"I am going to leave your door open so that you can listen. There is a man in there who is interesting."

I went back and asked Lampton what he was doing now. He began to tell me of a "small venture" he had begun in New Mexico through his son; "only a little thing—a mere trifle—partly to amuse my leisure, partly to keep my capital from lying idle, but mainly to develop the boy—develop the boy. Fortune's wheel is ever revolving; he may have to work for his living some day—as strange things have happened in this world. But it's only a little thing—a mere trifle, as I said."

And so it was—as he began it. But under his deft hands it grew and blossomed and spread—oh, beyond imagination. At the end of half an hour he finished; finished with the remark, uttered in an adorably languid manner:

"Yes, it is but a trifle, as things go nowadays—a bagatelle—but amusing. It passes the time. The boy thinks great things of it, but he is young, you know, and imaginative; lacks the experience which comes of handling large affairs, and which tempers the fancy and perfects the judgment. I suppose there's a couple of millions in it, possibly three, but not more, I think; still, for a boy, you know, just starting in life, it is not bad. I should not want him to make a fortune—let that come later. It could turn his head, at his time of life, and in many ways be a damage to him."

Then he said something about his having left his pocketbook lying on the table in the main drawing-room at home, and about its being after banking hours, now, and—

I stopped him there and begged him to honor Cable and me by being our guest at the lecture—with as many friends as might be willing to do us the like honor. He accepted. And he thanked me as a prince might who had granted us a grace. The reason I stopped his speech about the tickets was because I saw that he was going to ask me to furnish them to him and let him pay next day; and I knew that if he made the debt he would pay it if he had to pawn his clothes. After a little further chat he shook hands heartily and affectionately and took his leave. Cable put his head in at the door and said:

"That was Colonel Sellers."

As I have said, that vast plot of Tennessee land was held by my father twenty years—intact. When he died in 1847 we began to manage it ourselves. Forty years afterward we had managed it all away except 10,000 acres, and gotten nothing to remember the sales by. About 1887—possibly it was earlier—the 10,000 went. My brother found a chance to trade it for a house and lot in the town of Corry, in the oil regions of Pennsylvania. About 1894 he sold this property for $250. That ended the Tennessee land.

If any penny of cash ever came out of my father's wise investment but that, I have no recollection of it. No, I am overlooking a detail. It furnished me a field for Sellers and a book. Out of my half of the book I got $20,000, perhaps something more; out of the play I got $75,000— just about a dollar an acre. It is curious; I was not alive when my father made the investment, therefore he was not intending any partiality; yet I was the only member of the family that ever profited by it. I shall have occasion to mention this land again now and then, as I go along, for it influenced our life in one way or another during more than a generation. Whenever things grew dark it rose and put out its hopeful Sellers hand and cheered us up, and said, "Do not be afraid—trust in me—wait." It kept us hoping and hoping during forty years, and forsook us at last. It put our energies to sleep and made visionaries of us—dreamers and indolent. We were always going to be rich next year—no occasion to work. It is good to begin life poor; it is good to begin life rich—these are wholesome; but to begin it poor and prospectively rich! The man who has not experienced it cannot imagine the curse of it.

My parents removed to Missouri in the early 'thirties; I do not remember just when, for I was not born then and cared nothing for such things. It was a long journey in those days, and must have been a rough and tiresome one. The home was made in the wee village of Florida, in Monroe County, and I was born there in 1835. The village contained a hundred people and I increased the population by 1 per cent. It is more than many of the best men in history could have done for a town. It may not be modest in me to refer to this, but it is true. There is no record of a person doing as much—not even Shakespeare. But I did it for Florida, and it shows that I could have done it for any place—even London, I suppose.

Recently some one in Missouri has sent me a picture of the house I was born in. Heretofore I have always stated that it was a palace, but I shall be more guarded now.

I used to remember my brother Henry walking into a fire outdoors when he was a week old. It was remarkable in me to remember a thing like that, and it was still more remarkable that I should cling to the delusion, for thirty years, that I did remember it—for of course it never happened; he would not have been able to walk at that age. If I had stopped to reflect, I should not have burdened my memory with that impossible rubbish so long. It is believed by many people that an impression deposited in a child's memory within the first two years of its life cannot remain there five years, but that is an error. The incident of Benvenuto Cellini and the salamander must be accepted as authentic and trustworthy; and then that remarkable and indisputable instance in the experience of Helen Keller—However, I will speak of that at another time. For many years I believed that I remembered helping my grandfather drink his whisky toddy when I was six weeks old, but I do not tell about that any more, now; I am grown old and my memory is not as active as it used to be. When I was younger I could remember anything, whether it had happened or not; but my faculties are decaying now, and soon I shall be so I cannot remember any but the things that never happened. It is sad to go to pieces like this, but we all have to do it.

My uncle, John A. Quarles, was a farmer, and his place was in the country four miles from Florida. He had eight children and fifteen or twenty negroes, and was also fortunate in other ways, particularly in his character. I have not come across a better man than he was. I was his guest for two or three months every year, from the fourth year after we removed to Hannibal till I was eleven or twelve years old. I have never consciously used him or his wife in a book, but his farm has come very handy to me in literature once or twice. In Huck Finn and in Tom Sawyer, Detective I moved it down to Arkansas. It was all of six hundred miles, but it was no trouble; it was not a very large farm—five hundred acres, perhaps—but I could have done it if it had been twice as large. And as for the morality of it, I cared nothing for that; I would move a state if the exigencies of literature required it.

It was a heavenly place for a boy, that farm of my uncle John's. The house was a double log one, with a spacious floor (roofed in) connecting it with the kitchen. In the summer the table was set in the middle of that shady and breezy floor, and the sumptuous meals—well, it makes me cry to think of them. Fried chicken, roast pig; wild and tame turkeys, ducks, and geese; venison just killed; squirrels, rabbits, pheasants, partridges, prairie-chickens; biscuits, hot batter cakes, hot buckwheat cakes, hot "wheat bread," hot rolls, hot corn pone; fresh corn boiled on the ear, succotash, butter-beans, string-beans, tomatoes, peas, Irish potatoes, sweet potatoes; buttermilk, sweet milk, "clabber"; watermelons, muskmelons, cantaloupes—all fresh from the garden; apple pie, peach pie, pumpkin pie, apple dumplings, peach cobbler—I can't remember the rest. The way that the things were cooked was perhaps the main splendor—particularly a certain few of the dishes. For instance, the corn bread, the hot biscuits and wheat bread, and the fried chicken. These things have never been properly cooked in the North—in fact, no one there is able to learn the art, so far as my experience goes. The North thinks it knows how to make corn bread, but this is mere superstition. Perhaps no bread in the world is quite so good as Southern corn bread, and perhaps no bread in the world is quite so bad as the Northern imitation of it. The North seldom tries to fry chicken, and this is well; the art cannot be learned north of the line of Mason and Dixon, nor anywhere in Europe. This is not hearsay; it is experience that is speaking. In Europe it is imagined that the custom of serving various kinds of bread blazing hot is "American," but that is too broad a spread; it is custom in the South, but is much less than that in the North. In the North and in Europe hot bread is considered unhealthy. This is probably another fussy superstition, like the European superstition that ice-water is unhealthy. Europe does not need ice-water and does not drink it; and yet, notwithstanding this, its word for it is better than ours, because it describes it, whereas ours doesn't. Europe calls it "iced" water. Our word describes water made from melted ice—a drink which has a characterless taste and which we have but little acquaintance with.

It seems a pity that the world should throw away so many good things merely because they are unwholesome. I doubt if God has given us any refreshment which, taken in moderation, is unwholesome, except microbes. Yet there are people who strictly deprive themselves of each and every eatable, drinkable, and smokable which has in any way acquired a shady reputation. They pay this price for health. And health is all they get for it. How strange it is! It is like paying out your whole fortune for a cow that has gone dry.

The farmhouse stood in the middle of a very large yard, and the yard was fenced on three sides with rails and on the rear side with high palings; against these stood the smoke-house; beyond the palings was the orchard; beyond the orchard were the negro quarters and the tobacco fields. The front yard was entered over a stile made of sawed-off logs of graduated heights; I do not remember any gate. In a corner of the front yard were a dozen lofty hickory trees and a dozen black walnuts, and in the nutting season riches were to be gathered there.

Down a piece, abreast the house, stood a little log cabin against the rail fence; and there the woody hill fell sharply away, past the barns, the corn-crib, the stables, and the tobacco-curing house, to a limpid brook which sang along over its gravelly bed and curved and frisked in and out and here and there and yonder in the deep shade of overhanging foliage and vines—a divine place for wading, and it had swimming pools, too, which were forbidden to us and therefore much frequented by us. For we were little Christian children and had early been taught the value of forbidden fruit.

In the little log cabin lived a bedridden white-headed slave woman whom we visited daily and looked upon with awe, for we believed she was upward of a thousand years old and had talked with Moses. The younger negroes credited these statistics and had furnished them to us in good faith. We accommodated all the details which came to us about her; and so we believed that she had lost her health in the long desert trip coming out of Egypt, and had never been able to get it back again. She had a round bald place on the crown of her head, and we used to creep around and gaze at it in reverent silence, and reflect that it was caused by fright through seeing Pharaoh drowned. We called her "Aunt" Hannah, Southern fashion. She was superstitious, like the other negroes; also, like them, she was deeply religious. Like them, she had great faith in prayer and employed it in all ordinary exigencies, but not in cases where a dead certainty of result was urgent. Whenever witches were around she tied up the remnant of her wool in little tufts, with white thread, and this promptly made the witches impotent.

All the negroes were friends of ours, and with those of our own age we were in effect comrades. I say in effect, using the phrase as a modification. We were comrades, and yet not comrades; color and condition interposed a subtle line which both parties were conscious of and which rendered complete fusion impossible. We had a faithful and affectionate good friend, ally, and adviser in "Uncle Dan'l," a middle-aged slave whose head was the best one in the negro quarter, whose sympathies were wide and warm, and whose heart was honest and simple and knew no guile. He has served me well these many, many years. I have not seen him for more than half a century, and yet spiritually I have had his welcome company a good part of that time, and have staged him in books under his own name and as "Jim," and carted him all around—to Hannibal, down the Mississippi on a raft, and even across the Desert of Sahara in a balloon—and he has endured it all with the patience and friendliness and loyalty which were his birthright. It was on the farm that I got my strong liking for his race and my appreciation of certain of its fine qualities. This feeling and this estimate have stood the test of sixty years and more, and have suffered no impairment. The black face is as welcome to me now as it was then.

In my schoolboy days I had no aversion to slavery. I was not aware that there was anything wrong about it. No one arraigned it in my hearing; the local papers said nothing against it; the local pulpit taught us that God approved it, that it was a holy thing, and that the doubter need only look in the Bible if he wished to settle his mind—and then the texts were read aloud to us to make the matter sure; if the slaves themselves had an aversion to slavery, they were wise and said nothing. In Hannibal we seldom saw a slave misused; on the farm, never.

MARK TWAIN

There was, however, one small incident of my boyhood days which touched this matter, and it must have meant a good deal to me or it would not have stayed in my memory, clear and sharp, vivid and shadowless, all these slow-drifting years. We had a little slave boy whom we had hired from some one, there in Hannibal. He was from the eastern shore of Maryland, and had been brought away from his family and his friends, halfway across the American continent, and sold. He was a cheery spirit, innocent and gentle, and the noisiest creature that ever was, perhaps. All day long he was singing, whistling, yelling, whooping, laughing—it was maddening, devastating, unendurable. At last, one day, I lost all my temper, and went raging to my mother and said Sandy had been singing for an hour without a single break, and I couldn't stand it, and wouldn't she please shut him up. The tears came into her eyes and her lip trembled, and she said something like this:

"Poor thing, when he sings it shows that he is not remembering, and that comforts me; but when he is still I am afraid he is thinking, and I cannot bear it. He will never see his mother again; if he can sing, I must not hinder it, but be thankful for it. If you were older, you would understand me; then that friendless child's noise would make you glad."

It was a simple speech and made up of small words, but it went home, and Sandy's noise was not a trouble to me any more. She never used large words, but she had a natural gift for making small ones do effective work. She lived to reach the neighborhood of ninety years and was capable with her tongue to the last—especially when a meanness or an injustice roused her spirit. She has come handy to me several times in my books, where she figures as Tom Sawyer's Aunt Polly. I fitted her out with a dialect and tried to think up other improvements for her, but did not find any. I used Sandy once, also; it was in Tom Sawyer. I tried to get him to whitewash the fence, but it did not work. I do not remember what name I called him by in the book.

I can see the farm yet, with perfect clearness. I can see all its belongings, all its details; the family room of the house, with a "trundle" bed in one corner and a spinning-wheel in another—a wheel whose rising and falling wail, heard from a distance, was the mournfulest of all sounds to me, and made me homesick and low spirited, and filled my atmosphere with the wandering spirits of the dead; the vast fireplace, piled high, on winter nights, with flaming hickory logs from whose ends a sugary sap bubbled out, but did not go to waste, for we scraped it off and ate it; the lazy cat spread out on the rough hearthstones; the drowsy dogs braced against the jambs and blinking; my aunt in one chimney corner, knitting; my uncle in the other, smoking his corn-cob pipe; the slick and carpetless oak floor faintly mirroring the dancing flame tongues and freckled with black indentations where fire coals had popped out and died a leisurely death; half a dozen children romping in the background twilight; "split"-bottomed chairs here and there, some with rockers; a cradle—out of service, but waiting, with confidence; in the early cold mornings a snuggle of children, in shirts and chemises, occupying the hearthstone and procrastinating—they could not bear to leave that comfortable place and go out on the wind-swept floor space between the house and kitchen where the general tin basin stood, and wash.

Along outside of the front fence ran the country road, dusty in the summertime, and a good place for snakes—they liked to lie in it and sun themselves; when they were rattlesnakes or puff adders, we killed them; when they were black snakes, or racers, or belonged to the fabled "hoop" breed, we fled, without shame; when they were "house snakes," or "garters," we carried them home and put them in Aunt Patsy's work basket for a surprise; for she was prejudiced against snakes, and always when she took the basket in her lap and they began to climb out of it it disordered her mind. She never could seem to get used to them; her opportunities went for nothing. And she was always cold toward bats, too, and could not bear them; and yet I think a bat is as friendly a bird as there is. My mother was Aunt Patsy's sister and had the same wild superstitions. A bat is beautifully soft and silky; I do not know any creature that is pleasanter to the touch or is more grateful for caressings, if offered in the right spirit. I know all about these coleoptera, because our great cave, three miles below Hannibal, was multitudinously stocked with them, and often I brought them home to amuse my mother with. It was easy to manage if it was a school day, because then I had ostensibly been to school and hadn't any bats. She was not a suspicious person, but full of trust and confidence; and when I said, "There's something in my coat pocket for you," she would put her hand in. But she always took it out again, herself; I didn't have to tell her. It was remarkable, the way she couldn't learn to like private bats. The more experience she had, the more she could not change her views.

I think she was never in the cave in her life; but everybody else went there. Many excursion parties came from considerable distances up and down the river to visit the cave. It was miles in extent and was a tangled wilderness of narrow and lofty clefts and passages. It was an easy place to get lost in; anybody could do it—including the bats. I got lost in it myself, along with a lady, and our last candle burned down to almost nothing before we glimpsed the search party's lights winding about in the distance.

"Injun Joe," the half-breed, got lost in there once, and would have starved to death if the bats had run short. But there was no chance of that; there were myriads of them. He told me all his story. In the book called Tom Sawyer I starved him entirely to death in the cave, but that was in the interest of art; it never happened. "General" Gaines, who was our first town drunkard before Jimmy Finn got the place, was lost in there for the space of a week, and finally pushed his handkerchief out of a hole in a hilltop near Saverton, several miles down the river from the cave's mouth, and somebody saw it and dug him out. There is nothing the matter with his statistics except the handkerchief. I knew him for years and he hadn't any. But it could have been his nose. That would attract attention.

The cave was an uncanny place, for it contained a corpse—the corpse of a young girl of fourteen. It was in a glass cylinder inclosed in a copper one which was suspended from a rail which bridged a narrow passage. The body was preserved in alcohol, and it was said that loafers and rowdies used to drag it up by the hair and look at the dead face. The girl was the daughter of a St. Louis surgeon of extraordinary ability and wide celebrity. He was an eccentric man and did many strange things. He put the poor thing in that forlorn place himself.

BEYOND THE ROAD WHERE THE snakes sunned themselves was a dense young thicket, and through it a dim-lighted path led a quarter of a mile; then out of the dimness one emerged abruptly upon a level great prairie which was covered with wild strawberry plants, vividly starred with prairie pinks, and walled in on all sides by forests. The strawberries were fragrant and fine, and in the season we were generally there in the crisp freshness of the early morning, while the dew beads still sparkled upon the grass and the woods were ringing with the first songs of the birds.

Down the forest slopes to the left were the swings. They were made of bark stripped from hickory saplings. When they became dry they were dangerous. They usually broke when a child was forty feet in the air, and this was why so many bones had to be mended every year. I had no ill luck myself, but none of my cousins escaped. There were eight of them, and at one time and another they broke fourteen arms among them. But it cost next to nothing, for the doctor worked by the year—twenty-five dollars for the whole family. I remember two of the Florida doctors, Chowning and Meredith. They not only tended an entire family for twenty-five dollars a year, but furnished the medicines themselves. Good measure, too. Only the largest persons could hold a whole dose. Castor oil was the principal beverage. The dose was half a dipperful, with half a dipperful of New Orleans molasses added to help it down and make it taste good, which it never did. The next standby was calomel; the next, rhubarb; and the next, jalap. Then they bled the patient, and put mustard plasters on him. It was a dreadful system, and yet the death rate was not heavy. The calomel was nearly sure to salivate the patient and cost him some of his teeth. There were no dentists. When teeth became touched with decay or were otherwise ailing, the doctor knew of but one thing to do—he fetched his tongs and dragged them out. If the jaw remained, it was not his fault. Doctors were not called in cases of ordinary illness; the family grandmother attended to those. Every old woman was a doctor, and gathered her own medicines in the woods, and knew how to compound doses that would stir the vitals of a cast-iron dog. And then there was the "Indian doctor"; a grave savage, remnant of his tribe, deeply read in the mysteries of nature and the secret properties of herbs; and most backwoodsmen had high faith in his powers and could tell of wonderful cures achieved by him. In Mauritius, away off yonder in the solitudes of the Indian Ocean, there is a person who answers to our Indian doctor of the old times. He is a negro, and has had no teaching as a doctor, yet there is one disease which he is master of and can cure and the doctors can't. They send for him when they have a case. It is a child's disease of a strange and deadly sort, and the negro cures it with a herb medicine which he makes, himself, from a prescription which has come down to him from his father and grandfather. He will not let anyone see it. He keeps the secret of its components to himself, and it is feared that he will die without divulging it; then there will be consternation in Mauritius. I was told these things by the people there, in 1896.

We had the "faith doctor," too, in those early days—a woman. Her specialty was toothache. She was a farmer's old wife and lived five miles from Hannibal. She would lay her hand on the patient's jaw and say,

"Believe!" and the cure was prompt. Mrs. Utterback. I remember her very well. Twice I rode out there behind my mother, horseback, and saw the cure performed. My mother was the patient.

Doctor Meredith removed to Hannibal, by and by, and was our family physician there, and saved my life several times. Still, he was a good man and meant well. Let it go.

I was always told that I was a sickly and precarious and tiresome and uncertain child, and lived mainly on allopathic medicines during the first seven years of my life. I asked my mother about this, in her old age—she was in her eighty-eighth year—and said:

"I suppose that during all that time you were uneasy about me?"

"Yes, the whole time."

"Afraid I wouldn't live?"

After a reflective pause—ostensibly to think out the facts—"No—afraid you would."

The country schoolhouse was three miles from my uncle's farm. It stood in a clearing in the woods and would hold about twenty-five boys and girls. We attended the school with more or less regularity once or twice a week, in summer, walking to it in the cool of the morning by the forest paths, and back in the gloaming at the end of the day. All the pupils brought their dinners in baskets—corn dodger, buttermilk, and other good things—and sat in the shade of the trees at noon and ate them. It is the part of my education which I look back upon with the most satisfaction. My first visit to the school was when I was seven. A strapping girl of fifteen, in the customary sunbonnet and calico dress, asked me if I "used tobacco"—meaning did I chew it. I said no. It roused her scorn. She reported me to all the crowd, and said:

"Here is a boy seven years old who can't chew tobacco."

By the looks and comments which this produced I realized that I was a degraded object, and was cruelly ashamed of myself. I determined to reform. But I only made myself sick; I was not able to learn to chew tobacco. I learned to smoke fairly well, but that did not conciliate anybody and I remained a poor thing, and characterless. I longed to be respected, but I never was able to rise. Children have but little charity for one another's defects.

As I have said, I spent some part of every year at the farm until I was twelve or thirteen years old. The life which I led there with my cousins was full of charm, and so is the memory of it yet. I can call back the solemn twilight and mystery of the deep woods, the earthy smells, the faint odors of the wild flowers, the sheen of rain-washed foliage, the rattling clatter of drops when the wind shook the trees, the far-off hammering of woodpeckers and the muffled drumming of wood pheasants in the remoteness of the forest, the snapshot glimpses of disturbed wild creatures scurrying through the grass—I can call it all back and make it as real as it ever was, and as blessed. I can call back the prairie, and its loneliness and peace, and a vast hawk hanging motionless in the sky, with his wings spread wide and the blue of the vault showing through the fringe of their end feathers. I can see the woods in their autumn dress, the oaks purple, the hickories washed with gold, the maples and the sumachs luminous with crimson fires, and I can hear the rustle made by the fallen leaves as we plowed through them. I can see the blue clusters of wild grapes hanging among the foliage of the saplings, and I remember the taste of them and the smell. I know how the wild blackberries looked, and how they tasted, and the same with the pawpaws, the hazelnuts, and the persimmons; and I can feel the thumping rain, upon my head, of hickory nuts and walnuts when we were out in the frosty dawn to scramble for them with the pigs, and the gusts of wind loosed them and sent them down. I know the stain of blackberries, and how pretty it is, and I know the stain of walnut hulls, and how little it minds soap and water, also what grudged experience it had of either of them. I know the taste of maple sap, and when to gather it, and how to arrange the troughs and the delivery tubes, and how to boil down the juice, and how to hook the sugar after it is made, also how much better hooked sugar tastes than any that is honestly come by, let bigots say what they will. I know how a prize watermelon looks when it is sunning its fat rotundity among pumpkin vines and "simblins"; I know how to tell when it is ripe without "plugging" it; I know how inviting it looks when it is cooling itself in a tub of water under the bed, waiting; I know how it looks when it lies on the table in the sheltered great floor space between house and kitchen, and the children gathered for the sacrifice and their mouths watering; I know the crackling sound it makes when the carving knife enters its end, and I can see the split fly along in front of the blade as the knife cleaves its way to the other end; I can see its halves fall apart and display the rich red meat and the black seeds, and the heart standing up, a luxury fit for the elect; I know how a boy looks behind a yard-long slice of that melon, and I know how he feels; for I have been there. I know the taste of the watermelon which has been honestly come by, and I know the taste of the watermelon which has been acquired by art. Both taste good, but the experienced know which tastes best. I know the look of green apples and peaches and pears on the trees, and I know how entertaining they are when they are inside of a person. I know how ripe ones look when they are piled in pyramids under the trees, and how pretty they are and how vivid their colors. I know how a frozen apple looks, in a barrel down cellar in the wintertime, and how hard it is to bite, and how the frost makes the teeth ache, and yet how good it is, notwithstanding. I know the disposition of elderly people to select the specked apples for the children, and I once knew ways to beat the game. I know the look of an apple that is roasting and sizzling on a hearth on a winter's evening, and I know the comfort that comes of eating it hot, along with some sugar and a drench of cream. I know the delicate art and mystery of so cracking hickory nuts and walnuts on a flatiron with a hammer that the kernels will be delivered whole, and I know how the nuts, taken in conjunction with winter apples, cider, and doughnuts, make old people's old tales and old jokes sound fresh and crisp and enchanting, and juggle an evening away before you know what went with the time. I know the look of Uncle Dan'l's kitchen as it was on the privileged nights, when I was a child, and I can see the white and black children grouped on the hearth, with the firelight playing on their faces and the shadows flickering upon the walls, clear back toward the cavernous gloom of the rear, and I can hear Uncle Dan'l telling the immortal tales which Uncle Remus Harris was to gather into his book and charm the world with, by and by; and I can feel again the creepy joy which quivered through me when the time for the ghost story was reached—and the sense of regret, too, which came over me, for it was always the last story of the evening and there was nothing between it and the unwelcome bed.

I can remember the bare wooden stairway in my uncle's house, and the turn to the left above the landing, and the rafters and the slanting roof over my bed, and the squares of moonlight on the floor, and the white cold world of snow outside, seen through the curtainless window. I can remember the howling of the wind and the quaking of the house on stormy nights, and how snug and cozy one felt, under the blankets, listening; and how the powdery snow used to sift in, around the sashes, and lie in little ridges on the floor and make the place look chilly in the morning and curb the wild desire to get up—in case there was any. I can remember how very dark that room was, in the dark of the moon, and how packed it was with ghostly stillness when one woke up by accident away in the night, and forgotten sins came flocking out of the secret chambers of the memory and wanted a hearing; and how ill chosen the time seemed for this kind of business; and how dismal was the hoo-hooing of the owl and the wailing of the wolf, sent mourning by on the night wind.

I remember the raging of the rain on that roof, summer nights, and how pleasant it was to lie and listen to it, and enjoy the white splendor of the lightning and the majestic booming and crashing of the thunder. It was a very satisfactory room, and there was a lightning rod which was reachable from the window, an adorable and skittish thing to climb up and down, summer nights, when there were duties on hand of a sort to make privacy desirable.

I remember the 'coon and 'possum hunts, nights, with the negroes, and the long marches through the black gloom of the woods, and the excitement which fired everybody when the distant bay of an experienced dog announced that the game was treed; then the wild scramblings and stumblings through briers and bushes and over roots to get to the spot; then the lighting of a fire and the felling of the tree, the joyful frenzy of the dogs and the negroes, and the weird picture it all made in the red glare—I remember it all well, and the delight that everyone got out of it, except the 'coon.

I remember the pigeon seasons, when the birds would come in millions and cover the trees and by their weight break down the branches. They were clubbed to death with sticks; guns were not necessary and were not used. I remember the squirrel hunts, and prairie-chicken hunts, and wild-turkey hunts, and all that; and how we turned out, mornings, while it was still dark, to go on these expeditions, and how chilly and dismal it was, and how often I regretted that I was well enough to go. A toot on a tin horn brought twice as many dogs as were needed, and in their happiness they raced and scampered about, and knocked small people down, and made no end of unnecessary noise. At the word, they vanished away toward the woods, and we drifted silently after them in the melancholy gloom. But presently the gray dawn stole over the world, the birds piped up, then the sun rose and poured light and comfort all around, everything was fresh and dewy and fragrant, and life was a boon again. After three hours of tramping we arrived back wholesomely tired, overladen with game, very hungry, and just in time for breakfast.

Jane Lampton Clemens

THIS WAS MY MOTHER. WHEN she died, in October, 1890, she was well along in her eighty-eighth year, a mighty age, a well-contested fight for life for one who at forty was so delicate of body as to be accounted a confirmed invalid and destined to pass soon away. I knew her well during the first twenty-five years of my life; but after that I saw her only at wide intervals, for we lived many days' journey apart. I am not proposing to write about her, but merely to talk about her; not give her formal history, but merely make illustrative extracts from it, so to speak; furnish flashlight glimpses of her character, not a processional view of her career. Technically speaking, she had no career; but she had a character, and it was of a fine and striking and lovable sort.

What becomes of the multitudinous photographs which one's mind takes of people? Out of the million which my mental camera must have taken of this first and closest friend, only one clear and strongly defined one of early date remains. It dates back forty-seven years; she was forty years old then, and I was eight. She held me by the hand, and we were kneeling by the bedside of my brother, two years older than I, who lay dead, and the tears were flowing down her cheeks unchecked. And she was moaning. That dumb sign of anguish was perhaps new to me, since it made upon me a very strong impression—an impression which holds its place still with the picture which it helped to intensify and make memorable.

She had a slender, small body, but a large heart—a heart so large that everybody's grief and everybody's joys found welcome in it, and hospitable accommodation. The greatest difference which I find between her and the rest of the people whom I have known, is this, and it is a remarkable one: those others felt a strong interest in a few things, whereas to the very day of her death she felt a strong interest in the whole world and everything and everybody in it. In all her life she never knew such a thing as a half-hearted interest in affairs and people, or an interest which drew a line and left out certain affairs and was indifferent to certain people. The invalid who takes a strenuous and indestructible interest in everything and everybody but himself, and to whom a dull moment is an unknown thing and an impossibility, is a formidable adversary for disease and a hard invalid to vanquish. I am certain that it was this feature of my mother's makeup that carried her so far toward ninety.

Her interest in people and other animals was warm, personal, friendly. She always found something to excuse, and as a rule to love, in the toughest of them—even if she had to put it there herself. She was the natural ally and friend of the friendless. It was believed that, Presbyterian as she was, she could be beguiled into saying a soft word for the devil himself, and so the experiment was tried. The abuse of Satan began; one conspirator after another added his bitter word, his malign reproach, his pitiless censure, till at last, sure enough, the unsuspecting subject of the trick walked into the trap. She admitted that the indictment was sound, that Satan was utterly wicked and abandoned, just as these people had said; but would any claim that he had been treated fairly? A sinner was but a sinner; Satan was just that, like the rest. What saves the rest?—their own efforts alone? No—or none might ever be saved. To their feeble efforts is added the mighty help of pathetic, appealing, imploring prayers that go up daily out of all the churches in Christendom and out of myriads upon myriads of pitying hearts. But who prays for Satan? Who, in eighteen centuries, has had the common humanity to pray for the one sinner that needed it most, our one fellow and brother who most needed a friend yet had not a single one, the one sinner among us all who had the highest and clearest right to every Christian's daily and nightly prayers, for the plain and unassailable reason that his was the first and greatest need, he being among sinners the supremest?

This friend of Satan was a most gentle spirit, and an unstudied and unconscious pathos was her native speech. When her pity or her indignation was stirred by hurt or shame inflicted upon some defenseless person or creature, she was the most eloquent person I have heard speak. It was seldom eloquence of a fiery or violent sort, but gentle, pitying, persuasive, appealing; and so genuine and so nobly and simply worded and so touchingly uttered, that many times I have seen it win the reluctant and splendid applause of tears. Whenever anybody or any creature was being oppressed, the fears that belonged to her sex and her small stature retired to the rear and her soldierly qualities came promptly to the front. One day in our village I saw a vicious devil of a Corsican, a common terror in the town, chasing his grown daughter past cautious male citizens with a heavy rope in his hand, and declaring he would wear it out on her. My mother spread her door wide to the refugee, and then, instead of closing and locking it after her, stood in it and stretched her arms across it, barring the way. The man swore, cursed, threatened her with his rope; but she did not flinch or show any sign of fear; she only stood straight and fine, and lashed him, shamed him, derided him, defied him in tones not audible to the middle of the street, but audible to the man's conscience and dormant manhood; and he asked her pardon and gave her his rope and said with a most great and blasphemous oath that she was the bravest woman he ever saw; and so went his way without other word and troubled her no more. He and she were always good friends after that, for in her he had found a long-felt want—somebody who was not afraid of him.

One day in St. Louis she walked out into the street and greatly surprised a burly cartman who was beating his horse over the head with the butt of his heavy whip; for she took the whip away from him and then made such a persuasive appeal in behalf of the ignorantly offending horse that he was tripped into saying he was to blame; and also into volunteering a promise which of course he couldn't keep, for he was not built in that way—a promise that he wouldn't ever abuse a horse again.

That sort of interference in behalf of abused animals was a common thing with her all her life; and her manner must have been without offense and her good intent transparent, for she always carried her point, and also won the courtesy, and often the friendly applause, of the adversary. All the race of dumb animals had a friend in her. By some subtle sign the homeless, hunted, bedraggled, and disreputable cat recognized her at a glance as the born refuge and champion of his sort—and followed her home. His instinct was right, he was as welcome as the prodigal son. We had nineteen cats at one time, in 1845. And there wasn't one in the lot that had any character, not one that had any merit, except the cheap and tawdry merit of being unfortunate. They were a vast burden to us all—including my mother—but they were out of luck, and that was enough; they had to stay. However, better these than no pets at all; children must have pets, and we were not allowed to have caged ones. An imprisoned creature was out of the question—my mother would not have allowed a rat to be restrained of its liberty.

In the small town of Hannibal, Missouri, when I was a boy, everybody was poor, but didn't know it: and everybody was comfortable, and did know it. And there were grades of society—people of good family, people of unclassified family, people of no family. Everybody knew everybody, and was affable to everybody, and nobody put on any visible airs; yet the class lines were quite clearly drawn and the familiar social life of each class was restricted to that class. It was a little democracy which was full of liberty, equality, and Fourth of July, and sincerely so, too; yet you perceived that the aristocratic taint was there. It was there, and nobody found fault with the fact, or ever stopped to reflect that its presence was an inconsistency.

I suppose that this state of things was mainly due to the circumstance that the town's population had come from slave states and still had the institution of slavery with them in their new home. My mother, with her large nature and liberal sympathies, was not intended for an aristocrat, yet through her breeding she was one. Few people knew it, perhaps, for it was an instinct, I think, rather than a principle. So its outward manifestation was likely to be accidental, not intentional, and also not frequent. But I knew of that weak spot. I knew that privately she was proud that the Lambtons, now Earls of Durham, had occupied the family lands for nine hundred years; that they were feudal lords of Lambton Castle and holding the high position of ancestors of hers when the Norman Conqueror came over to divert the Englishry. I argued—cautiously, and with mollifying circumlocutions, for one had to be careful when he was on that holy ground, and mustn't cavort—that there was no particular merit in occupying a piece of land for nine hundred years, with the friendly assistance of an entail; anybody could do it, with intellect or without; therefore the entail was the thing to be proud of, just the entail and nothing else; consequently, she was merely descended from an entail, and she might as well be proud of being descended from a mortgage. Whereas my own ancestry was quite a different and superior thing, because it had the addition of an ancestor—one Clemens—who did something; something which was very creditable to him and satisfactory to me, in that he was a member of the court that tried Charles I and delivered him over to the executioner. Ostensibly this was chaff, but at the bottom it was not. I had a very real respect for that ancestor, and this respect has increased with the years, not diminished. He did what he could toward reducing the list of crowned shams of his day. However, I can say this for my mother, that I never heard her refer in any way to her gilded ancestry when any person not a member of the family was present, for she had good American sense. But with other Lamptons whom I have known, it was different. "Colonel Sellers" was a Lampton, and a tolerably near relative of my mother's; and when he was alive, poor old airy soul, one of the earliest things a stranger was likely to hear from his lips was some reference to the "head of our line," flung off with a painful casualness that was wholly beneath criticism as a work of art. It compelled inquiry, of course; it was intended to compel it. Then followed the whole disastrous history of how the Lambton heir came to this country a hundred and fifty years or so ago, disgusted with that foolish fraud, hereditary aristocracy, and married, and shut himself away from the world in the remotenesses of the wilderness, and went to breeding ancestors of future American claimants, while at home in England he was given up as dead and his titles and estates turned over to his younger brother, usurper and personally responsible for the perverse and unseatable usurpers of our day. And the colonel always spoke with studied and courtly deference of the claimant of his day—a second cousin of his—and referred to him with entire seriousness as "the earl." "The earl" was a man of parts, and might have accomplished something for himself but for the calamitous accident of his birth. He was a Kentuckian, and a well-meaning man; but he had no money, and no time to earn any; for all his time was taken up in trying to get me, and others of the tribe, to furnish him capital to fight his claim through the House of Lords with. He had all the documents, all the proofs; he knew he could win. And so he dreamed his life away, always in poverty, sometimes in actual want, and died at last, far from home, and was buried from a hospital by strangers who did not know he was an earl, for he did not look it. That poor fellow used to sign his letters "Durham," and in them he would find fault with me for voting the Republican ticket, for the reason that it was unaristocratic, and by consequence un-Lamptonian. And presently along would come a letter from some red-hot Virginian, son of my other branch, and abuse me bitterly for the same vote—on the ground that the Republican was an aristocratic party and it was not becoming in the descendant of a regicide to train with that kind of animals. And so I used to almost wish I hadn't had any ancestors, they were so much trouble to me.

As I have said, we lived in a slaveholding community; indeed, when slavery perished my mother had been in daily touch with it for sixty years. Yet, kind-hearted and compassionate as she was, I think she was not conscious that slavery was a bald, grotesque, and unwarrantable usurpation. She had never heard it assailed in any pulpit, but had heard it defended and sanctified in a thousand; her ears were familiar with Bible texts that approved it, but if there were any that disapproved it they had not been quoted by her pastors; as far as her experience went, the wise and the good and the holy were unanimous in the conviction that slavery was right, righteous, sacred, the peculiar pet of the Deity, and a condition which the slave himself ought to be daily and nightly thankful for. Manifestly, training and association can accomplish strange miracles. As a rule our slaves were convinced and content. So, doubtless, are the far more intelligent slaves of a monarchy; they revere and approve their masters, the monarch and the noble, and recognize no degradation in the fact that they are slaves—slaves with the name blinked, and less respectworthy than were our black ones, if to be a slave by meek consent is baser than to be a slave by compulsion—and doubtless it is.

However, there was nothing about the slavery of the Hannibal region to rouse one's dozing humane instincts to activity. It was the mild domestic slavery, not the brutal plantation article. Cruelties were very rare, and exceedingly and wholesomely unpopular. To separate and sell the members of a slave family to different masters was a thing not well liked by the people, and so it was not often done, except in the settling of estates. I have no recollection of ever seeing a slave auction in that town; but I am suspicious that that is because the thing was a common and commonplace spectacle, not an uncommon and impressive one. I vividly remember seeing a dozen black men and women chained to one another, once, and lying in a group on the pavement, awaiting shipment to the Southern slave market. Those were the saddest faces I have ever seen. Chained slaves could not have been a common sight, or this picture would not have made so strong and lasting an impression upon me.

The "nigger trader" was loathed by everybody. He was regarded as a sort of human devil who bought and conveyed poor helpless creatures to hell—for to our whites and blacks alike the Southern plantation was simply hell; no milder name could describe it. If the threat to sell an incorrigible slave "down the river" would not reform him, nothing would—his case was past cure.

It is commonly believed that an infallible effect of slavery was to make such as lived in its midst hard hearted. I think it had no such effect—speaking in general terms. I think it stupefied everybody's humanity, as regarded the slave, but stopped there. There were no hard-hearted people in our town—I mean there were no more than would be found in any other town of the same size in any other country; and in my experience hard-hearted people are very rare everywhere.

Playing "Bear"—Herrings—Jim Wolf and the Cats

This was in 1849. I was fourteen years old, then. We were still living in Hannibal, Missouri, on the banks of the Mississippi, in the new "frame" house built by my father five years before. That is, some of us lived in the new part, the rest in the old part back of it and attached to it. In the autumn my sister gave a party and invited all the marriageable young people of the village. I was too young for this society, and was too bashful to mingle with young ladies, anyway, therefore I was not invited—at least not for the whole evening. Ten minutes of it was to be my whole share. I was to do the part of a bear in a small fairy play. I was to be disguised all over in a close-fitting brown hairy stuff proper for a bear. About half past ten I was told to go to my room and put on this disguise, and be ready in half an hour. I started, but changed my mind, for I wanted to practice a little, and that room was very small. I crossed over to the large unoccupied house on the corner of Main Street, unaware that a dozen of the young people were also going there to dress for their parts. I took the little black boy, Sandy, with me, and we selected a roomy and empty chamber on the second floor. We entered it talking, and this gave a couple of half-dressed young ladies an opportunity to take refuge behind a screen undiscovered. Their gowns and things were hanging on hooks behind the door, but I did not see them; it was Sandy that shut the door, but all his heart was in the theatricals, and he was as unlikely to notice them as I was myself.

That was a rickety screen, with many holes in it, but, as I did not know there were girls behind it, I was not disturbed by that detail. If I had known, I could not have undressed in the flood of cruel moonlight that was pouring in at the curtainless windows; I should have died of shame. Untroubled by apprehensions, I stripped to the skin and began my practice. I was full of ambition, I was determined to make a hit, I was burning to establish a reputation as a bear and get further engagements; so I threw myself into my work with an abandon that promised great things. I capered back and forth from one end of the room to the other on all fours, Sandy applauding with enthusiasm; I walked upright and growled and snapped and snarled, I stood on my head, I flung handsprings, I danced a lubberly dance with my paws bent and my imaginary snout sniffing from side to side, I did everything a bear could do, and many things which no bear could ever do and no bear with any dignity would want to do, anyway; and of course I never suspected that I was making a spectacle of myself to anyone but Sandy. At last, standing on my head, I paused in that attitude to take a minute's rest. There was a moment's silence, then Sandy spoke up with excited interest and said:

"Mars Sam, has you ever seed a dried herring?"

"No. What is that?"

"It's a fish."

"Well, what of it? Anything peculiar about it?"

"Yes, suh, you bet you dey is. Dey eats 'em innards and all!"

There was a smothered burst of feminine snickers from behind the screen! All the strength went out of me and I toppled forward like an undermined tower and brought the screen down with my weight, burying the young ladies under it. In their fright they discharged a couple of piercing screams—and possibly others—but I did not wait to count. I snatched my clothes and fled to the dark hall below, Sandy following. I was dressed in half a minute, and out the back way. I swore Sandy to eternal silence, then we went away and hid until the party was over. The ambition was all out of me. I could not have faced that giddy company after my adventure, for there would be two performers there who knew my secret and would be privately laughing at me all the time. I was searched for, but not found, and the bear had to be played by a young gentleman in his civilized clothes. The house was still and everybody asleep when I finally ventured home. I was very heavy hearted and full of a bitter sense of disgrace. Pinned to my pillow I found a slip of paper which bore a line which did not lighten my heart, but only made my face burn. It was written in a laboriously disguised hand, and these were its mocking terms:

You probably couldn't have played bear, but you played bare very well—oh, very very well!

We think boys are rude, unsensitive animals, but it is not so in all cases. Each boy has one or two sensitive spots, and if you can find out where they are located you have only to touch them and you can scorch him as with fire. I suffered miserably over that episode. I expected that the facts would be all over the village in the morning, but it was not so. The secret remained confined to the two girls and Sandy and me. That was some appeasement of my pain, but it was far from sufficient—the main trouble remained: I was under four mocking eyes, and it might as well have been a thousand, for I suspected all girls' eyes of being the ones I so dreaded. During several weeks I could not look any young lady in the face; I dropped my eyes in confusion when any one of them smiled upon me and gave me greeting; I said to myself, "That is one of them," and got quickly away. Of course I was meeting the right girls everywhere, but if they ever let slip any betraying sign I was not bright enough to catch it. When I left Hannibal, four years later, the secret was still a secret; I had never guessed those girls out, and was no longer hoping or expecting to do it.

One of the dearest and prettiest girls in the village at the time of my mishap was one whom I will call Mary Wilson, because that was not her name. She was twenty years old; she was dainty and sweet, peach-blooming and exquisite, gracious and lovely in character. I stood in awe of her, for she seemed to me to be made out of angel clay and rightfully unapproachable by just any unholy ordinary kind of boy like me. I probably never suspected her. But—

The scene changes to Calcutta—forty-seven years later. It was in 1896. I arrived there on a lecturing trip. As I entered the hotel a vision passed out of it, clothed in the glory of the Indian sunshine—the Mary Wilson of my long-vanished boyhood! It was a startling thing. Before I could recover from the pleasant shock and speak to her she was gone. I thought maybe I had seen an apparition, but it was not so, she was flesh. She was the granddaughter of the other Mary. The other Mary, now a widow, was upstairs, and presently sent for me. She was old and gray-haired, but she looked young and was very handsome. We sat down and talked. We steeped our thirsty souls in the reviving wine of the past, the pathetic past, the beautiful past, the dear and lamented past; we uttered the names that had been silent upon our lips for fifty years, and it was as if they were made of music; with reverent hands we unburied our dead, the mates of our youth, and caressed them with our speech; we searched the dusty chambers of our memories and dragged forth incident after incident, episode after episode, folly after folly, and laughed such good laughs over them, with the tears running down; and finally Mary said, suddenly, and without any leading up:

"Tell me! What is the special peculiarity of dried herrings?"

It seemed a strange question at such a hallowed time as this. And so inconsequential, too. I was a little shocked. And yet I was aware of a stir of some kind away back in the deeps of my memory somewhere. It set me to musing—thinking—searching. Dried herrings? Dried herrings? The peculiarity of dri. . . I glanced up. Her face was grave, but there was a dim and shadowy twinkle in her eye which—All of a sudden I knew and far away down in the hoary past I heard a remembered voice murmur. "Dey eats 'em innards and all!"

"At—last! I've found one of you, anyway! Who was the other girl?"

But she drew the line there. She wouldn't tell me.

But a boy's life is not all comedy; much of the tragic enters into it. The drunken tramp—mentioned elsewhere—who was burned up in the village jail lay upon my conscience a hundred nights afterward and filled them with hideous dreams—dreams in which I saw his appealing face as I had seen it in the pathetic reality, pressed against the window bars, with the red hell glowing behind him—a face which seemed to say to me, "If you had not given me the matches, this would not have happened; you are responsible for my death." I was not responsible for it, for I had meant him no harm, but only good, when I let him have the matches; but no matter, mine was a trained Presbyterian conscience and knew but the one duty—to hunt and harry its slave upon all pretexts and on all occasions, particularly when there was no sense nor reason in it. The tramp—who was to blame—suffered ten minutes; I, who was not to blame, suffered three months.

The shooting down of poor old Smarr in the main street at noonday supplied me with some more dreams; and in them I always saw again the grotesque closing picture—the great family Bible spread open on the profane old man's breast by some thoughtful idiot, and rising and sinking to the labored breathings, and adding the torture of its leaden weight to the dying struggles. We are curiously made. In all the throng of gaping and sympathetic onlookers there was not one with common sense enough to perceive that an anvil would have been in better taste there than the Bible, less open to sarcastic criticism, and swifter in its atrocious work. In my nightmares I gasped and struggled for breath under the crush of that vast book for many a night.

All within the space of a couple of years we had two or three other tragedies, and I had the ill luck to be too near by, on each occasion. There was the slave man who was struck down with a chunk of slag for some small offense; I saw him die. And the young Californian emigrant who was stabbed with a bowie knife by a drunken comrade; I saw the red life gush from his breast. And the case of the rowdy young brothers and their harmless old uncle: one of them held the old man down with his knees on his breast while the other one tried repeatedly to kill him with an Allen revolver which wouldn't go off, I happened along just then, of course.

Then there was the case of the young Californian emigrant who got drunk and proposed to raid the "Welshman's house" all alone one dark and threatening night. This house stood halfway up Holliday's Hill and its sole occupants were a poor but quite respectable widow and her blameless daughter. The invading ruffian woke the whole village with his ribald yells and coarse challenges and obscenities. I went up there with a comrade—John Briggs, I think—to look and listen. The figure of the man was dimly visible; the women were on their porch, nor visible in the deep shadow of its roof, but we heard the elder woman's voice. She had loaded an old musket with slugs, and she warned the man that if he stayed where he was while she counted ten it would cost him his life. She began to count, slowly; he began to laugh. He stopped laughing at "six"; then through the deep stillness, in a steady voice, followed the rest of the tale: "Seven. . . eight. . . nine"—a long pause, we holding our breaths—"ten!" A red spout of flame gushed out into the night, and the man dropped with his breast riddled to rags. Then the rain and the thunder burst loose and the waiting town swarmed up the hill in the glare of the lightning like an invasion of ants. Those people saw the rest; I had had my share and was satisfied. I went home to dream, and was not disappointed.

My teaching and training enabled me to see deeper into these tragedies than an ignorant person could have done. I knew what they were for. I tried to disguise it from myself, but down in the secret deeps of my troubled heart I knew—and I knew I knew. They were inventions of Providence to beguile me to a better life. It sounds curiously innocent and conceited, now, but to me there was nothing strange about it; it was quite in accordance with the thoughtful and judicious ways of Providence as I understood them. It would not have surprised me, nor even overflattered me, if Providence had killed off that whole community in trying to save an asset like me. Educated as I had been, it would have seemed just the thing, and well worth the expense. Why Providence should take such an anxious interest in such a property, that idea never entered my head, and there was no one in that simple hamlet who would have dreamed of putting it there. For one thing, no one was equipped with it.

It is quite true, I took all the tragedies to myself, and tallied them off in turn as they happened, saying to myself in each case, with a sigh, "Another one gone—and on my account; this ought to bring me to repentance; the patience of God will not always endure." And yet privately I believed it would. That is, I believed it in the daytime; but not in the night. With the going down of the sun my faith failed and the clammy fears gathered about my heart. It was then that I repented. Those were awful nights, nights of despair, nights charged with the bitterness of death. After each tragedy I recognized the warning and repented; repented and begged; begged like a coward, begged like a dog; and not in the interest of those poor people who had been extinguished for my sake, but only in my own interest. It seems selfish, when I look back on it now.

My repentances were very real, very earnest; and after each tragedy they happened every night for a long time. But as a rule they could not stand the daylight. They faded out and shredded away and disappeared in the glad splendor of the sun. They were the creatures of fear and darkness, and they could not live out of their own place. The day gave me cheer and peace, and at night I repented again. In all my boyhood life I am not sure that I ever tried to lead a better life in the daytime— or wanted to. In my age I should never think of wishing to do such a thing. But in my age, as in my youth, night brings me many a deep remorse. I realize that from the cradle up I have been like the rest of the race—never quite sane in the night. When "Injun Joe" died. . . But never mind. Somewhere I have already described what a raging hell of repentance I passed through then. I believe that for months I was as pure as the driven snow. After dark.

Jim Wolf and the Cats

IT WAS BACK IN THOSE far-distant days—1848 or '49—that Jim Wolf came to us. He was from a hamlet thirty or forty miles back in the country, and he brought all his native sweetnesses and gentlenesses and simplicities with him. He was approaching seventeen, a grave and slender lad, trustful, honest, honorable, a creature to love and cling to. And he was incredibly bashful. He was with us a good while, but he could never conquer that peculiarity; he could not be at ease in the presence of any woman, not even in my good and gentle mother's; and as to speaking to any girl, it was wholly impossible. He sat perfectly still, one day—there were ladies chatting in the room—while a wasp up his leg stabbed him cruelly a dozen times; and all the sign he gave was a slight wince for each stab and the tear of torture in his eye. He was too bashful to move.

It is to this kind that untoward things happen. My sister gave a "candy-pull" on a winter's night. I was too young to be of the company, and Jim was too diffident. I was sent up to bed early, and Jim followed of his own motion. His room was in the new part of the house and his window looked out on the roof of the L annex. That roof was six inches deep in snow, and the snow had an ice crust upon it which was as slick as glass. Out of the comb of the roof projected a short chimney, a common resort for sentimental cats on moonlight nights—and this was a moonlight night. Down at the eaves, below the chimney, a canopy of dead vines spread away to some posts, making a cozy shelter, and after an hour or two the rollicking crowd of young ladies and gentlemen grouped themselves in its shade, with their saucers of liquid and piping-hot candy disposed about them on the frozen ground to cool. There was joyous chaffing and joking and laughter—peal upon peal of it.

About this time a couple of old, disreputable tomcats got up on the chimney and started a heated argument about something; also about this time I gave up trying to get to sleep and went visiting to Jim's room. He was awake and fuming about the cats and their intolerable yowling. I asked him, mockingly, why he didn't climb out and drive them away. He was nettled, and said overboldly that for two cents he would.

It was a rash remark and was probably repented of before it was fairly out of his mouth. But it was too late—he was committed. I knew him; and I knew he would rather break his neck than back down, if I egged him on judiciously.

"Oh, of course you would! Who's doubting it?"

It galled him, and he burst out, with sharp irritation, "Maybe you doubt it!"

"I? Oh no! I shouldn't think of such a thing. You are always doing wonderful things, with your mouth."

He was in a passion now. He snatched on his yarn socks and began to raise the window, saying in a voice quivering with anger:

"You think I dasn't—you do! Think what you blame please. I don't care what you think. I'll show you!"

The window made him rage; it wouldn't stay up.

I said, "Never mind, I'll hold it."

Indeed, I would have done anything to help. I was only a boy and was already in a radiant heaven of anticipation. He climbed carefully out, clung to the window sill until his feet were safely placed, then began to pick his perilous way on all-fours along the glassy comb, a foot and a hand on each side of it. I believe I enjoy it now as much as I did then; yet it is nearly fifty years ago. The frosty breeze flapped his short shirt about his lean legs; the crystal roof shone like polished marble in the intense glory of the moon; the unconscious cats sat erect upon the chimney, alertly watching each other, lashing their tails and pouring out their hollow grievances; and slowly and cautiously Jim crept on, flapping as he went, the gay and frolicsome young creatures under the vine canopy unaware, and outraging these solemnities with their misplaced laughter. Every time Jim slipped I had a hope; but always on he crept and disappointed it. At last he was within reaching distance. He paused, raised himself carefully up, measured his distance deliberately, then made a frantic grab at the nearest cat—and missed it. Of course he lost his balance. His heels flew up, he struck on his back, and like a rocket he darted down the roof feet first, crashed through the dead vines, and landed in a sitting position in fourteen saucers of red-hot candy, in the midst of all that party—and dressed as he was—this lad who could not look a girl in the face with his clothes on. There was a wild scramble and a storm of shrieks, and Jim fled up the stairs, dripping broken crockery all the way.

The incident was ended. But I was not done with it yet, though I supposed I was. Eighteen or twenty years later I arrived in New York from California, and by that time I had failed in all my other undertakings and had stumbled into literature without intending it. This was early in 1867. I was offered a large sum to write something for the Sunday Mercury, and I answered with the tale of "Jim Wolf and the Cats." I also collected the money for it—twenty-five dollars. It seemed over-pay, but I did not say anything about that, for I was not so scrupulous then as I am now.

A year or two later "Jim Wolf and the Cats" appeared in a Tennessee paper in a new dress—as to spelling; it was masquerading in a Southern dialect. The appropriator of the tale had a wide reputation in the West and was exceedingly popular. Deservedly so, I think. He wrote some of the breeziest and funniest things I have ever read, and did his work with distinguished ease and fluency. His name has passed out of my memory.

A couple of years went by; then the original story cropped up again and went floating around in the original spelling, and with my name to it. Soon, first one paper and then another fell upon me vigorously for "stealing" "Jim Wolf and the Cats" from the Tennessee man. I got a merciless basting, but I did not mind it. It's all in the game. Besides, I had learned, a good while before that, that it is not wise to keep the fires going under a slander unless you can get some large advantage out of keeping it alive. Few slanders can stand the wear of silence.

But I was not done with "Jim and the Cats" yet. In 1873 I was lecturing in London in the Queen's Concert Rooms, Hanover Square, and living at the Langham Hotel, Portland Place. I had no domestic household on that side of the water, and no official household except George Dolby, lecture agent, and Charles Warren Stoddard, the Californian poet, now professor of English literature in the Roman Catholic University, Washington. Ostensibly Stoddard was my private secretary; in reality he was merely my comrade—I hired him in order to have his company. As secretary there was nothing for him to do except to scrap-book the daily reports of the great trial of the Tichborne Claimant for perjury. But he made a sufficient job out of that, for the reports filled six columns a day and he usually postponed the scrap-booking until Sunday; then he had forty-two columns to cut out and paste in—a proper labor for Hercules. He did his work well, but if he had been older and feebler it would have killed him once a week. Without doubt he does his literary lectures well, but also without doubt he prepares them fifteen minutes before he is due on his platform and thus gets into them a freshness and sparkle which they might lack if they underwent the staling process of overstudy.

He was good company when he was awake. He was refined, sensitive, charming, gentle, generous, honest himself and unsuspicious of other people's honesty, and I think he was the purest male I have known, in mind and speech. George Dolby was something of a contrast to him, but the two were very friendly and sociable together, nevertheless. Dolby was large and ruddy, full of life and strength and spirits, a tireless and energetic talker, and always overflowing with good nature and bursting with jollity. It was a choice and satisfactory menagerie, this pensive poet and this gladsome gorilla. An indelicate story was a sharp distress to Stoddard; Dolby told him twenty-five a day. Dolby always came home with us after the lecture, and entertained Stoddard till midnight. Me, too. After he left I walked the floor and talked, and Stoddard went to sleep on the sofa. I hired him for company.

Dolby had been agent for concerts, and theaters, and Charles Dickens, and all sorts of shows and "attractions," for many years. He had known the human being in many aspects, and he didn't much believe in him. But the poet did. The waifs and estrays found a friend in Stoddard; Dolby tried to persuade him that he was dispensing his charities unworthily, but he was never able to succeed. One night a young American got access to Stoddard at the Concert Rooms and told him a moving tale. He said he was living on the Surrey side, and for some strange reason his remittances had failed to arrive from home; he had no money, he was out of employment and friendless; his girl wife and his new baby were actually suffering for food. For the love of Heaven could he lend him a sovereign until his remittance should resume? Stoddard was deeply touched, and gave him a sovereign on my account. Dolby scoffed, but Stoddard stood his ground. Each told me his story later in the evening, and I backed Stoddard's judgment. Dolby said we were women in disguise, and not a sane kind of woman, either. The next week the young man came again. His wife was ill with the pleurisy, the baby had the botts or something—I am not sure of the name of the disease; the doctor and the drugs had eaten up the money; the poor little family were starving. If Stoddard, "in the kindness of his heart, could only spare him another sovereign," etc., etc. Stoddard was much moved, and spared him a sovereign for me. Dolby was outraged. He spoke up and said to the customer:

"Now, young man, you are going to the hotel with us and state your case to the other member of the family. If you don't make him believe in you I shan't honor this poet's drafts in your interest any longer, for I don't believe in you myself."

The young man was quite willing. I found no fault in him. On the contrary, I believed in him at once and was solicitous to heal the wounds inflicted by Dolby's too frank incredulity; therefore I did everything I could think of to cheer him up and entertain him and make him feel at home and comfortable. I spun many yarns; among others the tale of "Jim Wolf and the Cats." Learning that he had done something in a small way in literature, I offered to try to find a market for him in that line. His face lighted joyfully at that, and he said that if I could only sell a small manuscript to Tom Hood's Annual for him it would be the happiest event of his sad life and he would hold me in grateful remembrance always. That was a most pleasant night for three of us, but Dolby was disgusted and sarcastic.

Next week the baby died. Meantime I had spoken to Tom Hood and gained his sympathy. The young man had sent his manuscript to him, and the very day the child died the money for the MS. came— three guineas. The young man came with a poor little strip of crape around his arm and thanked me, and said that nothing could have been more timely than that money and that his poor little wife was grateful beyond words for the service I had rendered. He wept, and in fact Stoddard and I wept with him, which was but natural. Also Dolby wept. At least he wiped his eyes and wrung out his handkerchief, and sobbed stertorously and made other exaggerated shows of grief. Stoddard and I were ashamed of Dolby and tried to make the young man understand that he meant no harm, it was only his way. The young man said sadly that he was not minding it, his grief was too deep for other hurts; that he was only thinking of the funeral and the heavy expenses which—

We cut that short and told him not to trouble about it, leave it all to us; send the bills to Mr. Dolby and—

"Yes," said Dolby, with a mock tremor in his voice, "send them to me and I will pay them. What, are you going? You must not go alone in your worn and broken condition. Mr. Stoddard and I will go with you. Come, Stoddard. We will comfort the bereaved mamma and get a lock of the baby's hair."

It was shocking. We were ashamed of him again, and said so. But he was not disturbed. He said:

"Oh, I know this kind; the woods are full of them. I'll make this offer: if he will show me his family I will give him twenty pounds. Come!"

The young man said he would not remain to be insulted, and he said good-night and took his hat. But Dolby said he would go with him and stay by him until he found the family. Stoddard went along to soothe the young man and modify Dolby. They drove across the river and all over Southwork, but did not find the family. At last the young man confessed that there wasn't any.

The thing he sold to Tom Hood's Annual for three guineas was "Jim Wolf and the Cats." And he did not put my name to it.

So that small tale was sold three times. I am selling it again now. It is one of the best properties I have come across.

Macfarlane

When I was turned twenty I wandered to Cincinnati, and was there several months. Our boarding-house crew was made up of commonplace people of various ages and both sexes. They were full of bustle, frivolity, chatter, and the joy of life, and were good-natured, clean-minded, and well-meaning; but they were oppressively uninteresting, for all that—with one exception. This was Macfarlane, a Scotchman. He was forty years old—just double my age—but we were opposite in most ways and comrades from the start. I always spent my evenings by the wood fire in his room, listening in comfort to his tireless talk and to the dulled complainings of the winter storms, until the clock struck ten. At that hour he grilled a smoked herring, after the fashion of an earlier friend in Philadelphia, the Englishman Sumner. His herring was his nightcap and my signal to go.

He was six feet high and rather lank, a serious and sincere man. He had no humor, nor any comprehension of it. He had a sort of smile, whose office was to express his good nature, but if I ever heard him laugh, the memory of it is gone from me. He was intimate with no one in the house but me, though he was courteous and pleasant with all. He had two or three dozen weighty books—philosophies, histories, and scientific works—and at the head of this procession were his Bible and his dictionary. After his herring he always read two or three hours in bed.

Diligent talker as he was, he seldom said anything about himself. To ask him a personal question gave him no offense—nor the asker any information; he merely turned the matter aside and flowed placidly on about other things. He told me once that he had had hardly any schooling, and that such learning as he had, he had picked up for himself. That was his sole biographical revelation, I believe. Whether he was bachelor, widower, or grass widower, remained his own secret. His clothes were cheap, but neat and caretakingly preserved. Ours was a cheap boarding house; he left the house at six, mornings, and returned to it toward six, evenings; his hands were not soft, so I reasoned that he worked at some mechanical calling ten hours a day, for humble wages—but I never knew. As a rule, technicalities of a man's vocation, and figures and metaphors drawn from it, slip out in his talk and reveal his trade; but if this ever happened in Macfarlane's case I was none the wiser, although I was constantly on the watch during half a year for those very betrayals. It was mere curiosity, for I didn't care what his trade was, but I wanted to detect it in true detective fashion and was annoyed because I couldn't do it. I think he was a remarkable man, to be able to keep the shop out of his talk all that time.

There was another noteworthy feature about him: he seemed to know his dictionary from beginning to end. He claimed that he did. He was frankly proud of this accomplishment and said I would not find it possible to challenge him with an English word which he could not promptly spell and define. I lost much time trying to hunt up a word which would beat him, but those weeks were spent in vain and I finally gave it up; which made him so proud and happy that I wished I had surrendered earlier.

He seemed to be as familiar with his Bible as he was with his dictionary. It was easy to see that he considered himself a philosopher and a thinker. His talk always ran upon grave and large questions; and I must do him the justice to say that his heart and conscience were in his talk and that there was no appearance of reasoning and arguing for the vain pleasure of hearing himself do it.

Of course his thinking and reasoning and philosophizings were those of a but partly taught and wholly untrained mind, yet he hit by accident upon some curious and striking things. For instance. The time was the early part of 1856—fourteen or fifteen years before Mr. Darwin's Descent of Man startled the world—yet here was Macfarlane talking the same idea to me, there in the boarding house in Cincinnati.

The same general idea, but with difference. Macfarlane considered that the animal life in the world was developed in the course of aeons of time from a few microscopic seed germs, or perhaps one microscopic seed germ deposited upon the globe by the Creator in the dawn of time, and that this development was progressive upon an ascending scale toward ultimate perfection until man was reached; and that then the progressive scheme broke pitifully down and went to wreck and ruin!

He said that man's heart was the only bad heart in the animal kingdom; that man was the only animal capable of feeling malice, envy, vindictiveness, revengefulness, hatred, selfishness, the only animal that loved drunkenness, almost the only animal that could endure personal uncleanliness and a filthy habitation, the sole animal in whom was fully developed the base instinct called patriotism, the sole animal that robs, persecutes, oppresses, and kills members of his own immediate tribe, the sole animal that steals and enslaves the members of any tribe. He claimed that man's intellect was a brutal addition to him and degraded him to a rank far below the plane of the other animals, and that there was never a man who did not use his intellect daily all his life to advantage himself at other people's expense. The divinest divine reduced his domestics to humble servitude under him by advantage of his superior intellect, and those servants in turn were above a still lower grade of people by force of brains that were still a little better than theirs.

Written in 1898

Old Lecture Days in Boston

Nasby, and others of Redpath's Lecture Bureau

I REMEMBER PETROLEUM VESUVIUS NASBY (Locke) very well. When the Civil War began he was on the staff of the Toledo Blade, an old and prosperous and popular weekly newspaper. He let fly a Nasby letter and it made a fine strike. He was famous at once. He followed up his new lead, and gave the Copperheads and the Democratic party a most admirable hammering every week, and his letters were copied everywhere, from the Atlantic to the Pacific, and read and laughed over by everybody—at least everybody except particularly dull and prejudiced Democrats and Copperheads. For suddenness, Nasby's fame was an explosion; for universality it was atmospheric. He was soon offered a company; he accepted and was straightway ready to leave for the front; but the Governor of the state was a wiser man than were the political masters of Körner and Petöfi; for he refused to sign Nasby's commission and ordered him to stay at home. He said that in the field Nasby would be only one soldier, handling one sword, but at home with his pen he was an army—with artillery! Nasby obeyed and went on writing his electric letters.

I saw him first when I was on a visit to Hartford; I think it was three or four years after the war. The Opera House was packed and jammed with people to hear him deliver his lecture on "Cussed be Canaan." He had been on the platform with that same lecture—and no other—during two or three years, and it had passed his lips several hundred times, yet even now he could not deliver any sentence of it without his manuscript—except the opening one. His appearance on the stage was welcomed with a prodigious burst of applause, but he did not stop to bow or in any other way acknowledge the greeting, but strode straight to the reading desk, spread his portfolio open upon it, and immediately petrified himself into an attitude which he never changed during the hour and a half occupied by his performance, except to turn his leaves— his body bent over the desk, rigidly supported by his left arm, as by a stake, the right arm lying across his back. About once in two minutes his right arm swung forward, turned a leaf, then swung to its resting-place on his back again—just the action of a machine, and suggestive of one; regular, recurrent, prompt, exact. You might imagine you heard it clash. He was a great, burly figure, uncouthly and provincially clothed, and he looked like a simple old farmer.

I was all curiosity to hear him begin. He did not keep me waiting. The moment he had crutched himself upon his left arm, lodged his right upon his back, and bent himself over his manuscript he raised his face slightly, flashed a glance upon the audience, and bellowed this remark in a thundering bull-voice:

"We are all descended from grandfathers!"

Then he went right on roaring to the end, tearing his ruthless way through the continuous applause and laughter, and taking no sort of account of it. His lecture was a volleying and sustained discharge of bull's-eye hits, with the slave power and its Northern apologists for target, and his success was due to his matter, not his manner; for his delivery was destitute of art, unless a tremendous and inspiring earnestness and energy may be called by that name. The moment he had finished his piece he turned his back and marched off the stage with the seeming of being not personally concerned with the applause that was booming behind him.

He had the constitution of an ox and the strength and endurance of a prize-fighter. Express trains were not very plenty in those days. He missed a connection, and in order to meet this Hartford engagement he had traveled two-thirds of a night and a whole day in a cattle car—it was midwinter. He went from the cattle car to his reading desk without dining; yet on the platform his voice was powerful and he showed no signs of drowsiness or fatigue. He sat up talking and supping with me until after midnight, and then it was I that had to give up, not he. He told me that in his first season he read his "Cussed be Canaan" twenty-five nights a month for nine successive months. No other lecturer ever matched that record, I imagine.

He said that as one result of repeating his lecture 225 nights straight along, he was able to say its opening sentence without glancing at his manuscript; and sometimes even did it, when in a daring mood. And there was another result: he reached home the day after his long campaign, and was sitting by the fire in the evening, musing, when the clock broke into his revery by striking eight. Habit is habit, and before he realized where he was he had thundered out, "We are all descended from grandfathers!"

I began as a lecturer in 1866, in California and Nevada; in 1867 lectured in New York once and in the Mississippi Valley a few times; in 1868 made the whole Western circuit; and in the two or three following seasons added the Eastern circuit to my route. We had to bring out a new lecture every season, now (Nasby with the rest), and expose it in the "Star Course," Boston, for a first verdict, before an audience of 2,500 in the old Music Hall; for it was by that verdict that all the lyceums in the country determined the lecture's commercial value. The campaign did not really begin in Boston, but in the towns around. We did not appear in Boston until we had rehearsed about a month in those towns and made all the necessary corrections and revisings.

This system gathered the whole tribe together in the city early in October, and we had a lazy and sociable time there for several weeks. We lived at Young's Hotel; we spent the days in Redpath's Bureau, smoking and talking shop; and early in the evenings we scattered out among the towns and made them indicate the good and poor things in the new lectures. The country audience is the difficult audience; a passage which it will approve with a ripple will bring a crash in the city. A fair success in the country means a triumph in the city. And so, when we finally stepped on to the great stage at the Music Hall we already had the verdict in our pocket.

But sometimes lecturers who were "new to the business" did not know the value of "trying it on the dog," and these were apt to come to the Music Hall with an untried product. There was one case of this kind which made some of us very anxious when we saw the advertisement. De Cordova—humorist—he was the man we were troubled about. I think he had another name, but I have forgotten what it was. He had been printing some dismally humorous things in the magazines; they had met with a deal of favor and given him a pretty wide name; and now he suddenly came poaching upon our preserve and took us by surprise. Several of us felt pretty unwell—too unwell to lecture. We got outlying engagements postponed and remained in town. We took front seats in one of the great galleries—Nasby, Billings, and I—and waited. The house was full. When De Cordova came on he was received with what we regarded as a quite overdone and almost indecent volume of welcome. I think we were not jealous, nor even envious, but it made us sick, anyway. When I found he was going to read a humorous story—from manuscript—I felt better and hopeful, but still anxious. He had a Dickens arrangement of tall gallows frame adorned with upholsteries, and he stood behind it under its overhead row of hidden lights. The whole thing had a quite stylish look and was rather impressive. The audience was so sure that he was going to be funny that they took a dozen of his first utterances on trust and laughed cordially—so cordially, indeed, that it was very hard for us to bear—and we felt very much disheartened. Still, I tried to believe he would fail, for I saw that he didn't know how to read. Presently the laughter began to relax; then it began to shrink in area; and next to lose spontaneity; and next to show gaps between; the gaps widened; they widened more; more yet; still more. It was getting to be almost all gaps and silence, with that untrained and unlively voice droning through them. Then the house sat dead and emotionless for a whole ten minutes. We drew a deep sigh; it ought to have been a sigh of pity for a defeated fellow craftsman, but it was not—for we were mean and selfish, like all the human race, and it was a sigh of satisfaction to see our unoffending brother fail.

He was laboring now, and distressed; he constantly mopped his face with his handkerchief, and his voice and his manner became a humble appeal for compassion, for help, for charity, and it was a pathetic thing to see. But the house remained cold and still, and gazed at him curiously and wonderingly.

There was a great clock on the wall, high up; presently the general gaze forsook the reader and fixed itself upon the clock face. We knew by dismal experience what that meant; we knew what was going to happen, but it was plain that the reader had not been warned and was ignorant. It was approaching nine now—half the house watching the clock, the reader laboring on. At five minutes to nine, twelve hundred people rose, with one impulse, and swept like a wave down the aisles toward the doors! The reader was like a person stricken with a paralysis; he stood choking and gasping for a few minutes, gazing in a white horror at that retreat, then he turned drearily away and wandered from the stage with the groping and uncertain step of one who walks in his sleep.

The management were to blame. They should have told him that the last suburban cars left at nine and that half the house would rise and go then, no matter who might be speaking from the platform. I think De Cordova did not appear again in public.

Written about 1898

Ralph Keeler

He was a Californian. I probably knew him in San Francisco in the early days—about 1865—when I was a newspaper reporter, and Bret Harte, Ambrose Bierce, Charles Warren Stoddard and Prentice Mulford were doing young literary work for Mr. Joe Lawrence's weekly periodical, the Golden Era. At any rate, I knew him in Boston a few years later, where he comraded with Howells, Aldrich, Boyle O'Reilly, and James T. Fields, and was greatly liked by them. I say he comraded with them, and that is the proper term, though he would not have given the relationship so familiar a name himself, for he was the modestest young fellow that ever was and looked humbly up to those distinguished men from his lowly obscurity, and was boyishly grateful for the friendly notice they took of him, and frankly grateful for it; and when he got a smile and a nod from Mr. Emerson and Mr. Whittier and Holmes and Lowell and Longfellow, his happiness was the prettiest thing in the world to see. He was not more than twenty-four at this time; the native sweetness of his disposition had not been marred by cares and disappointments; he was buoyant and hopeful, simple-hearted, and full of the most engaging and unexacting little literary ambitions. Whomsoever he met became his friend and—by some natural and unexplained impulse—took him under protection.

He probably never had a home or a boyhood. He had wandered to California as a little chap from somewhere or other, and had cheerfully achieved his bread in various humble callings, educating himself as he went along, and having a good and satisfactory time. Among his various industries was clog-dancing in a "nigger" show. When he was about twenty years old he scraped together eighty-five dollars—in greenbacks, worth about half that sum in gold—and on this capital he made the tour of Europe and published an account of his travels in the Atlantic Monthly. When he was about twenty-two he wrote a novel called Gloverson and His Silent Partners; and not only that, but found a publisher for it. But that was not really a surprising thing, in his case, for not even a publisher is hard-hearted enough to be able to say no to some people—and Ralph was one of those people. His gratitude for a favor granted him was so simple and sincere and so eloquent and touching that a publisher would recognize that if there was no money in the book there was still a profit to be had out of it beyond the value of money and above money's reach. There was no money in that book, not a single penny; but Ralph Keeler always spoke of his publisher as other people speak of divinities. The publisher lost two or three hundred dollars on the book, of course, and knew he would lose it when he made the venture, but he got much more than the worth of it back in the author's adoring admiration of him.

Ralph had little or nothing to do, and he often went out with me to the small lecture towns in the neighborhood of Boston. These lay within an hour of town, and we usually started at six or thereabouts, and returned to the city in the morning. It took about a month to do these Boston annexes, and that was the easiest and pleasantest month of the four or five which constituted the "lecture season." The "lyceum system" was in full flower in those days, and James Redpath's Bureau in School Street, Boston, had the management of it throughout the Northern States and Canada. Redpath farmed out the lectures in groups of six or eight to the lyceums all over the country at an average of about $100 a night for each lecture. His commission was 10 per cent; each lecture appeared about 110 nights in the season. There were a number of good drawing names in his list: Henry Ward Beecher; Anna Dickinson; John B. Gough; Horace Greeley; Wendell Phillips; Petroleum V. Nasby; Josh Billings; Hayes, the Arctic Explorer; Vincent, the English astronomer; Parsons, Irish orator; Agassiz; et al. He had in his list twenty or thirty men and women of light consequence and limited reputation who wrought for fees ranging from twenty-five dollars to fifty dollars. Their names have perished long ago. Nothing but art could find them a chance on the platform. Redpath furnished that art. All the lyceums wanted the big guns, and wanted them yearningly, longingly, strenuously. Redpath granted their prayers—on this condition: for each house-filler allotted them they must hire several of his house-emptiers. This arrangement permitted the lyceums to get through alive for a few years, but in the end it killed them all and abolished the lecture business.

Beecher, Gough, Nasby, and Anna Dickinson were the only lecturers who knew their own value and exacted it. In towns their fee was $200 and $250; in cities, $400. The lyceum always got a profit out of these four (weather permitting), but generally lost it again on the house-emptiers.

There were two women who should have been house-emptiers—Olive Logan and Kate Field—but during a season or two they were not. They charged $100, and were recognized house-fillers for certainly two years. After that they were capable emptiers and were presently shelved. Kate Field had made a wide, spasmodic notoriety in 1867 by some letters which she sent from Boston—by telegraph—to the Tribune about Dickens's readings there in the beginning of his triumphant American tour. The letters were a frenzy of praise—praise which approached idolatry—and this was the right and welcome key to strike, for the country was itself in a frenzy of enthusiasm about Dickens. Then the idea of telegraphing a newspaper letter was new and astonishing, and the wonder of it was in every one's mouth. Kate Field became a celebrity at once. By and by she went on the platform; but two or three years had elapsed and her subject—Dickens—had now lost its freshness and its interest. For a while people went to see her, because of her name; but her lecture was poor and her delivery repellently artificial; consequently, when the country's desire to look at her had been appeased, the platform forsook her.

She was a good creature, and the acquisition of a perishable and fleeting notoriety was the disaster of her life. To her it was infinitely precious, and she tried hard, in various ways, during more than a quarter of a century, to keep a semblance of life in it, but her efforts were but moderately successful. She died in the Sandwich Islands, regretted by her friends and forgotten of the world.

Olive Logan's notoriety grew out of—only the initiated knew what. Apparently it was a manufactured notoriety, not an earned one. She did write and publish little things in newspapers and obscure periodicals, but there was no talent in them, and nothing resembling it. In a century they would not have made her known. Her name was really built up out of newspaper paragraphs set afloat by her husband, who was a small-salaried minor journalist. During a year or two this kind of paragraphing was persistent; one could seldom pick up a newspaper without encountering it.

It is said that Olive Logan has taken a cottage at Nahant, and will spend the summer there.

MARK TWAIN

Olive Logan has set her face decidedly against the adoption of the short skirt for afternoon wear.

The report that Olive Logan will spend the coming winter in Paris is premature. She has not yet made up her mind.

Olive Logan was present at Wallack's on Saturday evening, and was outspoken in her approval of the new piece.

Olive Logan has so far recovered from her alarming illness that if she continues to improve her physicians will cease from issuing bulletins to-morrow.

The result of this daily advertising was very curious. Olive Logan's name was as familiar to the simple public as was that of any celebrity of the time, and people talked with interest about her doings and movements and gravely discussed her opinions. Now and then an ignorant person from the backwoods would proceed to inform himself, and then there were surprises in store for all concerned:

"Who is Olive Logan?"

The listeners were astonished to find that they couldn't answer the question. It had never occurred to them to inquire into the matter.

"What has she done?"

The listeners were dumb again. They didn't know. They hadn't inquired.

"Well, then, how does she come to be celebrated?"

"Oh, it's about something, I don't know what. I never inquired, but I supposed everybody knew."

For entertainment I often asked these questions myself, of people who were glibly talking about that celebrity and her doings and sayings. The questioned were surprised to find that they had been taking this fame wholly on trust and had no idea who Olive Logan was or what she had done—if anything.

On the strength of this oddly created notoriety Olive Logan went on the platform, and for at least two seasons the United States flocked to the lecture halls to look at her. She was merely a name and some rich and costly clothes, and neither of these properties had any lasting quality, though for a while they were able to command a fee of $100 a night. She dropped out of the memories of men a quarter of a century ago.

Ralph Keeler was pleasant company on my lecture flights out of Boston, and we had plenty of good talks and smokes in our rooms after the committee had escorted us to the inn and made their good-night. There was always a committee, and they wore a silk badge of office; they received us at the station and drove us to the lecture hall; they sat in a row of chairs behind me on the stage, minstrel fashion, and in the earliest days their chief used to introduce me to the audience; but these introductions were so grossly flattering that they made me ashamed, and so I began my talk at a heavy disadvantage. It was a stupid custom. There was no occasion for the introduction; the introducer was almost always an ass, and his prepared speech a jumble of vulgar compliments and dreary effort to be funny; therefore after the first season I always introduced myself—using, of course, a burlesque of the time-worn introduction. This change was not popular with committee chairmen. To stand up grandly before a great audience of his townsmen and make his little devilish speech was the joy of his life, and to have that joy taken from him was almost more than he could bear.

My introduction of myself was a most efficient "starter" for a while, then it failed. It had to be carefully and painstakingly worded, and very earnestly spoken, in order that all strangers present might be deceived into the supposition that I was only the introducer and not the lecturer; also that the flow of overdone compliments might sicken those strangers; then, when the end was reached and the remark casually dropped that I was the lecturer and had been talking about myself, the effect was very satisfactory. But it was a good card for only a little while, as I have said; for the newspapers printed it, and after that I could not make it go, since the house knew what was coming and retained its emotions.

Next I tried an introduction taken from my Californian experiences. It was gravely made by a slouching and awkward big miner in the village of Red Dog. The house, very much against his will, forced him to ascend the platform and introduce me. He stood thinking a moment, then said:

"I don't know anything about this man. At least I know only two things; one is, he hasn't been in the penitentiary, and the other is (after a pause, and almost sadly), I don't know why."

That worked well for a while, then the newspapers printed it and took the juice out of it, and after that I gave up introductions altogether.

Now and then Keeler and I had a mild little adventure, but none which couldn't be forgotten without much of a strain. Once we arrived late at a town and found no committee in waiting and no sleighs on the stand. We struck up a street in the gay moonlight, found a tide of people flowing along, judged it was on its way to the lecture hall—a correct guess—and joined it. At the hall I tried to press in, but was stopped by the ticket-taker.

"Ticket, please."

I bent over and whispered: "It's all right. I am the lecturer."

He closed one eye impressively and said, loud enough for all the crowd to hear: "No you don't. Three of you have got in, up to now, but the next lecturer that goes in here to-night pays."

Of course we paid; it was the least embarrassing way out of the trouble. The very next morning Keeler had an adventure. About eleven o'clock I was sitting in my room, reading the paper, when he burst into the place all atremble with excitement and said:

"Come with me—quick!"

"What is it? What's happened?"

"Don't wait to talk. Come with me."

We tramped briskly up the main street three or four blocks, neither of us speaking, both of us excited, I in a sort of panic of apprehension and horrid curiosity; then we plunged into a building and down through the middle of it to the farther end. Keeler stopped, put out his hand, and said:

"Look!"

I looked, but saw nothing except a row of books.

"What is it, Keeler?"

He said, in a kind of joyous ecstasy, "Keep on looking—to the right; farther—farther to the right. There—see it? Gloverson and His Silent Partners!"

And there it was, sure enough.

"This is a library! Understand? Public library. And they've got it!"

His eyes, his face, his attitude, his gestures, his whole being spoke his delight, his pride, his happiness. It never occurred to me to laugh; a supreme joy like that moves one the other way. I was stirred almost to the crying point to see so perfect a happiness.

He knew all about the book, for he had been cross-examining the librarian. It had been in the library two years and the records showed that it had been taken out three times.

"And read, too!" said Keeler. "See—the leaves are all cut!"

Moreover, the book had been "bought, not given—it's on the record." I think Gloverson was published in San Francisco. Other copies had been sold, no doubt, but this present sale was the only one Keeler was certain of. It seems unbelievable that the sale of an edition of one book could give an author this immeasurable peace and contentment, but I was there and I saw it.

Afterward Keeler went out to Ohio and hunted out one of Osawatomie Brown's brothers on his farm and took down in longhand his narrative of his adventures in escaping from Virginia after the tragedy of 1859—the most admirable piece of reporting, I make no doubt, that was ever done by a man destitute of a knowledge of shorthand writing. It was published in the Atlantic Monthly, and I made three attempts to read it, but was frightened off each time before I could finish. The tale was so vivid and so real that I seemed to be living those adventures myself and sharing their intolerable perils, and the torture of it was so sharp that I was never able to follow the story to the end.

By and by the Tribune commissioned Keeler to go to Cuba and report the facts of an outrage or an insult of some sort which the Spanish authorities had been perpetrating upon us according to their well-worn habit and custom. He sailed from New York in the steamer and was last seen alive the night before the vessel reached Havana. It was said that he had not made a secret of his mission, but had talked about it freely, in his frank and innocent way. There were some Spanish military men on board. It may be that he was not flung into the sea; still, the belief was general that that was what had happened.

Written in 1898. Vienna

BEAUTIES OF THE GERMAN LANGUAGE

February 3.—Lectured for the benefit of a charity last night, in the Börsendorfersaal. Just as I was going on the platform a messenger delivered to me an envelope with my name on it, and this written under it; "Please read one of these to-night." Inclosed were a couple of newspaper clippings—two versions of an anecdote, one German, the other English. I was minded to try the German one on those people, just to see what would happen, but my courage weakened when I noticed the formidable look of the closing word, and I gave it up. A pity, too, for it ought to read well on the platform and get an encore. That or a brickbat. There is never any telling what a new audience will do; their tastes are capricious. The point of this anecdote is a justifiable gibe at the German long word, and is not as much of an exaggeration as one might think. The German long word is not a legitimate construction, but an ignoble artificiality, a sham. It has no recognition by the dictionary and is not found there. It is made by jumbling a lot of words into one, in a quite unnecessary way; it is a lazy device of the vulgar and a crime against the language. Nothing can be gained, no valuable amount of space saved, by jumbling the following words together on a visiting card: "Mrs. Smith, widow of the late Commander-in-chief of the Police Department," yet a German widow can persuade herself to do it, without much trouble: "Mrs.-late-commander-in-chief-of-the-police-department's-widow-Smith." This is the English version of the anecdote:

A Dresden paper, the Weidmann, which thinks that there are kangaroos (Beutelratte) in South Africa, says the Hottentots (Hottentoten) put them in cages (kotter) provided with covers (lattengitter) to protect them from the rain. The cages are therefore called lattengitterwetterkotter, and the imprisoned kangaroo lattengitterwetterkotterbeutelratte. One day an assassin (attentäter) was arrested who had killed a Hottentot woman (Hottentotenmutter), the mother of two stupid and stuttering children in Strättertrotel. This woman, in the German language is entitled Hottentotenstrottertrottelmutter, and her assassin takes the name Hottentotenstrottermutterattentäter. The murderer was confined in a kangaroo's cage—Beutelrattenlattengitterwetterkotter—whence a few days later he escaped, but fortunately he was recaptured by a Hottentot, who presented himself at the mayor's office with beaming face. "I have captured the Beutelratte," said he. "Which one?" said the mayor; "we have several." "The Attentäterlattengitterwetterkotterbeutelratte." "Which attentäter are you talking about?" "About the Hottentotenstrotter-trottelmutterattentäter." "Then why don't you say at once the Hotten-totenstrottelmutterattentäterlattengitterwetterkotterbeutelratte?"

Written Sunday, June 26, 1898. Kaltenleutgeben

A Viennese Procession

I went in the eight-o'clock train to Vienna, to see the procession. It was a stroke of luck, for at the last moment I was feeling lazy and was minded not to go. But when I reached the station, five minutes late, the train was still there, a couple of friends were there also, and so I went.

At Liesing, half an hour out, we changed to a very long train and left for Vienna, with every seat occupied. That was no sign that this was a great day, for these people are not critical about shows; they turn out for anything that comes along. Half an hour later we were driving into the city. No particular bustle anywhere—indeed, less than is usual on an Austrian Sunday; bunting flying, and a decoration here and there—a quite frequent thing in this jubilee year; but as we passed the American Embassy I saw a couple of our flags out and the minister and his menservants arranging to have another one added. This woke me up—it seemed to indicate that something really beyond the common was to the fore.

As we neared the bridge which connects the First Bezirk with the Third, a pronounced and growing life and stir were noticeable—and when we entered the wide square where the Schwarzenberg palace is, there was something resembling a jam. As far as we could see down the broad avenue of the Park Ring both sides of it were packed with people in their holiday clothes. Our cab worked its way across the square, and then flew down empty streets, all the way, to Liebenberggasse No. 7— the dwelling we were aiming for. It stands on the corner of that street and the Park Ring, and its balconies command a mile stretch of the latter avenue. By a trifle after nine we were in the shade of the awnings of the first-floor balcony, with a dozen other guests, and ready for the procession. Ready, but it would not start for an hour yet, and would not reach us for half an hour afterward. As to numbers, it would be a large matter, for by report it would march 25,000 strong. But it isn't numbers that make the interest of a procession; I have seen a vast number of long processions which didn't pay. It is clothes that make a procession; where you have those of the right pattern you can do without length. Two or three months ago I saw one with the Emperor and an archbishop in it, and the archbishop was being carried along under a canopied arrangement and had his skullcap on, and the venerable Emperor was following him on foot and bareheaded. Even if that had been the entire procession, it would have paid. I am old, now, and may never be an emperor at all; at least in this world. I have been disappointed so many times that I am growing more and more doubtful and resigned every year; but if it ever should happen, the procession will have a fresh interest for the archbishop, for he will walk.

The wait on the balcony was not dull. There was the spacious avenue stretching into the distance, right and left, to look at, with its double wall of massed humanity, an eager and excited lot, broiling in the sun, and a comforting spectacle to contemplate from the shade. That is, on our side of the street they were in the sun, but not on the other side, where the park is; there was dense shade there. They were good-natured people, but they gave the policemen plenty of trouble, for they were constantly surging into the roadway and being hustled back again. They were in fine spirits, yet it was said that the most of them had been waiting there in the jam three or four hours—and two-thirds of them were women and girls.

At last a mounted policeman came galloping down the road in solitary state—first sign that pretty soon the show would open. After five minutes he was followed by a man on a decorated bicycle. Next, a marshal's assistant sped by on a polished and shiny black horse. Five minutes later, distant strains of music. Five more, and far up the street the head of the procession twinkles into view. That was a procession! I wouldn't have missed it for anything. According to my understanding, it was to be composed of shooting-match clubs from all over the Austrian Empire, with a club or two from France and Germany as guests. What I had in my imagination was 25,000 men in sober dress, drifting monotonously by, with rifles slung to their backs—a New York target excursion on a large scale. In my fancy I could see the colored brothers toting the ice pails and targets and swabbing off perspiration.

But this was a different matter. One of the most engaging spectacles in the world is a Wagner opera force marching on to the stage, with its music braying and its banners flying. This was that spectacle infinitely magnified, and with the glories of the sun upon it and a countless multitude of excited witnesses to wave the handkerchiefs and do the hurrahing. It was grand and beautiful and sumptuous; and no tinsel, no shams, no tin armor, no cotton velvet, no make-believe silk, no Birmingham Oriental rugs; everything was what it professed to be. It is the clothes that make a procession, and for these costumes all the centuries were drawn upon, even from times which were already ancient when Kaiser Rudolph himself was alive.

There were bodies of spearmen with plain steel casques of a date a thousand years ago; other bodies in more ornamental casques of a century or two later, and with breastplates added; other bodies with chain-mail elaborations, some armed with crossbows, some with the earliest crop of matchlocks; still other bodies clothed in the stunningly picturesque plate armor and plumed great helmets of the middle of the sixteenth century. And then there were bodies of men-at-arms in the darling velvets of the Middle Ages, and nobles on horseback in the same—doublets with huge puffed sleeves, wide brigand hats with great plumes; and the rich and effective colors—old gold, black, and scarlet; deep yellow, black, and scarlet; brown, black, and scarlet. A portly figure clothed like that, with a two-handed sword as long as a billiard cue, and mounted on a big draft horse finely caparisoned, with the sun flooding the splendid colors—a figure like that, with fifty duplicates marching in his rear, is procession enough, all by itself.

Yet that was merely a detail. All the centuries were passing by; passing by in glories of color and multiplicities of strange and quaint and curious and beautiful costumes not to be seen in this world now outside the opera and the picture books. And now and then, in the midst of this flowing tide of splendors appeared a sharply contrasting note—a mounted committee in evening dress—swallow-tails, white kids, and shiny new plug hats; and right in their rear, perhaps, a hundred capering clowns in thunder-and-lightning dress, or a band of silken pages out of ancient times, plumed and capped and daggered, dainty as rainbows, and mincing along in flesh-colored tights; and as handy at it, too, as if they had been born and brought up to it.

At intervals there was a great platform car bethroned and grandly canopied, upholstered in silks, carpeted with Oriental rugs, and freighted with girls clothed in gala costumes. There were several military companies dressed in uniforms of various bygone periods—among others, one dating back a century and a half, and another of Andreas Hofer's time and region; following this latter was a large company of men and women and girls dressed in the society fashions of a period stretching from the Directory down to about 1840—a thing worth seeing. Among the prettiest and liveliest and most picturesque costumes in the pageant were those worn by regiments and regiments of peasants, from the Tyrol and Bohemia and everywhere in the Empire. They are of ancient origin, but are still worn today.

I have seen no procession which evoked more enthusiasm than this one brought out. It would have made any country deliver its emotions, for it was a most stirring sight to see. At the end of this year I shall be sixty-three—if alive—and about the same if dead. I have been looking at processions for sixty years, and, curiously enough, all my really wonderful ones have come in the last three years—one in India in

'96, the Queen's Record procession in London last year, and now this one. As an appeal to the imagination—an object-lesson synopsizing the might and majesty and spread of the greatest empire the world has seen—the Queen's procession stands first; as a picture for the eye, this one beats it; and in this regard it even falls no very great way short, perhaps, of the Jeypore pageant—and that was a dream of enchantment.

Written 1898. Vienna

COMMENT ON TAUTOLOGY AND GRAMMAR

May 6 . . . I do not find that the repetition of an important word a few times—say, three or four times—in a paragraph troubles my ear if clearness of meaning is best secured thereby. But tautological repetition which has no justifying object, but merely exposes the fact that the writer's balance at the vocabulary bank has run short and that he is too lazy to replenish it from the thesaurus—that is another matter. It makes me feel like calling the writer to account. It makes me want to remind him that he is not treating himself and his calling with right respect, and, incidentally, that he is not treating me with proper reverence. At breakfast, this morning, a member of the family read aloud an interesting review of a new book about Mr. Gladstone in which the reviewer used the strong adjective "delightful" thirteen times. Thirteen times in a short review, not a long one. In five of the cases the word was distinctly the right one, the exact one, the best one our language can furnish, therefore it made no discord; but in the remaining cases it was out of tune. It sharped or flatted, one or the other, every time, and was as unpleasantly noticeable as is a false note in music. I looked in the thesaurus, and under a single head I found four words which would replace with true notes the false ones uttered by four of the misused "delightfuls"; and of course if I had hunted under related heads for an hour and made an exhaustive search I should have found right words, to a shade, wherewith to replace the remaining delinquents.

I suppose we all have our foibles. I like the exact word, and clarity of statement, and here and there a touch of good grammar for picturesqueness; but that reviewer cares for only the last mentioned of these things. His grammar is foolishly correct, offensively precise. It flaunts itself in the reader's face all along, and struts and smirks and shows off, and is in a dozen ways irritating and disagreeable. To be serious, I write good grammar myself, but not in that spirit, I am thankful to say. That is to say, my grammar is of a high order, though not at the top. Nobody's is. Perfect grammar—persistent, continuous, sustained—is the fourth dimension, so to speak; many have sought it, but none has found it. Even this reviewer, this purist, with all his godless airs, has made two or three slips. At least, I think he has. I am almost sure, by witness of my ear, but cannot be positive, for I know grammar by ear only, not by note, not by the rules. A generation ago I knew the rules—knew them by heart, word for word, though not their meanings—and I still know one of them: the one which says—which says—but never mind, it will come back to me presently. This reviewer even seems to know (or seems even to know, or seems to know even) how to put the word "even" in the right place; and the word "only," too. I do not like that kind of persons. I never knew one of them that came to any good. A person who is as self-righteous as that will do other things. I know this, because I have noticed it many a time. I would never hesitate to injure that kind of a man if I could. When a man works up his grammar to that altitude, it is a sign. It shows what he will do if he gets a chance; it shows the kind of disposition he has; I have noticed it often. I knew one once that did a lot of things. They stop at nothing.

But, anyway, this grammatical coxcomb's review is interesting, as I said before. And there is one sentence in it which tastes good in the mouth, so perfectly do the last five of its words report a something which we have all felt after sitting long over an absorbing book. The matter referred to is Mr. Gladstone's boswellized conversations and his felicitous handling of his subject.

One facet of the brilliant talker's mind flashes out on us after another till we tire with interest.

That is clearly stated. We recognize that feeling. In the morning paper I find a sentence of another breed.

There had been no death before the case of Cornelius Lean which had arisen and terminated in death since the special rules had been drawn up.

By the context I know what it means, but you are without that light and will be sure to get out of it a meaning which the writer of it was not intending to convey.

PRIVATE HISTORY OF A MS. THAT CAME TO GRIEF

It happened in London; not recently, and yet not very many years ago. An acquaintance had proposed to himself a certain labor of love, and when he told me about it I was interested. His idea was to have a fine translation made of the evidence given in the Joan of Arc Trials and Rehabilitation, and placed before the English-speaking world. A translation had been made and published a great many years before, but had achieved no currency, and in fact was not entitled to any, for it was a piece of mere shoemaker-work. But we should have the proper thing, now; for this acquaintance of mine was manifestly a Joan enthusiast, and as he had plenty of money and nothing to do but spend it, I took at par his remark that he had employed the most competent person in Great Britain to open this long-neglected mine and confer its riches upon the public. When he asked me to write an Introduction for the book, my pleasure was complete, my vanity satisfied.

At this moment, by good fortune, there chanced to fall into my hands a biographical sketch of me of so just and laudatory a character—particularly as concerned one detail—that it gave my spirit great contentment; and also set my head to swelling—I will not deny it. For it contained praises of the very thing which I most loved to hear praised—the good quality of my English; moreover, they were uttered by four English and American literary experts of high authority.

I am as fond of compliments as another, and as hard to satisfy as the average; but these satisfied me. I was as pleased as you would have been if they had been paid to you.

It was under the inspiration of that great several-voiced verdict that I set about that Introduction for Mr. X's book; and I said to myself that I would put a quality of English into it which would establish the righteousness of that judgment. I said I would treat the subject with the reverence and dignity due it; and would use plain, simple English words, and a phrasing undefiled by meretricious artificialities and affectations.

I did the work on those lines; and when it was finished I said to myself very privately. . .

But never mind. I delivered the MS. to Mr. X, and went home to wait for the praises. On the way I met a friend. Being in a happy glow over this pleasant matter, I could not keep my secret. I wanted to tell somebody, and I told him. For a moment he stood curiously measuring me up and down with his eye, without saying anything; then he burst into a rude, coarse laugh, which hurt me very much. He followed this up by saying:

"He is going to edit the translations of the Trials when it is finished? He?"

"He said he would."

"Why, what does he know about editing?"

"I don't know; but that is what he said. Do you think he isn't competent?"

"Competent? He is innocent, vain, ignorant, good-hearted, red-headed, and all that—there isn't a better-meaning man; but he doesn't know anything about literature and has had no literary training or experience; he can't edit anything."

"Well, all I know is, he is going to try."

"Indeed he will! He is quite unconscious of his incapacities; he would undertake to edit Shakespeare, if invited—and improve him, too. The world cannot furnish his match for guileless self-complacency; yet I give you my word he doesn't know enough to come in when it rains."

This gentleman's ability to judge was not to be questioned. Therefore, by the time I reached home I had concluded to ask Mr. X not to edit the translation, but to turn that work over to some expert whose name on the title page would be valuable.

Three days later Mr. X brought my Introduction to me, neatly typecopied. He was in a state of considerable enthusiasm, and said:

"Really I find it quite good—quite, I assure you."

There was an airy and patronizing complacency about this damp compliment which affected my head and healthfully checked the swelling which was going on there.

I said, with cold dignity, that I was glad the work had earned his approval.

"Oh, it has, I assure you!" he answered, with large cheerfulness. "I assure you it quite has. I have gone over it very thoroughly, yesterday and last night and to-day, and I find it quite creditable—quite. I have made a few corrections—that is, suggestions, and—"

"Do you mean to say that you have been ed—"

"Oh, nothing of consequence, nothing of consequence, I assure you," he said, patting me on the shoulder and genially smiling; "only a few little things that needed just a mere polishing touch—nothing of consequence, I assure you. Let me have it back as soon as you can, so that I can pass it on to the printers and let them get to work on it while I am editing the translation."

I sat idle and alone, a time, thinking grieved thoughts, with the edited Introduction unopened in my hand. I could not look at it yet awhile. I had no heart for it, for my pride was deeply wounded. It was the only time I had been edited in thirty-two years, except by Mr. Howells, and he did not intrude his help, but furnished it at my request. "And now here is a half-stranger, obscure, destitute of literary training, destitute of literary experience, destitute of—"

But I checked myself there; for that way lay madness. I must seek calm; for my self-respect's sake I must not descend to unrefined personalities. I must keep in mind that this person was innocent of injurious intent and was honorably trying to do me a service. To feel harshly toward him, speak harshly of him—this was not the right Christian spirit. These just thoughts tranquillized me and restored to me my better self, and I opened the Introduction at the middle.

I will not deny it, my feelings rose to 104 in the shade:

"The idea! That this long-eared animal—this literary kangaroo—this illiterate hostler, with his skull full of axle grease—this. . ."

But I stopped there, for this was not the right Christian spirit.

I subjected myself to an hour of calming meditation, then carried the raped Introduction to that friend whom I have mentioned above and showed it to him. He fluttered the leaves over, then broke into another of those ill-bred laughs which are such a mar to him.

"I knew he would!" he said—as if gratified. "Didn't I tell you he would edit Shakespeare?"

"Yes, I know; but I did not suppose he would edit me."

"Oh, you didn't! Well, now you see that he is even equal to that. I tell you there are simply no bounds to that man's irreverence."

"I realize it, now," I said.

"Well, what are you going to do? Let him put it in his book—either edited or unedited?"

"Of course not!"

"That is well. You are becoming rational again. But what are your plans? You are not going to stop where you are, are you? You will write him a letter and give him Hark from the Tomb?"

"No, I shall write him a letter, but not in that spirit, I trust."

"Why shan't you?"

"Because he has meant me a kindness, and I hope I am not the man to reward him for it in that way."

The friend looked me over awhile, pensively, then said—

"Mark, I am ashamed of you. This is mere schoolgirl sentimentality. You ought to baste him—you know it yourself."

I said I had no such feeling in my heart and should put nothing of the kind in my letter.

"I shall point out his errors to him in gentleness and in the unwounding language of persuasion. Many a literary beginner has been disheartened and defeated by the uncharitable word wantonly uttered; this one shall get none such from me. It is more Christian-like to do a good turn than an ill one, and you ought to encourage me in my attitude, not scoff at it. This man shall not be my enemy; I will make him my lasting and grateful friend."

I felt that I was in the right, and I went home and began the letter and found pleasure and contentment in the labor, for I had the encouragement and support of an approving conscience.

The letter will be found in its proper place in this chapter of my Autobiography; it follows:

The Letter

DEAR MR. X:

I find on my desk the first two pages of Miss Z's translation, with your emendations marked in them. Thank you for sending them.

I have examined the first page of my amended Introduction and will begin now and jot down some notes upon your corrections. If I find any changes which shall not seem to me to be improvements, I will point out my reasons for thinking so. In this way I may chance to be helpful to you and thus profit you, perhaps, as much as you have desired to profit me.

Notes

Section I. First Paragraph, "Jeanne d'Arc." This is rather cheaply pedantic, and is not in very good taste. Joan is not known by that name among plain people of our race and tongue. I notice that the name of the Deity occurs several times in the brief installment of the Trials which you have favored me with; to be consistent, it will be necessary that you strike out "God" and put in "Dieu." Do not neglect this.

First line. What is the trouble with "at the"? And why "Trial?" Has some uninstructed person deceived you into the notion that there was but one, instead of half a dozen?

Amongst. Wasn't "among" good enough?

Next half-dozen Corrections. Have you failed to perceive that by taking the word "both" out of its proper place you have made foolishness of the sentence? And don't you see that your smug "of which" has turned that sentence into reporter's English? "Quite." Why do you intrude that shopworn favorite of yours where there is nothing useful for it to do? Can't you rest easy in your literary grave without it?

Next sentence. You have made no improvement in it. Did you change it merely to be changing something?

Second Paragraph. Now you have begun on my punctuation. Don't you realize that you ought not to intrude your help in a delicate art like that, with your limitations? And do you think you have added just the right smear of polish to the closing clause of the sentence?

Second Paragraph. How do you know it was his "own" sword? It could have been a borrowed one, I am cautious in matters of history, and you should not put statements in my mouth for which you cannot produce vouchers. Your other corrections are rubbish.

Third Paragraph. Ditto.

Fourth Paragraph. Your word "directly" is misleading; it could be construed to mean "at once." Plain clarity is better than ornate obscurity. I note your sensitive marginal remark: "Rather unkind to French feelings—referring to Moscow." Indeed, I have not been concerning myself about French feelings, but only about stating the facts. I have said several uncourteous things about the French—calling them a "nation of ingrates," in one place—but you have been so busy editing commas and semicolons that you overlooked them and failed to get scared at them. The next paragraph ends with a slur at the French, but I have reasons for thinking you mistook it for a compliment. It is discouraging to try to penetrate a mind like yours. You ought to get it out and dance on it. That would take some of the rigidity out of it. And you ought to use it sometimes; that would help. If you had done this every now and then along through life, it would not have petrified.

Fifth Paragraph. Thus far, I regard this as your masterpiece! You are really perfect in the great art of reducing simple and dignified speech to clumsy and vapid commonplace.

Sixth Paragraph. You have a singularly fine and aristocratic disrespect for homely and unpretending English. Every time I use "go back" you get out your polisher and slick it up to "return." "Return" is suited only to the drawing-room—it is ducal, and says itself with a simper and a smirk.

Seventh Paragraph. "Permission" is ducal. Ducal and affected. "Her" great days were not "over"; they were only half over. Didn't you know that? Haven't you read anything at all about Joan of Arc? The truth is, you do not pay any attention; I told you on my very first page that the public part of her career lasted two years, and you have forgotten it already. You really must get your mind out and have it repaired; you see, yourself, that it is all caked together.

Eighth Paragraph. She "rode away to assault and capture a stronghold." Very well; but you do not tell us whether she succeeded or not. You should not worry the reader with uncertainties like that. I will remind you once more that clarity is a good thing in literature. An apprentice cannot do better than keep this useful rule in mind. Closing Sentences. Corrections which are not corrections.

Ninth Paragraph. "Known" history. That word is a polish which is too delicate for me; there doesn't seem to be any sense in it. This would have surprised me, last week.

Second Sentence. It cost me an hour's study before I found out what it meant. I see, now, that it is intended to mean what it meant before. It really does accomplish its intent, I think, though in a most intricate and slovenly fashion. What was your idea in reframing it? Merely in order that you might add this to your other editorial contributions and be able to say to people that the most of the Introduction was your work?

I am afraid that that was really your sly and unparliamentary scheme. Certainly we do seem to live in a very wicked world.

Closing Sentence. There is your empty "however" again. I cannot think what makes you so flatulent.

II. In Captivity. "Remainder." It is curious and interesting to notice what an attraction a fussy, mincing, nickel-plated artificial word has for you. This is not well.

Third Sentence. But she was held to ransom; it wasn't a case of "should have been" and it wasn't a case of "if it had been offered"; it was offered, and also accepted, as the second paragraph shows. You ought never to edit except when awake.

Fourth Sentence. Why do you wish to change that? It was more than "demanded"; it was required. Have you no sense of shades of meaning in words?

Fifth Sentence. Changing it to "benefactress" takes the dignity out of it. If I had called her a braggart, I suppose you would have polished her into a braggartess, with your curious and random notions about the English tongue.

Closing Sentence. "Sustained" is sufficiently nickel-plated to meet the requirements of your disease, I trust. "Wholly" adds nothing; the sentence means just what it meant before. In the rest of the sentence you sacrifice simplicity to airy fussiness.

Second Paragraph. It was not blood money, unteachable ass, any more than is the money that buys a house or a horse; it was an ordinary business transaction of the time, and was not dishonorable. "With her hands, feet and neck both chained," etc. The restricted word "both" cannot be applied to three things, but only to two. "Fence:" You "lifted" that word from further along—and with what valuable result? The next sentence—after your doctoring of it—has no meaning. The one succeeding it—after your doctoring of it—refers to nothing, wanders around in space, has no meaning and no reason for existing, and is by a shade or two more demented and twaddlesome than anything hitherto ground out of your strange and interesting editorial mill.

Closing Sentence, "Neither" for "either." Have you now debauched the grammar to your taste?

Third Paragraph. It was sound English before you decayed it. Sell it to the museum.

Fourth Paragraph. I note the compliment you pay yourself, margined opposite the closing sentence: "Easier translation." But it has two defects. In the first place it is a mistranslation, and in the second place it translates half of the grace out of Joan's remark.

Fifth Paragraph. Why are you so prejudiced against fact and so indecently fond of fiction? Her generalship was not" that of a tried and trained military experience," for she hadn't had any, and no one swore that she had had any. I had stated the facts; you should have reserved your fictions.

Note: To be intelligible, that whole paragraph must consist of a single sentence; in breaking it up into several, you have knocked the sense all out of it.

Eighth Paragraph. "When the flames leapt up and enveloped her frail form" is handsome, very handsome, even elegant, but it isn't yours; you hooked it out of "The Costermonger's Bride; or The Fire Fiend's Foe." To take other people's things is not right, and God will punish you. "Parched" lips? How do you know they were? Why do you make statements which you cannot verify, when you have no motive for it but to work in a word which you think is nobby?

III. The Rehabilitation. "Their statements were taken down as evidence." Wonderful! If you had failed to mention that particular, many persons might have thought they were taken down as entertainment.

IV. The Riddle of All Time. I note your marginal remark: "Riddle—Anglice?" Look in your spelling book. "We can understand how the genius was created," etc., "by steady and congenial growth." We can't understand anything of the kind; genius is not "created" by any farming process—it is born. You are thinking of potatoes. Note: Whenever I say "circumstances" you change it to "environment"; and you persistently change my thats into whiches and my whiches into thats. This is merely silly, you know.

Second Paragraph. I note your marginal remark, "2 comprehends." I suppose some one has told you that repetition is tautology, and then has left you to believe that repetition is always tautology. But let it go; with your limitations one would not be able to teach you how to distinguish between the repetition which isn't tautology and the repetition which is.

Closing Sentence. Your tipsy emendation, when straightened up on its legs and examined, is found to say this: "We fail to see her issue thus equipped, and we cannot understand why." That is to say, she did not issue so equipped, and you cannot make out why she didn't. That is the riddle that defeats you, labor at it as you may? Why, if that had happened, it wouldn't be a riddle at all—except to you—but a thing likely to happen to nearly anybody, and not matter for astonishment to any intelligent person standing by at the time—or later. There is a riddle, but you have mistaken the nature of it, I cannot tell how, labor at it as I may; and I will try to point it out to you so that you can see some of it. We do not fail to see her issue so equipped, we do see her. That is the whole marvel, mystery, riddle. That she, an ignorant country girl, sprang upon the world equipped with amazing natural gifts is not the riddle—it could have happened to you if you had been some one else; but the fact that those talents were instantly and effectively usable without previous training is the mystery which we cannot master, the riddle which we cannot solve. Do you get it?

Third Paragraph. Drunk.

V. As Prophet. "And in every case realized the complete fulfillment." How do you know she did that? There is no testimony to back up that wild assertion. I was particular not to claim that all her prophecies came true; for that would have been to claim that we have her whole list, whereas it is likely that she made some that failed and did not get upon the record. People do not record prophecies that failed. Such is not the custom.

VI. Her Character. "Comforted" is a good change, and quite sane. But you are not playing fair; you are getting some sane person to help you. Note: When I wrote "counselled her, advised her," that was tautology; the "2 comprehends" was a case of repetition which was not tautological. But I am sure you will never be able to learn the difference. Note: "But she, Jeanne d'Arc, when presently she found," etc. That is the funniest yet, and the common-placest. But it isn't original, you got it out of "How to Write Literary Without Any Apprenticeship," sixpence to the trade; retail, sevenpence farthing. Erased Passage. I note with admiration your marginal remark explaining your objection to it: "Is it warrantable to assert that she bragged? Is it in good taste? It was assuredly foreign to her character." I will admit that my small effort at playfulness was not much of a pearl; but such as it was, I realize that I threw it into the wrong trough.

VII. Her Face and Form. You have misunderstood me again. I did not mean that the artist had several ideas and one prevailing one; I meant that he had only one idea. In that same sentence, "omits" and "forgets" have just the same meaning; have you any clear idea, then, why you made the change? Is it your notion that "gross" is an improvement on "big," "perform" an improvement on "do," "inquiring" an improvement on "asking," and "in such wise" an improvement on "then," or have you merely been seduced by the fine, large sounds of those words? Are you incurably hostile to simplicity of speech? And finally, do you not see that you have edited all the dignity out of the paragraph and substituted simpering commonplace for it, and that your addition at the end is a deliciously flat and funny anticlimax? Still, I note your command in the margin, "Insert this remark," and I dutifully obey.

Second Paragraph. "Exploited" was worth a shilling, there; you have traded it for a word not worth tuppence ha'penny, and got cheated, and serves you right. Read "rightly," if it shocks you.

Close of Paragraph. You have exploited another anticlimax—and in the form, too, of an impudent advertisement of your book. It seems to me that for a person of your elegance of language you are curiously lacking in certain other delicacies.

Third Paragraph. I must reserve my thanks. "Moreover" is a parenthesis, when interjected in that fashion; a parenthesis is evidence that the man who uses it does not know how to write English or is too indolent to take the trouble to do it; a parenthesis usually throws the emphasis upon the wrong word, and has done it in this instance; a man who will wantonly use a parenthesis will steal. For these reasons I am unfriendly to the parenthesis. When a man puts one into my mouth his life is no longer safe. "Break another lance" is a knightly and sumptuous phrase, and I honor it for its hoary age and for the faithful service it has done in the prize-composition of the schoolgirl, but I have ceased from employing it since I got my puberty, and must solemnly object to fathering it here. And besides, it makes me hint that I have broken one of those things before, in honor of the Maid, an intimation not justified by the facts. I did not break any lances or other furniture, I only wrote a book about her.

Truly yours,

MARK TWAIN

It cost me something to restrain myself and say these smooth and half-flattering things to this immeasurable idiot, but I did it and have never regretted it. For it is higher and nobler to be kind to even a shad like him than just. If we should deal out justice only, in this world, who would escape? No, it is better to be generous, and in the end more profitable, for it gains gratitude for us, and love, and it is far better to have the love of a literary strumpet like this than the reproaches of his wounded spirit. Therefore I am glad I said no harsh things to him, but spared him, the same as I would a tapeworm. It is reward enough for me to know that my children will be proud of their father for this, when I am gone. I could have said hundreds of unpleasant things about this tadpole, but I did not even feel them.[1]

---

1. The letter was not sent, after all. The temptation was strong, but pity for the victim prevailed. The MS. was, however, recalled and later published in Harper's Magazine and in book form as St. Joan of Arc.

Author's Note

Finally in Florence, in 1904, I hit upon the right way to do an Autobiography: Start it at no particular time of your life; wander at your free will all over your life; talk only about the thing which interests you for the moment; drop it the moment its interest threatens to pale, and turn your talk upon the new and more interesting thing that has intruded itself into your mind meantime.

Also, make the narrative a combined Diary and Autobiography. In this way you have the vivid thing of the present to make a contrast with memories of like things in the past, and these contrasts have a charm which is all their own. No talent is required to make a Combined Diary and Autobiography interesting.

And so, I have found the right plan. It makes my labor amusement—mere amusement, play, pastime, and wholly effortless.[1]

---

1. The reader will realize, even if the author did not, that this had been his plan from the beginning.

MARK TWAIN

Florence, January, 1904

VILLA QUARTO

This villa is situated three or four miles from Florence, and has several names. Some call it the Villa Reale di Quarto, some call it the Villa Principessa, some call it the Villa Granduchessa; this multiplicity of names was an inconvenience to me for the first two or three weeks, for as I had heard the place called by only one name, when letters came for the servants directed to the care of one or the other of the other names, I supposed a mistake had been made and remailed them. It has been explained to me that there is reason for these several names. Its name Quarto it gets from the district which it is in, it being in the four-mile radius from the center of Florence. It is called Reale because the King of Würtemberg occupied it at one time; Principessa and Granduchessa because a Russian daughter of the Imperial house occupied it at another. There is a history of the house somewhere, and some time or other I shall get it and see if there are any details in it which could be of use in this chapter. I should like to see that book, for as an evolutionist I should like to know the beginning of this dwelling and the several stages of its evolution. Baedeker says it was built by Cosimo I, assisted by an architect. I have learned this within the past three minutes, and it wrecks my development scheme. I was surmising that the house began in a small and humble way, and was the production of a poor farmer whose idea of home and comfort it was; that following him a generation or two later came a successor of better rank and larger means who built an addition; that successor after successor added more bricks and more bulk as time dragged on, each in his turn leaving a detail behind him of paint or wallpaper to distinguish his reign from the others; that finally in the last century came the three that precede me, and added their specialties. The King of Würtemberg broke out room enough in the center of the building—about a hundred feet from each end of it—to put in the great staircase, a cheap and showy affair, almost the only wooden thing in the whole edifice, and as comfortable and sane and satisfactory as it is out of character with the rest of the asylum. The Russian princess, who came with native superstitions about cold weather, added the hot-air furnaces in the cellar and the vast green majolica stove in the great hall where the king's staircase is—a stove which I thought might possibly be a church—a nursery church for children, so imposing is it for size and so richly adorned with basso relievos of an ultra-pious sort. It is loaded and fired from a secret place behind the partition against which it is backed. Last of all came Satan also, the present owner of the house, an American product, who added a cheap and stingy arrangement of electric bells, inadequate acetylene gas plant, obsolete waterclosets, perhaps a dozen pieces of machine-made boarding-house furniture, and some fire-auction carpets which blaspheme the standards of color and art all day long, and never quiet down until the darkness comes and pacifies them.

However, if the house was built for Cosimo four hundred years ago and with an architect on deck, I suppose I must dismiss those notions about the gradual growth of the house in bulk. Cosimo would want a large house, he would want to build it himself so that he could have it just the way he wanted it. I think he had his will. In the architecture of this barrack there has been no development. There was no architecture in the first place and none has been added, except the king's meretricious staircase, the princess's ecclesiastical stove, and the obsolete water-closets. I am speaking of art-architecture; there is none.

There is no more architecture of that breed discoverable in this long stretch of ugly and ornamentless three-storied house front than there is about a rope walk or a bowling alley. The shape and proportions of the house suggest those things, it being two hundred feet long by sixty wide. There is no art-architecture inside the house, there is none outside.

We arrive now at practical architecture—the useful, the indispensable, which plans the inside of a house and by wisely placing and distributing the rooms, or by studiedly and ineffectually distributing them, makes the house a convenient and comfortable and satisfactory abiding place or the reverse. The inside of the house is evidence that Cosimo's architect was not in his right mind. And it seems to me that it is not fair and not kind in Baedeker to keep on exposing him and his crime down to this late date. I am nobler than Baedeker, and more humane, and I suppress it. I don't remember what it was, anyway.

I shall go into the details of this house, not because I imagine it differs much from any other old-time palace or new-time palace on the continent of Europe, but because every one of its crazy details interests me, and therefore may be expected to interest others of the human race, particularly women. When they read novels they usually skip the weather, but I have noticed that they read with avidity all that a writer says about the furnishings, decorations, conveniences, and general style of a home.

MARK TWAIN

The interior of this barrack is so chopped up and systemless that one cannot deal in exact numbers when trying to put its choppings-up into statistics.

In the basement or cellar there are as follows:

Stalls and boxes for many horses—right under the principal bedchamber. The horses noisily dance to the solicitations of the multitudinous flies all night.

Feed stores.

Carriage house.

Acetylene-gas plant.

A vast kitchen. Put out of use years ago.

Another kitchen.

Coal rooms.

Coke rooms.

Peat rooms.

Wood rooms.

3 furnaces.

Wine rooms.

Various storerooms for all sorts of domestic supplies.

Lot of vacant and unclassified rooms.

Labyrinth of corridors and passages, affording the stranger an absolute certainty of getting lost.

A vast cesspool! It is cleaned out every thirty years.

Couple of dark stairways leading up to the ground floor.

About twenty divisions, as I count them.

This cellar seems to be of the full dimension of the house's foundation—say two hundred feet by sixty.

The ground floor, where I am dictating—is cut up into twenty-three rooms, halls, corridors, and so forth. The next floor above contains eighteen divisions of the like sort, one of which is the billiard room and another the great drawing-room.

The top story consists of twenty bedrooms and a furnace. Large rooms they necessarily are, for they are arranged ten on a side, and they occupy that whole space of two hundred feet long by sixty wide, except that there is a liberal passage, or hallway, between them. There are good fireplaces up there, and they would make charming bedchambers if handsomely and comfortably furnished and decorated. But there would need to be a lift—not a European lift, with its mere stand-up space and its imperceptible movement, but a roomy and swift American one.

These rooms are reached now by the same process by which they were reached in Cosimo's time—by leg power. Their brick floors are bare and unpainted, their walls are bare and painted the favorite European color, which is now and always has been an odious stomach-turning yellow. It is said that these rooms were intended for servants only and that they were meant to accommodate two or three servants apiece. It seems certain that they have not been occupied by any but servants in the last fifty or one hundred years, otherwise they would exhibit some remains of decoration.

If, then, they have always been for the use of servants only, where did Cosimo and his family sleep? Where did the King of Würtemberg bestow his dear ones? For below that floor there are not any more than three good bedchambers and five devilish ones. With eighty cut-ups in the house and with but four persons in my family, this large fact is provable: that we can't invite a friend to come and stay a few days with us, because there is not a bedroom unoccupied by ourselves that we could offer him without apologies. In fact, we have no friend whom we love so little and respect so moderately as to be willing to stuff him into one of those vacant cells.

Yes—where did the vanished aristocracy sleep? I mean the real aristocracy, not the American successor who required no room to speak of. To go on with my details: this little room where I am dictating these informations on this eighth day of January, 1904, is on the east side of the house. It is level with the ground and one may step from its nine- or ten-feet-high vast door into the terrace garden, which is a great, square, level space surrounded by an ornamental iron railing with vases of flowers distributed here and there along its top. It is a pretty terrace with abundant green grass, with handsome trees, with a great fountain in the middle, and with roses of various tints nodding in the balmy air and flashing back the rays of the January sun. Beyond the railing to the eastward stretches the private park, and through its trees curves the road to the far-off iron gate on the public road, where there is neither porter nor porter's lodge nor any way to communicate with the mansion. Yet from time immemorial the Italian villa has been a fortress hermetically sealed up in high walls of masonry and with entrance guarded by locked iron gates. The gates of Italy have always been locked at nightfall and kept locked the night through. No Italian trusted his contadini neighbors in the old times, and his successor does not trust them now. There are bells and porters for the convenience of outsiders desiring to get in at other villas, but it is not the case with this one, and apparently never has been. Surely it must have happened now and then that these kings and nobilities got caught out after the gates were locked. Then how did they get in? We shall never know. The question cannot be answered. It must take its place with the other unsolved mystery of where the aristocracies slept during those centuries when they occupied this fortress.

To return to that glass door. Outside it are exceedingly heavy and coarse Venetian shutters, a fairly good defense against a catapult.

These, like the leaves of the glass door, swing open in the French fashion, and I will remark in passing that to my mind the French window is as rational and convenient as the English-American window is the reverse of this. Inside the glass door (three or four inches inside of it) are solid doors made of boards, good and strong and ugly. The shutters, the glass door, and these wooden-door defenses against intrusion of light and thieves are all armed with strong and heavy bolts which are shot up and down by the turning of a handle. These house walls being very thick, these doors and shutters and things do not crowd one another, there is plenty of space between them, and there is room for more in case we should get to feeling afraid. This shuttered glass door, this convenient exit to the terrace and garden, is not the only one on this side of the house from which one can as handily step upon the terrace. There is a procession of them stretching along, door after door, along the east, or rear, front of the house, from its southern end to its northern end—eleven in the procession. Beginning at the south end they afford exit from a parlor; a large bedroom (mine); this little twelve-by-twenty reception room where I am now at work; and a ten-by-twelve ditto, which is in effect the beginning of a corridor forty feet long by twelve wide, with three sets of triple glass doors for exit to the terrace. The corridor empties into a dining room, and the dining room into two large rooms beyond, all with glass-door exits to the terrace. When the doors which connect these seven rooms and the corridor are thrown open the two-hundred-foot stretch of variegated carpeting with its warring and shouting and blaspheming tumult of color makes a fine and almost contenting, receding, and diminishing perspective, and one realizes that if some sane person could have the privilege and the opportunity of burning the existing carpets and instituting harmonies of color in their place, the reformed perspective would be very beautiful. Above each of the eleven glass doors is a duplicate on the next floor—ten feet by six, of glass. And above each of these on the topmost floor is a smaller window—thirty-three good openings for light on this eastern front, the same on the western front, and nine of ampler size on each end of the house. Fifty-six of these eighty-four windows contain double enough glass to equip the average window of an American dwelling, yet the house is by no means correspondingly light. I do not know why; perhaps it is because of the dismal upholstering of the walls.

Villa di Quarto is a palace; Cosimo built it for that, his architect intended it for that, it has always been regarded as a palace, and an old resident of Florence told me the other day that it was a good average sample of the Italian palace of the great nobility, and that its grotesqueness and barbarities, incongruities and destitution of conveniences, are to be found in the rest. I am able to believe this because I have seen some of the others.

I think there is not a room in this huge confusion of rooms and halls and corridors and cells and waste spaces which does not contain some memento of each of its illustrious occupants, or at least two or three of them.

We will examine the parlor at the head of that long perspective which I have been describing. The arched ceiling is beautiful both in shape and in decoration. It is finely and elaborately frescoed. The ceiling is a memento of Cosimo. The doors are draped with heavy pale-blue silk, faintly figured; that is the King of Würtemberg relic. The gleaming-white brass-banded, porcelain pagoda which contains an open fireplace for wood is a relic of the Russian princess and a remembrancer of her native experiences of cold weather. The light-gray wallpaper figured with gold flowers is anybody's—we care not to guess its pedigree. The rest of the room is manifestly a result of the present occupation. The floor is covered with a felt-like filling of strenuous red; one can almost see Pharaoh's host floundering in it. There are four rugs scattered about like islands, violent rugs whose colors swear at one another and at the Red Sea. There is a sofa upholstered in a coarse material, a frenzy of green and blue and blood, a cheap and undeceptive imitation of Florentine embroidery. There is a sofa and two chairs upholstered in pale-green silk, figured; the wood is of three different breeds of American walnut, flimsy, cheap, machine-made. There is a French-walnut sofa upholstered in figured silk of a fiendish crushed-strawberry tint of a faded aspect, and there is an armchair which is a mate to it. There is a plain and naked black-walnut table without a cover to modify its nudity; under it is a large round ottoman covered with the palest of pale-green silk, a sort of glorified mushroom which curses with all its might at the Red Sea and the furious rugs and the crushed-strawberry relics. Against the wall stands a tall glass-fronted bookcase, machine-made—the material, American butternut. It stands near enough to the King of Würtemberg's heavy silken door-drapery to powerfully accent its cheapness and ugliness by contrast. Upon the walls hang three good water-colors, six or eight very bad ones, a pious-looking portrait, and a number of photographs, one of them a picture of a count, who has a manly and intelligent face and looks like a gentleman.

The whole literature of this vast house is contained in that fire-auction American bookcase. There are four shelves. The top one is made up of indiscriminate literature of good quality; the next shelf is made up of cloth-covered books devoted to Christian Science and spiritualism—forty thin books; the two remaining shelves contain fifty-four bound volumes of Blackwood, in date running backward from about 1870. This bookcase and its contents were probably imported from America.

The room just described must be dignified with that imposing title, library, on account of the presence in it of that butternut bookcase and its indigent contents. It does duty, now, as a private parlor for Mrs. Clemens during those brief and widely separated occasions when she is permitted to leave for an hour the bed to which she has been so long condemned. We are in the extreme south end of the house, if there is any such thing as a south end to a house, where orientation cannot be determined by me, because I am incompetent in all cases where an object does not point directly north or south. This one slants across between, and is therefore a confusion to me. This little private parlor is in one of the two corners of what I call the south end of the house. The sun rises in such a way that all the morning it is pouring its light in through the thirty-three glass doors or windows which pierce the side of the house which looks upon the terrace and garden, as already described; the rest of the day the light floods this south end of the house; as I call it; at noon the sun is directly above Florence yonder in the distance in the plain—directly above those architectural features which have been so familiar to the world in pictures for some centuries: the Duomo, the Campanile, the Tomb of the Medici, and the beautiful tower of the

Palazzo Vecchio; above Florence, but not very high above it, for it never climbs quite halfway to the zenith in these winter days; in this position it begins to reveal the secrets of the delicious blue mountains that circle around into the west, for its light discovers, uncovers, and exposes a white snowstorm of villas and cities that you cannot train yourself to have confidence in, they appear and disappear so mysteriously and so as if they might be not villas and cities at all, but the ghosts of perished ones of the remote and dim Etruscan times; and late in the afternoon the sun sinks down behind those mountains somewhere, at no particular time and at no particular place, so far as I can see.

This "library," or boudoir, or private parlor, opens into Mrs. Clemens's bedroom, and it and the bedroom together stretch all the way across the south end of the house. The bedroom gets the sun before noon, and is prodigally drenched and deluged with it the rest of the day. One of its windows is particularly well calculated to let in a liberal supply of sunshine, for it contains twelve great panes, each of them more than two feet square. The bedroom is thirty-one feet long by twenty-four wide, and there had been a time when it and the "library" had no partition between, but occupied the whole breadth of the south end of the house in an unbroken stretch. It must have been a ballroom or banqueting room at that time. I suggest this merely because perhaps not even Cosimo would need so much bedroom, whereas it would do very well indeed as a banqueting room because of its proximity to the cooking arrangements, which were not more than two or three hundred yards away, down cellar, a very eligible condition of things indeed in the old times. Monarchs cannot have the conveniences which we plebeians are privileged to luxuriate in—they can't, even to-day. If I were invited to spend a week in Windsor Castle it would gladden me and make me feel proud; but if there was any hint about regular boarders I should let on that I didn't hear. As a palace Windsor Castle is great; great for show, spaciousness, display, grandeur, and all that; but the bedrooms are small, uninviting, and inconvenient, and the arrangements for delivering food from the kitchen to the table are so clumsy and waste so much time, that a meal there probably suggests recent cold storage. This is only conjecture; I did not eat there. In Windsor Castle the courses are brought up by dumb waiter from the profound depth where the vast kitchen is; they are then transferred by rail on a narrow little tramway to the territory where the dinner is to have place. This trolley was still being worked by hand when I was there four years ago; still it was without doubt a great advance upon Windsor Castle transportation of any age before Queen Victoria's. It is startling to reflect that what we call convenience in a dwelling house, and which we regard as necessities, were born so recently that hardly one of them existed in the world when Queen Victoria was born. The valuable part—to my thinking the valuable part—of what we call civilization had no existence when she emerged upon the planet. She sat in her chair in that venerable fortress and saw it grow from its mustard seed to the stupendous tree which it had become before she died. She saw the whole of the new creation, she saw everything that was made, and without her witness was not anything made that was made. A very creditable creation indeed, taking all things into account; since man, quite unassisted, did it all out of his own head. I jump to this conclusion because I think that if Providence had been minded to help him, it would have occurred to Providence to do this some hundred thousand centuries earlier. We are accustomed to seeing the hand of Providence in everything. Accustomed, because if we missed it, or thought we missed it, we had discretion enough not to let on. We are a tactful race. We have been prompt to give Providence the credit of this fine and showy new civilization and we have been quite intemperate in our praises of this great benefaction; we have not been able to keep still over this splendid five-minute attention; we can only keep still about the ages of neglect which preceded it and which it makes so conspicuous. When Providence washes one of his worms into the sea in a tempest, then starves him and freezes him on a plank for thirty-four days, and finally wrecks him again on an uninhabited island, where he lives on shrimps and grasshoppers and other shell-fish for three months, and is at last rescued by some old whisky-soaked, profane, and blasphemous infidel of a tramp captain, and carried home gratis to his friends, the worm forgets that it was Providence that washed him overboard, and only remembers that Providence rescued him. He finds no fault, he has no sarcasms for Providence's crude and slow and labored ingenuities of invention in the matter of life-saving, he sees nothing in these delays and ineffectiveness but food for admiration; to him they seem a marvel, a miracle; and the longer they take and the more ineffective they are, the greater the miracle; meantime he never allows himself to break out in any good hearty unhandicapped thanks for the tough old shipmaster who really saved him, he damns him with faint praise as "the instrument," his rescuer "under Providence."

To get to that corner room with its bookcase freighted with twenty dollars' worth of ancient Blackwood and modern spiritualistic literature, I have passed through—undescribed—a room that is my bedroom. Its size is good, its shape is good—thirty feet by twenty-two. Originally it was fifty feet long, stretching from one side of the house to the other, in the true Italian fashion which makes everybody's bedroom a passageway into the next room—kings, nobles, serfs, and all; but this American countess, the present owner, cut off twenty feet of the room and reattached ten feet of it to the room as a bathroom, and devoted the rest to a hallway. This bedroom is lighted by one of those tall glass doors, already described, which give upon the terrace. It is divided across the middle by some polished white pillars as big as my body, with Doric capitals, supporting a small arch at each end and a long one in the middle; this is indeed grandeur and is quite imposing. The fireplace is of a good size, is of white marble, and the carvings upon it are of the dainty and graceful sort proper to its age, which is probably four hundred years. The fireplace and the stately columns are aristocratic, they recognize their kinship, and they smile at each other. That is, when they are not swearing at the rest of the room's belongings. The front half of the room is aglare with a paper loud of pattern, atrocious in color, and cheap beyond the dreams of avarice. The rear half is painted from floor to ceiling a dull, dead and repulsive yellow. It seems strange that yellow should be the favorite in Europe whereby to undecorate a wall; I have never seen the yellow wall which did not depress me and make me unhappy. The floor of the room is covered with a superannuated nightmare of a carpet whose figures are vast and riotous and whose indignant reds and blacks and yellows quarrel day and night and refuse to be reconciled. There is a door opening into the bathroom, and at that same end of the room is a door opening into a small box of a hall which leads to another convenience. Those two doors strictly follow the law of European dwellings, whether built for the prince or for the pauper. That is to say they are rude, thin, cheap planks, flimsy; the sort of door which in the South the negro attaches to his chicken coop. These doors, like all such doors on the Continent, have a gimlet handle in place of a door knob. It wrenches from the socket a bolt which has no springs and which will not return to that socket except upon compulsion. You can't slam a door like that; it would simply rebound. That gimlet handle catches on any garment that tries to get by; if tearable it tears it; if not tearable it stops the wearer with a suddenness and a violence and an unexpectedness which break down all his religious reserves, no matter who he may be.

The bedroom has a door on each side of the front end, so that anybody may tramp through that wants to at any time of the day or night, this being the only way to get to the room beyond, where the precious library is bookcased. Furniture: a salmon-colored silk sofa, a salmon-colored silk chair, a pair of ordinary wooden chairs, and a stuffed chair whose upholstery is of a species unknown to me but devilish; in the corner, an ordinary thin-legged kitchen table; against one wall a wardrobe and a dressing bureau; on the opposite side a rickety chest of drawers made of white pine painted black and ornamented with imitation brass handles; brass double bedstead. One will concede that this room is not over-embarrassed with furniture. The two clapboard doors already spoken of are mercifully concealed by parti-colored hangings of unknown country and origin; the three other doors already mentioned are hooded with long curtains that descend to the floor and are caught apart in the middle to permit the passage of people and light. These curtains have a proud and ostentatious look which deceives no one, it being based upon a hybrid silk with cotton for its chief ingredient. The color is a solid yellow, and deeper than the yellow of the rearward half of the walls; and now here is a curious thing: one may look from one of these colors to the other fifty times, and each time he will think that the one he is looking at is the ugliest. It is a most curious and interesting effect. I think that if one could get himself toned down to where he could look upon these curtains without passion he would then perceive that it takes both of them together to be the ugliest color known to art.

We have considered these two yellows, but they do not exhaust the matter; there is still another one in the room. This is a lofty and sumptuous canopy over the brass bedstead, made of brilliant and shiny and shouting lemon-colored satin—genuine satin, almost the only genuine thing in the whole room. It is of the nobility, it is of the aristocracy, it belongs with the majestic white pillars and the dainty old marble fireplace; all the rest of the room's belongings are profoundly plebeian, they are exiles, they are sorrowful outcasts from their rightful home, which is the poorhouse.

On the end wall of the yellow half of the room hang a couple of framed engravings, female angels engaged in their customary traffic of transporting departed persons to heaven over a distant prospect of city and plain and mountain.

The discords of this room, in colors, in humble poverty and showy and self-complacent pretentiousness, are repeated everywhere one goes in the huge house.

I am weary of particulars. One may travel two hundred feet down either side of the house, through an aimless jumble of useless little reception rooms and showy corridors, finding nothing sane or homelike till he reaches the dining room at the end.

On the next floor, over the Blackwood library, there is a good bedroom well furnished, and with a fine stone balcony and the majestic view, just mentioned, enlarged and improved, thence northward two hundred feet, cut up in much the same disarray as is that ground floor. But in the midst is a great drawing-room about forty feet square and perhaps as many high, handsomely and tastefully hung with brocaded silk and with a very beautifully frescoed ceiling. But the place has a most angry look, for scattered all about it are divans and sofas and chairs and lofty window hangings of that same fierce lemon-colored satin heretofore noted as forming the canopy of the brass bedstead downstairs. When one steps suddenly into that great place on a splendid Florentine day it is like entering hell on a Sunday morning when the brightest and yellowest brimstone fires are going.

I think I have said that the top floor has twenty rooms. They are not furnished, they are spacious, and from all of them one has a wide and charming view. Properly furnished they would be pleasant, homelike, and in every way satisfactory.

End of March. Now that we have lived in this house four and one-half months, my prejudices have fallen away one by one and the place has become very homelike to me. Under certain conditions I should like to go on living in it indefinitely. Indeed, I could reduce the conditions to two and be quite satisfied. I should wish the owner to move out of Italy; out of Europe; out of the planet.

I realize that there is no way of realizing this and so after two and a half months I have given it up and have been house hunting ever since. House hunting in any country is difficult and depressing; in the regions skirting Florence it leads to despair, and if persisted in will end in suicide. Professor Willard Fiske, the scholar, who bought the Walter Savage Landor villa fourteen or fifteen years ago, tells me that he examined three hundred villas before he found one that would suit him; yet he was a widower without child or dependent and merely needed a villa for his lone self. I was in it twelve years ago and it seemed to me that he had not bought a villa, but only a privilege—the privilege of building it over again and making it humanly habitable. During the first three weeks of February I climbed around over and prowled through an average of six large villas a week, but found none that would answer, in the circumstances. One of the circumstances, and the most important of all, being that we are in Italy by the command of physicians in the hope that in this mild climate Mrs. Clemens will get her health back. She suddenly lost it nineteen months ago, being smitten helpless by nervous prostration complicated with an affection of the heart of several years' standing, and the times since this collapse that she has been able to stand on her feet five minutes at a time have been exceedingly rare. I have examined two villas that were about as large as this one, but the interior architecture was so ill contrived that there was not comfortable room in them for my family of four persons. As a rule the bedchambers served as common hallways, which means that for centuries Tom, Dick, and Harry of both sexes and all ages have moved in procession to and fro through those ostensibly private rooms.

Every villa I examined had a number of the details which I was ordered to find; four possessed almost every one of them. In the case of the four the altitudes were not satisfactory to the doctors; two of them were too high, the other pair too low. These fifteen or twenty villas were all furnished. The reader of these notes will find that word in the dictionary, and it will be defined there; but that definition can have no value to a person who is desiring to know what the word means over here when it is attached to an advertisement proposing to let a dwelling house. Here it means a meager and scattering array of cheap and rickety chairs, tables, sofas, etc., upholstered in worn and damaged fragments of somber and melancholy hue that suggest the grave and compel the desire to retire to it. The average villa is properly a hospital for ailing and superannuated furniture. In its best days this furniture was never good nor comely nor attractive nor comfortable. When that best day was, was too long ago for anyone to be able to date it now.

Each time that I have returned from one of these quests I have been obliged to concede that the insurrection of color in this Villa di Quarto is rest to the eye after what I had been sighing and sorrowing over in those others, and that this is the only villa in the market so far as I know that has furniture enough in it for the needs of the occupants. Also I will concede that I was wrong in thinking this villa poverty-stricken in the matter of conveniences; for by contrast with those others this house is rich in conveniences.

Some time ago a lady told me that she had just returned from a visit to the country palace of a princess, a huge building standing in the midst of a great and beautiful and carefully kept flower garden, the garden in its turn being situated in a great and beautiful private park. She was received by a splendid apparition of the footman species, who ushered her into a lofty and spacious hall richly garnished with statuary, pictures, and other ornaments, fine and costly, and thence down an immensely long corridor which shone with a similar garniture, superb and showy to the last degree; and at the end of this enchanting journey she was delivered into the princess's bedchamber and received by the princess, who was ailing slightly and in bed. The room was very small, it was without bric-a-brac or prettinesses for the comfort of the eye and spirit, the bedstead was iron, there were two wooden chairs and a small table, and in the corner stood an iron tripod which supported a common white washbowl. The costly glories of the house were all for show; no money had been wasted on its mistress's comfort. I had my doubts about this story when I first acquired it; I am more credulous now.

A word or two more concerning the furnishings of the Villa di Quarto. The rooms contain an average of four pictures each, say two photographs or engravings and two oil- or water-color paintings of chromo degree.

High up on the walls of the great entrance hall hang several of those little shiny white cherubs which one associates with the name of Delia Robbia. The walls of this hall are further decorated, or at least relieved, by the usual great frameless oval oil portraits of long-departed aristocrats which one customarily finds thus displayed in all Florentine villas. In the present case the portraits were painted by artists of chromo rank, with the exception of one. As I have had no teaching in art, I cannot decide what is a good picture and what isn't, according to the established standards; I am obliged to depend on my own crude standards. According to these the picture which I am now considering sets forth a most noble, grave, and beautiful face, faultless in all details and with beautiful and faultless hands; and if it belonged to me I would never take a lesson in art lest the picture lose for me its finished, complete, and satisfying perfection.

WE HAVE LIVED IN A Florentine villa before. This was twelve years ago. This was the Villa Viviani, and was pleasantly and commandingly situated on a hill in the suburb of Settignano, overlooking Florence and the great valley. It was secured for us and put in comfortable order by a good friend, Mrs. Ross, whose stately castle was a twelve minutes' walk away. She still lives there, and had been a help to us more than once since we established relations with the titled owner of the Villa di Quarto. The year spent in the Villa Viviani was something of a contrast to the five months which we have now spent in this ducal barrack. Among my old manuscripts and random and spasmodic diaries I find some account of that pleasantly remembered year, and will make some extracts from the same and introduce them here.

When we were passing through Florence in the spring of '92 on our way to Germany, the diseased-world's bathhouse, we began negotiations for a villa, and friends of ours completed them after we were gone. When we got back three or four months later, everything was ready, even to the servants and the dinner. It takes but a sentence to state that, but it makes an indolent person tired to think of the planning and work and trouble that lie concealed in it. For it is less trouble and more satisfaction to bury two families than to select and equip a home for one.

The situation of the villa was perfect. It was three miles from Florence, on the side of a hill. The flowery terrace on which it stood looked down upon sloping olive groves and vineyards; to the right, beyond some hill spurs, was Fiesole, perched upon its steep terraces; in the immediate foreground was the imposing mass of the Ross castle, its walls and turrets rich with the mellow weather stains of forgotten centuries; in the distant plain lay Florence, pink and gray and brown, with the rusty huge dome of the cathedral dominating its center like a captive balloon, and flanked on the right by the smaller bulb of the Medici chapel and on the left by the airy tower of the Palazzo Vecchio; all around the horizon was a billowy rim of lofty blue hills, snowed white with innumerable villas. After nine months of familiarity with this panorama, I still think, as I thought in the beginning, that this is the fairest picture on our planet, the most enchanting to look upon, the most satisfying to the eye and the spirit. To see the sun sink down, drowned on his pink and purple and golden floods, and overwhelm Florence with tides of color that make all the sharp lines dim and faint and turn the solid city to a city of dreams, is a sight to stir the coldest nature and make a sympathetic one drunk with ecstasy.

Sept. 26, '92.—Arrived in Florence. Got my head shaved. This was a mistake. Moved to the villa in the afternoon. Some of the trunks brought up in the evening by the contadino—if that is his title. He is the man who lives on the farm and takes care of it for the owner, the marquis. The contadino is middle-aged and like the rest of the peasants—that is to say, brown, handsome, good-natured, courteous, and entirely independent without making any offensive show of it. He charged too much for the trunks, I was told. My informant explained that this was customary.

Sept. 27.—The rest of the trunks brought up this morning. He charged too much again, but I was told that this also was customary. It is all right, then. I do not wish to violate the customs. Hired landau, horses, and coachman. Terms, four hundred and eighty francs a month and a pourboire to the coachman, I to furnish lodging for the man and the horses, but nothing else. The landau has seen better days and weighs thirty tons. The horses are feeble and object to the landau; they stop and turn around every now and then and examine it with surprise and suspicion. This causes delay. But it entertains the people along the road. They came out and stood around with their hands in their pockets and discussed the matter with one another. I was told they said that a forty-ton landau was not the thing for horses like those—what they needed was a wheelbarrow.

I will insert in this place some notes made in October concerning the villa:

This is a two-story house. It is not an old house—from an Italian standpoint, I mean. No doubt there has always been a nice dwelling on this eligible spot since a thousand years B.C., but this present one is said to be only two hundred years old. Outside, it is a plain square building like a box, and is painted a light yellow and has green window shutters. It stands in a commanding position on an artificial terrace of liberal dimensions which is walled around with strong masonry. From the walls the vineyards and olive orchards of the estate slant away toward the valley; the garden about the house is stocked with flowers and a convention of lemon bushes in great crockery tubs; there are several tall trees—stately stone pines—also fig trees and trees of breeds not familiar to me; roses overflow the retaining walls and the battered and mossy stone urns on the gateposts in pink and yellow cataracts, exactly

MARK TWAIN

as they do on the drop curtains of theaters; there are gravel walks shut in by tall laurel hedges. A back corner of the terrace is occupied by a dense grove of old ilex trees. There is a stone table in there, with stone benches around it. No shaft of sunlight can penetrate that grove. It is always deep twilight in there, even when all outside is flooded with the intense sun glare common to this region. The carriage road leads from the inner gate eight hundred feet to the public road, through the vineyard, and there one may take the horse car for the city, and will find it a swifter and handier convenience than a sixty-ton landau. On the east (or maybe it is the south) front of the house is the Viviani coat of arms in plaster, and near it a sun dial which keeps very good time.

The house is a very fortress for strength. The main walls—of brick covered with plaster—are about three feet thick; the partitions of the rooms, also of brick, are nearly the same thickness. The ceilings of the rooms on the ground floor are more than twenty feet high; those of the upper floors are also higher than necessary. I have several times tried to count the rooms in the house, but the irregularities baffle me. There seem to be twenty-eight.

The ceilings are frescoed, the walls are papered. All the floors are of red brick covered with a coating or polished and shining cement which is as hard as stone and looks like it; for the surfaces have been painted in patterns, first in solid colors and then snowed over with varicolored freckles of paint to imitate granite and other stones. Sometimes the body of the floor is an imitation of gray granite with a huge star or other ornamental pattern of imitation fancy marbles in the center; with a two-foot band of imitation red granite all around the room, whose outer edge is bordered with a six-inch stripe of imitation lapis-lazuli; sometimes the body of the floor is red granite, then the gray is used as a bordering stripe. There are plenty of windows, and worlds of sun and light; these floors are slick and shiny and full of reflections, for each is a mirror in its way, softly imaging all objects after the subdued fashion of forest lakes.

There is a tiny family chapel on the main floor, with benches for ten or twelve persons, and over the little altar is an ancient oil painting which seems to me to be as beautiful and as rich in tone as any of those old-master performances down yonder in the galleries of the Pitti and the Uffizi. Botticelli, for instance; I wish I had time to make a few remarks about Botticelli—whose real name was probably Smith.

The curious feature of the house is the salon. This is a spacious and lofty vacuum which occupies the center of the house; all the rest of the house is built around it; it extends up through both stories and its roof projects some feet above the rest of the building. That vacuum is very impressive. The sense of its vastness strikes you the moment you step into it and cast your eyes around it and aloft. I tried many names for it: the Skating Rink, the Mammoth Cave, the Great Sahara, and so on, but none exactly answered. There are five divans distributed along its walls; they make little or no show, though their aggregate length is fifty-seven feet. A piano in it is a lost object. We have tried to reduce the sense of desert space and emptiness with tables and things, but they have a defeated look and do not do any good. Whatever stands or moves under that soaring painted vault is belittled.

Over the six doors are huge plaster medallions which are supported by great naked and handsome plaster boys, and in these medallions are plaster portraits in high relief of some grave and beautiful men in stately official costumes of a long-past day—Florentine senators and judges, ancient dwellers here and owners of this estate. The date of one of them is 1305—middle-aged, then, and a judge—he could have known, as a youth, the very creators of Italian art; he could have walked and talked with Dante, and probably did. The date of another is 1343—he could have known Boccaccio and spent his afternoons yonder in Fiesole gazing down on plague-reeking Florence and listening to that man's improper tales, and he probably did. The date of another is 1463—he could have met Columbus, and he knew the Magnificent Lorenzo, of course. These are all Cerretanis—or Cerretani-Twains, as I may say, for I have adopted myself into their family on account of its antiquity, my origin having been heretofore too recent to suit me.

But I am forgetting to state what it is about that Rink that is so curious—which is, that it is not really vast, but only seems so. It is an odd deception, and unaccountable; but a deception it is. Measured by the eye it is sixty feet square and sixty high; but I have been applying the tape line, and find it to be but forty feet square and forty high. These are the correct figures; and what is interestingly strange is that the place continues to look as big now as it did before I measured it.

This is a good house, but it cost very little and is simplicity itself, and pretty primitive in most of its features. The water is pumped to the ground floor from a well by hand labor, and then carried upstairs by hand. There is no drainage; the cesspools are right under the windows. This is the case with everybody's villa.

The doors in this house are like the doors of the majority of the houses and hotels of Italy—plain, thin, unpaneled boards painted white. This makes the flimsiest and most unattractive door known to history. The knob is not a knob, but a thing like the handle of a gimlet—you can get hold of it only with your thumb and forefinger. Still, even that is less foolish than our American door knob, which is always getting loose and turning futilely round and round in your hand, accomplishing nothing.

The windows are all of the rational continental breed; they open apart, like doors; and when they are bolted for the night they don't rattle and a person can go to sleep.

There are cunning little fireplaces in the bedrooms and sitting rooms, and lately a big, aggressive-looking German stove has been set up on the south frontier of the Great Sahara.

The stairs are made of granite blocks, the hallways of the second floor are of red brick. It is a safe house. Earthquakes cannot shake it down, fire cannot burn it. There is absolutely nothing burnable but the furniture, the curtains, and the doors. There is not much furniture; it is merely summer furniture—or summer bareness, if you like. When a candle set fire to the curtains in a room over my head the other night where samples of the family slept, I was wakened out of my sleep by shouts and screams, and was greatly terrified until an answer from the window told me what the matter was—that the window curtains and hangings were on fire. In America I should have been more frightened than ever, then, but this was not the case here. I advised the samples to let the fire alone and go to bed; which they did, and by the time they got to sleep there was nothing of the attacked fabrics left. We boast a good deal in America of our fire departments, the most efficient and wonderful in the world, but they have something better than that to boast of in Europe—a rational system of building which makes human life safe from fire and renders fire departments needless. We boast of a thing which we ought to be ashamed to require.

This villa has a roomy look, a spacious look; and when the sunshine is pouring in and lighting up the bright colors of the shiny floors and walls and ceilings there is a large and friendly suggestion of welcome about the aspects, but I do not know that I have ever seen a continental dwelling which quite met the American standard of a home in all the details. There is a trick about an American house that is like the deep-lying untranslatable idioms of a foreign language—a trick uncatchable by the stranger, a trick incommunicable and indescribable; and that elusive trick, that intangible something, whatever it is, is just the something that gives the home look and the home feeling to an American house and makes it the most satisfying refuge yet invented by men—and women, mainly women. The American house is opulent in soft and varied colors that please and rest the eye, and in surfaces that are smooth and pleasant to the touch, in forms that are shapely and graceful, in objects without number which compel interest and cover nakedness; and the night has even a higher charm than the day, there, for the artificial lights do really give light instead of merely trying and failing; and under their veiled and tinted glow all the snug coziness and comfort and charm of the place is at best and loveliest. But when night shuts down on the continental home there is no gas or electricity to fight it, but only dreary lamps of exaggerated ugliness and of incomparable poverty in the matter of effectiveness.

Sept. 29, '92.—I seem able to forget everything except that I have had my head shaved. No matter how closely I shut myself away from draughts it seems to be always breezy up there. But the main difficulty is the flies. They like it up there better than anywhere else; on account of the view, I suppose. It seems to me that I have never seen any flies before that were shod like these. These appear to have talons. Wherever they put their foot down they grab. They walk over my head all the time and cause me infinite torture. It is their park, their club, their summer resort. They have garden parties there, and conventions, and all sorts of dissipation. And they fear nothing. All flies are daring, but these are more daring than those of other nationalities. These cannot be scared away by any device. They are more diligent, too, than the other kinds; they come before daylight and stay till after dark. But there are compensations, not a trouble. There are very few of them, they are not noisy, and not much interested in their calling. A single unkind word will send them away; if said in English, which impresses them because they do not understand it, they come no more that night. We often see them weep when they are spoken to harshly. I have got some of the eggs to take home. If this breed can be raised in our climate they will be a great advantage. There seem to be no fleas here. This is the first time we have struck this kind of an interregnum in fifteen months. Everywhere else the supply exceeds the demand.

Oct. 1.—Finding that the coachman was taking his meals in the kitchen, I reorganized the contract to include his board, at thirty francs a month. That is what it would cost him up above us in the village, and I think I can feed him for two hundred, and save thirty out of it. Saving thirty is better than not saving anything.

That passage from the diary reminds me that I did an injudicious thing along about that time which bore fruit later. As I was to give the coachman, Vittorio, a monthly pourboire, of course I wanted to know the amount. So I asked the coachman's padrone (master), instead of asking somebody else—anybody else. He said thirty francs a month would be about right. I was afterward informed that this was an overcharge, but that it was customary, there being no customary charges except overcharges. However, at the end of that month the coachman demanded an extra pourboire of fifteen francs. When I asked why, he said his padrone had taken his other pourboire away from him. The padrone denied this in Vittorio's presence, and Vittorio seemed to retract. The padrone said he did, and he certainly had that aspect, but I had to take the padrone's word for it as interpreter of the coachman's Italian. When the padrone was gone the coachman resumed the charge, and as we liked him—and also believed him—we made his aggregate pourboire forty-five francs a month after that, and never doubted that the padrone took two-thirds of it. We were told by citizens that it was customary for the padrone to seize a considerable share of his dependent's pourboire, and also the custom for the padrone to deny it. That padrone is an accommodating man and a most capable and agreeable talker, speaking English like an archangel, and making it next to impossible for a body to be dissatisfied with him; yet his seventy-ton landau has kept us supplied with lame horses for nine months, whereas we were entitled to a light carriage suited to hill-climbing, and fastidious people would have made him furnish it.

The Cerretani family, of old and high distinction in the great days of the Republic, lived on this place during many centuries. Along in October we began to notice a pungent and suspicious odor which we were not acquainted with and which gave us some little apprehension, but I laid it on the dog, and explained to the family that that kind of a dog always smelled that way when he was up to windward of the subject, but privately I knew it was not the dog at all. I believed it was our adopted ancestors, the Cerretanis. I believed they were preserved under the house somewhere and that it would be a good scheme to get them out and air them. But I was mistaken. I made a secret search and had to acquit the ancestors. It turned out that the odor was a harmless one. It came from the wine crop, which was stored in a part of the cellars to which we had no access. This discovery gave our imaginations a rest and it turned a disagreeable smell into a pleasant one. But not until we had so long and lavishly flooded the house with odious disinfectants that the dog left and the family had to camp in the yard most of the time. It took two months to disinfect the disinfectants and persuade our wealth of atrocious stenches to emigrate. When they were finally all gone and the wine fragrance resumed business at the old stand, we welcomed it with effusion and have had no fault to find with it since.

Oct. 6.—I find myself at a disadvantage here. Four persons in the house speak Italian and nothing else, one person speaks German and nothing else, the rest of the talk is in the French, English, and profane languages. I am equipped with but the merest smattering in these tongues, if I except one or two. Angelo speaks French—a French which he could get a patent on, because he invented it himself; a French which no one can understand, a French which resembles no other confusion of sounds heard since Babel, a French which curdles the milk. He prefers it to his native Italian. He loves to talk it; loves to listen to himself; to him it is music; he will not let it alone. The family would like to get their little Italian savings into circulation, but he will not give change. It makes no difference what language he is addressed in, his reply is in French, his peculiar French, his grating, uncanny French, which sounds like shoveling anthracite down a coal chute. I know a few Italian words and several phrases, and along at first I used to keep them bright and fresh by whetting them on Angelo; but he partly couldn't understand them and partly didn't want to, so I have been obliged to withdraw them from the market for the present. But this is only temporary. I am practicing, I am preparing. Some day I shall be ready for him, and not in ineffectual French, but in his native tongue. I will seethe this kid in its mother's milk.

Oct. 27.—The first month is finished. We are wonted, now. It is agreed that life at a Florentine villa is an ideal existence. The weather is divine, the outside aspects lovely, the days and the nights tranquil and reposeful, the seclusion from the world and its worries as satisfactory as a dream. There is no housekeeping to do, no plans to make, no marketing to superintend—all these things do themselves, apparently. One is vaguely aware that somebody is attending to them, just as one is aware that the world is being turned over and the constellations worked

MARK TWAIN

and the sun shoved around according to the schedule, but that is all; one does not feel personally concerned, or in any way responsible. Yet there is no head, no chief executive; each servant minds his or her own department, requiring no supervision and having none. They hand in elaborately itemized bills once a week; then the machinery goes silently on again, just as before. There is no noise, or fussing, or quarreling, or confusion—upstairs. I don't know what goes on below. Late in the afternoons friends come out from the city and drink tea in the open air, and tell what is happening in the world; and when the great sun sinks down upon Florence and the daily miracle begins, they hold their breaths and look. It is not a time for talk.

A MEMORY OF JOHN HAY

A quarter of a century or so ago I was visiting John Hay, now Secretary of State, at Whitelaw Reid's house in New York, which Hay was occupying for a few months while Reid was absent on a holiday in Europe. Temporarily, also, Hay was editing Reid's paper, the New York Tribune. I remember two incidents of that Sunday visit particularly well, and I think I shall use them presently to illustrate something which I intend to say. One of the incidents is immaterial, and I hardly know why it is that it has stayed with me so many years. I must introduce it with a word or two. I had known John Hay a good many years; I had known him when he was an obscure young editorial writer on the Tribune in Horace Greeley's time, earning three or four times the salary he got, considering the high character of the work which came from his pen. In those earlier days he was a picture to look at, for beauty of feature, perfection of form, and grace of carriage and movement. He had a charm about him of a sort quite unusual, to my Western ignorance and inexperience—a charm of manner, intonation, apparently native and unstudied elocution, and all that—the groundwork of it, native, the ease of it, the polish of it, the winning naturalness of it, acquired in Europe, where he had been chargé d'affaires some time at the Court of Vienna. He was joyous, cordial, a most pleasant comrade.

Now I am coming to it. John Hay was not afraid of Horace Greeley.

I will leave that remark in a paragraph by itself; it cannot be made too conspicuous. John Hay was the only man who ever served Horace Greeley on the Tribune of whom that can be said. In the past few years, since Hay has been occupying the post of Secretary of State, with a succession of foreign difficulties on his hands such as have not fallen to the share of any previous occupant of that chair, perhaps, when we consider the magnitude of the matters involved, we have seen that that courage of his youth is his possession still and that he is not any more scarable by kings and emperors and their fleets and armies than he was by Horace Greeley.

I arrive at the application now. That Sunday morning, twenty-five years ago, Hay and I had been chatting and laughing and carrying on almost like our earlier selves of '67, when the door opened and Mrs. Hay, gravely clad, gloved, bonneted, and just from church, and fragrant with the odors of Presbyterian sanctity, stood in it. We rose to our feet at once, of course—rose through a swiftly falling temperature—a temperature which at the beginning was soft and summer-like, but which was turning our breath and all other damp things to frost crystals by the time we were erect—but we got no opportunity to say the pretty and polite thing and offer the homage due; the comely young matron forestalled us. She came forward, smileless, with disapproval written all over her face, said most coldly, "Good morning, Mr. Clemens," and passed on and out.

There was an embarrassed pause—I may say a very embarrassed pause. If Hay was waiting for me to speak, it was a mistake; I couldn't think of a word. It was soon plain to me that the bottom had fallen out of his vocabulary, too. When I was able to walk I started toward the door, and Hay, grown gray in a single night, so to speak, limped feebly at my side, making no moan, saying no word. At the door his ancient courtesy rose and bravely flickered for a moment, then went out. That is to say, he tried to ask me to call again, but at that point his ancient sincerity rose against the fiction and squelched it. Then he tried another remark, and that one he got through with. He said, pathetically and apologetically:

"She is very strict about Sunday."

More than once in these past years I have heard admiring and grateful people say, and have said it myself:

"He is not afraid of this whole nation of eighty millions when his duty requires him to do an unpopular thing."

Twenty-five years have gone by since then, and through manifold experiences I have learned that no courage is absolutely perfect; that there is always some one who is able to modify his pluck.

Another incident of that visit was this: in trading remarks concerning our ages I confessed to forty-two and Hay to forty. Then he asked if I had begun to write my autobiography, and I said I hadn't. He said that I ought to begin at once and that I had already lost two years. Then he said in substance this:

"At forty a man reaches the top of the hill of life and starts down on the sunset side. The ordinary man, the average man, not to particularize too closely and say the commonplace man, has at that age succeeded or failed; in either case he has lived all of his life that is likely to be worth recording; also in either case the life lived is worth setting down, and cannot fail to be interesting if he comes as near to telling the truth about himself as he can. And he will tell the truth in spite of himself, for his facts and his fictions will work loyally together for the protection of the reader; each fact and each fiction will be a dab of paint, each will fall in its right place, and together they will paint his portrait; not the portrait he thinks they are painting, but his real portrait, the inside of him, the soul of him, his character. Without intending to lie, he will lie all the time; not bluntly, consciously, not dully unconsciously, but half-consciously—consciousness in twilight; a soft and gentle and merciful twilight which makes his general form comely, with his virtuous prominences and projections discernible and his ungracious ones in shadow. His truths will be recognizable as truths, his modifications of facts which would tell against him will go for nothing, the reader will see the fact through the film and know his man. There is a subtle devilish something or other about autobiographical composition that defeats all the writer's attempts to paint his portrait his way."

Hay meant that he and I were ordinary average commonplace people, and I did not resent my share of the verdict, but nursed my wound in silence. His idea that we had finished our work in life, passed the summit, and were westward bound downhill, with me two years ahead of him and neither of us with anything further to do as benefactors to mankind, was all a mistake. I had written four books then, possibly five. I have been drowning the world in literary wisdom ever since, volume after volume; he has been the historian of Mr. Lincoln, and his book will never perish; he has been ambassador, brilliant orator, competent and admirable Secretary of State, and would be President next year if we were a properly honest and grateful nation instead of an ungrateful one, a nation which has usually not been willing to have a Chief Magistrate of gold when it could get one of tin.

I had lost two years, but I resolved to make up that loss. I resolved to begin my autobiography at once. I did begin it, but the resolve melted away and disappeared in a week and I threw my beginning away. Since then, about every three or four years I have made other beginnings and thrown them away. Once I tried the experiment of a diary, intending to inflate that into an autobiography when its accumulation should furnish enough material, but that experiment lasted only a week; it took me half of every night to set down the history of the day, and at the week's end I did not like the result.

Within the last eight or ten years I have made several attempts to do the autobiography in one way or another with a pen, but the result was not satisfactory; it was too literary. With the pen in one's hand, narrative is a difficult art; narrative should flow as flows the brook down through the hills and the leafy woodlands, its course changed by every bowlder it comes across and by every grass-clad gravelly spur that projects into its path; its surface broken, but its course not stayed by rocks and gravel on the bottom in the shoal places; a brook that never goes straight for a minute, but goes, and goes briskly, sometimes ungrammatically, and sometimes fetching a horseshoe three-quarters of a mile around, and at the end of the circuit flowing within a yard of the path it traversed an hour before; but always going, and always following at least one law, always loyal to that law, the law of narrative, which has no law. Nothing to do but make the trip; the how of it is not important, so that the trip is made.

With a pen in the hand the narrative stream is a canal; it moves slowly, smoothly, decorously, sleepily, it has no blemish except that it is all blemish. It is too literary, too prim, too nice; the gait and style and movement are not suited to narrative. That canal stream is always reflecting; it is its nature, it can't help it. Its slick shiny surface is interested in everything it passes along the banks—cows, foliage, flowers, everything. And so it wastes a lot of time in reflections.

Florence, April, 1904

Notes on "Innocents Abroad"

I will begin with a note upon the dedication. I wrote the book in the months of March and April, 1868, in San Francisco. It was published in August, 1869. Three years afterward Mr. Goodman of Virginia City, Nevada, on whose newspaper I had served ten years before and of whom I have had much to say in the book called Roughing It—I seem to be overloading the sentence and I apologize—came East, and we were walking down Broadway one day when he said:

"How did you come to steal Oliver Wendell Holmes's dedication and put it in your book?"

I made a careless and inconsequential answer, for I supposed he was joking. But he assured me that he was in earnest. He said:

"I'm not discussing the question of whether you stole it or didn't—for that is a question that can be settled in the first bookstore we come to. I am only asking you how you came to steal it, for that is where my curiosity is focalized."

I couldn't accommodate him with this information, as I hadn't it in stock. I could have made oath that I had not stolen anything, therefore my vanity was not hurt nor my spirit troubled. At bottom I supposed that he had mistaken another book for mine, and was now getting himself into an untenable place and preparing sorrow for himself and triumph for me. We entered a bookstore and he asked for The Innocents Abroad and for the dainty little blue-and-gold edition of Dr. Oliver Wendell Holmes's poems. He opened the books, exposed their dedications, and said:

"Read them. It is plain that the author of the second one stole the first one, isn't it?"

I was very much ashamed and unspeakably astonished. We continued our walk, but I was not able to throw any gleam of light upon that original question of his. I could not remember ever having seen Doctor Holmes's dedication. I knew the poems, but the dedication was new to me.

I did not get hold of the key to that secret until months afterward; then it came in a curious way, and yet it was a natural way; for the natural way provided by nature and the construction of the human mind for the discovery of a forgotten event is to employ another forgotten event for its resurrection.

I received a letter from the Reverend Doctor Rising, who had been rector of the Episcopal church in Virginia City in my time, in which letter Doctor Rising made reference to certain things which had happened to us in the Sandwich Islands six years before; among other things he made casual mention of the Honolulu Hotel's poverty in the matter of literature. At first I did not see the bearing of the remark; it called nothing to my mind. But presently it did—with a flash! There was but one book in Mr. Kirchhof's hotel, and that was the first volume of Doctor Holmes's blue-and-gold series. I had had a fortnight's chance to get well acquainted with its contents, for I had ridden around the big island (Hawaii) on horseback and had brought back so many saddle boils that if there had been a duty on them it would have bankrupted me to pay it. They kept me in my room, unclothed and in persistent pain, for two weeks, with no company but cigars and the little volume of poems. Of course I read them almost constantly; I read them from beginning to end, then began in the middle and read them both ways. In a word, I read the book to rags, and was infinitely grateful to the hand that wrote it.

Here we have an exhibition of what repetition can do when persisted in daily and hourly over a considerable stretch of time, where one is merely reading for entertainment, without thought or intention of preserving in the memory that which is read. It is a process which in the course of years tries all the juice out of a familiar verse of Scripture, leaving nothing but a dry husk behind. In that case you at least know the origin of the husk, but in the case in point I apparently preserved the husk, but presently forgot whence it came. It lay lost in some dim corner of my memory a year or two, then came forward when I needed a dedication, and was promptly mistaken by me as a child of my own happy fancy.

I was new, I was ignorant, the mysteries of the human mind were a sealed book to me as yet, and I stupidly looked upon myself as a tough and unforgivable criminal. I wrote to Doctor Holmes and told him the whole disgraceful affair, implored him in impassioned language to believe that I never intended to commit this crime, and was unaware that I had committed it until I was confronted with the awful evidence. I have lost his answer. I could better have afforded to lose an uncle. Of these I had a surplus, many of them of no real value to me, but that letter was beyond price and unsparable. In it Doctor Holmes laughed the kindest and healingest laugh over the whole matter, and at considerable length and in happy phrase assured me that there was no crime in unconscious plagiarism; that I committed it every day, that he committed it every day, that every man alive on the earth who writes or speaks commits it every day, and not merely once or twice, but every time he opens his mouth; that all our phrasings are spiritualized shadows cast multitudinously from our readings: that no happy phrase of ours is ever quite original with us; there is nothing of our own in it except some slight change born of our temperament, character, environment, teachings, and associations; that this slight change differentiates it from another man's manner of saying it, stamps it with our special style, and makes it our own for the time being; all the rest of it being old, moldy, antique, and smelling of the breath of a thousand generations of them that have used it before!

In the thirty-odd years which have elapsed since then I have satisfied myself that what Doctor Holmes said was true.

I wish to make a note upon the preface of the Innocents. In the last paragraph of that brief preface I speak of the proprietors of the Daily Alta Californian having "waived their rights" in certain letters which I wrote for that journal while absent on the Quaker City trip. I was young then, I am white-headed now, but the insult of that word rankles yet, now that I am reading that paragraph for the first time in many years, reading that paragraph for the first time since it was written, perhaps. There were rights, it is true—such rights as the strong are able to acquire over the weak and the absent. Early in '66 George Barnes invited me to resign my reportership on his paper, the San Francisco Morning Call, and for some months thereafter I was without money or work; then I had a pleasant turn of fortune. The proprietors of the Sacramento Union, a great and influential daily journal, sent me to the Sandwich Islands to write four letters a month at twenty dollars apiece. I was there four or five months, and returned to find myself about the best known man on the Pacific coast. Thomas McGuire, proprietor of several theaters, said that now was the time to make my fortune—strike while the iron was hot—break into the lecture field! I did it. I announced a lecture on the Sandwich Islands, closing the advertisement with the remark: "Admission one dollar; doors open at half past seven, the trouble begins at eight." A true prophecy. The trouble certainly did begin at eight, when I found myself in front of the only audience I had ever faced, for the fright which pervaded me from head to foot was paralyzing. It lasted two minutes and was as bitter as death; the memory of it is indestructible, but it had its compensations, for it made me immune from timidity before audiences for all time to come. I lectured in all the principal Californian towns and in Nevada, then lectured once or twice more in San Francisco, then retired from the field rich—for me—and laid out a plan to sail westward from San Francisco and go around the world. The proprietors of the Alta engaged me to write an account of the trip for that paper—fifty letters of a column and a half each, which would be about 2,000 words per letter, and the pay to be twenty dollars per letter.

I went east to St. Louis to say good-by to my mother, and then I was bitten by the prospectus of Captain Duncan of the Quaker City excursion, and I ended by joining it. During the trip I wrote and sent the fifty letters; six of them miscarried and I wrote six new ones to complete my contract. Then I put together a lecture on the trip and delivered it in San Francisco at great and satisfactory pecuniary profit; then I branched out into the country and was aghast at the result: I had been entirely forgotten, I never had people enough in my houses to sit as a jury of inquest on my lost reputation! I inquired into this curious condition of things and found that the thrifty owners of that prodigiously rich Alta newspaper had copyrighted all those poor little twenty-dollar letters and had threatened with prosecution any journal which should venture to copy a paragraph from them.

And there I was! I had contracted to furnish a large book, concerning the excursion, to the American Publishing Co. of Hartford, and I supposed I should need all those letters to fill it out with. I was in an uncomfortable situation—that is, if the proprietors of this stealthily acquired copyright should refuse to let me use the letters. That is what they did; Mr. Mac—something—I have forgotten the rest of his name[1]— said his firm were going to make a book out of the letters in order to get back the thousand dollars which they had paid for them. I said that if they had acted fairly and honorably, and had allowed the country press to use the letters or portions of them, my lecture skirmish on the coast would have paid me ten thousand dollars, whereas the Alta had lost me that amount. Then he offered a compromise: he would publish the book and allow me 10-per-cent royalty on it. The compromise did not appeal to me, and I said so. The book sale would be confined to San Francisco, and my royalty would not pay me enough to board me three months, whereas my Eastern contract, if carried out, could be profitable to me, for I had a sort of reputation on the Atlantic seaboard, acquired through the publication of six excursion letters in the New York Tribune and one or two in the Herald.

In the end Mr. Mac agreed to suppress his book, on certain conditions: in my preface I must thank the Alta for waiving its "rights" and granting me permission. I objected to the thanks. I could not with

1. May 20, 1906. I recall it now—MacCrellish.—M. T.

any large degree of sincerity thank the Alta for bankrupting my lecture raid. After considerable debate my point was conceded and the thanks left out.

Noah Brooks was editor of the Alta at the time, a man of sterling character and equipped with a right heart, also a good historian where facts were not essential. In biographical sketches of me written many years afterward (1902) he was quite eloquent in praises of the generosity of the Alta people in giving to me without compensation a book which, as history had afterward shown, was worth a fortune. After all the fuss, I did not levy heavily upon the Alta letters. I found that they were newspaper matter, not book matter. They had been written here and there and yonder, as opportunity had given me a chance working moment or two during our feverish flight around about Europe or in the furnace heat of my stateroom on board the Quaker City, therefore they were loosely constructed and needed to have some of the wind and water squeezed out of them. I used several of them—ten or twelve, perhaps. I wrote the rest of The Innocents Abroad in sixty days, and I could have added a fortnight's labor with the pen and gotten along without the letters altogether. I was very young in those days, exceedingly young, marvelously young, younger than I am now, younger than I shall ever be again, by hundreds of years. I worked every night from eleven or twelve until broad day in the morning, and as I did 200,000 words in the sixty days the average was more than 3,000 words a day—nothing for Sir Walter Scott, nothing for Louis Stevenson, nothing for plenty of other people, but quite handsome for me. In 1897, when we were living in Tedworth Square, London, and I was writing the book called Following the Equator, my average was 1,800 words a day; here in Florence (1904), my average seems to be 1,400 words per sitting of four or five hours.[1]

I was deducing from the above that I have been slowing down steadily in these thirty-six years, but I perceive that my statistics have a defect: 3,000 words in the spring of 1868, when I was working seven or eight or nine hours at a sitting, has little or no advantage over the sitting of to-day, covering half the time and producing half the output. Figures often beguile me, particularly when I have the arranging of them myself; in which case the remark attributed to Disraeli would often apply with justice and force:

"There are three kinds of lies: lies, damned lies, and statistics."

---

1. With the pen, I mean. This Autobiography is dictated, not written.

STEVENSON, ALDRICH, ETC.

. . . [1]But it was on a bench in Washington Square that I saw the most of Louis Stevenson. It was an outing that lasted an hour or more and was very pleasant and sociable. I had come with him from his house, where I had been paying my respects to his family. His business in the square was to absorb the sunshine. He was most scantily furnished with flesh, his clothes seemed to fall into hollows as if there might be nothing inside but the frame for a sculptor's statue. His long face and lank hair and dark complexion and musing and melancholy expression seemed to fit these details justly and harmoniously, and the altogether of it seemed especially planned to gather the rags of your observation and focalize them upon Stevenson's special distinction and commanding feature, his splendid eyes. They burned with a smoldering rich fire under the penthouse of his brows, and they made him beautiful.

I SAID I THOUGHT HE was right about the others, but mistaken as to Bret Harte; in substance I said that Harte was good company and a thin but pleasant talker; that he was always bright, but never brilliant; that in this matter he must not be classed with Thomas Bailey Aldrich, nor must any other man, ancient or modern; that Aldrich was always witty, always brilliant, if there was anybody present capable of striking his flint at the right angle; that Aldrich was as sure and prompt and unfailing as the red-hot iron on the blacksmith's anvil—you had only to hit it competently to make it deliver an explosion of sparks. I added:

"Aldrich has never had his peer for prompt and pithy and witty and humorous sayings. None has equaled him, certainly none has surpassed him, in the felicity of phrasing with which he clothed these children of his fancy. Aldrich was always brilliant, he couldn't help it; he is a fire opal set round with rose diamonds; when he is not speaking, you know that his dainty fancies are twinkling and glimmering around in him; when he speaks the diamonds flash. Yes, he was always brilliant; he will always be brilliant; he will be brilliant in hell—you will see."

Stevenson, smiling a chuckly smile, "I hope not."

---

1. Nothing is omitted from the MS. here, whatever may have been the thought in the author's mind.

"Well, you will, and he will dim even those ruddy fires and look like a blond Venus backed against a pink sunset."

THERE ON THAT BENCH WE struck out a new phrase—one, or the other of us, I don't remember which—"submerged renown." Variations were discussed: submerged fame, submerged reputation, and so on, and a choice was made; submerged renown was elected, I believe. This important matter rose out of an incident which had been happening to Stevenson in Albany. While in a bookshop or bookstall there he had noticed a long rank of small books cheaply but neatly gotten up and bearing such titles as Davis's Selected Speeches, Davis's Selected Poetry, Davis's this and Davis's that and Davis's the other thing; compilations every one of them, each with a brief, compact, intelligent, and useful introductory chapter by this same Davis, whose first name I have forgotten. Stevenson had begun the matter with this question:

"Can you name the American author whose fame and acceptance stretch widest and furthest in the States?"

I thought I could, but it did not seem to me that it would be modest to speak out, in the circumstances. So I diffidently said nothing. Stevenson noticed, and said:

"Save your delicacy for another time—you are not the one. For a shilling you can't name the American author of widest note and popularity in the States. But I can."

Then he went on and told about that Albany incident. He had inquired of the shopman, "Who is this Davis?"

The answer was, "An author whose books have to have freight trains to carry them, not baskets. Apparently you have not heard of him?"

Stevenson said no, this was the first time. The man said:

"Nobody has heard of Davis; you may ask all round and you will see. You never see his name mentioned in print, not even in advertisements; these things are of no use to Davis, not any more than they are to the wind and the sea. You never see one of Davis's books floating on top of the United States, but put on your diving armor and get yourself lowered away down and down and down till you strike the dense region, the sunless region of eternal drudgery and starvation wages—there you will find them by the million. The man that gets that market, his fortune is made, his bread and butter are safe, for those people will never go back on him. An author may have a reputation which is confined to the surface, and lose it and become pitied, then despised, then forgotten, entirely forgotten—the frequent steps in a surface reputation. A surface reputation, however great, is always mortal, and always killable if you go at it right—with pins and needles, and quiet slow poison, not with the club and the tomahawk. But it is a different matter with the submerged reputation—down in the deep water; once a favorite there, always a favorite; once beloved, always beloved; once respected, always respected, honored, and believed in. For what the reviewer says never finds its way down into those placid deeps, nor the newspaper sneers, nor any breath of the winds of slander blowing above. Down there they never hear of these things. Their idol maybe painted clay, up there at the surface, and fade and waste and crumble and blow away, there being much weather there; but down below he is gold and adamant and indestructible."

Florence, April, 1904

Henry H. Rogers

Mr. Rogers has been visiting the witness stand periodically in Boston for more than a year now. For eleven years he has been my closest and most valuable friend. His wisdom and steadfastness saved my copyrights from being swallowed up in the wreck and ruin of Charles L. Webster & Co., and his commercial wisdom has protected my pocket ever since in those lucid intervals wherein I have been willing to listen to his counsels and abide by his advice—a thing which I do half the time and half the time I don't.

He is four years my junior; he is young in spirit, and in looks, complexion, and bearing, easy and graceful in his movements, kind-hearted, attractive, winning, a natural gentleman, the best-bred gentleman I have met on either side of the ocean in any rank of life from the Kaiser of Germany down to the bootblack. He is affectionate, endowed with a fine quality of humor, and with his intimates he is a charming comrade. I am his principal intimate and that is my idea of him. His mind is a bewildering spectacle to me when I see it dealing with vast business complexities like the affairs of the prodigious Standard Oil Trust, the United States Steel, and the rest of the huge financial combinations of our time—for he and his millions are in them all, and his brain is a very large part of the machinery which keeps them alive and going. Many a time in the past eleven years my small and troublesome affairs have forced me to spend days and weeks of waiting time down in the city of New York, and my waiting refuge has been his private office in the Standard Oil Building, stretched out on a sofa behind his chair, observing his processes, smoking, reading, listening to his reasonings with the captains of industry, and intruding my advice where it was not invited, not desired, and in no instance adopted, so far as I remember. A patient man, I can say that for him.

The private office was a spacious, high-ceiled chamber on the eleventh floor of the Standard Oil Building, with large windows which looked out upon the moving life of the river, with the Colossus of Liberty enlightening the world holding up her torch in the distance. When I was not there it was a solitude, since in those intervals no one occupied the place except Mr. Rogers and his brilliant private secretary, Miss Katherine I. Harrison, whom he once called in on an emergency thirteen or fourteen years ago from among the 750 clerks laboring for the Standard Oil in the building. She was nineteen or twenty years old then and did stenographic work and typewriting at the wage of that day, which was fifteen or twenty dollars a week. He has a sharp eye for capacity, and after trying Miss Harrison for a week he promoted her to the post of chief of his private secretaries and raised her wages. She has held the post ever since; she has seen the building double its size and increase its clerical servants to 1,500, and her own salary climb to ten thousand dollars a year. She is the only private secretary who sits in the sanctum; the others are in the next room and come at the bell call. Miss Harrison is alert, refined, well read in the good literature of the day, is fond of paintings and buys them; she is a cyclopaedia in whose head is written down the multitudinous details of Mr. Rogers's business; order and system are a native gift with her; Mr. Rogers refers to her as he would to a book, and she responds with the desired information with a book's confidence and accuracy. Several times I have heard Mr. Rogers say that she is quite able to conduct his affairs, substantially without his help.

Necessarily Mr. Rogers's pecuniary aid was sought by his full share of men and women without capital who had ideas for sale—ideas worth millions if their exploitation could be put in charge of the right man. Mr. Rogers's share of these opportunities was so large that if he had received and conversed with all his applicants of that order he might have made many millions per hour, it is true, but he would not have had half an hour left in the day for his own business. He could not see all of these people, therefore he saw none of them, for he was a fair and just man. For his protection, his office was a kind of fortress with outworks, these outworks being several communicating rooms into which no one could get access without first passing through an outwork where several young colored men stood guard and carried in the cards and requests and brought back the regrets. Three of the communicating rooms were for consultations, and they were seldom unoccupied. Men sat in them waiting—men who were there by appointment—appointments not loosely specified, but specified by the minute hand of the clock. These rooms had ground-glass doors and their privacy was in other ways protected and secured. Mr. Rogers consulted with a good many men in those rooms in the course of his day's work of six hours; and whether the matter in hand was small and simple or great and complicated, it was discussed and dispatched with marvelous celerity. Every day these consultations supplied a plenty of vexations and exasperations for Mr. Rogers—I know this quite well—but if ever they found revealment in his face or manner it could have been for only a moment or two, for the signs were gone when he re-entered his private office and he was always his brisk and cheerful self again and ready to be chaffed and joked, and reply in kind. His spirit was often heavily burdened, necessarily, but it cast no shadow, and those about him sat always in the sunshine.

Sometimes the value of his securities went down by the million, day after day, sometimes they went up as fast, but no matter which it was, the face and bearing exhibited by him were only proper to a rising market. Several times every day Miss Harrison had to act in a diplomatic capacity. Men called whose position in the world was such that they could not be dismissed with the formula "engaged" along with Mr. Rogers's regrets, and to these Miss Harrison went out and explained, pleasantly and tactfully, and sent them away comfortable. Mr. Rogers transacted a vast amount of business during his six hours daily, but there always seemed time enough in the six hours for it.

That Boston gas lawsuit came on at a bad time for Mr. Rogers, for his health was poor and remained so during several months. Every now and then he had to stay in his country house at Fair Haven, Massachusetts, a week or two at a time, leaving his business in Miss Harrison's hands and conferring with her once or twice daily by long-distance telephone. To prepare himself for the witness stand was not an easy thing, but the materials for it were to be had, for Mr. Rogers never destroyed a piece of paper that had writing on it, and, as he was a methodical man, he had ways of tracing out any paper he needed, no matter how old it might be. The papers needed in the gas suit, wherein Mr. Rogers was sued for several millions of dollars, went back in date a good many years and were numberable by the hundreds; but Miss Harrison ferreted them all out from the stacks and bales of documents in the Standard Oil vaults and caused them to be listed and annotated by the other secretaries. This work cost weeks of constant labor, but it left Mr. Rogers in shape to establish for himself an unsurpassable reputation as a witness.

I wish to make a momentary digression here and call up an illustration of what I have been saying about Mr. Rogers's habits in the matter of order and system. When he was a young man of twenty-four, out in the oil regions of Pennsylvania and straitened in means, he had some business relations with another young man; time went on, they separated and lost sight of each other. After a lapse of twenty years this man's card came in one day and Mr. Rogers had him brought into the private office. The man showed age, his clothes showed that he was not prosperous, and his speech and manner indicated that hard luck had soured him toward the world and the fates. He brought a bill against Mr. Rogers, oral in form, for $1,500—a bill thirty years old. Mr. Rogers drew the check and gave it to him, saying he could not allow him to lose it, though he almost deserved to lose it for risking the claim thirty years without presenting it. When he was gone Mr. Rogers said:

"My memory is better than his. I paid the money at the time; knowing this, I know I took a receipt, although I do not remember that detail. To satisfy myself that I have not been careless, I will have that receipt searched out."

It took a day or two, but it was found and I saw it; then it was sent back to its place again among the archives.

Added in 1909

Henry H. Rogers (Continued)

The value of his advice.—His beautiful nature.

Since he passed from life many months have gone by, and still I have not found myself competent to put into words my feelings for him and my estimate of him. For he is as yet too near, the restraint of his spirit too effective.

All through my life I have been the easy prey of the cheap adventurer. He came, he lied, he robbed, and went his way, and the next one arrived by the next train and began to scrape up what was left. I was in the toils of one of these creatures sixteen years ago, and it was Mr. Rogers who got me out. We were strangers when we met, and friends when we parted, half an hour afterward. The meeting was accidental and unforeseen, but it had memorable and fortunate consequences for me. He dragged me out of that difficulty, and also out of the next one—a year or two later—which was still more formidable than its predecessor. He did these saving things at no cost to my self-love, no hurt to my pride; indeed, he did them with so delicate an art that I almost seemed to have done them myself. By no sign, no hint, no word did he ever betray any consciousness that I was under obligations to him. I have never been so great as that, and I have not known another who was. I have never approached it; it belongs among the loftiest of human attributes. This is a world where you get nothing for nothing; where you pay value for everything you get and 50 per cent over; and when it is gratitude you owe, you have to pay a thousand. In fact, gratitude is a debt which usually goes on accumulating, like blackmail; the more you pay, the more is exacted. In time you are made to realize that the kindness done you is become a curse and you wish it had not happened. You find yourself situated as was Mr. W., a friend of friends of mine, years ago. He was rich and good-hearted and appreciative. His wife's life was saved by a grocer's young man, who stopped her runaway horses. Her husband was grateful beyond words. For he supposed gratitude was a sentiment; he did not know it had a price and that he was not the one to determine the rate. But by and by he was educated. Then he said to the grocer's young man, "Take this five hundred dollars and vanish; I have had you and your tribe on my back three years, and if ever another man saves my wife's life, let him buy a coffin, for he will need it."

Mr. Rogers was a great man. No one denies him that praise. He was great in more ways than one—ways in which other men are great, ways in which he had not a monopoly; but in that fine trait which I have mentioned he was uniquely great; he held that high place almost alone, almost without a sharer. If nobilities of character were accorded decorations symbolizing degrees of merit and distinction, I think this one could claim rank, unchallenged, with the Garter and the Golden Fleece.

But what I am trying to place before unfamiliar eyes is the heart of him.

When the publishing house of Webster & Company failed, in the early '90's, its liabilities exceeded its assets by 66 per cent. I was morally bound for the debts, though not legally. The panic was on, business houses were falling to ruin everywhere, creditors were taking the assets—when there were any—and letting the rest go. Old business friends of mine said: "Business is business, sentiment is sentiment—and this is business. Turn the assets over to the creditors and compromise on that; other creditors are not getting 33 per cent." My wife said, "No, you will pay a hundred cents on the dollar." Mr. Rogers was certainly a business man—no one doubts that. People who know him only by printed report will think they know what his attitude would be in the matter. And they will be mistaken. He sided with my wife. He was the only man who had a clear eye for the situation, and could see that it differed from other apparently parallel situations. In substance he said this: "Business has its laws and customs, and they are justified; but a literary man's reputation is his life; he can afford to be money poor, but he cannot afford to be character poor; you must earn the cent per cent, and pay it." My nephew, the late Samuel E. Moffett— himself a literary man—felt in the same way, naturally enough; but I only mention him to recall and revivify a happy remark which he made, and which traveled around the globe: "Honor knows no statute of limitations."

So it was decided. I must cease from idling and take up work again. I must write a book; also I must return to the lecture platform. My wife said I could clear off the load of debt in four years. Mr. Rogers was more cautious, more conservative, more liberal. He said I could have as many years as I wanted—seven to start with. That was his joke. When he was not in the humor for pleasantry, it was because he was asleep. Privately I was afraid his seven might be nearer the mark than Mrs. Clemens's four.

One day I got a shock—a shock which disturbed me a good deal. I overheard a brief conversation between Mr. Rogers and a couple of other seasoned men of affairs.

First Man of Affairs. "How old is Clemens?"

Mr. Rogers. "Fifty-eight."

First Man of Affairs. "Ninety-five per cent of the men who fail at fifty-eight never get up again."

Second Man of Affairs. "You can make it ninety-eight per cent and be nearer right."

Those sayings haunted me for several days, troubling me with melancholy forebodings, and would not be reasoned away by me. There wasn't any room for reasoning, anyway, so far as I could see. If, at fifty-eight, ninety-eight men in a hundred who fail never get up again, what chance had I to draw No. 99 or No. 100? However, the depression did not last; it soon passed away, because Mrs. Clemens took her always-ready pencil and paper, when she learned my trouble, and clearly and convincingly ciphered out the intake of the four years and the resultant success. I could see that she was right. Indeed, she was always right. In foresight, wisdom, accurate calculation, good judgment, and the ability to see all sides of a problem, she had no match among people I have known, except Mr. Rogers.

Necessarily it took a good while to arrange the details and make the engagements for a lecture trip around the globe, but this labor was completed at last, and we made our start in the middle of July, 1895, booked ahead for twelve months.

Meantime he was in command, in the matter of the creditors—and had been from the beginning. There were ninety-six creditors. He had meetings with them, discussions, arguments, persuasions, but no quarrels. Mrs. Clemens wanted to turn over to the creditors the house she had built in Hartford, and which stood in her name, but he would not allow it. Neither would he allow my copyrights to go to them. Mrs. Clemens had lent the Webster firm $65,000 upon its notes, in its perishing days, in the hope of saving its life, and Mr. Rogers insisted upon making her a preferred creditor and letting her have the copyrights in liquidation of the notes. He would not budge from this position, and the creditors finally yielded the point.

Mr. Rogers insisted upon just two things besides the relinquishment of the copyrights: the creditors must be content with the Webster assets, for the present, and give me time to earn the rest of the firm's debt. He won them over. There were a clarity about his reasonings, and a charm about his manner, his voice, and the kindness and sincerity that looked out of his eyes, that could win anybody that had brains in his head and a heart in his body. Of the ninety-six creditors, only three or four stood out for rigorous and uncompromising measures against me and refused to relent. The others said I could go free and take my own time. They said they would obstruct me in no way and would bring no actions; and they kept their word. As to the three or four, I have never resented their animosity, except in my Autobiography. And even there, not in spite, not in malice, but only frankly and in only a brief chapter—a chapter which can never wound them, for I have every confidence that they will be in hell before it is printed.

The long, long head that Mr. Rogers carried on his shoulders! When he was so strenuous about my copyrights, and so determined to keep them in the family, I was not able to understand why he should think the matter so important. He insisted that they were a great asset. I said they were not an asset at all; I couldn't even give them away. He said, wait—let the panic subside and business revive, and I would see; they would be worth more than they had ever been worth before.

That was his idea—the idea of a financier, familiar with finance; of a capitalist, deep in railroads, oil, banks, iron, copper, telegraphs, and so on, and familiar with those things, but what could he know about books? What was his opinion about copyright values worth, if it clashed with the opinion of experienced old publishers? Which it did. The Webster failure threw seven of my books on my hands. I had offered them to three first-class publishers; they didn't want them. If Mr. Rogers had let Mrs. Clemens and me have our way, the copyrights would have been handed over to the publishers.

I am grateful to his memory for many a kindness and many a good service he did me, but gratefulest of all for the saving of my copyrights—a service which saved me and my family from want and assured us permanent comfort and prosperity.

How could he look into the future and see all that, when the men whose trade and training it was to exercise that technical vision were forecast blind and saw no vestige of it? This is only one example of the wonders of his mind; his intimates could cite many others, products of that rich treasury.

I was never able to teach him anything about finance, though I tried hard and did the best I could. I was not able to move him. Once I had hopes for a little while. The Standard Oil declared one of its customary fury-breeding 40- or 50-per-cent dividends on its $100,000,000 capital, and the storm broke out, as usual. To the unposted public a 40- or 50-per-cent dividend could mean only one thing—the giant Trust was squeezing an utterly and wickedly unfair profit out of the helpless people; whereas in truth the giant Trust was not doing anything of the kind, but was getting only 5 or 6 per cent on the money actually invested in its business, which was eight or ten times a hundred millions. In my quality of uneducated financial expert I urged that the nominal capital be raised to $1,000,000,000; then next year's dividend would drop to 4 or 5 per cent, the year's profit would be the same as usual, but the usual storm would not happen. If I remember rightly, I think he offered the objection that the tenfold increase of taxes would be too heavy, and I rejoined that by the ill-veiled exultation in his eye I knew he regarded my suggestion as of vast value and was trying to invent some plausible way of getting out of paying a commission on it. I often gave him fresh financial ideas, quite uninvited; and in return—uninvited—he told me how to write my literature better; but nothing came of it, both of us remained as poor as ever.

Unconsciously we all have a standard by which we measure other men, and if we examine closely we find that this standard is a very simple one, and is this: we admire them, we envy them, for great qualities which we ourselves lack. Hero worship consists in just that. Our heroes are the men who do things which we recognize, with regret, and sometimes with a secret shame, that we cannot do. We find not much in ourselves to admire, we are always privately wanting to be like somebody else. If everybody was satisfied with himself, there would be no heroes.

Mr. Rogers was endowed with many great qualities; but the one which I most admired, and which was to me a constant reproach because I lacked it, was his unselfishness where a friend or a cause that was near his heart was concerned, and his native readiness to come forward and take vigorous hold of the difficulty involved and abolish it. I was born to indolence, idleness, procrastination, indifference—the qualities that constitute a shirk; and so he was always a wonder to me, and a delight—he who never shirked anything, but kept his master brain and his master hands going all day long, and every day, and was happiest when he was busiest, and apparently lightest of heart when his burden of labor and duty was heaviest.

He could take trouble; I could not take trouble, either for myself or for anyone else. I dreaded anything that might disturb my ease and comfort, and would put that thing from me even when it cost me shame to do it; and so to see him take trouble, no end of trouble, days and days of trouble, and take it so patiently, so placidly, so interestedly—and so affectionately, too, if it was for somebody else—was to me a strange and marvelous thing, and beautiful. It probably never occurred to him to admire it; no, he would be occupied in admiring some quality in some one else which was lacking in his own composition.

The question of what is a gentleman was being thrashed out in the newspapers shortly after Mr. Rogers's death, and many definitions were furnished, but no decision reached. The larger part of the definitions were in substance alike, differing only in small details and delicate shadings. They painted a lofty and charming and lovable personality. Mr. Rogers could have sat for that portrait.

INTERVAL OF TWO YEARS

The final dictation, beginning January 9, 1906.
Present Mr. Clemens, Mr. Paine,
Miss Hobby, stenographer.

January 9, 1906

Mr. Clemens (to Mr. Paine):

The more I think of this (the biography), the more nearly impossible the project seems. The difficulties of it grow upon me all the time. For instance, the idea of blocking out a consecutive series of events which have happened to me, or which I imagine have happened to me—I can see that that is impossible for me. The only thing possible for me is to talk about the thing that something suggests at the moment—something in the middle of my life, perhaps, or something that happened only a few months ago. It is my purpose to extend these notes to 600,000 words, and possibly more. But that is going to take a long time—a long time.

My idea is this: that I write an autobiography. When that autobiography is finished—or before it is finished, but no doubt after it is finished—then you take the manuscript and decide on how much of a biography to make. But this is no holiday excursion—it is a journey.

We will try this—see whether it is dull or interesting—whether it will bore us and we will want to commit suicide. I hate to get at it. I hate to begin, but I imagine if you are here to make suggestions from time to time, we can make it go along, instead of having it drag.

Now let me see, there was something I wanted to talk about, and I supposed it would stay in my head. I know what it is—about the Big Bonanza in Nevada.

I want to read from the commercial columns of the New York Times, of a day or two ago, what practically was the beginning of the great Bonanza in Nevada, and these details seem to me to be correct—that in Nevada, during 1871, John Mackay and Fair got control of the Consolidated Virginia Mine for $26,000; that in 1873, two years later, its 108,000 shares sold at $45 per share; and that it was at that time that Fair made the famous silver ore find of the great Bonanza. Also, according to these statistics, in November, '74 the stock went to 115, and in the following month—January, '75—it reached 700. The shares of the companion mine, the California, rose in four months from 37 to 780—a total property which in 1869 was valued on the Mining Exchange at $40,000, was quoted six years later at $160,000,000. I think those dates are correct. That great Bonanza occupies a rather prominent place in my mind for the reason that I knew persons connected with it. For instance, I knew John Mackay very well—that would be in

1862, '63, and '64, I should say. I don't remember what he was doing when I came to Virginia in 1862, from starving to death down in the so-called mines of Esmeralda, which consisted in that day merely of silver-bearing quartz—plenty of bearing, and didn't have much load to carry in the way of silver—and it was a happy thing for me when I was summoned to come up to Virginia City to be local editor of the Virginia City Enterprise during three months, while Mr. William H. Wright (Dan de Quille) should go east, to Iowa, and visit his family, whom he hadn't seen for some years. I took the position of local editor with joy, because there was a salary of forty dollars a week attached to it and I knew that that was all of forty dollars more than I was worth, and I had always wanted a position which paid in the opposite proportion of value to amount of work. I took that position with pleasure, not with confidence—but I had a difficult job—a difficult job. I was to furnish one column of leaded nonpareil every day, and as much more as I could get on paper before the paper should go to press at two o'clock in the morning. By and by, in the course of a few months, I met John Mackay, with whom I had already been well acquainted for some time. He had established a broker's office on C Street, in a new frame house, and it was rather sumptuous for that day and place, for it had part of a carpet on the floor and two chairs instead of a candle box. I was envious of Mackay, who had not been in such very smooth circumstances as this before, and I offered to trade places with him—take his business and let him have mine—and he asked me how much mine was worth. I said forty dollars a week. He said: "I never swindled anybody in my life, and I don't want to begin on you. This business of mine is not worth forty dollars a week. You stay where you are and I will try to get a living out of this."

I left Nevada in 1864 to avoid a term in the penitentiary (in another chapter I shall have to explain that) so that it was all of ten years, apparently, before John Mackay developed suddenly into the first of the hundred-millionaires. Apparently his prosperity began in '71—that discovery was made in '71. I know how it was made. I remember those details, for they came across the country to me in Hartford. There was a tunnel 1,700 feet long which struck in from way down on the slope of the mountain and passed under some portion of Virginia City, at a great depth. It was striking for a lode which it did not find, and I think it had been long abandoned. Now it was in groping around in that tunnel that Mr. Fair (afterward U. S. Senator and great multi-millionaire, who was at that time a day laborer working with pick and shovel at five dollars a day)—groping around in that abandoned tunnel to see what he could find—no doubt looking for cross lodes and blind veins—came across a body of rich ore—so the story ran—and he came and reported that to John Mackay. They examined this body of rich ore and found that there was a very great deposit of it. They prospected it in the usual way and proved its magnitude and that it was extremely rich. They thought it was a "chimney," belonging probably to the California, away up on the mountain-side, which had an abandoned shaft—or possibly the Virginia mine which was not worked then—nobody caring anything about the Virginia, an empty mine. And these men determined that this body of ore properly belonged to the California mine and by some trick of nature had been shaken down the mountain-side. They got O'Brien—who was a silver expert in San Francisco—to come in as capitalist, and they bought up a controlling interest in that abandoned mine, and no doubt got it at that figure—$26,000—six years later to be worth $160,000,000.

As I say, I was not there. I had been here in the East, six, seven, or eight years—but friends of mine were interested. John P. Jones, who has lately resigned as U. S. Senator after an uninterrupted term of perhaps thirty years—John P. Jones was not a Senator yet, but was living in San Francisco. And he had a great affection for a couple of old friends of mine—Joseph T. Goodman and Dennis McCarthy. They had been proprietors of that paper that I served—the Virginia City Enterprise—and had enjoyed great prosperity in that position. They were young journeymen printers, typesetting in San Francisco in 1858, and they went over the mountains—the Sierras—for they heard of the discovery of silver in that unknown region of Nevada, to push their fortunes. When they arrived at that miserable little camp, Virginia City, they had no money to push their fortunes with. They had only youth, energy, hope. They found Williams there ("Stud" Williams was his society name), who had started a weekly newspaper, and he had one journeyman, who set up the paper, and printed it on a hand press with Williams's help and the help of a Chinaman—and they all slept in one room—cooked and slept and worked, and disseminated intelligence in this paper of theirs. Well, Williams was in debt fourteen dollars. He didn't see any way to get out of it with his newspaper, and so he sold the paper to Dennis McCarthy and Goodman for two hundred dollars, they to assume the debt of fourteen dollars and to pay the $200, in this world or the next—there was no definite promise about that. But as Virginia City developed they discovered new mines, new people began to flock in, and there was talk of a faro bank and a church and all those things that go to make a frontier Christian city, and there was vast prosperity there, and Goodman and Dennis reaped the advantage of that. Their prosperity was so great that they built a three-story brick building, which was a wonderful thing for that town, and their business increased so mightily that they would often plant out eleven columns of new ads on a standing galley and leave them there to sleep and rest and breed income. When any man objected, after searching the paper in the hope of seeing his advertisement, they would say. "We are doing the best we can." Now and then the advertisements would appear, but the standing galley was doing its work all the time. But after a time, when that territory was turned into a state, in order to furnish office for some people who needed office, their paper, from paying those boys twenty to forty thousand dollars a year, had ceased to pay anything. I suppose they were very glad to get rid of it, and probably on the old terms, to some journeyman who was willing to take the old fourteen dollars indebtedness and pay it when he could.

These boys went down to San Francisco, setting type again. They were delightful fellows, always ready for a good time, and that meant that everybody got their money except themselves. And when the Bonanza was about to be discovered Joe Goodman arrived here from somewhere that he'd been—I suppose trying to make business, or a livelihood, or something—and he came to see me to borrow three hundred dollars to take him out to San Francisco. And if I remember rightly he had no prospect in front of him at all, but thought he would be more likely to find it out there among the old friends, and he went to San Francisco. He arrived there just in time to meet Jones (afterwards U. S. Senator), who was a delightful man. Jones met him and said privately, "There has been a great discovery made in Nevada, and I am on the inside." Dennis was setting type in one of the offices there. He was married and was building a wooden house to cost $1,800, and he had paid a part and was building it on installments out of his wages. And Jones said: "I am going to put you and Dennis in privately on the big Bonanza. I am on the inside, I will watch it, and we will put this money up on a margin. Therefore when I say it is time to sell, it will be very necessary to sell." So he put up 20-per-cent margins for those two boys—and that is the time when this great spurt must have happened which sent that stock up to the stars in one flight—because, as the history was told to me by Joe Goodman, when that thing happened Jones said to Goodman and Dennis:

"Now then, sell. You can come out $600,000 ahead, each of you, and that is enough. Sell."

"No," Joe objected, "it will go higher."

Jones said: "I am on the inside; you are not. Sell."

Joe's wife implored him to sell. He wouldn't do it. Dennis's family implored him to sell. Dennis wouldn't sell. And so it went on during two weeks. Each time the stock made a flight Jones tried to get the boys to sell. They wouldn't do it. They said, "It is going higher." When he said, "Sell at $900,000," they said, "No. It will go to million."

Then the stock began to go down very rapidly. After a little, Joe sold, and he got out with $600,000 cash, Dennis waited for the million, but he never got a cent. His holding was sold for the "mud"—so that he came out without anything and had to begin again setting type.

That is the story as it was told to me many years ago—I imagine by Joe Goodman; I don't remember now. Dennis, by and by, died poor—never got a start again.

Joe Goodman immediately went into the broker business. Six hundred thousand dollars was just good capital. He wasn't in a position to retire yet. And he sent me the $300, and said that now he had started in the broking business and that he was making an abundance of money. I didn't hear any more then for a long time; then I learned that he had not been content with mere broking, but had speculated on his own account and lost everything he had. And when that happened, John Mackay, who was always a good friend of the unfortunate, lent him $4,000 to buy a grape ranch with, in Fresno County, and Joe went up there. He didn't know anything about the grape culture, but he and his wife learned it in a very little while. He learned it a little better than anybody else, and got a good living out of it until 1886 or '87; then he sold it for several times what he paid for it originally.

He was here a year ago and I saw him. He lives in the garden of California—in Alameda. Before this Eastern visit he had been putting in twelve years of his time in the most unpromising and difficult and stubborn study that anybody has undertaken since Champollion's time; for he undertook to find out what those sculptures mean that they find down there in the forests of Central America. And he did find out and published a great book, the result of his twelve years of study.

In this book he furnishes the meanings of those hieroglyphs, and his position as a successful expert in that complex study is recognized by the scientists in that line in London and Berlin and elsewhere. But he is no better known than he was before—he is known only to those people. His book was published in about 1901.

This account in the New York Times says that in consequence of that strike in the great Bonanza a tempest of speculation ensued, and that the group of mines right around that center reached a value in the stock market of close upon $400,000,000; and six months after that, that value had been reduced by three-quarters; and by 1880, five years later, the stock of the Consolidated Virginia was under $2 a share, and the stock in the California was only $1.75—for the Bonanza was now confessedly exhausted.

New York, January 10, 1906

I have to make several speeches within the next two or three months, and I have been obliged to make a few speeches during the last two months—and all of a sudden it is borne in upon me that people who go out that way to make speeches at gatherings of one kind or another, and at social banquets particularly, put themselves to an unnecessary amount of trouble, often, in the way of preparation. As a rule, your speech at a social banquet is not an important part of your equipment for that occasion, for the reason that as a rule the banquet is merely given to celebrate some event of merely momentary interest, or to do honor to some guest of distinction—and so there is nothing of large consequence—nothing, I mean, that one should feel bound to concentrate himself upon in talking upon such an occasion, whereas the really important matter, perhaps, is that the speaker make himself reasonably interesting while he is on his feet, and avoid wearying and exasperating the people who are not privileged to make speeches, and also not privileged to get out of the way when other people begin. So, common charity for those people should require that the speaker make some kind of preparation, instead of going to the place absolutely empty.

The person who makes frequent speeches can't afford much time for their preparation, and he probably goes to that place empty (just as I am in the habit of doing), purposing to gather texts from other unprepared people who are going to speak before he speaks. Now it is perfectly true that if you can get yourself located along about number three, and from that lower down on the program, it can be depended on with certainty that one or another of those previous speakers will furnish all the texts needed. In fact, you are likely to have more texts than you do need, and so they can become an embarrassment. You would like to talk to all of those texts, and of course that is a dangerous thing. You should choose one of them and talk to that one—and it is a hundred to one that before you have been on your feet two minutes you will wish you had taken the other one. You will get away from the one you have chosen, because you will perceive that there was another one that was better.

I am reminded of this old, old fact in my experience by what happened the other night at the Players', where twenty-two of my friends of ancient days in the Players' Club gave me a dinner[1] in testimony of their satisfaction in having me back again after an absence of three years, occasioned by the stupidity of the board of management of that club—a board which had been in office ever since the founding of the club; and if it were not the same old board that they had in the beginning it amounted to the same, because they must have been chosen, from time to time, from the same asylum that had furnished the original board. On this occasion Brander Matthews was chairman, and he opened the proceedings with an easy and comfortable and felicitous speech. Brander is always prepared and competent when he is going to make a speech. Then he called up Gilder, who came empty, and probably supposed he was going to be able to fill from Brander's tank, whereas he struck a disappointment. He labored through and sat down, not entirely defeated, but a good deal crippled. Frank Millet (painter) was next called up. He struggled along through his remarks, exhibiting two things—one, that he had prepared and couldn't remember the details of his preparation, and the other that his text was a poor text. In his talk the main sign of preparation was that he tried to recite two considerable batches of poetry—good poetry—but he lost confidence and turned it into bad poetry by bad recitation. Sculpture was to have been represented, and Saint-Gaudens had accepted and had promised a speech, but at the last moment he was not able to come and a man who was thoroughly unprepared had to get up and make a speech in Saint-Gaudens's place. He did not hit upon anything original or disturbing in his remarks, and, in fact, they were so tottering and

---

1. It was at this dinner that the idea of the biography which led to these dictations developed.

hesitating and altogether commonplace that really he seemed to have hit upon something new and fresh when he finished by saying that he had not been expecting to be called upon to make a speech! I could have finished his speech for him, I had heard it so many times.

Those people were unfortunate because they were thinking—that is Millet and Gilder were—all the time that Matthews was speaking; they were trying to keep in mind the little preparations which they had made, and this prevented them from getting something new and fresh in the way of a text out of what Brander was saying. In the same way Millet was still thinking about his preparation while Gilder was talking, and so he overlooked possible texts furnished by Gilder. But as I had asked Matthews to put me last on the list of speakers, I had all the advantages possible to the occasion. For I came without a text, and these boys furnished plenty of texts for me, because my mind was not absorbed in trying to remember my preparations—they didn't exist. I spoiled, in a degree, Brander's speech, because his speech had been prepared with direct reference to introducing me, the guest of the occasion—and he had to turn that all around and get out of it, which he did very gracefully, explaining that his speech was a little lopsided and wrong end first because I had asked to be placed last in the list of speakers. I had a plenty good-enough time, because Gilder had furnished me a text; Brander had furnished me a text; Millet had furnished me a text. These texts were fresh, hot from the bat, and they produced the same eager disposition to take hold of them and talk that they would have produced in ordinary conversation around a table in a beer mill.

Now then, I know how banquet speeches should be projected, because I have been thinking over this matter. This is my plan. Where it is merely a social banquet for a good time—such as the one which I am to attend in Washington on the 27th, where the company will consist of the membership of the Gridiron Club (newspaper correspondents exclusively, I think), with as guests the President and Vice-President of the United States and two others—certainly that is an occasion where a person will be privileged to talk about any subject except politics and theology, and even if he is asked to talk to a toast he needn't pay any attention to the toast, but talk about anything. Now then, the idea is this—to take the newspaper of that day, or the newspaper of that evening, and glance over the headings in the telegraphic page—a perfect bonanza of texts, you see! I think a person could pull that day's newspaper out of his pocket and talk that company to death before he would run out of material. If it were to-day, you have the Morris incident. And that reminds me how unexciting the Morris incident will be two or three years from now—maybe six months from now—and yet what an irritating thing it is to-day, and has been for the past few days. It brings home to one this large fact: that the events of life are mainly small events—they only seem large when we are close to them. By and by they settle down and we see that one doesn't show above another. They are all about one general low altitude, and inconsequential. If you should set down every day, by shorthand, as we are doing now, the happenings of the previous day, with the intention of making out of the massed result an autobiography, it would take from one to two hours—and from that to four hours—to set down the autobiographical matter of that one day, and the result would be a consumption of from five to forty thousand words. It would be a volume. Now one must not imagine that because it has taken all day Tuesday to write up the autobiographical matter of Monday, there will be nothing to write on Wednesday. No, there will be just as much to write on Wednesday as Monday had furnished for Tuesday. And that is because life does not consist mainly—or even largely—of facts and happenings. It consists mainly of the storm of thoughts that is forever blowing through one's head. Could you set them down stenographically? No. Could you set down any considerable fraction of them stenographically? No. Fifteen stenographers hard at work couldn't keep up. Therefore a full autobiography has never been written, and it never will be. It would consist of 365 double-size volumes per year—and so if I had been doing my whole autobiographical duty ever since my youth, all the library buildings on the earth could not contain the result.

I wonder what the Morris incident will look like in history fifty years from now. Consider these circumstances: that here at our own doors the mighty insurance upheaval has not settled down to a level yet. Even yesterday, and day before, the discredited millionaire insurance magnates had not all been flung out and buried from sight under the maledictions of the nation, but some of the McCurdies, McCalls, Hydes, and Alexanders were still lingering in positions of trust, such as directorships in banks. Also we have to-day the whole nation's attention centered upon the Standard Oil corporation, the most prodigious commercial force existing upon the planet. All the American world are standing breathless and wondering if the Standard Oil is going to come out of its Missourian battle crippled, and if crippled, how much crippled. Also we have Congress threatening to overhaul the Panama Canal Commission to see what it has done with the fifty-nine millions, and to find out what it proposes to do with the recently added eleven millions. Also there are three or four other matters of colossal public interest on the board to-day. And on the other side of the ocean we have Church and State separated in France; we have a threat of war between France and Germany upon the Morocco question; we have a crushed revolution in Russia, with the Tsar and his family of thieves—the grand dukes—recovering from their long fright and beginning to butcher the remnants of the revolutionaries in the old confident way that was the Russian way in former days for three centuries; we have China furnishing a solemn and awful mystery. Nobody knows what it is, but we are sending three regiments in a hurry from the Philippines to China, under the generalship of Funston, the man who captured Aguinaldo by methods which would disgrace the lowest blatherskite that is doing time in any penitentiary. Nobody seems to know what the Chinese mystery is, but everybody seems to think that a giant convulsion is impending there.

That is the menu as it stands to-day. These are the things which offer themselves to the world's attention to-day. Apparently they are large enough to leave no space for smaller matters, yet the Morris incident comes up and blots the whole thing out. The Morris incident is making a flurry in Congress, and for several days now it has been rioting through the imagination of the American nation and setting every tongue afire with excited talk. This autobiography will not see the light of print until after my death. I do not know when that is going to happen, and do not feel a large interest in the matter, anyway. It may be some years yet, but if it does not occur within the next three months I am confident that by that time the nation, encountering the Morris incident in my autobiography, would be trying to remember what the incident was, and not succeeding. That incident, which is so large to-day, will be so small three or four months from now it will then have taken its place with the abortive Russian revolution and these other large matters, and nobody will be able to tell one from the other by difference of size.

This is the Morris incident. A Mrs. Morris, a lady of culture, refinement, and position, called at the White House and asked for a moment's conversation with President Roosevelt. Mr. Barnes, one of the private secretaries, declined to send in her card, and said that she couldn't see the President, that he was busy. She said she would wait. Barnes wanted to know what her errand was, and she said that some time ago her husband had been dismissed from the public service and she wanted to get the President to look into his case. Barnes, finding that it was a military case, suggested that she go to the Secretary of War. She said she had been to the War Office, but could not get admission to the Secretary—she had tried every means she could think of, but had failed. Now she had been advised by the wife of a member of the Cabinet to ask for a moment's interview with the President.

Well, without going into a multiplicity of details, the general result was that Barnes still persisted in saying that she could not see the President, and he also persisted in inviting her, in the circumstances, to go away. She was quiet, but she still insisted on remaining until she could see the President. Then the "Morris incident" happened. At a sign from Barnes a couple of policemen on guard there rushed forward and seized this lady, and began to drag her out of the place. She was frightened and she screamed. Barnes says she screamed repeatedly, and in a way which "aroused the whole White House"—though nobody came to see what was happening. This might give the impression that this was something that was happening six or seven times a day, since it didn't cause any excitement. But this was not so. Barnes has been a private secretary long enough to work his imagination, probably, and that accounts for most of the screaming—though the lady did some of it herself, as she concedes. The woman was dragged out of the White House. She says that in the course of dragging her along the roadway her clothes were soiled with mud and some of them stripped in rags from her back. A negro gathered up her ankles, and so relieved her from contact with the ground. He supporting her by the ankles, and the two policemen carrying her at the other end, they conveyed her to a place— apparently a police station of some kind, a couple of blocks away—and she was dripping portemonnaies and keys, and one thing or another, along the road, and honest people were picking them up and fetching them along. Barnes entered a charge against her of insanity. Apparently the police inspector regarded that as rather a serious charge, and, as he probably had not had one like it before and did not quite know how it ought to be handled, he would not allow her to be delivered to her friends until she had deposited five dollars in his till. No doubt this was to keep her from disappearing from the United States—and he might want to take up this serious charge presently and thresh it out.

That lady still lies in her bed at the principal hotel in Washington, disabled by the shock, and naturally very indignant at the treatment which she has received—but her calm and mild, unexcited, and well-worded account of her adventure is convincing evidence that she was not insane, even to the moderate extent of five dollars' worth.

There you have the facts. It is as I have said—for a number of days they have occupied almost the entire attention of the American nation; they have swept the Russian revolution out of sight, the China mystery, and all the rest of it. It is this sort of thing which makes the right material for an autobiography. You set the incident down which for the moment is to you the most interesting. If you leave it alone three or four weeks you wonder why you ever thought of setting such a thing down—it has no value, no importance. The champagne that made you drunk with delight or exasperation at the time has all passed away; it is stale. But that is what human life consists of—little incidents and big incidents, and they are all of the same size if we let them alone. An autobiography that leaves out the little things and enumerates only the big ones is no proper picture of the man's life at all; his life consists of his feelings and his interests, with here and there an incident apparently big or little to hang the feelings on.

That Morris incident will presently have no importance whatever, and yet the biographer of President Roosevelt will find it immensely valuable if he will consider it—examine it—and be sagacious, enough to perceive that it throws a great deal of light upon the President's character. Certainly a biography's chiefest feature is the exhibition of the character of the man whose biography is being set forth. Roosevelt's biographer will light up the President's career step by step, mile after mile, through his life's course, with illuminating episodes and incidents. He should set one of the lamps by the Morris incident, for it indicates character. It is a thing which probably could not have happened in the White House under any other President who has ever occupied those premises. Washington wouldn't call the police and throw a lady out over the fence! I don't mean that Roosevelt would. I mean that Washington wouldn't have any Barneses in his official family. It is the Roosevelts that have the Barneses around. That private secretary was perfectly right in refusing access to the President—the President can't see everybody on everybody's private affairs, and it is quite proper, then, that he should refuse to see anybody on a private affair—treat all the nation alike. That is a thing which has been done, of course, from the beginning until now—people have always been refused admission to the President on private matters, every day, from Washington's time to ours. The secretaries have always carried their point; Mr. Barnes carried his. But, according to the President in office at the time, the methods have varied—one President's secretary has managed it in one way, another President's secretary has managed it in another way—but it never would have occurred to any previous secretary to manage it by throwing the lady over the fence.

Theodore Roosevelt is one of the most impulsive men in existence. That is the reason why he has impulsive secretaries. President Roosevelt probably never thinks of the right way to do anything. That is why he has secretaries who are not able to think of the right way to do anything. We naturally gather about us people whose ways and dispositions agree with our own. Mr. Roosevelt is one of the most likable men that I am acquainted with. I have known him, and have occasionally met him, dined in his company, lunched in his company, for certainly twenty years. I always enjoy his society, he is so hearty, so straightforward, outspoken, and, for the moment, so absolutely sincere. These qualities endear him to me when he is acting in his capacity of private citizen, they endear him to all his friends. But when he is acting under their impulse as President, they make of him a sufficiently queer President. He flies from one thing to another with incredible dispatch—throws a somersault and is straightway back again where he was last week. He will then throw some more somersaults and nobody can foretell where he is finally going to land after the series. Each act of his, and each opinion expressed, is likely to abolish or controvert some previous act or expressed opinion. This is what is happening to him all the time as President. But every opinion that he expresses is certainly his sincere opinion at that moment, and it is as certainly not the opinion which he was carrying around in his system three or four weeks earlier, and which was just as sincere and honest as the latest one. No, he can't be accused of insincerity—that is not the trouble. His trouble is that his newest interest is the one that absorbs him; absorbs the whole of him from his head to his feet, and for the time being it annihilates all previous opinions and feelings and convictions. He is the most popular human being that has ever existed in the United States, and that popularity springs from just these enthusiasms of his—these joyous ebullitions of excited sincerity. It makes him so much like the rest of the people. They see themselves reflected in him. They also see that his impulses are not often mean. They are almost always large, fine, generous. He can't stick to one of them long enough to find out what kind of a chick it would hatch if it had a chance, but everybody recognizes the generosity of the intention and admires it and loves him for it.

New York, January 12, 1906

My seventieth birthday arrived recently—that is to say, it arrived on the 30th of November, but Colonel Harvey[1] was not able to celebrate it on that date because that date had been pre-empted by the President to be used as the usual and perfunctory Thanksgiving Day, a function which originated in New England two or three centuries ago when those people recognized that they really had something to be thankful for—annually, not oftener—if they had succeeded in exterminating their neighbors, the Indians, during the previous twelve months instead of getting exterminated by their neighbors, the Indians. Thanksgiving Day became a habit, for the reason that in the course of time, as the years drifted on, it was perceived that the exterminating had ceased to be mutual and was all on the white man's side, consequently on the Lord's side; hence it was proper to thank the Lord for it and extend the usual annual compliments. The original reason for a Thanksgiving Day has long ago ceased to exist—the Indians have long ago been comprehensively and satisfactorily exterminated and the account closed with the Lord, with the thanks due. But, from old habit, Thanksgiving Day has remained with us, and every year the President of the United States and the Governors of all the several states and territories set themselves the task, every November, to hunt up something to be thankful for, and then they put those thanks into a few crisp and reverent phrases, in the form of a proclamation, and this is read from all the pulpits in the land, the national conscience is wiped clean with one swipe, and sin is resumed at the old stand.

The President and the Governors had to have my birthday—the 30th—for Thanksgiving Day, and this was a great inconvenience to Colonel Harvey, who had made much preparation for a banquet to be given to me on that day in celebration of the fact that it marked my seventieth escape from the gallows, according to his idea—a fact which he regarded with favor and contemplated with pleasure, because he is

---

1. Col. George Harvey, at the time president of Harper & Brothers, later American Ambassador to the Court of St. James's.

my publisher and commercially interested. He went to Washington to try to get the President to select another day for the national Thanksgiving, and I furnished him with arguments to use which I thought persuasive and convincing, arguments which ought to persuade him even to put off Thanksgiving Day a whole year—on the ground that nothing had happened during the previous twelvemonth except several vicious and inexcusable wars, and King Leopold of Belgium's usual annual slaughters and robberies in the Congo State, together with the insurance revelations in New York, which seemed to establish the fact that if there was an honest man left in the United States, there was only one, and we wanted to celebrate his seventieth birthday. But the colonel came back unsuccessful, and put my birthday celebration off to the 5th of December.

In the birthday speech which I made were concealed many facts. I expected everybody to discount those facts 95 per cent, and that is probably what happened. That does not trouble me; I am used to having my statements discounted. My mother had begun it before I was seven years old. But all through my life my facts have had a substratum of truth, and therefore they were not without value. Any person who is familiar with me knows how to strike my average, and therefore knows how to get at the jewel of any fact of mine and dig it out of its blue-clay matrix. My mother knew that art. When I was seven or eight or ten or twelve years old—along there—a neighbor said to her, "Do you ever believe anything that that boy says?" My mother said, "He is the wellspring of truth, but you can't bring up the whole well with one bucket"—and she added, "I know his average, therefore he never deceives me. I discount him 90 per cent for embroidery, and what is left is perfect and priceless truth, without a flaw in it anywhere."

Now to make a jump of forty years, without breaking the connection, one of those words was used again in my presence and concerning me, when I was fifty years old, one night at Rev. Frank Goodwin's house in Hartford, at a meeting of the Monday Evening Club. The Monday Evening Club still exists. It was founded about forty-five years ago by that theological giant, Reverend Doctor Bushnell, and some comrades of his, men of large intellectual caliber and more or less distinction, local or national. I was admitted to membership in it in the fall of 1871, and was an active member thenceforth until I left Hartford in the summer of 1891. The membership was restricted, in those days, to eighteen—possibly twenty. The meetings began about the 1st of

October and were held in the private houses of the members every fortnight thereafter throughout the cold months until the 1st of May. Usually there were a dozen members present—sometimes as many as fifteen. There were an essay and a discussion. The essayists followed one another in alphabetical order through the season. The essayist could choose his own subject and talk twenty minutes on it. from MS. or orally, according to his preference. Then the discussion followed, and each member present was allowed ten minutes in which to express his views. The wives of these people were always present. It was their privilege. It was also their privilege to keep still. They were not allowed to throw any light upon the discussion. After the discussion there was a supper, and talk, and cigars. This supper began at ten o'clock promptly, and the company broke up and went away at midnight. At least they did except upon one occasion. In my birthday speech I have remarked upon the fact that I have always bought cheap cigars, and that is true. I have never smoked costly ones, and whenever I go to a rich man's house to dinner I conceal cheap cigars about my person, as a protection against his costly ones. There are enough costly Havana cigars in my house to start a considerable cigar shop with, but I did not buy one of them—I doubt if I have ever smoked one of them. They are Christmas presents from wealthy and ignorant friends, extending back for a long series of years. Among the lot, I found, the other day, a double handful of J. Pierpont Morgan's cigars, which were given to me three years ago by his particular friend, the late William E. Dodge, one night when I was at dinner in Mr. Dodge's house. Mr. Dodge did not smoke, and so he supposed that those were superexcellent cigars, because they were made for Mr. Morgan in Havana out of special tobacco and cost $1.66 apiece. Now whenever I buy a cigar that costs six cents I am suspicious of it. When it costs four and a quarter or five cents I smoke it with confidence. I carried those sumptuous cigars home, after smoking one of them at Mr. Dodge's house to show that I had no animosity, and here they lie ever since. They cannot beguile me. I am waiting for somebody to come along whose lack of education will enable him to smoke them and enjoy them.

Well, that night at the club—as I was saying—George, our colored butler, came to me when the supper was nearly over, and I noticed that he was pale. Normally his complexion was a clear black and very handsome, but now it had modified to old amber. He said:

"Mr. Clemens, what are we going to do? There is not a cigar in the house but those old Wheeling 'long nines.' Can't nobody smoke them but you. They kill at thirty yards. It is too late to telephone—we couldn't get any cigars out from town. What can we do? Ain't it best to say nothing and let on that we didn't think?"

"No," I said, "that would not be honest. Fetch out the 'long nines'"— which he did.

I had just come across those "long nines" a few days or a week before. I hadn't seen a "long nine" for years. When I was a cub pilot on the Mississippi in the late '60's I had had a great affection for them, because they were not only—to my mind—perfect, but you could get a basketful of them for a cent—or a dime—they didn't use cents out there in those days. So when I saw them advertised in Hartford I sent for a thousand at once. They were sent out to me in badly battered and disreputable-looking old square pasteboard boxes, about two hundred in a box. George brought the box, which had caved in on all sides, looking the worst it could, and began to pass them around. The conversation had been brilliantly animated up to that moment—but now a frost fell upon the company. That is to say, not all of a sudden, but the frost fell upon each man as he took up a cigar and held it poised in the air—and there, in the middle, his sentence broke off. And that kind of thing went all around the table, until, when George had completed his crime the whole place was full of a thick solemnity and silence.

Those men began to light the cigars. Reverend Doctor Parker was the first man to light. He took three or four heroic whiffs—then gave it up. He got up with the excuse that he had to go to the bedside of a dying parishioner, which I knew was a lie, because if that had been the truth he would have gone earlier. He started out. Reverend Doctor Burton was the next man. He took only one whiff, and followed Parker. He furnished a pretext, and you could see by the sound of his voice that he didn't think much of the pretext, and was vexed with Parker for getting in ahead with a dying client. Rev. Joe Twichell followed, with a good hearty pretext—nothing in it, and he didn't expect anybody to find anything in it, but Twichell is always more or less honest, to this day, and it cost him nothing to say that he had to go now because he must take the midnight train for Boston. Boston was the first place that occurred to him—he would have said Jerusalem if he had thought of it.

It was only a quarter to eleven when they began to hand out pretexts. At five minutes to eleven all those people were out of the house and praying, no doubt, that the pretext might be overlooked, in consideration of the circumstances. When nobody was left but George and me I was cheerful—I was glad—had no compunctions of conscience, no griefs of any kind. But George was beyond speech, because he held the honor and credit of the family above his own, and he was ashamed that this smirch had been put upon it. I told him to go to bed and try to sleep it off. I went to bed myself. At breakfast in the morning, when George was taking a cup of coffee from Mrs. Clemens's hand, I saw it tremble in his hand. I knew by that sign there was something on his mind. He brought the cup to me and asked impressively:

"Mr. Clemens, how far is it from the front door to the upper gate?"

I said, "It is one hundred and twenty-five steps."

He said, "Mr. Clemens, you know, you can start at the front door and you can go plumb to the upper gate and tread on one of them cigars every time."

Now by this roundabout and gradual excursion I have arrived at that meeting of the club at Rev. Frank Goodwin's house which I spoke of awhile back, and where that same word was used in my presence, and to me, which I mentioned as having been used by my mother as much as forty years before. The subject under discussion was dreams. The talk passed from mouth to mouth in the usual serene way. The late Charles Dudley Warner delivered his views in the smooth and pleasantly flowing fashion which he had learned in his early manhood when he was an apprentice to the legal profession. He always spoke pleasingly, always smoothly, always choicely, never excitedly, never aggressively, always kindly, gently, and always with a lambent and playful and inconspicuous thread of humor appearing and disappearing along through his talk, like the tinted lights in an opal. To my thinking, there was never much body to what he said, never much juice in it; never anything very substantial, to carry away and think about, yet it was always a pleasure to listen to him. Always his art was graceful and charming. Then came the late Colonel Greene, who had been a distinguished soldier in the Civil War and who at the time that I speak of was high up in the Connecticut Mutual and on his way to become its president presently, and in time to die in that harness and leave behind him a blemishless reputation, at a time when the chiefs of the New York insurance companies were approaching the eternal doom of their reputations. Colonel Greene discussed the dream question in his usual way—that is to say, he began a sentence and went on and on, dropping a comma in here and there at intervals of eighteen inches, never hesitating for a word, drifting straight along like a river at half bank with no reefs in it; the surface of his talk as smooth as a mirror; his construction perfect and fit for print without correction, as he went along. And when the hammer fell, at the end of his ten minutes, he dumped in a period right where he was and stopped—and it was just as good there as it would have been anywhere else in that ten minutes' sentence. You could look back over that speech and you'd find it dimly milestoned along with those commas which he had put in and which could have been left out just as well, because they merely staked out the march, and nothing more. They could not call attention to the scenery, because there wasn't any. His speech was always like that— perfectly smooth, perfectly constructed; and when he had finished, no listener could go into court and tell what it was he had said. It was a curious style. It was impressive—you always thought, from one comma to another, that he was going to strike something presently, but he never did. But this time that I speak of, the burly and magnificent Reverend Doctor Burton sat with his eyes fixed upon Greene from the beginning of the sentence until the end of it. He looked as the lookout on a whaleship might look who was watching where a whale had gone down and was waiting and watching for it to reappear; and no doubt that was the figure that was in Burton's mind, because, when at last Greene finished, Burton threw up his hands and shouted, "There she blows!"

The elder Hammersley took his appointed ten minutes, easily, comfortably, with good phrasing, and most entertainingly—and this was always to be expected of the elder Hammersley.

Then his son, Will Hammersley, a young lawyer, now this many years a judge of the Connecticut Supreme Court, took his chance in the dream question. And I can't imagine anything more distressing than a talk from Will Hammersley—a talk from the Will Hammersley of those days. You always knew that before he got through he would certainly say something—something that you could carry away, something that you could consider, something that you couldn't easily put out of your mind. But you also knew that you would suffer many a torture before he got that thing out. He would hesitate and hesitate, get to the middle of a sentence and search around and around and around for a word, get the wrong word, search again, get another wrong one, search again and again—and so he would go on in that way till everybody was in misery on his account, hoping that he would arrive in the course of time, and yet sinking deeper and deeper toward despair, with the conviction that this time he was not going to arrive. He would seem to get so far away from any possible goal that you would feel convinced that he could not cover the intervening space and get there before his ten minutes would come to an end and leave him suspended between heaven and earth. But, sure as a gun, before that ten minutes ended Will Hammersley would arrive at his point and fetch it out with such a round and complete and handsome and satisfying unostentatious crash that you would be lifted out of your chair with admiration and gratitude.

Joe Twichell sometimes took his turn. If he talked, it was easily perceptible that it was because he had something to say, and he was always able to say it well. But almost as a rule, he said nothing, and gave his ten minutes to the next man. And whenever he gave it to—, he ran the risk of getting lynched on his way home by the rest of the membership.— was the dullest white man in Connecticut—and he probably remains that to this day: I have not heard of any real competitor.—would moon along, and moon along, and moon along, using the most commonplace, the most dreary, the most degraded English, with never an idea in it by any chance. But he never gave his ten minutes to anybody. He always used it up to the last second. Then there was always a little gap—had to be for the crowd to recover before the next man could begin—when he would get entirely lost in his talk and didn't know where he was in his idiotic philosophizings, would grasp at narrative, as the drowning man grasps at a straw. If a drowning man ever does that—which I doubt. Then he would tell something in his experiences, thinking perhaps it had something to do with the question in hand. It generally hadn't—and this time he told about a long and arduous and fatiguing chase which he had had in the Maine woods on a hot summer's day, after some kind of a wild animal that he wanted to kill, and how at last, chasing eagerly after this creature across a wide stream, he slipped and fell on the ice, and injured his leg—whereupon a silence and confusion.—noticed that something was wrong, and then it occurred to him that there was a kind of discrepancy in hunting animals on the ice in summertime, so he switched off to theology. He always did that. He was a rabid Christian, and member of Joe Twichell's church. Joe Twichell could get together the most impossible Christians that ever assembled in anybody's congregation; and as a usual thing he couldn't run his church systematically on account of new deacons who didn't understand the business—the recent deacons having joined their predecessors in the penitentiary down there at Wethersfield.—would

MARK TWAIN

wind up with some very pious remarks—and in fact they all did that. Take the whole crowd—the crowd that was almost always present— and this remark applies to them. There was J. Hammond Trumbull, the most learned man in the United States. He knew everything— everything in detail that had ever happened in this world, and a lot that was going to happen, and a lot that couldn't ever possibly happen. He would close with some piety. Henry C. Robinson—Governor Henry C. Robinson—a brilliant man, a most polished and effective and eloquent speaker, an easy speaker, a speaker who had no difficulties to encounter in delivering himself—always closed with some piety. A. C. Dunham, a man really great in his line—that is to say the commercial line—a great manufacturer, an enterprising man, a capitalist, a most competent and fascinating talker, a man who never opened his mouth without a stream of practical pearls flowing from it—he always closed with some piety.

New York, January 13, 1906
The piety ending was used also by Franklin and Johnson, and possibly by the rest of the club—most likely by the rest of the club. But I recall that that ending was a custom with Franklin and with Johnson. Franklin was a bluff old soldier. He was a West Pointer and, I think, had served in the Mexican War. He commanded one of McClellan's armies in the Civil War at the time that McClellan was commander-in-chief. He was an ideal soldier, simple-hearted, good, kind, affectionate; set in his opinions, his partialities and his prejudices, believing everything which he had been taught to believe about politics, religion, and military matters; thoroughly well educated in the military science—in fact, I have already said that, because I have said he was a West Pointer. He knew all that was worth knowing in that specialty and was able to reason well upon his knowledge, but his reasoning faculty did not shine when he was discussing other things. Johnson was a member of Trinity, and was easily the most brilliant member of the club. But his fine light shone not in public, but in the privacy of the club, and his qualities were not known outside of Hartford.

I had long been suffering from these intolerable and inexcusable exudations of misplaced piety, and for years had wanted to enter a protest against them, but had struggled against the impulse and had always been able to conquer it, until now. But this time—was too much for me. He was the feather that broke the camel's back. The substance of his wandering twaddle—if by chance it had substance—was that there is nothing in dreams. Dreams merely proceed from indigestion—there is no quality of intelligence in them—they are thoroughly fantastic and without beginning, logical sequence, or definite end. Nobody, in our day, but the stupid or the ignorant attaches any significance to them. And then he went on blandly and pleasantly to say that dreams had once had a mighty importance, that they had had the illustrious honor of being used by the Almighty as a means of conveying desires, warnings, commands, to people whom He loved or hated—that these dreams are set down in Holy Writ; that no sane man challenges their authenticity, their significance, their verity.

I followed—and I remember with satisfaction that I said not one harsh thing, vexed as I was, but merely remarked, without warmth, that these tiresome damned prayer-meetings might better be adjourned to the garret of some church, where they belonged. It is centuries ago that I did that thing. It was away back, back, back, so many, many years ago—and yet I have always regretted it, because from that time forth, to the last meeting which I attended (which would be at the beginning of the spring of 1891) the piety ending was never used again. No, perhaps I am going too far; maybe I am putting too much emphasis upon my regret. Possibly when I said that about regret, I was doing what people so often unconsciously do, trying to place myself in a favorable light after having made a confession that makes such a thing more or less difficult. No, I think it quite likely that I never regretted it at all.

Anybody could see that the "piety ending" had no importance, for the reason that it was manifestly perfunctory. The club was founded by a great clergyman; it always had more clergymen in it than good people. Clergymen are not able to sink the shop without falling under suspicion. It was quite natural that the original members should introduce that kind of ending to their speeches. It was also quite natural that the rest of the membership, being church members, should take up the custom, turn it into a habit, and continue it without ever happening to notice that it was merely a mouth function, had no heart in it, and therefore was utterly valueless to themselves and to everybody else.

I do not now remember what form my views concerning dreams took at that time. I don't remember now what my notion about dreams was then, but I do remember telling a dream by way of illustrating some detail of my speech, and I also remember that when I had finished it Reverend Doctor Burton made that remark which contained that word I have already spoken of sixteen or seventeen times as having been uttered by my mother, in some such connection, forty or fifty years before. I was probably engaged in trying to make those people believe that now and then, by some accident, or otherwise, a dream which was prophetic turned up in the dreamer's mind. The date of my memorable dream was about the beginning of May, 1858. It was a remarkable dream, and I had been telling it several times every year for more than fifteen years—and now I was telling it again, here in the club.

In 1858 I was a steersman on board the swift and popular New Orleans and St. Louis packet, Pennsylvania, Captain Kleinfelter. I had been lent to Mr. Brown, one of the pilots of the Pennsylvania, by my owner. Mr. Horace E. Bixby, and I had been steering for Brown about eighteen months, I think. Then in the early days of May, 1858, came a tragic trip—the last trip of that fleet and famous steamboat. I have told all about it in one of my books, called Life on the Mississippi. But it is not likely that I told the dream in that book. I will ask my secretary to see—but I will go on and dictate the dream now, and it can go into the waste basket if it shall turn out that I have already published it. It is impossible that I can have published it, I think, because I never wanted my mother to know about that dream, and she lived several years after I published that volume.

I had found a place on the Pennsylvania for my brother Henry, who was two years my junior. It was not a place of profit, it was only a place of promise. He was "mud" clerk. Mud clerks received no salary, but they were in the line of promotion. They could become, presently, third clerk and second clerk, then chief clerk—that is to say, purser. The dream begins when Henry had been mud clerk about three months. We were lying in port at St. Louis. Pilots and steersmen had nothing to do during the three days that the boat lay in port in St. Louis and New Orleans, but the mud clerk had to begin his labors at dawn and continue them into the night, by the light of pine-knot torches. Henry and I, moneyless and unsalaried, had billeted ourselves upon our brother-in-law, Mr. Moffett, as night lodgers while in port. We took our meals on board the boat. No, I mean I lodged at the house, not Henry. He spent the evenings at the house, from nine until eleven, then went to the boat to be ready for his early duties. On the night of the dream he started away at eleven, shaking hands with the family, and said good-by according to custom. I may mention that handshaking as a good-by was not merely the custom of that family, but the custom of the region—the custom of Missouri, I may say. In all my life, up to that time, I had never seen one member of the Clemens family kiss another one—except once. When my father lay dying in our home in Hannibal, Missouri—the 24th of March, 1847—he put his arm around my sister's neck and drew her down and kissed her, saying, "Let me die." I remember that, and I remember the death rattle which swiftly followed those words, which were his last. These good-bys were always executed in the family sitting room on the second floor, and Henry went from that room and downstairs without further ceremony. But this time my mother went with him to the head of the stairs and said good-by again. As I remember it, she was moved to this by something in Henry's manner, and she remained at the head of the stairs while he descended. When he reached the door he hesitated, and climbed the stairs and shook hands good-by again. In the morning, when I awoke, I had been dreaming, and the dream was so vivid, so like reality, that it deceived me, and I thought it was real. In the dream I had seen Henry a corpse. He lay in a metallic burial case. He was dressed in a suit of my clothing, and on his breast lay a great bouquet of flowers, mainly white roses, with a red rose in the center. The casket stood upon a couple of chairs. I dressed, and moved toward that door, thinking I would go in there and look at it, but I changed my mind. I thought I could not yet bear to meet my mother. I thought I would wait awhile and make some preparation for that ordeal. The house was in Locust Street, a little above Thirteenth, and I walked to Fourteenth and to the middle of the block beyond before it suddenly flashed upon me that there was nothing real about this—it was only a dream. I can still feel something of the grateful upheaval of joy of that moment, and I can also still feel the remnant of doubt, the suspicion that maybe it was real, after all. I returned to the house almost on a run, flew up the stairs two or three steps at a jump, and rushed into that sitting room, and was made glad again, for there was no casket there.

We made the usual eventless trip to New Orleans—no, it was not eventless, for it was on the way down that I had the fight with Mr. Brown[1] which resulted in his requiring that I be left ashore at New Orleans. In New Orleans I always had a job. It was my privilege to watch the freight piles from seven in the evening until seven in the morning, and get three dollars for it. It was a three-night job and

---

1. See Life on the Mississippi.

MARK TWAIN

occurred every thirty-five days. Henry always joined my watch about nine in the evening, when his own duties were ended, and we often walked my rounds and chatted together until midnight. This time we were to part, and so the night before the boat sailed I gave Henry some advice. I said: "In case of disaster to the boat, don't lose your head— leave that unwisdom to the passengers—they are competent—they'll attend to it. But you rush for the hurricane deck, and astern to the solitary lifeboat lashed aft the wheelhouse on the port side, and obey the mate's orders—thus you will be useful. When the boat is launched, give such help as you can in getting the women and children into it, and be sure you don't try to get into it yourself. It is summer weather, the river is only a mile wide, as a rule, and you can swim ashore without any trouble." Two or three days afterward the boat's boilers exploded at Ship Island, below Memphis, early one morning—and what happened afterward I have already told in Life on the Mississippi. As related there, I followed the Pennsylvania about a day later, on another boat, and we began to get news of the disaster at every port we touched at, and so by the time we reached Memphis we knew all about it.

I found Henry stretched upon a mattress on the floor of a great building, along with thirty or forty other scalded and wounded persons, and was promptly informed, by some indiscreet person, that he had inhaled steam, that his body was badly scalded, and that he would live but a little while; also, I was told that the physicians and nurses were giving their whole attention to persons who had a chance of being saved. They were short-handed in the matter of physicians and nurses, and Henry and such others as were considered to be fatally hurt were receiving only such attention as could be spared, from time to time, from the more urgent cases. But Doctor Peyton, a fine and large-hearted old physician of great reputation in the community, gave me his sympathy and took vigorous hold of the case, and in about a week he had brought Henry around. He never committed himself with prognostications which might not materialize, but at eleven o'clock one night he told me that Henry was out of danger and would get well. Then he said, "At midnight these poor fellows lying here and there and all over this place will begin to mourn and mutter and lament and make outcries, and if this commotion should disturb Henry it will be bad for him; therefore ask the physicians on watch to give him an eighth of a grain of morphine, but this is not to be done unless Henry shall show signs that he is being disturbed."

Oh, well, never mind the rest of it. The physicians on watch were young fellows hardly out of the medical college, and they made a mistake—they had no way of measuring the eighth of a grain of morphine, so they guessed at it and gave him a vast quantity heaped on the end of a knife blade, and the fatal effects were soon apparent. I think he died about dawn, I don't remember as to that. He was carried to the dead-room and I went away for a while to a citizen's house and slept off some of my accumulated fatigue—and meantime something was happening. The coffins provided for the dead were of unpainted white pine, but in this instance some of the ladies of Memphis had made up a fund of sixty dollars and bought a metallic case, and when I came back and entered the dead-room Henry lay in that open case, and he was dressed in a suit of my clothing. I recognized instantly that my dream of several weeks before was here exactly reproduced, so far as these details went—and I think I missed one detail, but that one was immediately supplied, for just then an elderly lady entered the place with a large bouquet consisting mainly of white roses, and in the center of it was a red rose, and she laid it on his breast.

I told the dream there in the club that night just as I have told it here, I suppose.

New York, January 15, 1906

Reverend Doctor Burton swung his leonine head around, focused me with his eye, and said:

"When was it that this happened?"

"In June, '58."

"It is a good many years ago. Have you told it several times since?"

"Yes, I have, a good many times."

"How many?"

"Why, I don't know how many."

"Well, strike an average. How many times a year do you think you have told it?"

"Well, I have told it as many as six times a year, possibly oftener."

"Very well, then, you've told it, we'll say, seventy or eighty times since it happened?"

"Yes," I said, "that's a very conservative estimate."

"Now then, Mark, a very extraordinary thing happened to me a great many years ago, and I used to tell it a number of times—a good many times—every year, for it was so wonderful that it always astonished the hearer, and that astonishment gave me a distinct pleasure every time. I never suspected that that tale was acquiring any auxiliary advantages through repetition until one day after I had been telling it ten or fifteen years it struck me that either I was getting old and slow in delivery, or that the tale was longer than it was when it was born. Mark, I diligently and prayerfully examined that tale, with this result: that I found that its proportions were now, as nearly as I could make out, one part fact, straight fact, fact pure and undiluted, golden fact, and twenty-four parts embroidery. I never told that tale afterward—I was never able to tell it again, for I had lost confidence in it, and so the pleasure of telling it was gone, and gone permanently. How much of this tale of yours is embroidery?"

"Well," I said, "I don't know, I don't think any of it is embroidery. I think it is all just as I have stated it, detail by detail."

"Very well," he said, "then it is all right, but I wouldn't tell it any more; because if you keep on, it will begin to collect embroidery sure. The safest thing is to stop now."

That was a great many years ago. And to-day is the first time that I have told that dream since Doctor Burton scared me into fatal doubts about it. No, I don't believe I can say that. I don't believe that I ever had any doubts whatever concerning the salient points of the dream, for those points are of such a nature that they are pictures, and pictures can be remembered, when they are vivid, much better than one can remember remarks and unconcreted facts. Although it has been so many years since I have told that dream, I can see those pictures now just as clearly defined as if they were before me in this room. I have not told the entire dream. There was a good deal more of it. I mean I have not told all that happened in the dream's fulfillment. After the incident in the death-room I may mention one detail, and that is this. When I arrived in St. Louis with the casket it was about eight o'clock in the morning, and I ran to my brother-in-law's place of business, hoping to find him there, but I missed him, for while I was on the way to his office he was on his way from the house to the boat. When I got back to the boat the casket was gone. He had had it conveyed out to his house. I hastened thither, and when I arrived the men were just removing the casket from the vehicle to carry it upstairs. I stopped that procedure, for I did not want my mother to see the dead face, because one side of it was drawn and distorted by the effects of the opium. When I went upstairs there stood the two chairs which I had seen in my dream, and if I had arrived there two or three minutes later the casket would have been resting upon those two chairs, just as in my dream of several weeks before.

A very curious thing happened at the house of James Goodwin, father of Rev. Francis Goodwin and also father of the great Connecticut Mutual Insurance Company. Mr. James Goodwin was an old man at the time that I speak of, but in his young days, when he used to drive stage between Hartford and Springfield, he conceived the idea of starting a Mutual Insurance Company, and he collected a little capital in the way of subscriptions—enough to start the business in a modest way—and he gave away the rest of the stock where he could find people willing to accept it (though they were rather scarce)—and now he had lived to see that stock worth 250 and nobody willing to sell at that price, or any other. He had long ago forgotten how to drive stage—but it was no matter. He was worth seven millions, and didn't need to work for a living any longer. Rev. Frank Goodwin, his son, an Episcopal clergyman, was a man of many accomplishments; and, among others, he was an architect. He planned and built a huge granite mansion for his father, and I think it was in this mansion that that curious thing happened. No, it happened in Francis Goodwin's own house in the neighborhood. It happened in this way. Frank Goodwin had a burglar alarm in his house. The annunciator was right at his ear, on the port side of his bed. He would put the whole house on the alarm—every window and every door—at bedtime; then, at five o'clock in the morning, the cook would descend from her bedroom and open the kitchen door, and that would set the alarm to buzzing in Goodwin's ear. Now as that happened every morning straight along, week in and week out, Goodwin soon became so habituated to it that it didn't disturb him. It aroused him, partly, from his sleep sometimes—sometimes it probably did not affect his sleep at all, but from old habit he would automatically put out his left hand and shut off that alarm. By that act he shut off the alarm from the entire house, leaving not a window or a door on it from five o'clock in the morning thenceforth until he should set the alarm the next night at bedtime.

The night that I speak of was one of those dismal New England November nights, close upon the end of the month, when the pestiferous New England climate furnishes those regions a shake-down just in the way of experiment and to get its hand in for business when the proper time comes, which is December. Well, the wind howled and the snow blew along in clouds when we left that house about midnight. It was a wild night. It was like a storm at sea, for boom and crash and roar and furious snow-drive. It was no kind of a night for burglars to be out in, and yet they were out. Goodwin was in bed, with his house on the alarm by half past twelve. Not very long afterward the burglars arrived. Evidently they knew all about the burglar alarm, because, instead of breaking into the kitchen, they sawed their way in—that is to say, they sawed a great panel out of the kitchen door and stepped in without alarming the alarm. They went all over the house at their leisure; they collected all sorts of trinkets and trumpery, all of the silverware. They carried these things to the kitchen, put them in bags, and then they gathered together a sumptuous supper, with champagne and Burgundy and so on, and ate that supper at their leisure. Then when they were ready to leave—say at three o'clock in the morning—the champagne and the Burgundy had had an influence, and they became careless for a moment; but one moment was enough. In that careless moment a burglar unlocked and opened the kitchen door, and of course the alarm went off. Rev. Mr. Goodwin put out his left hand and shut off the alarm and went on sleeping peacefully, but the burglars bounded out of the place and left all their swag behind them. A burglar alarm is a valuable thing if you know how to utilize it.

When Reverend Frank was finishing his father's mansion, I was passing by one day. I thought I would go in and see how the house was coming along, and in the first room I entered I found Mr. Goodwin and a paperhanger. Then Mr. Goodwin told me this curious story. He said: "This room has been waiting a good while. This is Morris paper, and it didn't hold out. You will see there is one space there, from the ceiling halfway to the floor, which is blank. I sent to New York and ordered some more of the paper—it couldn't be furnished. I applied in Philadelphia and in Boston, with the same result. There was not a bolt of that paper left in America, so far as any of these people knew. I wrote to London. The answer came back in those same monotonous terms—that paper was out of print—not a yard of it to be found. Then I told the paperhanger to strip the paper off and we would replace it with some other pattern, and I was very sorry, because I preferred that pattern to any other. Just then a farmer-looking man halted in front of the house, started to walk that single-plank approach that you just walked, and came in; but he saw that sign up there—'No admittance'—a sign which did not obstruct your excursion into this place—but it halted him. I said: 'Come in! Come in!' He came in, and, this being the first room on the route, he naturally glanced in. He saw the paper on the wall and remarked, casually: 'I am acquainted with that pattern. I've got a bolt of it at home down on my farm in Glastonbury.' It didn't take long to strike up a trade with him for that bolt, which had been lying in his farmhouse for he didn't know how long, and he hadn't any use for it— and now we are finishing up that lacking patch there."

Mrs Morris's Illness Takes A Serious Turn

Cabinet Officers Urge President to Disavow Violence to Her

A Discussion in the Case

Mr. Sheppard Criticizes the President and Republican Leaders Try to Stop Him.

(Special to The New York Times.)

Washington, Jan. 10.—Mrs. Minor Morris, who on Thursday was dragged from the White House, is tonight in a critical condition.

She seemed to be on the road to recovery on Saturday, and her physicians held out hopes that she would be able to be out by Monday. At the beginning of this week her condition took an unfavorable turn, and she has been growing steadily worse. She had a congestive chill to-day and has continued to grow worse. It is evident to-night that her nervous system has suffered something approaching a collapse.

The bruises inflicted upon her by the policemen have not disappeared, a striking evidence of their severity. Her arms, shoulders, and neck still bear testimony to the nature of her treatment. Mentally and physically she is suffering severely.

It was learned to-day that two Cabinet officers, one of whom is Secretary Taft, have been laboring with the President for two days to get him to issue a statement disavowing the action of Assistant Secretary Barnes, who ordered Mrs. Morris expelled, and expressing his regret for the way she was treated. They have also urged him to promise to take action which will make impossible the repetition of such an occurrence.

The President has held out stoutly against the advice of these two Cabinet officers. He authorized Mr. Barnes to make the statement that he gave out, in which the treatment of Mrs. Morris was justified, and it is not easy to take the other tack now. On high authority, however, it is learned that the two Cabinet officers have not ceased their labors. They both look on the matter not as "a mere incident," but as a serious affair.

The Morris incident was brought up in the House to-day just before adjournment by Mr. Sheppard of Texas. He was recognized for fifteen minutes, in the ordinary course of the debate on the Philippine Tariff bill, and began at once to discuss the resolution he introduced Monday calling for an investigation of the expulsion. He excused himself for speaking on the resolution at this time, saying that as it was not privileged he could not obtain its consideration without the consent of the Committee on Rules.

He went on to describe the incident at the White House. He had proceeded only a minute or two when he was interrupted by General Grosvenor, who rose to the point of order that the remarks were not germane to the Philippine Tariff bill.

"I will show the gentleman that it is germane," cried Mr. Sheppard. "It is just as proper for this country to have a Chinese wall around the White House as it is to have such a wall around the United States."

"Well, if he thinks it is proper to thus arraign the President and his household," said Mr. Grosvenor, "let him go on."

"If the President had heard the howl of a wolf or the growl of a bear from the adjacent offices," retorted Mr. Sheppard, "the response would have been immediate, but the wail of an American woman fell upon unresponsive ears."

There had been several cries of protest when General Grosvenor interrupted Mr. Sheppard, many of whose Democratic friends gathered about him and urged him to proceed. They applauded his reply to Mr. Grosvenor, and the Ohioan did not press his point.

"These unwarrantable and unnecessary brutalities," continued Mr. Sheppard, "demand an investigation. Unless Congress takes some action we shall soon witness in a free republic a condition where citizens cannot approach the President they have created without fear of bodily harm from arbitrary subordinates."

Mr. Sheppard had nearly reached the close of his remarks when Mr. Payne, the titular floor leader of the Republicans, renewed the Grosvenor point of order. Mr. Olmstead of Pennsylvania, in the chair, however, ruled that with the House sitting in Committee of the Whole on the state of the Union, remarks need not be germane.

Mr. Payne interrupted again, to ask a question.

"If a gentleman has the facts upon which to found his attack," he said, "does he not think the police court is the better place to air them?"

"The suggestion is a reflection upon the gentleman himself, although he is a friend of mine," replied Sheppard.

When the speech was finished Grosvenor got the floor and said he had been aware of the rules when he did not press his point.

"But I made the point," he continued, "merely to call the attention of the young gentleman from Texas in a mild and fatherly manner to my protest against his remarks. I hoped he would refrain from further denunciation of the President. He has introduced a resolution which is now pending before the proper committee. That resolution asks for facts and I supposed that the gentleman would wait for the facts until that resolution is brought into the House.

"I know no difference in proper conduct between the President's office and household and the humblest home in this Nation, but I don't believe a condition has arisen such that the husband of this woman cannot take care of the situation."

A high government official to-night added to the accounts of the expulsion an incident, which he said was related to him by an eye-witness. While the policemen and their negro assistant were dragging Mrs. Morris through the grounds the scene was witnessed by the women servants, some of whom called out, "Shame!" One of the policemen pressed his hand down on Mrs. Morris's mouth to stifle her cries for help, and at that sight a man servant, a negro, rushed forward and shouted:

"Take your hand off that white woman's face! Don't treat a white woman that way!"

The policeman paid no attention to the man, and continued his efforts to stifle Mrs. Morris's cries.

THE REASON I WANT TO insert that account of the Morris case, which is making such a lively stir all over the United States, and possibly the entire world, in these days, is this. Some day, no doubt, these autobiographical notes will be published. It will be after my death. It may be five years from now, it may be ten, it may be fifty—but whenever the time shall come, even if it should be a century hence—I claim that the reader of that day will find the same strong interest in that narrative that the world has in it to-day, for the reason that the account speaks of the thing in the language we naturally use when we are talking about something that has just happened. That form of narrative is able to carry along with it for ages and ages the very same interest which we find in it to-day. Whereas if this had happened fifty years ago, or a hundred, and the historian had dug it up and was putting it in his language, and furnishing you a long-distance view of it, the reader's interest in it would be pale. You see, it would not be news to him, it would be history; merely history; and history can carry on no successful competition with news, in the matter of sharp interest. When an eye-witness sets down in narrative form some extraordinary occurrence which he has witnessed, that is news—that is the news form, and its interest is absolutely indestructible; time can have no deteriorating effect upon that episode. I am placing that account there largely as an experiment. If any stray copy of this book shall, by any chance, escape the paper-mill for a century or so, and then be discovered and read, I am betting that that remote reader will find that it is still news and that it is just as interesting as any news he will find in the newspapers of his day and morning—if newspapers shall still be in existence then—though let us hope they won't.

These notions were born to me in the fall of 1867, in Washington. That is to say, thirty-nine years ago. I had come back from the Quaker City excursion. I had gone to Washington to write The Innocents Abroad, but before beginning that book it was necessary to earn some money to live on meantime, or borrow it—which would be difficult, or to take it where it reposed unwatched—which would be unlikely. So I started the first Newspaper Correspondence Syndicate that an unhappy world ever saw. I started it in conjunction with William Swinton, a brother of the admirable John Swinton. William Swinton was a brilliant creature, highly educated, accomplished. He was such a contrast to me that I did not know which of us most to admire, because both ends of a contrast are equally delightful to me. A thoroughly beautiful woman and a thoroughly homely woman are creations which I love to gaze upon, and which I cannot tire of gazing upon, for each is perfect in her own line, and it is perfection, I think, in many things, and perhaps most things, which is the quality that fascinates us. A splendid literature charms us; but it doesn't charrn me any more than its opposite does—"hog-wash" literature. At another time I will explain that word, "hog-wash" and offer an example of it which lies here on the bed—a book which was lately sent to me from England, or Ireland.

Swinton kept a jug. It was sometimes full, but seldom as full as himself—and it was when he was fullest that he was most competent with his pen. We wrote a letter apiece once a week and copied them and sent them to twelve newspapers, charging each of the newspapers a dollar apiece. And although we didn't get rich, it kept the jug going and partly fed the two of us. We earned the rest of our living with magazine articles. My trade in that line was better than his, because I had written six letters for the New York Tribune while I was out on the Quaker City excursion, fifty-three for the Alta Californian, and one pretty breezy one for the New York Herald after I got back, and so I had a good deal of a reputation to trade on. Every now and then I was able to get twenty-five dollars for a magazine article.

I had a chance to write a magazine article about an ancient and moss-grown claim which was disturbing Congress that session, a claim which had been disturbing Congress ever since the War of 1812, and was always getting paid, but never satisfied. The claim was for Indian corn and for provender consumed by the American troops in Maryland or somewhere around there, in the War of 1812. I wrote the article, and it is in one of my books, and is there called "Concerning the Great Beef Contract." It was necessary to find out the price of Indian corn in 1812, and I found that detail a little difficult. Finally I went to A. R. Spofford, who was the Librarian of Congress then—Spofford the man with the prodigious memory—and I put my case before him. He knew every volume in the Library, and what it contained, and where it was located. He said promptly, "I know of only two sources which promise to afford this information, 'Tooke on Prices'" (he brought me the book) "and the New York Evening Post. In those days newspapers did not publish market reports, but about 1809 the New York Evening Post began to print market reports on sheets of paper about note-paper size, and fold these in the journal." He brought me a file of the Evening Post for 1812. I examined "Tooke" and then began to examine the Post—and I was in a great hurry. I had less than an hour at my disposal. But in the Post I found a personal narrative which chained my attention at once. It was a letter from a gentleman who had witnessed the arrival of the British and the burning of the Capitol. The matter was bristling with interest for him and he delivered his words hot from the bat. That letter must have been read with fiery and absorbing interest three days later in New York, but not with any more absorbing interest than the interest which was making my blood leap fifty-nine years later. When I finished that account I found I had used up all the time that was at my disposal, and more.

That incident made a strong impression upon me. I believed I had made a discovery—the discovery already indicated—the discovery of the wide difference in interest between "news" and "history"; that news is history in its first and best form, its vivid and fascinating form, and that history is the pale and tranquil reflection of it.

This reminds me that in this daily dictation of autobiographical notes I am mixing these two forms together all the time. I am hoping by this method of procedure to secure the values of both. I am sure I have found the right way to spin an autobiography at last, after my many experiments. Years ago I used to make skeleton notes to use as texts in writing autobiographical chapters, but really those notes were worth next to nothing. If I expanded them upon the page at once, while their interest was fresh in my mind, they were useful, but if I left them unused for several weeks, or several months, their power to suggest and excite had usually passed away. They were faded flowers, their fragrance was gone. But I believe in this present plan. When you arrive with your stenographic plant at eleven, every morning, you find me placid and comfortable in bed, smoking, untroubled by the fact that I must presently get to work and begin to dictate this history of mine. And if I were depending upon faded notes for inspiration, I should have trouble and my work would soon become distasteful. But by my present system I do not need any notes. The thing uppermost in a person's mind is the thing to talk about or write about. The thing of new and immediate interest is the pleasantest text he can have—and you can't come here at eleven o'clock, or any other hour, and catch me without a new interest—a perfectly fresh interest—because I have either been reading the infernal newspapers and got it there, or I have been talking with somebody; and in either case the new interest is present—the interest which I most wish to dictate about. So you see the result is that this narrative of mine is sure to begin every morning in diary form, because it is sure to begin with something which I have just read, or something which I have just been talking about. That text, when I am done with it—if I ever get done with it, and I don't seem to get done with any text—but it doesn't matter, I am not interested in getting done with anything. I am only interested in talking along and wandering around as much as I want to, regardless of results to the future reader. By consequence, here we have diary and history combined; because as soon as I wander from the present text—the thought of to-day—that digression takes me far and wide over an uncharted sea of recollection, and the result of that is history. Consequently my autobiography is diary and history combined. The privilege of beginning every day in the diary form is a valuable one. I may even use a larger word, and say it is a precious one, for it brings together widely separated things that are in a manner related to each other, and consequently pleasant surprises and contrasts are pretty sure to result every now and then.

Did I dictate something about John Malone three or four days ago? Very well, then, if I didn't I must have been talking with somebody about John Malone. I remember now, it was with Mr. Volney Streamer. He is a librarian of the Players' Club. He called here to bring me a book which he has published, and, in a general way, to make my acquaintance. I was a foundation member of the Players' Club, but ceased to be a member three years ago, through an absurdity committed by the management of that club, a management which has always been idiotic; a management which from the beginning has been selected from, not the nearest asylum in the city, but the most competent one (and some time I wish to talk about that). Several times, during this lapse of three years, old friends of mine and comrades in the club—David Munro, that charming Scot, editor of the North American Review; Robert Reid, the artist; Saint-Gaudens, the sculptor; John Malone, the ex-actor; and others—have been resenting the conduct of that management—the conduct, I mean, which resulted in my segregation from the club—and they have always been trying to find a way of restoring me to the fold without damaging my pride. At last they found a way. They made me an honorary member. This handsome honor afforded me unlimited gratification and I was glad to get back under such flattering conditions. (I don't like that word, but let it go, I can't think of the right one at the moment.) Then David Munro and the others put up the fatted calf for the lost sheep in the way of a dinner to me. Midway of the dinner I got a glimpse, through a half-open pantry door, of that pathetic figure, John Malone. There he was, left out, of course. Sixty-five years old; and his history may be summarized—his history for fifty years—in those two words, those eloquent words—"left out." He has been left out, and left out, and left out, as the years drifted by for nearly two generations. He was always expecting to be counted in. He was always pathetically hoping to be counted in; and that hope never deserted him through all those years, and yet was never in any instance realized. During all those years that

I used to drop in at the Players' for a game of billiards and a chat with the boys, John Malone was always there until midnight and after. He had a cheap lodging in the Square—somewhere on Gramercy Park, but the club was his real home. He told me his history once. His version of it was this:

He was an apprentice in a weekly little newspaper office in Willamette, Oregon, and by and by Edwin Booth made a one-night stand there with his troupe, and John got stage-struck and joined the troupe, and traveled with it around about the Pacific coast in various useful histrionic capacities—capacities suited to a beginner, sometimes assisting by appearing on the stage to say, "My lord, the carriage waits," later appearing armored in shining tin, as a Roman soldier, and so on, gradually rising to higher and higher eminences, and by and by he stood shoulder to shoulder with John McCullough, and the two stood next in rank after Edwin Booth himself on the tragic stage. It was a question which of the two would succeed Booth when Booth should retire or die. According to Malone, his celebrity quite equaled McCullough's in those days, and the chances were evenly balanced. A time came when there was a great opportunity—a great part to be played in Philadelphia. Malone was chosen for the part. He missed his train. John McCullough was put into that great place and achieved a success which made him for life. Malone was sure that if he had not missed the train he would have achieved that success himself; he would have secured the enduring fame which fell to John McCullough's lot; he would have moved on through life serene, comfortable, fortunate, courted, admired, applauded, as was John McCullough's case from that day until the day of his death. Malone believed with all his heart that fame and fortune were right there within his reach at that time, and that he lost them merely through missing his train. He dated his decline from that day. He declined, and declined, and declined, little by little, and little by little, and year after year, until there came a time when he was no longer wanted on the stage; when even minor part after minor part slipped from his grasp; and at last engagements ceased altogether—engagements of any kind. Yet he was always believing, and always expecting, that a turn of fortune would come; that he would get a chance on the stage in some great part; and that one chance, he said, was all he wanted. He was convinced that the world would not question that he was the rightful successor of Edwin Booth, and from that day forth he would be a famous and happy and fortunate man. He never gave up that hope. Three or four years ago,

I remember his jubilation over the fact that he had been chosen by some private theatrical people to play Othello in one of the big theaters of New York. And I remember his grief and deep depression when those private theatrical people gave up the enterprise, at the last moment, and canceled Malone's engagement, snatching from him the greatness which had once more been just within his reach.

As I was saying, at mid-dinner that night I saw him through the half-open door. There he remained through the rest of the dinner, "left out," always left out. But at the end of the speeches, when a number of us were standing up in groups and chatting, he crept meekly in and found his way to the vacant chair at my side, and sat down. I sat down at once and began to talk with him. I was always fond of him—I think everybody was. And presently the president of the New York City College came and bent over John and asked me something about my last summer, and how I had liked it up in the New Hampshire hills, at Dublin. Then, in order to include John in the conversation, he asked him if he was acquainted with that region and if he had ever been in Dublin. Malone said dreamily, and with the air of a man who was trying to think up long-gone things, "How does it lie as regards Manchester?" President Finley told him, and then John said, "I have never been to Dublin, but I have a sort of recollection of Manchester. I am pretty sure I was there once—but it was only a one-night stand, you know."

It filled my soul with a gentle delight, a gracious satisfaction, the way he said that—"Only a one-night stand." It seemed to reveal that in his half century of daydreaming he had been an Edwin Booth and unconscious that he was only John Malone—that he was an Edwin Booth, with a long and great and successful career behind him, in which "one-night stands" sank into insignificance and the memory unused to treasuring such little things could not keep tally of them. He said it with the splendid indifference and serenity of a Napoleon who was making an indolent effort to remember a skirmish in which a couple of soldiers had been killed, but was not finding it really worth while to dig deep after such a fact.

Yesterday I spoke to Volney Streamer about John Malone. I had a purpose in this, though I did not tell Streamer what it was. David Munro was not able to be at that dinner, and so, to get satisfaction, he is providing another, for the 6th of February. David told me the guests he was inviting, and said that if there was anybody that I would like to invite, think it over and send him the name. I did think it over, and I

have written down here on this pad the name of the man I selected—
John Malone—hoping that he would not have to be left out this time,
and knowing he wouldn't be left out unless David should desire it, and
I didn't think David would desire it. However, I took the opportunity
to throw out a feeler or two in talking with Volney Streamer, merely
asking him how John Malone stood with the membership of the
Players' now—and that question was quickly and easily answered—that
everybody liked John Malone and everybody pitied him.

Then he told me John Malone's history. It differed in some points
from the history which Malone had given me, but not in essentials, I
should say. One fact came out which I had not known about—that John
was not a bachelor, but had a married daughter living here somewhere in
New York. Then, as Streamer went on, came this surprise: that he was
a member of Edwin Booth's company when John Malone joined it a
thousand years ago, and that he had been a comrade of John's in the
company all over the Pacific coast and the rest of the states for years
and years. There, you see, an entire stranger drops in here in the most
casual way, and the first thing I know he is an ancient and moss-grown
and mildewed comrade of the man who is for the moment uppermost
in my mind. That is the way things happen when you are doing a diary
and a history combined, and you can't catch these things in any other
way but just that. If you try to remember them, with the intention of
writing them down in the form of history a month or a year hence, why,
when you get to them the juice is all out of them—you can't bring to
mind the details. And moreover, they have lost their quality of surprise
and joy, anyway. That has all wasted and passed away.

Very well. Yesterday Rev. Joe Twichell arrived from Hartford to take
dinner and stay all night and swap some lies, and he sat here by the
bed the rest of the afternoon, and we talked, and I told him all about
John Malone. Twichell came in after breakfast this morning (the 16th)
to chat again, and he brought me this, which he had cut out of the
morning paper:

Veteran Actor Dead

John Malone Was Historian of The Players' Club

John Malone, the historian of the Players' Club and one of the oldest
actors in the country, was stricken with apoplexy yesterday afternoon in

front of Bishop Greer's residence, 7 Gramercy Park, a few doors from the club. Bishop Greer saw him fall, and, with the assistance of his servants, carried Mr. Malone into his house. He was unconscious, and the Bishop telephoned to Police Headquarters.

An ambulance was sent from Bellevue Hospital, and Mr. Malone was taken to the institution by Dr. Hawkes. Later the Players' had him removed to the Post-Graduate Hospital, where he died last night.

Mr. Malone was sixty-five years old, and supported all the notable actors of a past generation. For a long time he was associated with Booth and Barrett. He had appeared on the stage but infrequently of late years, devoting the greater part of his time to magazine work. He lived with a married daughter in West 147th Street, but visited the Players' Club nearly every day. He was on his way to the club when stricken.

So THERE IS ANOTHER SURPRISE, you see. While Twichell and I were talking about John Malone he was passing from this life. His disappointments are ended. At last he is not "left out." It was a long wait, but the best of all fortunes is his at last.

I started to say, a while ago, that when I had seemingly made that discovery of the difference between "news" and "history" thirty-nine years ago, I conceived the idea of a magazine, to be called The Back Number and to contain nothing but ancient news; narratives culled from moldy old newspapers and moldy old books; narratives set down by eye-witnesses at the time that the episodes treated of happened.

ABOUT GENERAL SICKLES

New York, January 16th, continued
Dictated Wednesday, January 17th

With considerable frequency, since then, I have tried to get publishers to make the experiment of such a magazine, but I was never successful. I was never able to convince a publisher that The Back Number would interest the public. Not one of them was able to conceive of the idea of a sane human being finding interest in stale things. I made my latest effort three years ago. Again I failed to convince. But I, myself, am not convinced. I am quite sure that The Back Number would succeed and become a favorite. I am also sure of another thing—that The Back Number would have this advantage over any other magazine that was ever issued, to wit: that the man who read the first paragraph in it would go on and read the magazine entirely through, skipping nothing—whereas there is no magazine in existence which ever contains three articles which can be depended upon to interest the reader. It is necessary to put a dozen articles into a magazine of the day in order to hit six or eight tastes. One man buys the magazine for one of its articles, another is attracted by another, another by a third; but no man buys the magazine because of the whole of its contents. I contend that The Back Number would be bought for the whole of its contents and that each reader would read the whole.

Mr. Paine, you and I will start that magazine, and try the experiment, if you are willing to select the ancient news from old books and newspapers and do the rest of the editorial work. Are you willing?

Mr. Paine. "I should be very willing, when we get time to undertake it."

"Very well, then we will, by and by, make that experiment."

Twichell and I stepped across the street, that night, in the rain, and spent an hour with General Sickles. Sickles is eighty-one years old, now. I had met him only once or twice before, although there has been only the width of Ninth Street between us for a year. He is too old to make visits, and I am too lazy. I remember when he killed Philip Barton Key, son of the author of "The Star-spangled Banner," and I remember the prodigious excitement it made in the country. I think it cannot be far from fifty years ago. My vague recollection of it is that it happened in Washington and that I was there at the time.[1]

I have felt well acquainted with General Sickles for thirty-eight or thirty-nine years, because I have known Twichell that long. Twichell was a chaplain in Sickles's brigade in the Civil War, and he was always fond of talking about the general. Twichell was under Sickles all through the war. Whenever he comes down from Hartford he makes it his duty to go and pay his respects to the general. Sickles is a genial old fellow; a handsome and stately military figure; talks smoothly, in well-constructed English—I may say perfectly constructed English. His talk is full of interest and bristling with points, but as there are no emphases scattered through it anywhere, and as there is no animation in it, it soon becomes oppressive by its monotony and it makes the listener drowsy. Twichell had to step on my foot once or twice. The late Bill Nye once said, "I have been told that Wagner's music is better than it sounds."

---

1. Key was shot by Sickles as a result of a complication which concerned Sickles's wife.

That felicitous description of a something which so many people have tried to describe, and couldn't, does seem to fit the general's manner of speech exactly. His talk is much better than it is. No, that is not the idea—there seems to be a lack there somewhere. Maybe it is another case of the sort just quoted. Maybe Nye would say that "it is better than it sounds." I think that is it. His talk does not sound entertaining, but it is distinctly entertaining.

Sickles lost a leg at Gettysburg, and I remember Twichell's account of that circumstance. He talked about it on one of our long walks, a great many years ago, and, although the details have passed out of my memory, I still carry the picture in my mind as presented by Twichell. The leg was taken off by a cannon ball. Twichell and others carried the general out of the battle, and they placed him on a bed made of boughs, under a tree. There was no surgeon present, and Twichell and Rev. Father O'Hagan, a Catholic priest, made a makeshift tourniquet and stopped the gush of blood—checked it, perhaps is the right term. A newspaper correspondent appeared first. Gen. Sickles considered himself a dying man, and (if Twichell is as truthful a person as the character of his cloth requires him to be) General Sickles put aside everything connected with a future world in order to go out of this one in becoming style. And so he dictated his "last words" to that newspaper correspondent. That was Twichell's idea—I remember it well—that the general, no doubt influenced by the fact that several people's last words have been so badly chosen—whether by accident or intention—that they have outlived all the rest of the man's fame, was moved to do his last words in a form calculated to petrify and preserve them for the future generations. Twichell quoted that speech. I have forgotten what it was, now, but it was well chosen for its purpose.

Now when we sat there in the general's presence, listening to his monotonous talk—it was about himself, and is always about himself, and always seems modest and unexasperating, inoffensive—it seemed to me that he was just the kind of man who would risk his salvation in order to do some "last words" in an attractive way. He murmured and warbled, and warbled, and it was all just as simple and pretty as it could be. And also I will say this: that he never made an ungenerous remark about anybody. He spoke severely of this and that and the other person—officers in the war—but he spoke with dignity and with courtesy. There was no malignity in what he said. He merely pronounced what he evidently regarded as just criticisms upon them.

I noticed then, what I had noticed once before, four or five months ago, that the general valued his lost leg away above the one that is left. I am perfectly sure that if he had to part with either of them he would part with the one that he has got. I have noticed this same thing in several other generals who had lost a portion of themselves in the Civil War. There was General Fairchild of Wisconsin. He lost an arm in one of the great battles. When he was consul-general in Paris and we Clemenses were sojourning there some time or other, and grew to be well acquainted with him and with his family, I know that whenever a proper occasion—an occasion which gave General Fairchild an opportunity to elevate the stump of the lost arm and wag it with effect, occurred—that is what he did. It was easy to forgive him for it, and I did it.

General Noyes was our minister to France at the time. He had lost a leg in the war. He was a pretty vain man, I will say that for him, and anybody could see—certainly I saw—that whenever there was a proper gathering around, Noyes presently seemed to disappear. There wasn't anything left of him but the leg which he didn't have.

Well, General Sickles sat there on the sofa, and talked. It was a curious place. Two rooms of considerable size—parlors opening together with folding-doors—and the floors, the walls, the ceilings cluttered up and overlaid with lion skins, tiger skins, leopard skins, elephant skins; photographs of the general at various times of life—photographs en civil; photographs in uniform; gushing sprays of swords fastened in trophy form against the wall; flags of various kinds stuck here and there and yonder; more animals; more skins; here and there and everywhere more and more skins; skins of wild creatures, always, I believe; beautiful skins. You couldn't walk across that floor anywhere without stumbling over the hard heads of lions and things. You couldn't put out a hand anywhere without laying it upon a velvety, exquisite tiger-skin or leopard skin, and so on—oh, well, all the kinds of skins were there; it was as if a menagerie had undressed in the place. Then there was a most decided and rather unpleasant odor, which proceeded from disinfectants and preservatives and things such as you have to sprinkle on skins in order to discourage the moths—so it was not altogether a pleasant place, on that account. It was a kind of museum, and yet it was not the sort of museum which seemed dignified enough to be the museum of a great soldier—and so famous a soldier. It was the sort of museum which should delight and entertain little boys and girls.

I suppose that that museum reveals a part of the general's character and make. He is sweetly and winningly childlike.

Once, in Hartford, twenty or twenty-five years ago, just as Twichell was coming out of his gate one Sunday morning to walk to his church and preach, a telegram was put into his hand. He read it immediately, and then, in a manner, collapsed. It said, "General Sickles died last night at midnight."

Well, you can see, now, that it wasn't so. But no matter—it was so to Joe at the time. He walked along—walked to the church—but his mind was far away. All his affection and homage and worship of his general had come to the fore. His heart was full of these emotions. He hardly knew where he was. In his pulpit, he stood up and began the service, but with a voice over which he had almost no command. The congregation had never seen him thus moved, before, in his pulpit. They sat there and gazed at him and wondered what was the matter; because he was now reading, in this broken voice and with occasional tears trickling down his face, what to them, seemed a quite unemotional chapter—that one about Moses begat Aaron, and Aaron begat Deuteronomy, and Deuteronomy begat St. Peter, and St. Peter begat Cain, and Cain begat Abel—and he was going along with this, and half crying—his voice continually breaking. The congregation left that church that morning without being able to account for this most extraordinary thing—as it seemed to them. That a man who had been a soldier for more than four years, and who had preached in that pulpit so many, many times on really moving subjects, without even the quiver of a lip, should break all down over the begattings, was a thing which they couldn't understand. But there it is—any one can see how such a mystery as that would arouse the curiosity of those people to the boiling-point.

Twichell has had many adventures. He has more adventures in a year than anybody else has in five. One Saturday night he noticed a bottle on his wife's dressing bureau. He thought the label said "Hair Restorer," and he took it in his room and gave his head a good drenching and sousing with it and carried it back and thought no more about it. Next morning when he got up his head was a bright green! He sent around everywhere and couldn't get a substitute preacher, so he had to go to his church himself and preach—and he did it. He hadn't a sermon in his barrel—as it happened—of any lightsome character, so he had to preach a very grave one—a very serious one—and it made the matter worse. The gravity of the sermon did not harmonize with the gayety of his head, and the people sat all through it with handkerchiefs stuffed in their mouths—any way to try to keep down their joy. And Twichell told me that he was sure he never had seen his congregation—he had never seen the whole body of his congregation—the entire body of his congregation—absorbed in interest in his sermon, from beginning to end, before. Always there had been an aspect of indifference, here and there, or wandering, somewhere; but this time there was nothing of the kind. Those people sat there as if they thought, "Good for this day and train only; we must have all there is of this show, not waste any of it." And he said that when he came down out of the pulpit more people waited to shake him by the hand and tell him what a good sermon it was, than ever before. And it seemed a pity that these people should do these fictions in such a place—right in the church—when it was quite plain they were not interested in the sermon at all; they only wanted to get a near view of his head.

Well, Twichell said—no, Twichell didn't say, I say, that as the days went on and Sunday followed Sunday, the interest in Twichell's hair grew and grew; because it didn't stay green. It took on deeper and deeper shades of green; and then it would change and become reddish, and would go from that to some other color; but it was never a solid color. It was always mottled. And each Sunday it was a little more interesting than it was the Sunday before—and Twichell's head became famous while his hair was undergoing these various and fascinating mottlings. And it was a good thing in several ways, because the business had been languishing a little, and now a lot of people joined the church so that they could have the show, and it was the beginning of a prosperity for that church which has never diminished in all these years. Nothing so fortunate ever happened to Joe as that.

But I have wandered from that tree where General Sickles lay bleeding and arranging his last words. It was three-quarters of an hour before a surgeon could be found, for that was a tremendous battle and surgeons were needed everywhere. When the surgeon arrived it was after nightfall. It was a still and windless July night, and there was a candle burning—I think somebody sat near the general's head and held this candle in his hand. It threw just light enough to make the general's face distinct, and there were several dim figures waiting around about. Into this group, out of the darkness, bursts an aide; springs lightly from his horse; approaches this white-faced expiring general; straightens himself up soldier fashion; salutes; and reports in the most soldierly and matter-of-fact way that he has carried out an order given him by the general, and that the movement of the regiments to the supporting point designated has been accomplished.

The general thanked him courteously. I am sure Sickles must have been always polite. It takes training to enable a person to be properly courteous when he is dying. Many have tried it. I suppose very few have succeeded.

New York, Thursday, January 18, 1906

Senator Tillman of South Carolina has been making a speech—day before yesterday—of frank and intimate criticism of the President—the President of the United States, as he calls him; whereas, so far as my knowledge goes, there has been no such functionary as President of the United States for forty years, perhaps, if we except Cleveland. I do not call to mind any other President of the United States—there may have been one or two—perhaps one or two, who were not always and persistently presidents of the Republican party, but were now and then for a brief interval really Presidents of the United States. Tillman introduces into this speech the matter of the expulsion of Mrs. Morris from the White House, and I think his arraignment of the President was a good and capable piece of work. At any rate, his handling of it suited me very well and tasted very good in my mouth. I was glad that there was somebody to take this matter up, whether from a generous motive or from an ungenerous one, and give it an airing. It was needed. The whole nation, and the entire press, have been sitting by in meek and slavish silence, everybody privately wishing—just as was my own case—that some person with some sense of the proprieties would rise up and denounce this outrage as it ought to be denounced. Tillman makes a point which charms me. I wanted to use it myself, days ago, but I was already arranging a scheme in another matter of public concern which may invite a brick or two in my direction, and one entertainment of this sort at a time is plenty for me. That point was this: that the President is always prodigal of letters and telegrams to Tom, Dick, and Harry, about everything and nothing. He seems never to lack time from his real duties to attend to duties that do not exist. So, at the very time when he should have been throwing off one or two little lines to say to Mrs. Morris and her friends that, being a gentleman, he was hastening to say he was sorry that his assistant secretary had been turning the nation's official mansion into a sailor boarding-house, and that he would admonish Mr. Barnes, and the rest of the reception-room garrison, to deal more gently with the erring in future, and to abstain from any conduct in the White House which would rank as disgraceful in any other respectable dwelling in the land. . .

I don't like Tillman. His second cousin killed an editor, three years ago, without giving that editor a chance to defend himself. I recognize that it is almost always wise, and is often in a manner necessary, to kill an editor, but I think that when a man is a United States Senator he ought to require his second cousin to refrain as long as he can, and then do it in a handsome way, running some personal risk himself. I have not known Tillman to do many things that were greatly to his credit during his political life, but I am glad of the position which he has taken this time. The President has persistently refused to listen to such friends of his as are not insane—men who have tried to persuade him to disavow Mr. Barnes's conduct and express regret for that occurrence. And now Mr. Tillman uses that point which I spoke of a minute ago, and uses it with telling effect. He reminds the Senate that at the very time that the President's dignity would not allow him to send to Mrs. Morris or her friends a kindly and regretful line, he had time enough to send a note of compliment and admiration to a prize-fighter in the far West. If the President had been an unpopular person, that point would have been seized upon early, and much and disastrous notice taken of it. But, as I have suggested before, the nation and the newspapers have maintained a loyal and humiliated silence about it, and have waited prayerfully and hopefully for some reckless person to say the things which were in their hearts, and which they could not bear to utter. Mrs. Morris embarrasses the situation, and extends and keeps alive the discomfort of eighty millions of people, by lingering along near to death, yet neither rallying nor dying; to do either would relieve the tension. For the present, the discomfort must continue. Mr. Tillman certainly has not chloroformed it.

We buried John Malone this morning. His old friends of the Players' Club attended in a body. It was the second time in my life that I had been present at a Catholic funeral. And as I sat in the church my mind went back, by natural process, to that other one, and the contrast strongly interested me. That first one was the funeral of the Empress of Austria, who was assassinated six or eight years ago. There was a great concourse of the ancient nobility of the Austrian Empire; and as that patchwork of old kingdoms and principalities consists of nineteen states and eleven nationalities, and as these nobles came clothed in the costumes which their ancestors were accustomed to wear on state occasions three, four, or five centuries ago, the variety and magnificence of the costumes made a picture which cast far into the shade all the notions of splendor and magnificence which in the course of my life I had accumulated from the opera, the theater, the picture galleries, and from books. Gold, silver, jewels, silks, satins, velvets—they were all there in brilliant and beautiful confusion, and in that sort of perfect harmony which Nature herself observes and is master of, when she paints and groups her flowers and her forests and floods them with sunshine. The military and civic milliners of the Middle Ages knew their trade. Infinite as was the variety of the costumes displayed, there was not an ugly one, not one that was a discordant note in the harmony, or an offense to the eye. When those massed costumes were still, they were transcendently beautiful; when the mass stirred, the slightest movement set the jewels and metals and bright colors afire and swept it with flashing lights which sent a sort of ecstasy of delight through me.

But it was different this morning. This morning the clothes were all alike. They were simple and devoid of color. The Players were clothed as they are always clothed, except that they wore the high silk hat of ceremony. Yet, in its way, John Malone's funeral was as impressive as had been that of the Empress. There was no inequality between John Malone and the Empress except the artificial inequalities which have been invented and established by man's childish vanity. The Empress and John were just equals in the essentials of goodness of heart and a blameless life. Both passed by the onlooker, in their coffins, respected, esteemed, honored; both traveled the same road from the church, bound for the same resting-place—according to Catholic doctrine, Purgatory—to be removed thence to a better land or to remain in Purgatory accordingly as the contributions of their friends, in cash or prayer, shall determine. The priest told us, in an admirably framed speech, about John's destination, and the terms upon which he might continue his journey or must remain in Purgatory. John was poor; his friends are poor. The Empress was rich; her friends are rich. John Malone's prospects are not good, and I lament it.

Perhaps I am in error in saying I have been present at only two Catholic funerals. I think I was present at one in Virginia City, Nevada, in the neighborhood of forty years ago—or perhaps it was down in

Esmeralda, on the borders of California—but if it happened, the memory of it can hardly be said to exist, it is so indistinct. I did attend one or two funerals—maybe a dozen—out there; funerals of desperadoes who had tried to purify society by exterminating other desperadoes—and did accomplish the purification, though not according to the program which they had laid out for this office.

Also, I attended some funerals of persons who had fallen in duels—and maybe it was a duelist whom I helped to ship. But would a duelist be buried by the church? In inviting his own death, wouldn't he be committing suicide, substantially? Wouldn't that rule him out? Well, I don't remember how it was, now, but I think it was a duelist.

New York, Friday, January 19, 1906

About Dueling

In those early days dueling suddenly became a fashion in the new territory of Nevada, and by 1864 everybody was anxious to have a chance in the new sport, mainly for the reason that he was not able to thoroughly respect himself so long as he had not killed or crippled somebody in a duel or been killed or crippled in one himself.

At that time I had been serving as city editor on Mr. Goodman's Virginia City Enterprise for a matter of two years. I was twenty-nine years old. I was ambitious in several ways, but I had entirely escaped that particular fashion. I had had no desire to fight a duel. I had no intention of provoking one. I did not feel respectable, but I got a certain amount of satisfaction out of feeling safe. I was ashamed of myself, the rest of the staff were ashamed of me—but I got along well enough. I had always been accustomed to feeling ashamed of myself, for one thing or another, so there was no novelty for me in the situation. I bore it very well. Plunkett was on the staff. R. M. Daggett was on the staff. These had tried to get into duels, but, for the present, had failed and were waiting. Goodman was the only one of us who had done anything to shed credit upon the paper. The rival paper was the Virginia Union. Its editor for a little while was Fitch, called the "silver-tongued orator of Wisconsin"—that was where he came from. He tuned up his oratory in the editorial columns of the Union, and Mr. Goodman invited him out and modified him with a bullet. I remember the joy of the staff when Goodman's challenge was accepted by Fitch. We ran late that night, and made much of Joe Goodman. He was only twenty-four years old; he lacked the wisdom which a person has at twenty-nine, and he was as glad of being it as I was that I wasn't. He chose Major Graves for his second (that name is not right, but it's close enough, I don't remember the major's name). Graves came over to instruct Joe in the dueling art. He had been a major under Walker, the "gray-eyed man of destiny," and had fought all through that remarkable man's filibustering campaign in Central America. That fact gauges the major. To say that a man was a major under Walker, and came out of that struggle ennobled by Walker's praise, is to say that the major was not merely a brave man, but that he was brave to the very utmost limit of that word. All of Walker's men were like that. I knew the Gillis family intimately. The father made the campaign under Walker, and with him one son. They were in the memorable Plaza fight, and stood it out to the last against overwhelming odds, as did also all of the Walker men. The son was killed at the father's side. The lather received a bullet through the eye. The old man—for he was an old man at the time—wore spectacles, and the bullet and one of the glasses went into his skull, and the bullet remained there. There were some other sons—Steve, George, and Jim, very young chaps—the merest lads—who wanted to be in the Walker expedition, for they had their father's dauntless spirit. But Walker wouldn't have them; he said it was a serious expedition, and no place for children.

The major was a majestic creature, with a most stately and dignified and impressive military bearing, and he was by nature and training courteous, polite, graceful, winning; and he had that quality which I think I have encountered in only one other man—Bob Rowland—that quality which resides in the eye; and when that eye is turned upon an individual or a squad, in warning, that is enough. The man that has that eye doesn't need to go armed; he can move upon an armed desperado and quell him and take him prisoner without saying a single word. I saw Bob Howland do that once—a slender, good-natured, amiable, gentle, kindly little skeleton of a man, with a sweet blue eye that would win your heart when it smiled upon you, or turn cold and freeze it, according to the nature of the occasion.

The major stood Joe up straight; stood Steve Gillis up fifteen paces away; made Joe turn his right side toward Steve, cock his navy six-shooter—that prodigious weapon—and hold it straight down against his leg; told him that that was the correct position for the gun—that the position ordinarily in use at Virginia City (that is to say, the gun straight up in the air, bring it slowly down to your man) was all wrong. At the word "One," you must raise the gun slowly and steadily to the place on the other man's body that you desire to convince. "One, two, three—fire—Stop!" At the word "stop," you may fire—but not earlier. You may give yourself as much time as you please after that word. Then, when you fire, you may advance and go on firing at your leisure and pleasure, if you can get any pleasure out of it. And, in the meantime, the other man, if he has been properly instructed and is alive to his privileges, is advancing on you, and firing—and it is always likely that more or less trouble will result.

Naturally, when Joe's revolver had risen to a level it was pointing at Steve's breast, but the major said: "No, that is not wise. Take all the risks of getting murdered yourself, but don't run any risk of murdering the other man. If you survive a duel you want to survive it in such a way that the memory of it will not linger along with you through the rest of your life, and interfere with your sleep. Aim at your man's leg; not at the knee, not above the knee, for those are dangerous spots. Aim below the knee; cripple him, but leave the rest of him to his mother."

By grace of these truly wise and excellent instructions, Joe tumbled his man down with a bullet through his lower leg, which furnished him a permanent limp. And Joe lost nothing but a lock of hair, which he could spare better then than he could now. For when I saw him here a year ago his crop was gone; he had nothing much left but a fringe, with a dome rising above.

About a year later I got my chance. But I was not hunting for it. Goodman went off to San Francisco for a week's holiday, and left me to be chief editor, I had supposed that that was an easy berth, there being nothing to do but write one editorial per day; but I was disappointed in that superstition. I couldn't find anything to write an article about, the first day. Then it occurred to me that inasmuch as it was the 22d of April, 1864, the next morning would be the three-hundredth anniversary of Shakespeare's birthday—and what better theme could I want than that? I got the Cyclopedia and examined it, and found out who Shakespeare was and what he had done, and I borrowed all that and laid it before a community that couldn't have been better prepared for instruction about Shakespeare than if they had been prepared by art. There wasn't enough of what Shakespeare had done to make an editorial of the necessary length, but I filled it out with what he hadn't done—which in many respects was more important and striking and readable than the handsomest things he had really accomplished. But next day I was in trouble again. There were no more Shakespeares to work up. There was nothing in past history, or in the world's future possibilities, to make an editorial out of suitable to that community; so there was but one theme left. That theme was Mr. Laird, proprietor of the Virginia Union. His editor had gone off to San Francisco, too, and Laird was trying his hand at editing. I woke up Mr. Laird with some courtesies of the kind that were fashionable among newspaper editors in that region, and he came back at me the next day in a most vitriolic way. So we expected a challenge from Mr. Laird, because according to the rules—according to the etiquette of dueling as reconstructed and reorganized and improved by the duelists of that region—whenever you said a thing about another person that he didn't like, it wasn't sufficient for him to talk back in the same, or a more offensive spirit; etiquette required him to send a challenge. So we waited for a challenge—waited all day. It didn't come. And as the day wore along, hour after hour, and no challenge came, the boys grew depressed. They lost heart. But I was cheerful; I felt better and better all the time. They couldn't understand it, but I could understand it. It was my make that enabled me to be cheerful when other people were despondent. So then it became necessary for us to waive etiquette and challenge Mr. Laird. When we reached that decision, they began to cheer up, but I began to lose some of my animation. However, in enterprises of this kind you are in the hands of your friends; there is nothing for you to do but to abide by what they consider to be the best course. Daggett wrote a challenge for me, for Daggett had the language—the right language—the convincing language—and I lacked it. Daggett poured out a stream of unsavory epithets upon Mr. Laird, charged with a vigor and venom of a strength calculated to persuade him; and Steve Gillis, my second, carried the challenge and came back to wait for the return. It didn't come. The boys were exasperated, but I kept my temper. Steve carried another challenge, hotter than the other, and we waited again. Nothing came of it, I began to feel quite comfortable. I began to take an interest in the challenges myself. I had not felt any before; but it seemed to me that I was accumulating a great and valuable reputation at no expense, and my delight in this grew and grew as challenge after challenge was declined, until by midnight I was beginning to think that there was nothing in the world so much to be desired as a chance to fight a duel. So I hurried

Daggett up; made him keep on sending challenge after challenge. Oh, well, I overdid it. I might have suspected that that would happen—Laird was a man you couldn't depend on.

The boys were jubilant beyond expression. They helped me make my will, which was another discomfort—and I already had enough. Then they took me home. I didn't sleep any—didn't want to sleep. I had plenty of things to think about, and less than four hours to do it in—because five o'clock was the hour appointed for the tragedy, and I should have to use up one hour—beginning at four—in practicing with the revolver and finding out which end of it to level at the adversary. At four we went down into a little gorge, about a mile from town, and borrowed a barn door for a mark—borrowed it of a man who was over in California on a visit—and we set the barn door up and stood a fence rail up against the middle of it. The rail was no proper representative of Mr. Laird, for he was longer than a rail and thinner. Nothing would ever fetch him but a line shot, and then, as like as not, he would split the bullet—the worst material for dueling purposes that could be imagined. I began on the rail. I couldn't hit the rail; I couldn't hit the barn door. There was nobody in danger except stragglers around on the flanks of that mark. I was thoroughly discouraged, and I didn't cheer up any when we presently heard pistol shots over in the next little ravine. I knew what that was—that was Laird's gang out practicing him. They would hear my shots, and of course they would come up over the ridge to see what kind of a record I was making—see what their chances were against me. Well, I hadn't any record; and I knew that if Laird came over that ridge and looked at my barn door without a scratch on it, he would be as anxious to fight as I was—or as I had been at midnight, before that disastrous acceptance came.

Now just at this moment a little bird, no bigger than a sparrow, flew along by and lit on a sage-bush about thirty yards away. Steve whipped out his revolver and shot its head off. Oh, he was a marksman—much better than I was. We ran down there to pick up the bird, and just then, sure enough, Mr. Laird and his people came over the ridge, and they joined us. And when Laird's second saw that bird with its head shot off, he lost color, and you could see that he was interested.

He said:

"Who did that?"

Before I could answer, Steve spoke up and said quite calmly, and in a matter-of-fact way, "Clemens did it."

The second said, "Why, that is wonderful! How far off was that bird?"

Steve said, "Oh, not far—about thirty yards."

The second said, "Well, that is astonishing shooting. How often can he do that?"

Steve said, languidly, "Oh, about four times out of five!"

I knew the little rascal was lying, but I didn't say anything. The second said:

"Why, that is wonderful shooting! Why, I supposed he couldn't hit a church!"

He was supposing very sagaciously, but I didn't say anything. Well, they said good morning. The second took Mr. Laird home, a little tottery on his legs, and Laird sent back a note in his own hand declining to fight a duel with me on any terms whatever.

Well, my life was saved—saved by that accident.

I don't know what the bird thought about that interposition of Providence, but I felt very, very comfortable over it—satisfied and content. Now we found out, later, that Laird had hit his mark four times out of six, right along. If the duel had come off, he would have so filled my skin with bullet holes that it wouldn't have held my principles.

By breakfast time the news was all over town that I had sent a challenge and Steve Gillis had carried it. Now that would entitle us to two years apiece in the penitentiary, according to the brand-new law. Governor North sent us no message as coming from himself, but a message came from a close friend of his. He said it would be a good idea for us to leave the territory by the first stage-coach. This would sail next morning at four o'clock—and in the meantime we would be searched for, but not with avidity; and if we were in the territory after that stage-coach left, we would be the first victims of the new law. Judge North was anxious to have some victims for that law, and he would absolutely keep us in the prison the full two years. He wouldn't pardon us out to please anybody.

Well, it seemed to me that our society was no longer desirable in Nevada; so we stayed in our quarters and observed proper caution all day—except that once Steve went over to the hotel to attend to another customer of mine. That was a Mr. Cutler. You see, Laird was not the only person whom I had tried to reform during my occupancy of the editorial chair. I had looked around and selected several other people, and delivered a new zest of life into them through warm criticism and disapproval—so that when I laid clown my editorial pen I had four horse-whippings and two duels owing to me. We didn't care for the horse-whippings; there was no glory in them; they were not worth the trouble of collecting. But honor required that some notice should be taken of that other duel. Mr. Cutler had come up from Carson City, and sent a man over with a challenge from the hotel. Steve went over to pacify him. Steve weighed only ninety-five pounds, but it was well known throughout the territory that with his fists he could whip anybody that walked on two legs, let his weight and science be what they might. Steve was a Gillis, and when a Gillis confronted a man and had a proposition to make the proposition always contained business. When Cutler found that Steve was my second he cooled down; he became calm and rational, and was ready to listen. Steve gave him fifteen minutes to get out of the hotel, and half an hour to get out of town, or there would be results. So that duel went off successfully, because Mr. Cutler went off toward Carson, a convinced and reformed man.

I have never had anything to do with duels since. I thoroughly disapprove of duels. I consider them unwise, and I know they are dangerous. Still, I have always taken a great interest in other people's duels. One always feel an abiding interest in any heroic thing which has entered into his own experience.

In 1878, fourteen years after my unmaterialized duel, Messieurs Fortu and Gambetta fought a duel which made heroes of both of them in France, and made them ridiculous throughout the rest of the world. I was living in Munich that fall and winter, and I was so interested in that duel that I wrote a long account of it, and it is in one of my books, somewhere[1]—an account which had some inaccuracies in it, but as an exhibition of the spirit of that duel, I think it was correct and trustworthy.

END OF VOLUME ONE

---

1. A Tramp Abroad.

VOLUME 2

New York, Tuesday, January 23, 1906
About a meeting at Carnegie Hall, in the interest of Booker Washington's Tuskegee Institute.—An unpleasant political incident which happened to Mr. Twichell.

There was a great mass meeting at Carnegie Hall last night, in the interest of Booker Washington's Tuskegee Educational Institute in the South, and the interest which New York people feel in that Institute was quite manifest, in the fact that although it was not pleasant weather there were three thousand people inside the Hall and two thousand outside, who were trying to get in when the performances were ready to begin at eight o'clock.[1] Mr. Choate presided, and was received with a grand welcome when he marched in upon the stage. He is fresh from his long stay in England, as our Ambassador, where he won the English people by the gifts of his heart, and won the royalties and the Government by his able diplomatic service, and captured the whole nation with his fine and finished oratory. For thirty-five years Choate has been the handsomest man in America. Last night he seemed to me to be just as handsome as he was thirty-five years ago, when I first knew him. And when I used to see him in England, five or six years ago, I thought him the handsomest man in that country.

It was at a Fourth of July reception in Mr. Choate's house in London that I first met Booker Washington. I have met him a number of times since, and he always impresses me pleasantly. Last night he was a mulatto. I didn't notice it until he turned, while he was speaking, and said something to me. It was a great surprise to me to see that he was a mulatto and had blue eyes. How unobservant a dull person can be! Always, before, he was black, to me, and I had never noticed whether he had eyes at all, or not. He has accomplished a wonderful work in this quarter of a century. When he finished his education at the Hampton Colored School twenty-five years ago he was unknown and hadn't a penny, nor a friend outside his immediate acquaintanceship. But by the persuasions of his carriage and address and the sincerity and honesty that look out of his eyes he has been enabled to gather money by the hatful here in the North, and with it he has built up and firmly established his great school for the colored people of the two sexes in

---

1. They were largely attracted by the announcement that Mark Twain was to be present and would speak.—A. B. P.

the South. In that school the students are not merely furnished a book education, but are taught thirty-seven useful trades. Booker Washington has scraped together many hundreds of thousands of dollars, in the twenty-five years, and with this money he has taught and sent forth into Southern fields among the colored people six thousand trained colored men and women; and his student roll now numbers fifteen hundred names. The Institute's property is worth a million and a half, and the establishment is in a flourishing condition. A most remarkable man is Booker Washington. And he is a fervent and effective speaker on the platform.

When the affair was over and the people began to climb up on the stage and pass along and shake hands, the usual thing happened. It always happens. I shake hands with people who used to know my mother intimately in Arkansas, in New Jersey, in California, in Jericho—and I have to seem so glad and so happy to meet these persons who knew in this intimate way one who was so near and dear to me. And this is the kind of thing that gradually turns a person into a polite liar and deceiver, for my mother was never in any of those places.

One pretty creature was glad to see me again, and remembered being at my house in Hartford—I don't know when, a great many years ago, it was. Now she was mistaking herself for somebody else. It couldn't have happened to her. But I was very cordial, because she was very pretty. We might have had a good long chat except for the others that I had to talk with and work up reminiscences that belonged in somebody else's experiences, not theirs or mine.

There was one young fellow, brisk, but not bright, overpoweringly pleasant and cordial, in his way. He said his mother used to teach school in Elmira, New York, where he was born and bred and where the family continued to reside, and that she would be very glad to know that he had met me and shaken hands, for he said: "She is always talking about you. She holds you in high esteem, although, as she says, she has to confess that of all the boys that ever she had in her school, you were the most troublesome."

"Well," I said, "those were my last school days, and through long practice in being troublesome, I had reached the summit by that time, because I was more than thirty-three years old."

It didn't affect him in the least. I don't think he even heard what I said, he was so eager to tell me all about it, and I said to him once more, so as to spare him, and me, that I was never in a schoolhouse in Elmira,

New York, even on a visit, and that his mother must be mistaking me for some of the Langdons, the family into which I married. No matter, he didn't hear it—kept on his talk with animation and delight, and has gone to tell his mother, I don't know what. He didn't get anything out of me to tell her, for he never heard anything I said.

These episodes used to vex me, years and years ago. But they don't vex me now. I am older. If a person thinks that he has known me at some time or other, all I require of him is that he shall consider it a distinction to have known me; and then, as a rule, I am perfectly willing to remember all about it and add some things that he has forgotten.

Twichell came down from Hartford to be present at that meeting, and we chatted and smoked after we got back home. And reference was made again to that disastrous Boston speech which I made at Whittier's seventieth-birthday dinner; and Joe asked me if I was still minded to submit that speech to that club in Washington, day after to-morrow, where Colonel Harvey and I are to be a couple of the four guests. And I said, "No," I had given that up—which was true. Because I have examined that speech a couple of times since, and have changed my notion about it—changed it entirely. I find it gross, coarse—well, I needn't go on with particulars. I didn't like any part of it, from the beginning to the end. I found it always offensive and detestable. How do I account for this change of view? I don't know. I can't account for it. I am the person concerned. If I could put myself outside of myself and examine it from the point of view of a person not personally concerned in it, then no doubt I could analyze it and explain to my satisfaction the change which has taken place. As it is, I am merely moved by instinct. My instinct said, formerly, that it was an innocent speech, and funny. The same instinct, sitting cold and judicial, as a court of last resort, has reversed that verdict. I expect this latest verdict to remain.

Twichell's congregation—the only congregation he has ever had since he entered the ministry—celebrated the fortieth anniversary of his accession to that pulpit, a couple of weeks ago. Joe entered the army as chaplain in the very beginning of the Civil War. He was a young chap, and had just been graduated from Yale and the Yale Theological Seminary. He made all the campaigns of the Army of the Potomac. When he was mustered out, that congregation I am speaking of called him, and he has served them ever since, and always to their satisfaction—except once.

I have found among my old MSS. one which I perceive to be about twenty-two years old. It has a heading and looks as if I had meant it to serve as a magazine article. I can clearly see, now, why I didn't print it. It is full of indications that its inspiration was what happened to Twichell about that time, and which produced a situation for him which he will not forget until he is dead, if he even forgets it then. I think I can see, all through this artful article, that I was trying to hint at Twichell, and the episode of that preacher whom I met on the street, and hint at various things that were exasperating me. And now that I read that old article, I perceive that I probably saw that my art was not ingenious enough— that I hadn't covered Twichell up, and hadn't covered up the episode that I was hinting at—that anybody in Hartford could read everything between the lines that I was trying to conceal.

I will insert this venerable article in this place, and then take up that episode in Joe's history and tell about it.

The Character of Man

Concerning Man—he is too large a subject to be treated as a whole; so I will merely discuss a detail or two of him at this time. I desire to contemplate him from this point of view—this premise: that he was not made for any useful purpose, for the reason that he hasn't served any; that he was most likely not even made intentionally; and that his working himself up out of the oyster bed to his present position was probably matter of surprise and regret to the Creator. . . For his history, in all climes, all ages and all circumstances, furnishes oceans and continents of proof that of all the creatures that were made he is the most detestable. Of the entire brood he is the only one—the solitary one—that possesses malice.

That is the basest of all instincts, passions, vices—the most hateful. That one thing puts him below the rats, the grubs, the trichinae. He is the only creature that inflicts pain for sport, knowing it to be pain. But if the cat knows she is inflicting pain when she plays with the frightened mouse, then we must make an exception here; we must grant that in one detail man is the moral peer of the cat. All creatures kill—there seems to be no exception; but of the whole list, man is the only one that kills for fun; he is the only one that kills in malice, the only one that kills for revenge. Also—in all the list he is the only creature that has a nasty mind.

Shall he be extolled for his noble qualities, for his gentleness, his sweetness, his amiability, his lovingness, his courage, his devotion, his patience, his fortitude, his prudence, the various charms and graces of his spirit? The other animals share all these with him, yet are free from the blacknesses and rottennesses of his character.

. . . There are certain sweet-smelling sugar-coated lies current in the world which all politic men have apparently tacitly conspired together to support and perpetuate. One of these is, that there is such a thing in the world as independence: independence of thought, independence of opinion, independence of action. Another is, that the world loves to see independence—admires it, applauds it. Another is, that there is such a thing in the world as toleration—in religion, in politics, and such matters; and with it trains that already mentioned auxiliary lie that toleration is admired and applauded. Out of these trunk-lies spring many branch ones: to wit, the lie that not all men are slaves: the lie that men are glad when other men succeed; glad when they prosper; glad to see them reach lofty heights; sorry to see them fall again. And yet other branch lies: to wit, that there is heroism in man; that he is not mainly made up of malice and treachery; that he is sometimes not a coward; that there is something about him that ought to be perpetuated—in heaven, or hell, or somewhere. And these other branch lies, to wit: that conscience, man's moral medicine chest, is not only created by the Creator, but is put into man ready charged with the right and only true and authentic correctives of conduct—and the duplicate chest, with the self-same correctives, unchanged, unmodified, distributed to all nations and all epochs. And yet one other branch lie: to wit, that I am I, and you are you; that we are units, individuals, and have natures of our own, instead of being the tail end of a tapeworm eternity of ancestors extending in linked procession back and back and back—to our source in the monkeys, with this so-called individuality of ours a decayed and rancid mush of inherited instincts and teachings derived, atom by atom, stench by stench, from the entire line of that sorry column, and not so much new and original matter in it as you could balance on a needle point and examine under a microscope. This makes well-nigh fantastic the suggestion that there can be such a thing as a personal, original, and responsible nature in a man, separable from that in him which is not original, and findable in such quantity as to enable the observer to say, This is a man, not a procession.

. . . Consider the first-mentioned lie: that there is such a thing in the world as independence; that it exists in individuals; that it exists in bodies of men. Surely if anything is proven, by whole oceans and continents of evidence, it is that the quality of independence was almost wholly left out of the human race. The scattering exceptions to the rule only emphasize it, light it up, make it glare. The whole population of New England meekly took their turns, for years, in standing up in the railway trains, without so much as a complaint above their breath, till at last these uncounted millions were able to produce exactly one single independent man, who stood to his rights and made the railroad give him a seat. Statistics and the law of probabilities warrant the assumption that it will take New England forty years to breed his fellow. There is a law, with a penalty attached, forbidding trains to occupy the Asylum Street crossing more than five minutes at a time. For years people and carriages used to wait there nightly as much as twenty minutes on a stretch while New England trains monopolized that crossing. I used to hear men use vigorous language about that insolent wrong—but they waited, just the same.

We are discreet sheep; we wait to see how the drove is going, and then go with the drove. We have two opinions: one private, which we are afraid to express; and another one—the one we use—which we force ourselves to wear to please Mrs. Grundy, until habit makes us comfortable in it, and the custom of defending it presently makes us love it, adore it, and forget how pitifully we came by it. Look at it in politics. Look at the candidates whom we loathe, one year, and are afraid to vote against, the next; whom we cover with unimaginable filth, one year, and fall down on the public platform and worship, the next—and keep on doing it until the habitual shutting of our eyes to last year's evidences brings us presently to a sincere and stupid belief in this year's. Look at the tyranny of party—at what is called party allegiance, party loyalty—a snare invented by designing men for selfish purposes—and which turns voters into chattels, slaves, rabbits, and all the while their masters, and they themselves are shouting rubbish about liberty, independence, freedom of opinion, freedom of speech, honestly unconscious of the fantastic contradiction; and forgetting or ignoring that their fathers and the churches shouted the same blasphemies a generation earlier when they were closing their doors against the hunted slave, beating his handful of humane defenders with Bible texts and billies, and pocketing the insults and licking the shoes of his Southern master.

If we would learn what the human race really is at bottom, we need only observe it in election times. A Hartford clergyman met me in the street and spoke of a new nominee—denounced the nomination, in strong, earnest words—words that were refreshing for their independence, their manliness.[1] He said, "I ought to be proud, perhaps, for this nominee is a relative of mine; on the contrary, I am humiliated and disgusted, for I know him intimately—familiarly—and I know that he is an unscrupulous scoundrel, and always has been." You should have seen this clergyman preside at a political meeting forty days later, and urge, and plead, and gush—and you should have heard him paint the character of this same nominee. You would have supposed he was describing the Cid, and Greatheart, and Sir Galahad, and Bayard the Spotless all rolled into one. Was he sincere? Yes—by that time; and therein lies the pathos of it all, the hopelessness of it all. It shows at what trivial cost of effort a man can teach himself to lie, and learn to believe it, when he perceives, by the general drift, that that is the popular thing to do. Does he believe his lie yet? Oh, probably not; he has no further use for it. It was but a passing incident; he spared to it the moment that was its due, then hastened back to the serious business of his life.

And what a paltry poor lie is that one which teaches that independence of action and opinion is prized in men, admired, honored, rewarded. When a man leaves a political party, he is treated as if the party owned him—as if he were its bond slave, as most party men plainly are—and had stolen himself, gone off with what was not his own. And he is traduced, derided, despised, held up to public obloquy and loathing. His character is remorselessly assassinated; no means, however vile, are spared to injure his property and his business.

The preacher who casts a vote for conscience' sake runs the risk of starving. And is rightly served, for he has been teaching a falsity—that men respect and honor independence of thought and action.

Mr. Beecher may be charged with a crime, and his whole following will rise as one man, and stand by him to the bitter end; but who so poor to be his friend when he is charged with casting a vote for conscience' sake? Take the editor so charged—take—take anybody.

---

1. Jan, 11, '06.—I can't remember his name. It began with K, I think. He was one of the American revisers of the New Testament, and was nearly as great a scholar as Hammond Trumbull.

All the talk about tolerance, in anything or anywhere, is plainly a gentle lie. It does not exist. It is in no man's heart; but it unconsciously, and by moss-grown inherited habit, drivels and slobbers from all men's lips. Intolerance is everything for oneself, and nothing for the other person. The mainspring of man's nature is just that—selfishness. Let us skip the other lies, for brevity's sake. To consider them would prove nothing, except that man is what he is—loving toward his own, lovable to his own—his family, his friends—and otherwise the buzzing, busy, trivial enemy of his race—who tarries his little day, does his little dirt, commends himself to God, and then goes out into the darkness, to return no more, and send no messages back—selfish even in death.

New York, Wednesday, January 24, 1906
Tells of the defeat of Mr. Blaine for the Presidency, and how Mr. Clemens's, Mr. Twichell's, and Mr. Goodwin's votes were cast for Cleveland.

It is plain, I think, that this old article was written about twenty-two years ago, and that it followed by about three or four months the defeat of James G. Blaine for the Presidency and the election of Grover Cleveland, the Democratic candidate—a temporary relief from a Republican-party domination which had lasted a generation. I had been accustomed to vote for Republicans more frequently than for Democrats, but I was never a Republican and never a Democrat. In the community, I was regarded as a Republican, but I had never so regarded myself. As early as 1865 or '66 I had had this curious experience: that whereas up to that time I had considered myself a Republican, I was converted to a no-party independence by the wisdom of a rabid Republican. This was a man who was afterward a United States Senator, and upon whose character rests no blemish that I know of, except that he was the father of the William R. Hearst of to-day, and therefore grandfather of Yellow Journalism—that calamity of calamities.

Hearst was a Missourian; I was a Missourian. He was a long, lean, practical, common-sense, uneducated man of fifty or thereabouts. I was shorter and better informed—at least I thought so. One day, in the Lick House in San Francisco, he said:

"I am a Republican; I expect to remain a Republican always. It is my purpose, and I am not a changeable person. But look at the condition of things. The Republican party goes right along, from year to year,

MARK TWAIN

scoring triumph after triumph, until it has come to think that the political power of the United States is its property and that it is a sort of insolence for any other party to aspire to any part of that power. Nothing can be worse for a country than this. To lodge all power in one party and keep it there is to insure bad government and the sure and gradual deterioration of the public morals. The parties ought to be so nearly equal in strength as to make it necessary for the leaders on both sides to choose the very best men they can find. Democratic fathers ought to divide up their sons between the two parties if they can, and do their best in this way to equalize the powers. I have only one son. He is a little boy, but I am already instructing him, persuading him, preparing him, to vote against me when he comes of age, let me be on whichever side I may. He is already a good Democrat, and I want him to remain a good Democrat—until I become a Democrat myself. Then I shall shift him to the other party, if I can."

It seemed to me that this unlettered man was at least a wise one. And I have never voted a straight ticket from that day to this. I have never belonged to any party from that day to this. I have never belonged to any church from that day to this. I have remained absolutely free in those matters. And in this independence I have found a spiritual comfort and a peace of mind quite above price.

When Blaine came to be talked of by the Republican leaders as their probable candidate for the Presidency, the Republicans of Hartford were very sorry, and they thought they foresaw his defeat, in case he should be nominated. But they stood in no great fear of his nomination. The convention met in Chicago and the balloting began. In my house we were playing billiards. Sam Dunham was present; also F. G. Whitmore, Henry C. Robinson, Charles E. Perkins, and Edward M. Bunce. We took turns in the game, and, meanwhile, discussed the political situation. George, the colored butler, was down in the kitchen on guard at the telephone. As fast as a ballot was received at the political headquarters downtown, it was telephoned out to the house, and George reported it to us through the speaking-tube. Nobody present was seriously expecting the nomination of Mr. Blaine. All these men were Republicans, but they had no affection for Blaine. For two years the Hartford Courant had been holding Blaine up to scorn and contumely. It had been denouncing him daily. It had been mercilessly criticizing his political conduct and backing up the criticisms with the deadly facts. Up to that time the Courant had been a paper which could be depended on to speak its sincere mind about the prominent men of both parties, and its judgments could be depended upon as being well and candidly considered, and sound. It had been my custom to pin my faith to the Courant and accept its verdicts at par.

The billiard game and the discussion went on and on, and by and by, about mid-afternoon, George furnished us a paralyzing surprise through the speaking-tube. Mr. Blaine was the nominee! The butts of the billiard cues came down on the floor with a bump, and for a while the players were dumb. They could think of nothing to say. Then Henry Robinson broke the silence. He said, sorrowfully, that it was hard luck to have to vote for that man. I said:

"But we don't have to vote for him."

Robinson said, "Do you mean to say that you are not going to vote for him?"

"Yes," I said, "that is what I mean to say. I am not going to vote for him."

The others began to find their voices. They sang the same note. They said that when a party's representatives choose a man, that ends it. If they choose unwisely it is a misfortune, but no loyal member of the party has any right to withhold his vote. He has a plain duty before him and he can't shirk it. He must vote for that nominee.

I said that no party held the privilege of dictating to me how I should vote. That if party loyalty was a form of patriotism, I was no patriot, and that I didn't think I was much of a patriot, anyway, for oftener than otherwise what the general body of Americans regarded as the patriotic course was not in accordance with my views; that if there was any valuable difference between being an American and a monarchist it lay in the theory that the American could decide for himself what is patriotic and what isn't; whereas the king could dictate the monarchist's patriotism for him—a decision which was final and must be accepted by the victim; that in my belief I was the only person in the sixty millions—with Congress and the Administration back of the sixty millions—who was privileged to construct my patriotism for me.

They said, "Suppose the country is entering upon a war—where do you stand then? Do you arrogate to yourself the privilege of going your own way in the matter, in the face of the nation?"

"Yes," I said, "that is my position. If I thought it an unrighteous war I would say so. If I were invited to shoulder a musket in that cause and march under that flag, I should decline. I would not voluntarily march under this country's flag, or any other, when it was my private judgment that the country was in the wrong. If the country obliged me to shoulder the musket, I could not help myself, but I would never volunteer. To volunteer would be the act of a traitor to myself, and consequently traitor to my country. If I refused to volunteer, I should be called a traitor, I am well aware of that—but that would not make me a traitor. The unanimous vote of the sixty millions could not make me a traitor. I should still be a patriot, and, in my opinion, the only one in the whole country."

There was a good deal of talk, but I made no converts. They were all candid enough to say that they did not want to vote for Mr. Blaine, but they all said they would do it, nevertheless. Then Henry Robinson said:

"It is a good while yet before election. There is time for you to come around, and you will come around. The influences about you will be too strong for you. On election day you will vote for Blaine."

I said I should not go to the polls at all.

The Courant had an uncomfortable time thence until midnight. General Hawley, the editor-in-chief (and he was also commander-in-chief of the paper), was at his post in Congress, and the telegraphing to and fro between the Courant and him went on diligently until midnight. For two years the Courant had been making a "tar baby" of Mr. Blaine, and adding tar every day—and now it was called upon to praise him, hurrah for him, and urge its well-instructed clientele to elevate the "tar baby" to the Chief Magistracy of the nation. It was a difficult position and it took the Courant people and General Hawley nine hours to swallow the bitter pill. But at last General Hawley reached a decision and at midnight the pill was swallowed. Within a fortnight the Courant had acquired some facility in praising where it had so long censured; within another month the change in its character was become complete—and to this day it has never recovered its virtue entirely, though under Charles Hopkins Clark's editorship it has gotten back 90 per cent of it, by my estimate.

Charles Dudley Warner was the active editor of the time. He could not stomach the new conditions. He found himself unable to turn his pen in the other direction and make it proceed backward, therefore he decided to retire his pen altogether. He withdrew from the editorship, resigned his salary, lived thenceforth upon his income as a part proprietor of the paper and upon the proceeds of magazine work and lecturing, and kept his vote in his pocket on election day.

The conversation with the learned American member of the board of scholars which revised the New Testament did occur as I have outlined it in that old article. He was vehement in his denunciation of Blaine, his relative, and said he should never vote for him. But he was so used to revising New Testaments that it took him only a few days to revise this one. I had hardly finished with him when I came across James G. Batterson. Batterson was president of the great Travelers' Insurance Company. He was a fine man, a strong man, and a valuable citizen. He was fully as vehement as that clergyman had been in his denunciations of Blaine—but inside of two weeks he was presiding at a great Republican ratification meeting; and to hear him talk about Blaine and his perfections, a stranger would have supposed that the Republican party had had the good fortune to secure an archangel as its nominee.

Time went on. Election day was close at hand. Late one frosty night, Twichell, the Rev. Francis Goodwin, and I were tramping homeward through the deserted streets in the face of a wintry gale, after a séance of our Monday Evening Club, and after a supper-table debate over the political situation, in which the fact had come out—to the astonishment and indignation of everybody, the ladies included—that three traitors were present. That Goodwin, Twichell, and I were going to keep our votes in our pockets instead of casting them for the archangel. Along in that homeward tramp, somewhere, Goodwin had a happy idea, and brought it out. He said:

"Why are we keeping back these three votes from Blaine? Plainly the answer is, to do what we can to defeat Blaine. Very well, then, these are three votes against Blaine. The common-sense procedure would be to cast six votes against him by turning in our three votes for Cleveland."

Even Twichell and I could see that there was sense in that, and we said:

"That is a very good thing to do and we'll do it."

On election day we went to the polls and consummated our hellish design. At that time the voting was public. Any spectator could see how a man was voting—and straightway this crime was known to the whole community. This double crime—in the eyes of the community. To withhold a vote from Blaine was bad enough, but to add to that iniquity by actually voting for the Democratic candidate was criminal

MARK TWAIN

to a degree for which there was no adequate language discoverable in the dictionary.

From that day forth, for a good while to come, Twichell's life was a good deal of a burden to him. To use a common expression, his congregation "soured" on him and he found small pleasure in the exercise of his clerical office—unless, perhaps, he got some healing for his hurts, now and then, through the privilege of burying some of those people of his. It would have been a benevolence to bury the whole of them, I think, and a profit to the community. But if that was Twichell's feeling about it, he was too charitable in his nature and too kindly to expose it. He never said it to me, and I think that if he would have said it to anyone, I should have been the one.

Twichell had most seriously damaged himself with his congregation. He had a young family to support. It was a large family already, and it was growing. It was becoming a heavier and heavier burden every year—but his salary remained always the same. It became less and less competent to keep up with the domestic drain upon it, and if there had ever been any prospect of increasing this salary, that prospect was gone now. It was not much of a salary. It was four thousand dollars. He had not asked for more, and it had not occurred to the congregation to offer it. Therefore his vote for Cleveland was a distinct disaster to him. That exercise of his ostensible great American privilege of being free and independent in his political opinions and actions proved a heavy calamity. But the Rev. Francis Goodwin continued to be respected as before—that is, publicly; privately he was damned. But publicly he had suffered no harm. Perhaps it was because the public approval was not a necessity in his case. His father was worth seven millions, and was old. The Rev. Francis was in the line of promotion and would soon inherit.

As far as I was myself concerned, I did not need to worry. I did not draw my living from Hartford. It was quite sufficient for my needs. Hartford's opinion of me could not affect it, and besides it had long been known among my friends that I had never voted a straight ticket, and was therefore so accustomed to crime that it was unlikely that disapproval of my conduct could reform me—and maybe I wasn't worth the trouble, anyway.

By and by, about a couple of months later, New-Year's Eve arrived, and with it the annual meeting of Joe's congregation and the annual sale of the pews.

New York, Thursday, February 1, 1906
Subject of January 24th continued.
—Mr. Twichell's unpopular vote.

Joe was not quite present. It was not etiquette for him to be within hearing of the business talks concerning the church's affairs. He remained in the seclusion of the church parlor, ready to be consulted if that should be necessary. The congregation was present in full force; every seat was occupied. The moment the house was called to order, a member sprang to his feet and moved that the connection between Twichell and the church be dissolved. The motion was promptly seconded. Here, and there, and yonder, all over the house, there were calls of, "Question! Question!" But Mr. Hubbard, a middle-aged man, a wise and calm and collected man, business manager and part owner of the Courant, rose in his place and proposed to discuss the motion before rushing it to a vote. The substance of his remarks was this (which I must put in my own language, of course, as I was not there):

"Mr. Twichell was the first pastor you have ever had. You have never wanted another until two months ago. You have had no fault to find with his ministrations as your pastor, but he has suddenly become unfit to continue them because he is unorthodox in his politics, according to your views. Very well, he was fit; he has become unfit. He was valuable; his value has passed away, apparently—but only apparently. His highest value remains—if I know this congregation. When he assumed this pastorate this region was an outlying district, thinly inhabited, its real estate worth next to nothing. Mr. Twichell's personality was a magnet which immediately began to draw population in this direction. It has continued to draw it from that day to this. As a result, your real estate, almost valueless in the beginning, ranges now at very high prices. Reflect before you vote upon this resolution. The church in West Hartford is waiting upon this vote with deep solicitude. That congregation's real estate stands at a low figure. What they are anxious to have now above everything else under God, is a price-raiser. Dismiss Mr. Twichell tonight, and they will hire him to-morrow. Prices there will go up; prices here will go down. That is all. I move the vote."

Twichell was not dismissed. That was twenty-two years ago. It was Twichell's first pulpit after his consecration to his vocation. He occupies it yet, and has never had another. The fortieth anniversary of his accession to it was celebrated by that congregation and its descendants a couple of weeks ago, and there was great enthusiasm. Twichell has never made any political mistakes since. His persistency in voting right has been an exasperation to me these many years and has been the cause and inspiration of more than one vicious letter from me to him. But the viciousness was all a pretense. I have never found any real fault with him for voting his infernal Republican ticket, for the reason that, situated as he was, with a large family to support, his first duty was not to his political conscience, but to his family conscience. A sacrifice had to be made; a duty had to be performed. His very first duty was to his family, not to his political conscience. He sacrificed his political independence, and saved his family by it. In the circumstances, this was the highest loyalty, and the best. If he had been a Henry Ward Beecher it would not have been his privilege to sacrifice his political conscience, because in case of dismissal a thousand pulpits would have been open to him, and his family's bread secure. In Twichell's case, there would have been some risk—in fact, a good deal of risk. That he, or any other expert, could have raised the prices of real estate in West Hartford is, to my mind, exceedingly doubtful. I think Mr. Hubbard worked his imagination to the straining point when he got up that scare that night. I believe it was safest for Twichell to remain where he was if he could. He saved his family, and that was his first duty, in my opinion.

In this country there are perhaps eighty thousand preachers. Not more than twenty of them are politically independent—the rest cannot be politically independent. They must vote the ticket of their congregations. They do it, and are justified. They themselves are mainly the reason why they have no political independence, for they do not preach political independence from their pulpits. They have their large share in the fact that the people of this nation have no political independence.

New York, February 1, 1906

To-morrow will be the thirty-sixth anniversary of our marriage. My wife passed from this life one year and eight months ago, in Florence, Italy, after an unbroken illness of twenty-two months' duration.

I saw her first in the form of an ivory miniature in her brother Charley's stateroom in the steamer Quaker City in the Bay of Smyrna, in the summer of 1867, when she was in her twenty-second year. I saw her in the flesh for the first time in New York in the following December. She was slender and beautiful and girlish—and she was both girl and woman. She remained both girl and woman to the last day of her life. Under a grave and gentle exterior burned inextinguishable fires of sympathy, energy, devotion, enthusiasm, and absolutely limitless affection. She was always frail in body, and she lived upon her spirit, whose hopefulness and courage were indestructible. Perfect truth, perfect honesty, perfect candor, were qualities of her character which were born with her. Her judgments of people and things were sure and accurate. Her intuitions almost never deceived her. In her judgments of the characters and acts of both friends and strangers there was always room for charity, and this charity never failed. I have compared and contrasted her with hundreds of persons, and my conviction remains that hers was the most perfect character I have ever met. And I may add that she was the most winningly dignified person I have ever known. Her character and disposition were of the sort that not only invite worship, but command it. No servant ever left her service who deserved to remain in it. And as she could choose with a glance of her eye, the servants she selected did in almost all cases deserve to remain, and they did remain. She was always cheerful; and she was always able to communicate her cheerfulness to others. During the nine years that we spent in poverty and debt she was always able to reason me out of my despairs and find a bright side to the clouds and make me see it. In all that time I never knew her to utter a word of regret concerning our altered circumstances, nor did I ever know her children to do the like. For she had taught them, and they drew their fortitude from her. The love which she bestowed upon those whom she loved took the form of worship, and in that form it was returned—returned by relatives, friends, and the servants of her household. It was a strange combination which wrought into one individual, so to speak by marriage—her disposition and character and mine. She poured out her prodigal affections in kisses and caresses, and in a vocabulary of endearments whose profusion was always an astonishment to me. I was born reserved as to endearments of speech, and caresses, and hers broke upon me as the summer waves break upon Gibraltar. I was reared in that atmosphere of reserve. As I have already said, I never knew a member of my father's family to kiss another member of it except once, and that at a deathbed. And our village was not a kissing community. The kissing and caressing ended with courtship—along with the deadly piano-playing of that day.

She had the heart-free laugh of a girl. It came seldom, but when it broke upon the ear it was as inspiring as music. I heard it for the last time when she had been occupying her sick bed for more than a year, and I made a written note of it at the time—a note not to be repeated.

To-morrow will be the thirty-sixth anniversary. We were married in her father's house in Elmira, New York, and went next day, by special train, to Buffalo, along with the whole Langdon family, and with the Beechers and the Twichells, who had solemnized the marriage. We were to live in Buffalo, where I was to be one of the editors of the Buffalo Express and a part owner of the paper. I knew nothing about Buffalo, but I had made my household arrangements there through a friend, by letter. I had instructed him to find a boarding-house of as respectable a character as my light salary as editor would command. We were received at about nine o'clock at the station in Buffalo and were put into several sleighs and driven all over America, as it seemed to me—for apparently we turned all the corners in the town and followed all the streets there were—I scolding freely and characterizing that friend of mine in very uncomplimentary ways for securing a boarding-house that apparently had no definite locality. But there was a conspiracy—and my bride knew of it, but I was in ignorance. Her father, Jervis Langdon, had bought and furnished a new house for us in the fashionable street, Delaware Avenue, and had laid in a cook and housemaids and a brisk and electric young coachman, an Irishman, Patrick McAleer—and we were being driven all over that city in order that one sleighful of these people could have time to go to the house and see that the gas was lighted all over it, and a hot supper prepared for the crowd. We arrived at last, and when I entered that fairy place my indignation reached high-water mark, and without any reserve I delivered my opinion to that friend of mine for being so stupid as to put us into a boarding-house whose terms would be far out of my reach. Then Mr. Langdon brought forward a very pretty box and opened it and took from it a deed of the house. So the comedy ended very pleasantly and we sat down to supper.

The company departed about midnight, and left us alone in our new quarters. Then Ellen, the cook, came in to get orders for the morning's marketing—and neither of us knew whether beefsteak was sold by the barrel or by the yard. We exposed our ignorance, and Ellen was full of Irish delight over it. Patrick McAleer, that brisk young Irishman, came in to get his orders for next day—and that was our first glimpse of him.

Thirty-six years have gone by. And this letter from Twichell comes this morning, from Hartford:

HARTFORD, January 31

DEAR MARK:

I am sorry to say that the news about Patrick is very bad. I saw him Monday. He looked pretty well and was in cheerful spirits. He told me that he was fast recovering from an operation performed on him last week Wednesday, and would soon be out again. But a nurse who followed me from the room when I left told me that the poor fellow was deceived. The operation had simply disclosed the fact that nothing could be done for him.

Yesterday I asked the surgeon (Johnson, living opposite us) if that were so. He said "Yes," that the trouble was cancer of the liver and that there was no help for it in surgery; the case was quite hopeless; the end was not many weeks off. A pitiful case, indeed!

Poor Patrick! His face brightened when he saw me. He told me, the first thing, that he had just heard from Jean. His wife and son were with him. Whether they suspect the truth I don't know. I doubt if the wife does; but the son looked very sober. Maybe he only has been told.

Yrs. aff.,
JOE

Jean had kept watch of Patrick's case by correspondence with Patrick's daughter Nancy, and so we already knew that it was hopeless. In fact, the end seems to be nearer than Twichell suspects. Last night I sent Twichell word that I knew Patrick had only a day or two to live, and he must not forget to provide a memorial wreath and pin a card to it with my name and Clara's and Jean's signed to it, worded, "In loving remembrance of Patrick McAleer, faithful and valued friend of our family for thirty-six years."

I wanted to say that he had served us thirty-six years, but some people would not have understood that. He served us constantly for twenty-one years. Then came that break when we spent nine or ten years in Europe. But if Patrick himself could see his funeral wreath—then I should certainly say, in so many words, that he served us thirty-six years.

For last summer, when we were located in the New Hampshire hills, at Dublin, we had Patrick with us. Jean had gone to Hartford the 1st of May and secured his services for the summer. Necessarily, a part of our household was Katy Leary, who has been on our roster for twenty-six years, and one day Jean overheard Katy and Patrick disputing about this length of service. Katy said she had served the family longer than Patrick had. Patrick said it was nothing of the kind; that he had already served the family ten years when Katy came, and that he had now served it thirty-six years.

He was just as brisk there in the New Hampshire hills as he was thirty-six years ago. He was sixty-four years old, but was just as slender and trim and handsome, and just as alert and springy on his feet, as he was in those long-vanished days of his youth. He was the most perfect man in his office that I have ever known, for this reason: that he never neglected any detail, howsoever slight, of his duties, and there was never any occasion to give him an order about anything. He conducted his affairs without anybody's help. There was always plenty of feed for the horses; the horses were always shod when they needed to be shod; the carriages and sleighs were always attended to; he kept everything in perfect order. It was a great satisfaction to have such a man around. I was not capable of telling anybody what to do about anything. He was my particular servant, and I didn't need to tell him anything at all. He was just the same in the New Hampshire hills. I never gave him an order while he was there, the whole five months; and there was never anything lacking that belonged in his jurisdiction.

When we had been married a year or two Patrick took a wife, and they lived in a house which we built and added to the stable. They reared eight children. They lost one, two or three years ago—a thriving young man, assistant editor of a Hartford daily paper, I think. The children were all educated in the public schools and in the high school. They are all men and women now, of course...

Our first child, Langdon Clemens, was born the 7th of November, 1870, and lived twenty-two months. Susy was born the 19th of March, 1872, and passed from life in the Hartford home, the 18th of August, 1896. With her, when the end came, were Jean, and Katy Leary, and John and Ellen (the gardener and his wife). Clara and her mother and I arrived in England from around the world on the 31st of July, and took a house in Guildford. A week later, when Susy, Katy, and Jean should have been arriving from America, we got a letter instead.

Subject of February first continued.—The death of Susy Clemens. Ends with mention of Dr. John Brown.

It explained that Susy was slightly ill—nothing of consequence. But we were disquieted and began to cable for later news. This was Friday. All day no answer—and the ship to leave Southampton next day, at noon. Clara and her mother began packing, to be ready in case the news should be bad. Finally came a cablegram saying, "Wait for cablegram in the morning." This was not satisfactory—not reassuring. I cabled again, asking that the answer be sent to Southampton, for the day was now closing. I waited in the post-office that night till the doors were closed, toward midnight, in the hope that good news might still come, but there was no message. We sat silent at home till one in the morning, waiting—waiting for we knew not what. Then we took the earliest morning train, and when we reached Southampton the message was there. It said the recovery would be long, but certain. This was a great relief to me, but not to my wife. She was frightened. She and Clara went aboard the steamer at once and sailed for America, to nurse Susy. I remained behind to search for another and larger house in Guildford.

That was the 15th of August, 1896. Three days later, when my wife and Clara were about halfway across the ocean, I was standing in our dining-room, thinking of nothing in particular, when a cablegram was put into my hand. It said, "Susy was peacefully released to-day."

It is one of the mysteries of our nature that a man, all unprepared, can receive a thunder-stroke like that and live. There is but one reasonable explanation of it. The intellect is stunned by the shock and but gropingly gathers the meaning of the words. The power to realize their full import is mercifully wanting. The mind has a dumb sense of vast loss—that is all. It will take mind and memory months, and possibly years, to gather together the details and thus learn and know the whole extent of the loss. A man's house burns down. The smoking wreckage represents only a ruined home that was dear through years of use and pleasant associations. By and by, as the days and weeks go on, first he misses this, then that, then the other thing. And when he casts about for it he finds that it was in that house. Always it is an essential—there was but one of its kind. It cannot be replaced. It was in that house. It is irrevocably lost. He did not realize that it was an essential when he had it; he only discovers it now when he finds himself balked, hampered, by its absence. It will be years before the tale of lost essentials is complete, and not till then can he truly know the magnitude of his disaster.

The 18th of August brought me the awful tidings. The mother and the sister were out there in mid-Atlantic, ignorant of what was happening, flying to meet this incredible calamity. All that could be done to protect them from the full force of the shock was done by relatives and good friends. They went down the Bay and met the ship at night, but did not show themselves until morning, and then only to Clara. When she returned to the stateroom she did not speak, and did not need to. Her mother looked at her and said, "Susy is dead."

At half past ten o'clock that night Clara and her mother completed their circuit of the globe, and drew up at Elmira by the same train and in the same car which had borne them and me westward from it one year, one month, and one week before. And again Susy was there—not waving her welcome in the glare of the lights as she had waved her farewell to us thirteen months before, but lying white and fair in her coffin, in the house where she was born.

The last thirteen days of Susy's life were spent in our own house in Hartford, the home of her childhood and always the dearest place in the earth to her. About her she had faithful old friends—her pastor, Mr. Twichell, who had known her from the cradle and who had come a long journey to be with her; her uncle and aunt, Mr. and Mrs. Theodore Crane; Patrick, the coachman; Katy, who had begun to serve us when Susy was a child of eight years; John and Ellen, who had been with us many years. Also Jean was there.

At the hour when my wife and Clara set sail for America, Susy was in no danger. Three hours later there came a sudden change for the worse. Meningitis set in, and it was immediately apparent that she was death-struck. That was Saturday, the 15th of August.

"That evening she took food for the last time." (Jean's letter to me.) The next morning the brain fever was raging. She walked the floor a little in her pain and delirium, then succumbed to weakness and returned to her bed. Previously she had found hanging in a closet a gown which she had seen her mother wear. She thought it was her mother, dead, and she kissed it and cried. About noon she became blind (an effect of the disease) and bewailed it to her uncle.

From Jean's letter I take this sentence, which needs no comment:
"About one in the afternoon Susy spoke for the last time."

It was only one word that she said when she spoke that last time, and it told of her longing. She groped with her hands and found Katy, and caressed her face and said, "Mamma."

How gracious it was that in that forlorn hour of wreck and ruin, with the night of death closing around her, she should have been granted that beautiful illusion—that the latest vision which rested upon the clouded mirror of her mind should have been the vision of her mother, and the latest emotion she should know in life the joy and peace of that dear imagined presence.

About two o'clock she composed herself as if for sleep, and never moved again. She fell into unconsciousness and so remained two days and five hours, until Tuesday evening at seven minutes past seven, when the release came. She was twenty-four years and five months old.

On the 23d her mother and her sisters saw her laid to rest—she that had been our wonder and our worship.

The summer seasons of Susy's childhood were spent at Quarry Farm on the hills east of Elmira, New York; the other seasons of the year at the home in Hartford. Like other children, she was blithe and happy, fond of play; unlike the average of children, she was at times much given to retiring within herself and trying to search out the hidden meanings of the deep things that make the puzzle and pathos of human existence, and in all the ages have baffled the inquirer and mocked him. As a little child aged seven, she was oppressed and perplexed by the maddening repetition of the stock incidents of our race's fleeting sojourn here, just as the same thing has oppressed and perplexed maturer minds from the beginning of time. A myriad of men are born; they labor and sweat and struggle for bread; they squabble and scold and fight; they scramble for little mean advantages over each other. Age creeps upon them; infirmities follow; shames and humiliations bring down their prides and their vanities. Those they love are taken from them, and the joy of life is turned to aching grief. The burden of pain, care, misery, grows heavier year by year. At length ambition is dead; pride is dead; vanity is dead; longing for release is in their place. It comes at last—the only unpoisoned gift earth ever had for them—and they vanish from a world where they were of no consequence; where they achieved nothing; where they were a mistake and a failure and a foolishness; where they have left no sign that they have existed—a world which will lament them a day and forget them forever. Then another myriad takes their place, and copies all they did, and goes along the same profitless road, and

MARK TWAIN

vanishes as they vanished—to make room for another and another and a million other myriads to follow the same arid path through the same desert and accomplish what the first myriad, and all the myriads that came after it, accomplished—nothing!

"Mamma, what is it all for?" asked Susy, preliminarily stating the above details in her own halting language, after long brooding over them alone in the privacy of the nursery.

A year later, she was groping her way alone through another sunless bog, but this time she reached a rest for her feet. For a week, her mother had not been able to go to the nursery, evenings, at the child's prayer hour. She spoke of it—was sorry for it, and said she would come to-night, and hoped she could continue to come every night and hear Susy pray, as before. Noticing that the child wished to respond, but was evidently troubled as to how to word her answer, she asked what the difficulty was. Susy explained that Miss Foote (the governess) had been teaching her about the Indians and their religious beliefs, whereby it appeared that they had not only a god, but several. This had set Susy to thinking. As a result of this thinking she had stopped praying. She qualified this statement—that is, she modified it—saying she did not now pray "in the same way" as she had formerly done. Her mother said, "Tell me about it, dear."

"Well, mamma, the Indians believed they knew, but now we know they were wrong. By and by it can turn out that we are wrong. So now I only pray that there may be a God and a heaven—or something better."

I wrote down this pathetic prayer in its precise wording, at the time, in a record which we kept of the children's sayings, and my reverence for it has grown with the years that have passed over my head since then. Its untaught grace and simplicity are a child's, but the wisdom and the pathos of it are of all the ages that have come and gone since the race of man has lived, and longed, and hoped, and feared, and doubted.

To go back a year—Susy aged seven. Several times her mother said to her, "There, there, Susy, you mustn't cry over little things."

This furnished Susy a text for thought. She had been breaking her heart over what had seemed vast disasters—a broken toy; a picnic canceled by thunder and lightning and rain; the mouse that was growing tame and friendly in the nursery caught and killed by the cat—and now came this strange revelation. For some unaccountable reason, these were not vast calamities. Why? How is the size of calamities measured? What is the rule? There must be some way to tell the great ones from the small ones; what is the law of these proportions? She examined the problem earnestly and long. She gave it her best thought, from time to time, for two or three days—but it baffled her—defeated her. And at last she gave up and went to her mother for help.

"Mamma, what is 'little things'?"

It seemed a simple question—at first. And yet before the answer could be put into words, unsuspected and unforeseen difficulties began to appear. They increased; they multiplied; they brought about another defeat. The effort to explain came to a standstill. Then Susy tried to help her mother out—with an instance, an example, an illustration. The mother was getting ready to go downtown, and one of her errands was to buy a long-promised toy watch for Susy.

"If you forgot the watch, mamma, would that be a little thing?"

She was not concerned about the watch, for she knew it would not be forgotten. What she was hoping for was that the answer would unriddle the riddle and bring rest and peace to her perplexed little mind.

The hope was disappointed, of course—for the reason that the size of a misfortune is not determinable by an outsider's measurement of it, but only by the measurements applied to it by the person specially affected by it. The king's lost crown is a vast matter to the king, but of no consequence to the child. The lost toy is a great matter to the child, but in the king's eyes it is not a thing to break the heart about. A verdict was reached, but it was based upon the above model, and Susy was granted leave to measure her disasters thereafter with her own tape-line.

I will throw in a note or two here touching the time when Susy was seventeen. She had written a play modeled upon Greek lines, and she and Clara and Margaret Warner, and other young comrades, had played it to a charmed houseful of friends in our house in Hartford. Charles Dudley Warner and his brother, George, were present. They were near neighbors and warm friends of ours. They were full of praises of the workmanship of the play, and George Warner came over the next morning and had a long talk with Susy. The result of it was this verdict:

"She is the most interesting person I have ever known, of either sex."

Remark of a lady—Mrs. Cheney, I think, author of the biography of her father, Rev. Dr. Bushnell:

"I made this note after one of my talks with Susy: 'She knows all there is of life and its meanings. She could not know it better if she had lived it out to its limit. Her intuitions and ponderings and analyzings seem to have taught her all that my sixty years have taught me.'"

Remark of another lady; she is speaking of Susy's last days:

"In those last days she walked as if on air, and her walk answered to the buoyancy of her spirits and the passion of intellectual energy and activity that possessed her."

I return now to the point where I made this diversion. From her earliest days, as I have already indicated, Susy was given to examining things and thinking them out by herself. She was not trained to this; it was the make of her mind. In matters involving questions of fair or unfair dealing, she reviewed the details patiently and surely arrived at a right and logical conclusion. In Munich, when she was six years old, she was harassed by a recurrent dream, in which a ferocious bear figured. She came out of the dream each time sorely frightened, and crying. She set herself the task of analyzing this dream. The reasons of it? The purpose of it? The origin of it? No—the moral aspect of it. Her verdict, arrived at after candid and searching investigation, exposed it to the charge of being one-sided and unfair in its construction: for (as she worded it) she was "never the one that ate, but always the one that was eaten."

Susy backed her good judgment in matters of morals with conduct to match—even upon occasions when it caused her sacrifice to do it. When she was six and her sister Clara four, the pair were troublesomely quarrelsome. Punishments were tried as a means of breaking up this custom—these failed. Then rewards were tried. A day without a quarrel brought candy. The children were their own witnesses—each for or against her own self. Once Susy took the candy, hesitated, then returned it with a suggestion that she was not fairly entitled to it. Clara kept hers, so, here was a conflict of evidence—one witness for a quarrel, and one against it. But the better witness of the two was on the affirmative side, and the quarrel stood proved, and no candy due to either side. There seemed to be no defense for Clara—yet there was, and Susy furnished it; and Clara went free. Susy said, "I don't know whether she felt wrong in her heart, but I didn't feel right in my heart."

It was a fair and honorable view of the case, and a specially acute analysis of it for a child of six to make. There was no way to convict Clara now, except to put her on the stand again and review her evidence. There was a doubt as to the fairness of this procedure, since her former evidence had been accepted, and not challenged at the time. The doubt was examined, and canvassed—then she was given the benefit of it and acquitted; which was just as well, for in the meantime she had eaten the candy, anyway.

Whenever I think of Susy I think of Marjorie Fleming. There was but one Marjorie Fleming. There can never be another. No doubt I think of Marjorie when I think of Susy mainly because Dr. John Brown, that noble and beautiful soul—rescuer of marvelous Marjorie from oblivion—was Susy's great friend in her babyhood—her worshiper and willing slave.

In 1873, when Susy was fourteen months old, we arrived in Edinburgh from London, fleeing thither for rest and refuge, after experiencing what had been to us an entirely new kind of life—six weeks of daily lunches, teas, and dinners away from home. We carried no letters of introduction; we hid ourselves away in Veitch's family hotel in George Street and prepared to have a comfortable season all to ourselves. But by good fortune this did not happen. Straightway Mrs. Clemens needed a physician, and I stepped around to 23 Rutland Street to see if the author of Rab and His Friends was still a practicing physician. He was. He came, and for six weeks thereafter we were together every day, either in his house or in our hotel.

New York, Monday, February 5, 1906

Dr. John Brown continued.—Incidents connected with Susy Clemens's childhood.—Bad spelling, etc.

His was a sweet and winning face—as beautiful a face as I have ever known. Reposeful, gentle, benignant—the face of a saint at peace with all the world and placidly beaming upon it the sunshine of love that filled his heart. Doctor John was beloved by everybody in Scotland; and I think that on its downward sweep southward it found no frontier, I think so because when, a few years later, infirmities compelled Doctor John to give up his practice, and Mr. Douglas, the publisher, and other friend set themselves the task of raising a fund of a few thousand dollars, whose income was to be devoted to the support of himself and his maiden sister (who was in age), the fund was not only promptly made up, but so very promptly that the books were closed before friends a hundred miles south of the line had had an opportunity to contribute. No public appeal was made. The matter was never mentioned in print. Mr. Douglas and the other friends applied for contributions by private letter only. Many complaints came from London, and everywhere between, from people who had not been allowed an opportunity to contribute. This sort of complaint is so new to the world—so strikingly unusual—that I think it worth while to mention it.

Doctor John was very fond of animals, and particularly of dogs. No one needs to be told this who has read that pathetic and beautiful masterpiece, Rab and His Friends. After his death, his son, Jock, published a brief memorial of him which he distributed privately among the friends; and in it occurs a little episode which illustrates the relationship that existed between Doctor John and the other animals. It is furnished by an Edinburgh lady whom Doctor John used to pick up and carry to school or back in his carriage frequently at a time when she was twelve years old. She said that they were chatting together tranquilly one day, when he suddenly broke off in the midst of a sentence and thrust his head out of the carriage window eagerly—then resumed his place with a disappointed look on his face. The girl said: "Who is it? Some one you know?" He said, "No, a dog I don't know."

He had two names for Susy—"Wee wifie" and "megalopis." This formidable Greek title was conferred in honor of her big, big dark eyes. Susy and the Doctor had a good deal of romping together. Daily he unbent his dignity and played "bear" with the child, I do not now remember which of them was the bear, but I think it was the child. There was a sofa across a corner of the parlor with a door behind it opening into Susy's quarters, and she used to lie in wait for the Doctor behind the sofa—not lie in wait, but stand in wait; for you could only get just a glimpse of the top of her yellow head when she stood upright. According to the rules of the game, she was invisible, and this glimpse did not count. I think she must have been the bear, for I can remember two or three occasions when she sprang out from behind the sofa and surprised the Doctor into frenzies of fright, which were not in the least modified by the fact that he knew that the "bear" was there and was coming.

It seems incredible that Doctor John should ever have wanted to tell a grotesque and rollicking anecdote. Such a thing seems so out of character with that gentle and tranquil nature that—but no matter. I tried to teach him the anecdote, and he tried his best for two or three days to perfect himself in it—and he never succeeded. It was the most impressive exhibition that ever was. There was no human being, nor dog, of his acquaintance in all Edinburgh that would not have been paralyzed with astonishment to step in there and see Doctor John trying to do that anecdote. It was one which I have told some hundreds of times on the platform, and which I was always very fond of, because it worked the audience so hard. It was a stammering man's account of how he got cured of his infirmity—which was accomplished by introducing a whistle into the midst of every word which he found himself unable to finish on account of the obstruction of the stammering. And so his whole account was an absurd mixture of stammering and whistling—which was irresistible to an audience properly keyed up for laughter. Doctor John learned to do the mechanical details of the anecdote, but he was never able to inform these details with expression. He was preternaturally grave and earnest all through, and so when he fetched up with the climaxing triumphant sentence at the end—but I must quote that sentence, or the reader will not understand. It was this:

"The doctor told me that whenever I wanted to sta—(whistle) sta—(whistle) sta—(whistle) am-mer, I must whistle; and I did, and it k—(whistle) k- (whistle) k- (whistle) k- ured me entirely!"

The Doctor could not master that triumphant note. He always gravely stammered and whistled and whistled and stammered it through, and it came out at the end with the solemnity and the gravity of the judge delivering sentence to a man with the black cap on.

He was the loveliest creature in the world—except his aged sister, who was just like him. We made the round of his professional visits with him in his carriage every day for six weeks. He always brought a basket of grapes, and we brought books. The scheme which we began with on the first round of visits was the one which was maintained until the end—and was based upon this remark, which he made when he was disembarking from the carriage at his first stopping place, to visit a patient, "Entertain yourselves while I go in here and reduce the population."

As a child, Susy had a passionate temper; and it cost her much remorse and many tears before she learned to govern it, but after that it was a wholesome salt, and her character was the stronger and healthier for its presence. It enabled her to be good with dignity; it preserved her not only from being good for vanity's sake, but from even the appearance of it. In looking back over the long-vanished years it seems but natural and excusable that I should dwell with longing affection and preference upon incidents of her young life which made it beautiful to us, and that I should let its few and small offenses go unsummoned and unreproached.

In the summer of 1880, when Susy was just eight years of age, the family were at Quarry Farm, on top of a high hill, three miles from Elmira, New York, where we always spent our summers, in those days. Hay-cutting time was approaching, and Susy and Clara were counting the hours, for the time was big with a great event for them; they had been promised that they might mount the wagon and ride home from the fields on the summit of the hay mountain. This perilous privilege, so dear to their age and species, had never been granted them before. Their excitement had no bounds. They could talk of nothing but this epoch-making adventure, now. But misfortune overtook Susy on the very morning of the important day. In a sudden outbreak of passion she corrected Clara—with a shovel, or stick, or something of the sort. At any rate, the offense committed was of a gravity clearly beyond the limit allowed in the nursery. In accordance with the rule and custom of the house, Susy went to her mother to confess and to help decide upon the size and character of the punishment due. It was quite understood that as a punishment could have but one rational object and function—to act as a reminder and warn the transgressor against transgressing in the same way again—the children would know about as well as any how to choose a penalty which would be rememberable and effective. Susy and her mother discussed various punishments, but none of them seemed adequate. This fault was an unusually serious one, and required the setting up of a danger signal in the memory that would not blow out nor burn out, but remain a fixture there and furnish its saving warning indefinitely. Among the punishments mentioned was deprivation of the hay-wagon ride. It was noticeable that this one hit Susy hard. Finally, in the summing up, the mother named over the list and asked, "Which one do you think it ought to be, Susy?"

Susy studied, shrank from her duty, and asked, "Which do you think, mamma?"

"Well, Susy, I would rather leave it to you. You make the choice, yourself."

It cost Susy a struggle, and much and deep thinking and weighing—but she came out where anyone who knew her could have foretold she would:

"Well, mamma, I'll make it the hay wagon, because, you know, the other things might not make me remember not to do it again, but if I don't get to ride on the hay wagon I can remember it easily."

In this world the real penalty, the sharp one, the lasting one, never falls otherwise than on the wrong person. It was not I that corrected Clara, but the remembrance of poor Susy's lost hay ride still brings me a pang—after twenty-six years.

Apparently Susy was born with humane feelings for the animals and compassion for their troubles. This enabled her to see a new point in an old story, once, when she was only six years old—a point which had been overlooked by older, and perhaps duller, people for many ages. Her mother told her the moving story of the sale of Joseph by his brethren, the staining of his coat with the blood of the slaughtered kid, and the rest of it. She dwelt upon the inhumanity of the brothers, their cruelty toward their helpless young brother, and the unbrotherly treachery which they practiced upon him; for she hoped to teach the child a lesson in gentle pity and mercifulness which she would remember. Apparently her desire was accomplished, for the tears came into Susy's eyes and she was deeply moved. Then she said, "Poor little kid!"

A child's frank envy of the privileges and distinctions of its elders is often a delicately flattering attention and the reverse of unwelcome, but sometimes the envy is not placed where the beneficiary is expecting it to be placed. Once when Susy was seven, she sat breathlessly absorbed in watching a guest of ours adorn herself for a ball. The lady was charmed by this homage, this mute and gentle admiration, and was happy in it. And when her pretty labors were finished, and she stood at last perfect, unimprovable, clothed like Solomon in his glory, she paused, confident and expectant, to receive from Susy's tongue the tribute that was burning in her eyes. Susy drew an envious little sigh and said, "I wish I could have crooked teeth and spectacles!"

Once, when Susy was six months along in her eighth year, she did something one day in the presence of company which subjected her to criticism and reproof. Afterward, when she was alone with her mother, as was her custom she reflected a little while over the matter. Then she set up what I think—and what the shade of Burns would think—was a quite good philosophical defense: "Well, mamma, you know I didn't see myself, and so I couldn't know how it looked."

In homes where the near friends and visitors are mainly literary people—lawyers, judges, professors, and clergymen—the children's ears become early familiarized with wide vocabularies. It is natural for them to pick up any words that fall in their way; it is natural for them

MARK TWAIN

to pick up big and little ones indiscriminately; it is natural for them to use without fear any word that comes to their net, no matter how formidable it may be as to size. As a result, their talk is a curious and funny musketry-clatter of little words, interrupted at intervals by the heavy-artillery crash of a word of such imposing sound and size that it seems to shake the ground and rattle the windows. Sometimes the child gets a wrong idea of a word which it has picked up by chance, and attaches to it a meaning which impairs its usefulness—but this does not happen as often as one might expect it would. Indeed, it happens with an infrequency which may be regarded as remarkable. As a child, Susy had good fortune with her large words, and she employed many of them. She made no more than her fair share of mistakes. Once when she thought something very funny was going to happen (but it didn't) she was racked and torn with laughter, by anticipation. But apparently she still felt sure of her position, for she said, "If it had happened, I should have been transformed (transported) with glee."

And earlier, when she was a little maid of five years, she informed a visitor that she had been in a church only once, and that was the time when Clara was "crucified" (christened).

In Heidelberg, when she was six, she noticed that the Schloss gardens—

Dear me, how remote things do come together! I break off that sentence to remark that at a luncheon uptown yesterday, I reminded the hostess that she had not made me acquainted with all the guests. She said yes, she was aware of that—that by request of one of the ladies she had left me to guess that lady out for myself; that I had known that lady for a day, more than a quarter of a century ago, and that the lady was desirous of finding out how long it would take me to dig her up out of my memory. The rest of the company were in the game and were anxious to see whether I would succeed or fail. It seemed to me, as the time drifted along, that I was never going to be able to locate that woman; but at last, when the luncheon was nearly finished, a discussion broke out as to where the most comfortable hotel in the world was to be found. Various hotels on the several sides of the ocean were mentioned, and at last somebody reminded her that she had not put forward a preference yet, and she was asked to name the hotel that she thought was, from her point of view, the most satisfactory and comfortable hotel on the planet, and she said, promptly, "The 'Slosh,' at Heidelberg."

I said at once, "I am sincerely glad to meet you again, Mrs. Jones, after this long stretch of years—but you were Miss Smith in those days. Have I located you?"

"Yes," she said, "you have."

I knew I had. During that day at Heidelberg, so many ages ago, many charitable people tried furtively to get that young Miss Smith to adopt the prevailing pronunciation of Schloss, by saying Schloss softly and casually every time she said "Slosh," but nobody succeeded in converting her. And I knew perfectly well that this was that same old Smith girl, because there could not be two persons on this planet at one and the same time who could preserve and stick to a mispronunciation like that for nearly a generation.

As I was saying, when I interrupted myself—in Heidelberg, when Susy was six, she noticed that the Schloss gardens were populous with snails creeping all about everywhere. One day she found a new dish on her table and inquired concerning it, and learned that it was made of snails. She was awed and impressed, and said, "Wild ones, mamma?"

She was thoughtful and considerate of others—an acquired quality, no doubt. No one seems to be born with it. One hot day, at home in Hartford, when she was a little child, her mother borrowed her fan several times (a Japanese one, value five cents), refreshed herself with it a moment or two, then handed it back with a word of thanks. Susy knew her mother would use the fan all the time if she could do it without putting a deprivation upon its owner. She also knew that her mother could not be persuaded to do that. A relief must be devised somehow; Susy devised it. She got five cents out of her money box and carried it to Patrick and asked him to take it downtown (a mile and a half) and buy a Japanese fan and bring it home. He did it—and thus thoughtfully and delicately was the exigency met and the mother's comfort secured. It is to the child's credit that she did not save herself expense by bringing down another and more costly kind of fan from upstairs, but was content to act upon the impression that her mother desired the Japanese kind—content to accomplish the desire and stop with that, without troubling about the wisdom or unwisdom of it.

Sometimes while she was still a child, her speech fell into quaint and strikingly expressive forms. Once—aged nine or ten—she came to her mother's room when her sister Jean was a baby and said Jean was crying in the nursery, and asked if she might ring for the nurse. Her mother asked, "Is she crying hard?"—meaning cross, ugly.

"Well, no, mamma. It is a weary, lonesome cry."

It is a pleasure to me to recall various incidents which reveal the delicacies of feeling which were so considerable a part of her budding character. Such a revelation came once in a way which, while creditable to her heart, was defective in another direction. She was in her eleventh year, then. Her mother had been making the Christmas purchases, and she allowed Susy to see the presents which were for Patrick's children. Among these was a handsome sled for Jimmy, on which a stag was painted; also in gilt capitals the word "DEER." Susy was excited and joyous over everything until she came to this sled. Then she became sober and silent—yet the sled was the choicest of all the gifts. Her mother was surprised and also disappointed, and said:

"Why, Susy, doesn't it please you? Isn't it fine?"

Susy hesitated, and it was plain that she did not want to say the thing that was in her mind. However, being urged, she brought it haltingly out:

"Well, mamma, it is fine, and of course it did cost a good deal—but—but—why should that be mentioned?"

Seeing that she was not understood, she reluctantly pointed to that word "DEER." It was her orthography that was at fault, not her heart. She had inherited both from her mother.

The ability to spell is a natural gift. The person not born with it can never become perfect in it. I was always able to spell correctly. My wife and her sister, Mrs. Crane, were always bad spellers. Once when Clara was a little chap her mother was away from home for a few days, and Clara wrote her a small letter every day. When her mother returned, she praised Clara's letters. Then she said, "But in one of them, Clara, you spelled a word wrong."

Clara said, with quite unconscious brutality, "Why, mamma, how did you know?"

More than a quarter of a century has elapsed, and Mrs. Crane is under our roof here in New York for a few days. Her head is white now, but she is as pretty and winning and sweet as she was in those ancient times at her Quarry Farm, where she was an idol and the rest of us were the worshipers. Her gift of imperfect orthography remains unimpaired. She writes a great many letters. This was always a passion of hers. Yesterday she asked me how to spell New Jersey, and I knew by her look, after she got the information, that she was regretting she hadn't asked somebody years ago. The miracles which she and her sister, Mrs. Clemens, were able to perform without help of dictionary or spelling book are incredible. During the year of my engagement—1869—while I was out on the lecture platform, the daily letter that came for me generally brought me news from the front—by which expression I refer to the internecine war that was always going on in a friendly way between these two orthographists about the spelling of words. One of these words was scissors. They never seemed to consult a dictionary; they always wanted something or somebody that was more reliable. Between them, they had spelled scissors in seven different ways, a feat which I am certain no person now living, educated or uneducated, can match. I have forgotten how I was required to say which of the seven ways was the right one. I couldn't do it. If there had been fourteen ways, none of them would have been right. I remember only one of the instances offered—the other six have passed from my memory. That one was "sicisiors." That way of spelling it looked so reasonable—so plausible, to the discoverer of it, that I was hardly believed when I decided against it. Mrs. Crane keeps by her, to this day, a little book of about thirty pages of note-paper, on which she has written, in a large hand, words which she needs to use in her letters every day—words which the cat could spell without prompting or tuition, and yet are words which Mrs. Crane never allows herself to risk upon paper without looking at that vocabulary of hers, each time, to make certain.

During my engagement year, thirty-seven years ago, a considerable company of young people amused themselves in the Langdon homestead one night with the game of Verbarium, which was brand new at the time and very popular. A text word was chosen and each person wrote that word in large letters across the top of a sheet of paper, then sat with pencil in hand and ready to begin as soon as game was called. The player could begin with the first letter of that text word and build words out of the text word during two minutes by the watch. But he must not use a letter that was not in the text word and he must not use any letter in the text word twice, unless the letter occurred twice in the text word. I remember the first bout that we had at that game. The text word was California. When game was called everybody began to set down words as fast as he could make his pencil move—"corn," "car," "cone," and so on, digging out the shortest words first because they could be set down more quickly than the longer ones. When the two minutes were up, the scores were examined, and the prize went to the person who had achieved the largest number of words. The good scores ranged along between thirty and fifty or sixty words. But Mrs. Crane would not allow her score to be examined. She was plainly doubtful about getting that prize. But when persuasion failed to avail we chased her about the place, captured her, and took her score away from her by force. She had achieved only one word, and that was calf—which she had spelled "caff." And she never would have gotten even that one word honestly—she had to introduce a letter that didn't belong in the text word in order to get it.

New York, Tuesday, February 6, 1906
Playing "The Prince and the Pauper."—Acting charades, etc.

When Susy was twelve and a half years old, I took to the platform again, after a long absence from it, and raked the country for four months in company with George W. Cable. Early in November we gave a reading one night in Chickering Hall, in New York, and when I was walking home in a dull gloom of fog and rain I heard one invisible man say to another invisible man, this, in substance: "General Grant has actually concluded to write his autobiography." That remark gave me joy, at the time, but if I had been struck by lightning in place of it, it would have been better for me and mine. However, that is a long story, and this is not the place for it.

To Susy, as to all Americans, General Grant was the supremest of heroes, and she longed for a sight of him. I took her to see him one day—However, let that go. It belongs elsewhere. I will return to it by and by.

In the midst of our reading campaign, I returned to Hartford from the far West, reaching home one evening just at dinner time. I was expecting to have a happy and restful season by a hickory fire in the library with the family, but was required to go at once to George Warner's house, a hundred and fifty yards away, across the grounds. This was a heavy disappointment, and I tried to beg off, but did not succeed. I couldn't even find out why I must waste this precious evening in a visit to a friend's house when our own house offered so many and superior advantages. There was a mystery somewhere, but I was not able to get to the bottom of it. So we tramped across in the snow, and I found the Warner drawing-room crowded with seated people. There was a vacancy in the front row, for me—in front of a curtain. At once the curtain was drawn, and before me, properly costumed, was the little maid, Margaret Warner, clothed in Tom Canty's rags, and beyond an intercepting railing was Susy Clemens, arrayed in the silks and satins of the prince. Then followed with good action and spirit the rest of that first meeting between the prince and the pauper. It was a charming surprise, and to me a moving one. Other episodes of the tale followed, and I have seldom in my life enjoyed an evening so much as I enjoyed that one. This lovely surprise was my wife's work. She had patched the scenes together from the book and had trained the six or eight young actors in their parts, and had also designed and furnished the costumes.

Afterward, I added a part for myself (Miles Hendon), also a part for Katy and a part for George. I think I have not mentioned George before. He was a colored man—the children's darling and a remarkable person. He had been a member of the family a number of years at that time. He had been born a slave, in Maryland, was set free by the Proclamation when he was just entering young manhood. He was body servant to General Devens all through the war, and then had come North and for eight or ten years had been earning his living by odd jobs. He came out to our house once, an entire stranger, to clean some windows—and remained eighteen years. Mrs. Clemens could always tell enough about a servant by the look of him—more, in fact, than she, or anybody else, could tell about him by his recommendations.

We played "The Prince and the Pauper" a number of times in our house to seated audiences of eighty-four persons, which was the limit of our space, and we got great entertainment out of it. As we played the piece it had several superiorities over the play as presented on the public stage in England and America, for we always had both the prince and the pauper on deck, whereas these parts were always doubled on the public stage—an economical but unwise departure from the book, because it necessitated the excision of the strongest and most telling of the episodes. We made a stirring and handsome thing out of the coronation scene. This could not be accomplished otherwise than by having both the prince and the pauper present at the same time. Clara was the little Lady Jane Grey, and she performed the part with electrifying spirit. Twichell's littlest cub, now a grave and reverend clergyman, was a page. He was so small that people on the back seats could not see him without an opera-glass, but he held up Lady Jane's train very well. Jean was only something past three years old, therefore was too young to have a part, but she produced the whole piece every day independently, and played all the parts herself. For a one-actor piece it was not bad. In fact, it was very good—very entertaining. For she was in very deep earnest, and, besides, she used an English which none but herself could handle with effect.

Our children and the neighbors' children played well; easily, comfortably, naturally, and with high spirit. How was it that they were able to do this? It was because they had been in training all the time from their infancy. They grew up in our house, so to speak, playing charades. We never made any preparation. We selected a word, whispered the parts of it to the little actors; then we retired to the hall where all sorts of costumery had been laid out ready for the evening. We dressed the parts in three minutes and each detachment marched into the library and performed its syllable, then retired, leaving the fathers and mothers to guess that syllable if they could. Sometimes they could.

Will Gillette, now world-famous actor and dramatist, learned a part of his trade by acting in our charades. Those little chaps, Susy and Clara, invented charades themselves in their earliest years, and played them for the entertainment of their mother and me. They had one high merit—none but a high-grade intellect could guess them. Obscurity is a great thing in a charade. These babies invented one once which was a masterpiece in this regard. They came in and played the first syllable, which was a conversation in which the word red occurred with suggestive frequency. Then they retired—came again, continuing an angry dispute which they had begun outside, and in which several words like just, fair, unfair, unjust, and so on, kept occurring; but we noticed that the word just was in the majority—so we set that down along with the word red and discussed the probabilities while the children went out to recostume themselves. We had thus "red," "just." They soon appeared and began to do a very fashionable morning call, in which the one made many inquiries of the other concerning some lady whose name was persistently suppressed, and who was always referred to as "her," even when the grammar did not permit of that form of the pronoun. The children retired. We took an account of stock and, so far as we could see, we had three syllables, "red," "just," "her." But that was all. The combination did not seem to throw any real glare on the future completed word. The children arrived again, and stooped down and began to chat and quarrel and carry on, and fumble and fuss at the register!—(red—just—her). With the exception of myself, this family was never strong on spelling.

In "The Prince and the Pauper" days, and earlier and later—especially later, Susy and her nearest neighbor, Margaret Warner, often devised tragedies and played them in the school-room, with little Jean's help—with closed doors—no admission to anybody. The chief characters were always a couple of queens, with a quarrel in stock—historical when possible, but a quarrel anyway, even if it had to be a work of the imagination. Jean always had one function—only one. She sat at a little table about a foot high and drafted death warrants for these queens to sign. In the course of time they completely wore out Elizabeth and Mary, Queen of Scots—also all of Mrs. Clemens's gowns that they could get hold of—for nothing charmed these monarchs like having four or five feet of gown dragging on the floor behind. Mrs. Clemens and I spied upon them more than once, which was treacherous conduct—but I don't think we very seriously minded that. It was grand to see the queens stride back and forth and reproach each other in three- or four-syllable words dripping with blood; and it was pretty to see how tranquil Jean was through it all. Familiarity with daily death and carnage had hardened her to crime and suffering in all their forms, and they were no longer able to hasten her pulse by a beat. Sometimes when there was a long interval between death warrants she even leaned her head on her table and went to sleep. It was then a curious spectacle of innocent repose and crimson and volcanic tragedy.

Wednesday, February 7, 1906

Susy Clemens's biography of her father.—Mr. Clemens's opinion of critics, etc.

When Susy was thirteen, and was a slender little maid with plaited tails of copper-tinged brown hair down her back, and was perhaps the busiest bee in the household hive, by reason of the manifold studies, health exercises, and recreations she had to attend to, she secretly, and of her own motion, and out of love, added another task to her labors—the writing of a biography of me. She did this work in her bedroom at night, and kept her record hidden. After a little, the mother discovered it and filched it, and let me see it; then told Susy what she had done, and how pleased I was and how proud. I remember that time with a deep pleasure. I had had compliments before, but none that touched me like this; none that could approach it for value in my eyes. It has kept that place always since. I have had no compliment, no praise, no tribute from any source, that was so precious to me as this one was and still is. As I read it now, after all these many years, it is still a king's message to me, and brings me the same dear surprise it brought me then—with the pathos added of the thought that the eager and hasty hand that sketched it and scrawled it will not touch mine again—and I feel as the humble and unexpectant must feel when their eyes fall upon the edict that raises them to the ranks of the noble.

Yesterday while I was rummaging in a pile of ancient note-books of mine which I had not seen for years, I came across a reference to that biography. It is quite evident that several times, at breakfast and dinner, in those long-past days, I was posing for the biography. In fact, I clearly remember that I was doing that—and I also remember that Susy detected it. I remember saying a very smart thing, with a good deal of an air, at the breakfast table one morning, and that Susy observed to her mother privately, a little later, that papa was doing that for the biography.

I cannot bring myself to change any line or word in Susy's sketch of me, but will introduce passages from it now and then just as they came in—their quaint simplicity out of her honest heart, which was the beautiful heart of a child. What comes from that source has a charm and grace of its own which may transgress all the recognized laws of literature, if it choose, and yet be literature still, and worthy of hospitality.

The spelling is frequently desperate, but it was Susy's, and it shall stand. I love it, and cannot profane it. To me, it is gold. To correct it would alloy it, not refine it. It would spoil it. It would take from it its freedom and flexibility and make it stiff and formal. Even when it is most extravagant I am not shocked. It is Susy's spelling, and she was doing the best she could—and nothing could better it for me.

She learned languages easily; she learned history easily, she learned music easily; she learned all things easily, quickly, and thoroughly—except spelling. She even learned that, after a while. But it would have grieved me but little if she had failed in it—for, although good spelling was my one accomplishment, I was never able to greatly respect it. When I was a schoolboy, sixty years ago, we had two prizes in our school. One was for good spelling, the other for amiability. These things were thin, smooth, silver disks, about the size of a dollar. Upon the one was engraved in flowing Italian script the words "Good Spelling," on the other was engraved the word "Amiability." The holders of these prizes hung them about the neck with a string—and those holders were the envy of the whole school. There wasn't a pupil that wouldn't have given a leg for the privilege of wearing one of them a week, but no pupil ever got a chance except John RoBards and me. John RoBards was eternally and indestructibly amiable. I may even say devilishly amiable; fiendishly amiable; exasperatingly amiable. That was the sort of feeling that we had about that quality of his. So he always wore the amiability medal. I always wore the other medal. That word "always" is a trifle too strong. We lost the medals several times. It was because they became so monotonous. We needed a change—therefore several times we traded medals. It was a satisfaction to John RoBards to seem to be a good speller—which he wasn't. And it was a satisfaction to me to seem to be amiable, for a change. But of course these changes could not long endure—for some schoolmate or other would presently notice what had been happening, and that schoolmate would not have been human if he had lost any time in reporting this treason. The teacher took the medals away from us at once, of course—and we always had them back again before Friday night. If we lost the medals Monday morning, John's amiability was at the top of the list Friday afternoon when the teacher came to square up the week's account. The Friday-afternoon session always closed with "spelling down." Being in disgrace, I necessarily started at the foot of my division of spellers, but I always slaughtered both divisions and stood alone with the medal around my neck when the campaign was finished. I did miss on a word once, just at the end of one of these conflicts, and so lost the medal. I left the first r out of February—but that was to accommodate a sweetheart. My passion was so strong just at that time that I would have left out the whole alphabet if the word had contained it.

As I have said before, I never had any large respect for good spelling. That is my feeling yet. Before the spelling-book came with its arbitrary forms, men unconsciously revealed shades of their characters, and also added enlightening shades of expression to what they wrote by their spelling, and so it is possible that the spelling-book has been a doubtful benevolence to us.

Susy began the biography in 1885, when I was in the fiftieth year of my age, and she in the fourteenth of hers. She begins in this way:

WE ARE A VERY HAPPY family. We consist of Papa, Mamma, Jean, Clara and me. It is papa I am writing about, and I shall have no trouble in not knowing what to say about him, as he is a very striking character.

But wait a minute—I will return to Susy presently. In the matter of slavish imitation, man is the monkey's superior all the time. The average man is destitute of independence of opinion. He is not interested in contriving an opinion of his own, by study and reflection, but is only anxious to find out what his neighbor's opinion is and slavishly adopt it. A generation ago, I found out that the latest review of a book was pretty sure to be just a reflection of the earliest review of it. That whatever the first reviewer found to praise or censure in the book would be repeated in the latest reviewer's report, with nothing fresh added.[1] Therefore more than once I took the precaution of sending my book, in manuscript, to Mr. Howells, when he was editor of the Atlantic Monthly, so that he could prepare a review of it at leisure. I knew he would say the truth about the book—I also knew that he would find more merit than demerit in it, because I already knew that that was the condition of the book. I allowed no copy of that book to go out to the press until after Mr. Howells's notice of it had appeared. That book was always safe. There wasn't a man behind a pen in all America that had the courage to find anything in the book which Mr. Howells had not found—there wasn't a man behind a pen in America that had spirit enough to say a brave and original thing about the book on his own responsibility.

I believe that the trade of critic, in literature, music, and the drama, is the most degraded of all trades, and that it has no real value—certainly no large value. When Charles Dudley Warner and I were about to bring out The Gilded Age, the editor of the Daily Graphic persuaded me to let him have an advance copy, he giving me his word of honor that no notice of it should appear in his paper until after the Atlantic Monthly notice should have appeared. This reptile published a review of the book within three days afterward, I could not really complain, because he had only given me his word of honor as security. I ought to have required of him something substantial. I believe his notice did not deal mainly with the merit of the book, or the lack of it, but with my moral attitude toward the public. It was charged that I had used my reputation to play a swindle upon the public—that Mr. Warner had written as much as half of the book, and that I had used my name to float it and

---

1. Hardly true to-day.—A. B. P.

give it currency—a currency which it could not have acquired without my name—and that this conduct of mine was a grave fraud upon the people. The Graphic was not an authority upon any subject whatever. It had a sort of distinction in that it was the first and only illustrated daily newspaper that the world had seen; but it was without character, it was poorly and cheaply edited, its opinion of a book or of any other work of art was of no consequence. Everybody knew this, yet all the critics in America, one after the other, copied the Graphic's criticism, merely changing the phraseology, and left me under that charge of dishonest conduct. Even the great Chicago Tribune, the most important journal in the Middle West, was not able to invent anything fresh, but adopted the view of the humble Daily Graphic, dishonesty charge and all. However, let it go. It is the will of God that we must have critics, and missionaries, and congressmen, and humorists, and we must bear the burden.

What I have been traveling toward all this time is this: The first critic that ever had occasion to describe my personal appearance littered his description with foolish and inexcusable errors whose aggregate furnished the result that I was distinctly and distressingly unhandsome. That description floated around the country in the papers, and was in constant use and wear for a quarter of a century. It seems strange to me that apparently no critic in the country could be found who could look at me and have the courage to take up his pen and destroy that lie. That lie began its course on the Pacific coast, in 1864, and it likened me in personal appearance to Petroleum V. Nasby, who had been out there lecturing. For twenty-five years afterward, no critic could furnish a description of me without fetching in Nasby to help out my portrait. I knew Nasby well, and he was a good fellow, but in my life I have not felt malignantly enough about any more than three persons to charge those persons with resembling Nasby. It hurts me to the heart, these things. To this day, it hurts me to the heart, and it had long been a distress to my family—including Susy—that the critics should go on making this wearisome mistake, year after year, when there was no foundation for it. Even when a critic wanted to be particularly friendly and complimentary to me, he didn't dare to go beyond my clothes. He did not venture beyond that frontier. When he had finished with my clothes he had said all the kind things, the pleasant things, the complimentary things he could risk. Then he dropped back on Nasby.

Yesterday I found this clipping in the pocket of one of those ancient memorandum-books of mine. It is of the date of thirty-nine years ago, and both the paper and the ink are yellow with the bitterness that I felt in that old day when I clipped it out to preserve it and brood over it and grieve about it. I will copy it here, to wit:

A correspondent of the Philadelphia Press, writing of one of Schuyler Colfax's receptions, says of our Washington correspondent: "Mark Twain, the delicate humorist, was present; quite a lion, as he deserves to be. Mark is a bachelor, faultless in taste, whose snowy vest is suggestive of endless quarrels with Washington washerwomen; but the heroism of Mark is settled for all time, for such purity and smoothness were never seen before. His lavender gloves might have been stolen from some Turkish harem, so delicate were they in size; but more likely— anything else were more likely than that. In form and feature he bears some resemblance to the immortal Nasby; but whilst Petroleum is brunette to the core, Twain is golden, amber-hued, melting, blonde."

Let us return to Susy's biography now, and get the opinion of one who is unbiased.

Papa's appearance has been described many times, but very incorrectly. He has beautiful gray hair, not any too thick or any too long, but just right; a Roman nose, which greatly improves the beauty of his features; kind blue eyes and a small mustache. He has a wonderfully shaped head and profile. He has a very good figure—in short, he is an extrodinarily fine looking man. All his features are perfect, exept that he hasn't extrodinary teeth. His complexion is very fair, and he doesn't ware a beard. He is a very good man and a very funny one. He has got a temper, but we all of us have in this family. He is the loveliest man I ever saw or ever hope to see—and oh, so absent-minded. He does tell perfectly delightful stories. Clara and I used to sit on each arm of his chair and listen while he told us stories about the pictures on the wall.

I remember the story-telling days vividly. They were a difficult and exacting audience—those little creatures.

New York, Thursday, February 8, 1906

Susy Clemens's biography continued.—Romancer to the children.— Incident of the spoon-shaped drive.—The burglar alarm does its whole duty.

Along one side of the library, in the Hartford home, the bookshelves joined the mantelpiece—in fact, there were shelves on both sides of the mantelpiece. On these shelves, and on the mantelpiece, stood various ornaments. At one end of the procession was a framed oil-painting of a cat's head; at the other end was a head of a beautiful young girl, life size, called Emmeline, an impressionist water-color. Between the one picture and the other there were twelve or fifteen of the bric-à-brac things already mentioned, also an oil-painting by Elihu Vedder, "The Young Medusa." Every now and then the children required me to construct a romance—always impromptu—not a moment's preparation permitted—and into that romance I had to get all that bric-à-brac and the three pictures. I had to start always with the cat and finish with Ernmeline. I was never allowed the refreshment of a change, end for end. It was not permissible to introduce a bric-à-brac ornament into the story out of its place in the procession. These bric-à-bracs were never allowed a peaceful day, a reposeful day, a restful Sabbath. In their lives there was no Sabbath. In their lives there was no peace. They knew no existence but a monotonous career of violence and bloodshed. In the course of time the bric-à-brac and the pictures showed wear. It was because they had had so many and such violent adventures in their romantic careers.

As romancer to the children I had a hard time, even from the beginning. If they brought me a picture and required me to build a story to it, they would cover the rest of the page with their pudgy hands to keep me from stealing an idea from it. The stories had to be absolutely original and fresh. Sometimes the children furnished me simply a character or two, or a dozen, and required me to start out at once on that slim basis and deliver those characters up to a vigorous and entertaining life of crime. If they heard of a new trade, or an unfamiliar animal, or anything like that, I was pretty sure to have to deal with those things in the next romance. Once Clara required me to build a sudden tale out of a plumber and a "bawgun stricter," and I had to do it. She didn't know what a boa-constrictor was until he developed in the tale—then she was better satisfied with it than ever.

From Susy's Biography

Papa's favorite game is billiards, and when he is tired and wishes to rest himself he stays up all night and plays billiards, it seems to rest his head. He smokes a great deal almost incessantly. He has the mind of an author exactly, some of the simplest things he can't understand. Our burglar alarm is often out of order, and papa had been obliged to take the mahogany room off from the alarm altogether for a time, because the burglar alarm had been in the habit of ringing even when the mahogany-room window was closed. At length he thought that perhaps the burglar alarm might be in order, and he decided to try and see; accordingly he put it on and then went down and opened the window; consequently the alarm bell rang, it would even if the alarm had been in order. Papa went despairingly upstairs and said to mamma, "Livy the mahogany room won't go on. I have just opened the window to see."

"Why, Youth," mamma replied. "If you've opened the window, why of course the alarm will ring!"

"That's what I've opened it for, why I just went down to see if it would ring!"

Mamma tried to explain to papa that when he wanted to go and see whether the alarm would ring while the window was closed he mustn't go and open the window—but in vain, papa couldn't understand, and got very impatient with mamma for trying to make him believe an impossible thing true.

This is a frank biographer, and an honest one; she uses no sandpaper on me. I have, to this day, the same dull head in the matter of conundrums and perplexities which Susy had discovered in those long-gone days. Complexities annoy me; then irritate me; then this progressive feeling presently warms into anger. I cannot get far in the reading of the commonest and simplest contract—with its "parties of the first part," and "parties of the second part," and "parties of the third part,"—my temper is all gone.

In the days which Susy is talking about, a perplexity fell to my lot one day. F. G. Whitmore was my business agent, and he brought me out from town in his buggy. We drove by the porte-cochère and toward the stable. Now this was a single road, and was like a spoon whose handle stretched from the gate to a great round flower bed in the neighborhood of the stable. At the approach to the flower bed the road divided and circumnavigated it, making a loop, which I have likened to the bowl of the spoon. I was sitting on the starboard side. As we neared the loop, I sitting as I say, on the starboard side (and that was the side on which the house was), I saw that Whitmore was laying his course to port and was going to start around that spoon bowl on that left-hand side. I said: "Don't do that, Whitmore; take the right-hand side. Then I shall be next to the house when we get to the door."

He said: "That will happen in any case. It doesn't make any difference which way I go around this flower bed."

I explained to him that he was an ass, but he stuck to his proposition, and I said, "Go on and try it, and see."

He went on and tried it, and sure enough he fetched me up at the door on the side that he said I would be. I was not able to believe it then, and I don't believe it yet. I said: "Whitmore, that is merely an accident. You can't do it again." He said he could—and we drove down into the street, fetched around, came back—did it again. I was stupefied, paralyzed, petrified, with these strange results, but they did not convince me. I didn't believe he could do it another time, but he did. He said he could do it all day and fetch up the same way every time— and by that time my temper was gone, and I asked him to go home and apply to the asylum and I would pay the expenses. I didn't want to see him any more for a week. I went upstairs in a rage and started to tell Livy about it, expecting to get her sympathy for me and to breed aversion in her for Whitmore; but she merely burst into peal after peal of laughter as the tale of my adventure went on, for her head was like Susy's. Riddles and complexities had no terrors for it. Her mind and Susy's were analytical. I have tried to make it appear that mine was different. Many and many a time I have told that buggy experiment, hoping against hope that I would some time or other find somebody who would be on my side—but it has never happened. And I am never able to go glibly forward and state the circumstances of that buggy's progress without having to halt and consider, and call up in my mind the spoon handle, the bowl of the spoon, the buggy and the horse, and my position in the buggy—and the minute I have got that far and try to turn it to the left, it goes to ruin. I can't see how it is ever going to fetch me out right when we get to the door. Susy is right in her estimate. I can't understand things.

That burglar alarm which Susy mentions led a gay and careless life, and had no principles. It was generally out of order at one point or another, and there was plenty of opportunity, because all the windows and doors in the house, from the cellar up to the top floor, were connected with it. In its seasons of being out of order it could trouble us for only a very little while. We quickly found out that it was fooling us and that it was buzzing its bloodcurdling alarm merely for its own amusement. Then we would shut it off and send to New York for the electrician— there not being one in all Hartford in those days. Then when the repairs were finished we would set the alarm again and reestablish our confidence in it. It never did any real business except upon one single occasion. All the rest of its expensive career was frivolous and without purpose. Just that one time it performed its duty, and its whole duty— gravely, seriously, admirably. It let fly about two o'clock one black and dreary March morning, and I turned out promptly, because I knew that it was not fooling, this time. The bathroom door was on my side of the bed. I stepped in there, turned up the gas, looked at the annunciator, turned off the alarm—so far as the door indicated was concerned—thus stopping the racket. Then I came back to bed.

Mrs. Clemens said, "What was it?"

I said, "It was the cellar door."

She said, "Was it a burglar, do you think?"

"Yes," I said, "of course it was. Do you suppose it was a Sunday-school superintendent?"

She said, "What do you suppose he wants?"

I said: "I suppose he wants jewelry, but he is not acquainted with the house and he thinks it is in the cellar. I don't like to disappoint a burglar whom I am not acquainted with and who has done me no harm, but if he had had common sagacity enough to inquire, I could have told him we kept nothing down there but coal and vegetables. Still, it may be that he is acquainted with this place and that what he really wants is coal and vegetables. On the whole, I think it is vegetables he is after."

She said, "Are you going down to see?"

"No," I said; "I could not be of any assistance. Let him select for himself."

Then she said, "But suppose he comes up to the ground floor!"

I said: "That's all right. We shall know it the minute he opens a door on that floor. It will set off the alarm."

Just then the terrific buzzing broke out again. I said: "He has arrived. I told you he would. I know all about burglars and their ways. They are systematic people."

I went into the bathroom to see if I was right, and I was. I shut off the dining-room and stopped the buzzing and came back to bed. My wife said:

"What do you suppose he is after now?"

I said: "I think he has got all the vegetables he wants and is coming up for napkin rings and odds and ends for the wife and the children. They all have families—burglars have—and they are always thoughtful of them; always take a few necessaries of life for themselves, and the rest as tokens of remembrance for the family. In taking them they do not forget us. Those very things represent tokens of his remembrance of us also. We never get them again. The memory of the attention remains embalmed in our hearts."

She said. "Are you going down to see what it is he wants now?"

"'No," I said; "I am no more interested than I was before. These are experienced people. They know what they want. I should be no help to him. I think he is after ceramics and bric-à-brac and such things. If he knows the house he knows that that is all that he can find on the dining-room floor."

She said, "Suppose he comes up here!"

I said: "It is all right. He will give us notice."

She said, "What shall we do then?"

I said, "Climb out of the window."

She said, "Well, what is the use of a burglar alarm for us?"

I said, "You have seen that it has been useful up to the present moment, and I have explained to you how it will be continuously useful after he gets up here."

That was the end of it. He didn't ring any more alarms.

Presently I said: "He is disappointed, I think. He has gone off with the vegetables and the bric-à-brac and I think he is dissatisfied."

We went to sleep, and at a quarter before eight in the morning I was out, and hurrying, for I was to take the 8:29 train for New York. I found the gas burning brightly—full head—all over the first floor. My new overcoat was gone; my old umbrella was gone; my new patent-leather shoes, which I had never worn, were gone. The large window which opened into the ombra at the rear of the house was standing wide. I passed out through it and tracked the burglar down the hill through the trees; tracked him without difficulty, because he had blazed his progress with imitation-silver napkin rings and my umbrella, and various other things which he had disapproved of; and I went back in triumph and proved to my wife that he was a disappointed burglar. I had suspected he would be, from the start, and from his not coming up to our floor to get human beings.

Things happened to me that day in New York. I will tell about them another time.

From Susy's Biography

Papa has a peculiar gait we like, it seems just to sute him, but most people do not; he always walks up and down the room while thinking and between each coarse at meals.

A LADY DISTANTLY RELATED TO us came to visit us once in those days. She came to stay a week, but all our efforts to make her happy failed, and we could not imagine why. We did much guessing, but could not solve the mystery. Later we found out what the trouble was. It was my tramping up and down between the courses. She conceived the idea that I could not stand her society.

That word "Youth," as the reader has perhaps already guessed, was my wife's pet name for me. It was gently satirical, but also affectionate. I had certain mental and material peculiarities and customs proper to a much younger person than I was.

From Susy's Biography

Papa is very fond of animals particularly of cats, we had a dear little gray kitten once that he named "Lazy" (papa always wears gray to match his hair and eyes) and he would carry him around on his shoulder, it was a mighty pretty sight! the gray cat sound asleep against papa's gray coat and hair. The names that he has given our different cats, are realy remarkably funny, they are namely Stray Kit, Abner, Motley, Fraeulein, Lazy, Buffalo Bill, Soapy Sall, Cleveland, Sour Mash, and Pestilence and Famine.

AT ONE TIME WHEN THE children were small we had a very black mother-cat named Satan, and Satan had a small black offspring named Sin. Pronouns were a difficulty for the children. Little Clara came in one day, her black eyes snapping with indignation, and said: "Papa, Satan ought to be punished. She is out there at the greenhouse and there she stays and stays, and his kitten is downstairs, crying."

Papa uses very strong language, but I have an idea not nearly so strong as when he first maried mamma. A lady acquaintance of his is rather apt to interupt what one is saying, and papa told mamma that he thought he should say to the lady's husband "I am glad your wife wasn't present when the Deity said Let there be light."

IT IS AS I HAVE said before. This is a frank historian. She doesn't cover up one's deficiencies, but gives them an equal showing with one's handsomer qualities. Of course I made the remark which she has quoted—and even at this distant day I am still as much as half persuaded that if the lady mentioned had been present when the Creator said "Let there be light" she would have interrupted him, and we shouldn't ever have got it.

Papa said the other day, "I am a mugwump and a mugwump is pure from the marrow out." (Papa knows that I am writing this biography of him, and he said this for it.) He doesn't like to go to church at all, why I never understood, until just now, he told us the other day that he couldn't bear to hear any one talk but himself, but that he could listen to himself talk for hours without getting tired, of course he said this in joke, but I've no dought it was founded on truth.

New York, Friday, February 9, 1906

The "strong language" episode in the bathroom. Susy's reference to "The Prince and the Pauper."—The mother and the children help edit the books.—Reference to ancestors.

Susy's remark about my strong language troubles me, and I must go back to it. All through the first ten years of my married life I kept a constant and discreet watch upon my tongue while in the house, and went outside and to a distance when circumstances were too much for me and I was obliged to seek relief. I prized my wife's respect and approval above all the rest of the human race's respect and approval. I dreaded the day when she should discover that I was but a whited sepulcher partly freighted with suppressed language, I was so careful, during ten years, that I had not a doubt that my suppressions had been successful. Therefore I was quite as happy in my guilt as I could have been if I had been innocent.

But at last an accident exposed me. I went into the bathroom one morning to make my toilet, and carelessly left the door two or three inches ajar. It was the first time that I had ever failed to take the precaution of closing it tightly. I knew the necessity of being particular about this, because shaving was always a trying ordeal for me, and I could seldom carry it through to a finish without verbal helps. Now this time I was unprotected, and did not suspect it. I had no extraordinary trouble with my razor on this occasion, and was able to worry through with mere mutterings and growlings of an improper sort, but with nothing noisy or emphatic about them—no snapping and barking. Then I put on a shirt. My shirts are an invention of my own. They open in the back, and are buttoned there—when there are buttons. This time the button was missing. My temper jumped up several degrees in a moment and my remarks rose accordingly, both in loudness and vigor of expression. But I was not troubled, for the bathroom door was a solid one and I supposed it was firmly closed. I flung up the window and threw the shirt out. It fell upon the shrubbery where the people on their way to church could admire it if they wanted to; there was merely fifty feet of grass between the shirt and the passer-by. Still rumbling and thundering distantly, I put on another shirt. Again the button was absent. I augmented my language to meet the emergency and threw that shirt out of the window. I was too angry—too insane—to examine the third shirt, but put it furiously on. Again the button was absent, and that shirt followed its comrades out of the window. Then I straightened up, gathered my reserves, and let myself go like a cavalry charge. In the midst of that great assault, my eye fell upon that gaping door, and I was paralyzed.

It took me a good while to finish my toilet. I extended the time unnecessarily in trying to make up my mind as to what I would best do in the circumstances. I tried to hope that Mrs. Clemens was asleep, but I knew better. I could not escape by the window. It was narrow and suited only to shirts. At last I made up my mind to boldly loaf through the bedroom with the air of a person who had not been doing anything. I made half the journey successfully. I did not turn my eyes in her direction, because that would not be safe. It is very difficult to look as if you have not been doing anything when the facts are the other way, and my confidence in my performance oozed steadily out of me as I went along. I was aiming for the left-hand door because it was farthest from my wife. It had never been opened from the day that the house was built, but it seemed a blessed refuge for me now. The bed was this one, wherein I am lying now and dictating these histories morning after morning with so much serenity. It was this same old elaborately carved black Venetian bedstead—the most comfortable bedstead that ever was, with space enough in it for a family, and carved angels enough surmounting its twisted columns and its headboard and footboard to bring peace to the sleepers, and pleasant dreams. I had to stop in the middle of the room. I hadn't the strength to go on. I believed that I was under accusing eyes—that even the carved angels were inspecting me with an unfriendly gaze. You know how it is when you are convinced that somebody behind you is looking steadily at you. You have to turn your face—you can't help it. I turned mine. The bed was placed as it is now, with the foot where the head ought to be. If it had been placed as it should have been, the high headboard would have sheltered me. But the footboard was no sufficient protection and I could be seen over it. I was exposed. I was wholly without protection. I turned, because I couldn't help it—and my memory of what I saw is still vivid, after all these years.

Against the white pillows I saw the black head—I saw that young and beautiful face; and I saw the gracious eyes with a something in them which I had never seen there before. They were snapping and flashing with indignation. I felt myself crumbling; I felt myself shrinking away to nothing under that accusing gaze. I stood silent under that desolating fire for as much as a minute, I should say—it seemed a very, very long time. Then my wife's lips parted, and from them issued—my latest bathroom remark. The language perfect, but the expression unpractical, apprentice-like, ignorant, inexperienced, comically inadequate, absurdly weak and unsuited to the great language. In my lifetime I had never heard anything so out of tune, so inharmonious, so incongruous, so ill suited to each other as were those mighty words set to that feeble music. I tried to keep from laughing, for I was a guilty person in deep need of charity and mercy. I tried to keep from bursting, and I succeeded—until she gravely said, "There, now you know how it sounds."

Oh, then I exploded! I said, "Oh, Livy, if it sounds like that, God forgive me, I will never do it again."

Then she had to laugh, herself. Both of us broke into convulsions, and went on laughing until we were exhausted.

The children were present at breakfast—Clara, aged six, and Susy, eight—and the mother made a guarded remark about strong language; guarded because she did not wish the children to suspect anything—a guarded remark which censured strong language. Both children broke out in one voice with this comment, "Why, mamma, papa uses it!" I was astonished. I had supposed that that secret was safe in my own breast and that its presence had never been suspected. I asked, "How did you know, you little rascals?"

"Oh," they said, "we often listen over the balusters when you are in the hall explaining things to George."

FROM SUSY'S BIOGRAPHY

One of papa's latest books is "The Prince and the Pauper" and it is unquestionably the best book he has ever written, some people want him to keep to his old style, some gentleman wrote him, "I enjoyed Huckleberry Finn immensely and am glad to see that you have returned to your old style." That enoyed me that enoyed me greatly, because it trobles me (Susy was troubled by that word, and uncertain; she wrote a u above it in the proper place, but reconsidered the matter and struck it out) to have so few people know papa, I mean realy know him, they think of Mark Twain as a humorist joking at everything; "And with a mop of reddish brown hair which sorely needs the barbars brush a roman nose, short stubby mustache, a sad care-worn face, with maney crow's feet," etc. That is the way people picture papa, I have wanted papa to write a book that would reveal something of his kind sympathetic nature, and "The Prince and the Pauper" partly does it. The book is full of lovely charming ideas, and oh the language! It is perfect. I think that one of the most touching scenes in it, is where the pauper is riding horseback with his nobles in the "recognition procession" and he sees his mother oh and then what followed! How she runs to his side, when she sees him throw up his hand palm outward, and is rudely pushed off by one of the King's officers, and then how the little pauper's consceince troubles him when he remembers the shameful words that were falling from his lips, when she was turned from his side "I know you not woman" and how his grandeurs were stricken valueless, and his pride consumed to ashes. It is a wonderfully beautiful and touching little scene, and papa has described it so wonderfully. I never saw a man with so much variety of feeling as papa has; now the "Prince and the Pauper" is full of touching places, but there is most always a streak of humor in them somewhere. Now in the coronation—in the stirring coronation, just after the little king has got his crown back again papa brings that in about the Seal, where the pauper says he used the Seal "to crack nuts with." Oh it is so funny and nice! Papa very seldom writes a passage without some humor in it somewhere, and I dont think he ever will.

THE CHILDREN ALWAYS HELPED THEIR mother to edit my books in manuscript. She would sit on the porch at the farm and read aloud, with her pencil in her hand, and the children would keep an alert and suspicious eye upon her right along, for the belief was well grounded in them that whenever she came across a particularly satisfactory passage she would strike it out. Their suspicions were well founded. The passages which were so satisfactory to them always had an element of strength in them which sorely needed modification or expurgation, and was always sure to get it at their mother's hand.

For my own entertainment, and to enjoy the protests of the children, I often abused my editor's innocent confidence. I often interlarded remarks of a studied and felicitously atrocious character purposely to achieve the children's delight and see the pencil do its fatal work. I often joined my supplications to the children's for mercy, and strung the argument out and pretended to be in earnest. They were deceived, and so was their mother. It was three against one, and most unfair. But it was very delightful, and I could not resist the temptation. Now and then we gained the victory and there was much rejoicing. Then I privately struck the passage out myself. It had served its purpose. It had furnished three of us with good entertainment, and in being removed from the book by me it was only suffering the fate originally intended for it.

FROM THE BIOGRAPHY

Papa was born in Missouri. His mother is Grandma Clemens (Jane Lampton Clemens) of Kentucky. Grandpa Clemens was of the F. F. V's of Virginia.

Without doubt it was I that gave Susy that impression. I cannot imagine why, because I was never in my life much impressed by grandeurs which proceed from the accident of birth. I did not get this indifference from my mother. She was always strongly interested in the ancestry of the house. She traced her own line back to the Lambtons of Durham, England—a family which had been occupying broad lands there since Saxon times. I am not sure, but I think that those Lambtons got along without titles of nobility for eight or nine hundred years, then produced a great man, three-quarters of a century ago, and broke into the peerage. My mother knew all about the Clemenses of Virginia, and loved to aggrandize them to me, but she has long been dead. There has been no one to keep those details fresh in my memory, and they have grown dim.

New York, Monday, February 12, 1906
Susy's biography continued.—Some of the tricks played in "Tom Sawyer."—The broken sugar bowl.—Skating on the Mississippi with Tom Nash, etc.

From Susy's Biography

Clara and I are sure that papa played the trick on Grandma, about the whipping, that is related in "The Adventures of Tom Sawyer": "Hand me that switch." The switch hovered in the air, the peril was desperate— "My, look behind you Aunt!" The old lady whirled around and snatched her skirts out of danger. The lad fled on the instant, scrambling up the high board fence and disappeared over it.

Susy and Clara were quite right about that.
    Then Susy says:

And we know papa played "Hookey" all the time. And how readily would papa pretend to be dying so as not to have to go to school!

These revelations and exposures are searching, but they are just. If I am as transparent to other people as I was to Susy, I have wasted much effort in this life.

Grandma couldn't make papa go to school, so she let him go into a printing-office to learn the trade. He did so, and gradually picked up enough education to enable him to do about as well as those who were more studious in early life.

IT IS NOTICEABLE THAT SUSY does not get overheated when she is complimenting me, but maintains a proper judicial and biographical calm. It is noticeable, also, and it is to her credit as a biographer, that she distributes compliment and criticism with a fair and even hand.

My mother had a good deal of trouble with me, but I think she enjoyed it. She had none at all with my brother Henry, who was two years younger than I, and I think that the unbroken monotony of his goodness and truthfulness and obedience would have been a burden to her but for the relief and variety which I furnished in the other direction. I was a tonic. I was valuable to her. I never thought of it before, but now I see it. I never knew Henry to do a vicious thing toward me, or toward anyone else—but he frequently did righteous ones that cost me as heavily. It was his duty to report me, when I needed reporting and neglected to do it myself, and he was very faithful in discharging that duty. He is Sid in Tom Sawyer. But Sid was not Henry. Henry was a very much finer and better boy than ever Sid was.

It was Henry who called my mother's attention to the fact that the thread with which she had sewed my collar together to keep me from going in swimming had changed color. My mother would not have discovered it but for that, and she was manifestly piqued when she recognized that that prominent bit of circumstantial evidence had escaped her sharp eye. That detail probably added a detail to my punishment. It is human. We generally visit our shortcomings on somebody else when there is a possible excuse for it—but no matter. I took it out of Henry. There is always compensation for such as are unjustly used. I often took it out of him—sometimes as an advance payment for something which I hadn't yet done. These were occasions when the opportunity was too strong a temptation, and I had to draw on the future. I did not need to copy this idea from my mother, and probably didn't. It is most likely that I invented it for myself. Still, she wrought upon that principle upon occasion.

If the incident of the broken sugar bowl is in Tom Sawyer—I don't remember whether it is or not—that is an example of it. Henry never stole sugar. He took it openly from the bowl. His mother knew he wouldn't take sugar when she wasn't looking, but she had her doubts about me. Not exactly doubts, either. She knew very well I would. One day when she was not present Henry took sugar from her prized and precious old-English sugar bowl, which was an heirloom in the family—

and he managed to break the bowl. It was the first time I had ever had a chance to tell anything on him, and I was inexpressibly glad. I told him I was going to tell on him, but he was not disturbed. When my mother came in and saw the bowl lying on the floor in fragments, she was speechless for a minute. I allowed that silence to work; I judged it would increase the effect. I was waiting for her to ask, "Who did that?"—so that I could fetch out my news. But it was an error of calculation. When she got through with her silence she didn't ask anything about it—she merely gave me a crack on the skull with her thimble that I felt all the way down to my heels. Then I broke out with my injured innocence, expecting to make her very sorry that she had punished the wrong one. I expected her to do something remorseful and pathetic. I told her that I was not the one—it was Henry. But there was no upheaval. She said, without emotion: "It's all right. It isn't any matter. You deserve it for something you've done that I didn't know about; and if you haven't done it, why then you deserve it for something that you are going to do that I shan't hear about."

There was a stairway outside the house, which led up to the rear part of the second story. One day Henry was sent on an errand, and he took a tin bucket along. I knew he would have to ascend those stairs, so I went up and locked the door on the inside, and came down into the garden, which had been newly plowed and was rich in choice, firm clods of black mold. I gathered a generous equipment of these and ambushed him. I waited till he had climbed the stairs and was near the landing and couldn't escape. Then I bombarded him with clods, which he warded off with his tin bucket the best he could, but without much success, for I was a good marksman. The clods smashing against the weather-boarding fetched my mother out to see what was the matter, and I tried to explain that I was amusing Henry. Both of them were after me in a minute, but I knew the way over that high board fence and escaped for that time. After an hour or two, when I ventured back, there was no one around and I thought the incident was closed. But it was not so. Henry was ambushing me. With an unusually competent aim for him, he landed a stone on the side of my head which raised a bump there which felt like the Matterhorn. I carried it to my mother straightway for sympathy, but she was not strongly moved. It seemed to be her idea that incidents like this would eventually reform me if I harvested enough of them. So the matter was only educational. I had had a sterner view of it than that before.

Whenever my conduct was of such exaggerated impropriety that my mother's extemporary punishments were inadequate, she saved the matter up for Sunday and made me go to church Sunday night—which was a penalty sometimes bearable, perhaps, but as a rule it was not, and I avoided it for the sake of my constitution. She would never believe that I had been to church until she had applied her test. She made me tell her what the text was. That was a simple matter—caused me no trouble. I didn't have to go to church to get a text. I selected one for myself. This worked very well until one time when my text and the one furnished by a neighbor, who had been to church, didn't tally. After that my mother took other methods. I don't know what they were now.

In those days men and boys wore rather long cloaks in the wintertime. They were black, and were lined with very bright and showy Scotch plaids. One winter's night when I was starting to church to square a crime of some kind committed during the week. I hid my cloak near the gate and went off and played with the other boys until church was over. Then I returned home. But in the dark I put the cloak on wrong side out, entered the room, threw the cloak aside, and then stood the usual examination. I got along very well until the temperature of the church was mentioned. My mother said, "It must have been impossible to keep warm there on such a night."

I didn't see the art of that remark, and was foolish enough to explain that I wore my cloak all the time that I was in church. She asked if I kept it on from church home, too. I didn't see the bearing of that remark. I said that that was what I had done. She said: "You wore it with that red Scotch plaid outside and glaring? Didn't that attract any attention?"

Of course to continue such a dialogue would have been tedious and unprofitable, and I let it go and took the consequences.

That was about 1849. Tom Nash was a boy of my own age—the postmaster's son. The Mississippi was frozen across, and he and I went skating one night, probably without permission. I cannot see why we should go skating in the night unless without permission, for there could be no considerable amusement to be gotten out of skating at midnight if nobody was going to object to it. About midnight, when we were more than half a mile out toward the Illinois shore, we heard some ominous rumbling and grinding and crashing going on between us and the home side of the river, and we knew what it meant—the river was breaking up. We started for home, pretty badly scared. We flew along at full speed whenever the moonlight sifting down between the clouds enabled us to tell which was ice and which was water. In the pauses we waited, started again whenever there was a good bridge of ice, paused again when we came to naked water, and waited in distress until a floating vast cake should bridge that place. It took us an hour to make the trip—a trip which we made in a misery of apprehension all the time. But at last we arrived within a very brief distance of the shore. We waited again. There was another place that needed bridging. All about us the ice was plunging and grinding along and piling itself up in mountains on the shore, and the dangers were increasing, not diminishing. We grew very impatient to get to solid ground, so we started too early and went springing from cake to cake. Tom made a miscalculation and fell short. He got a bitter bath, but he was so close to shore that he only had to swim a stroke or two—then his feet struck hard bottom and he crawled out. I arrived a little later, without accident. We had been in a drenching perspiration and Tom's bath was a disaster for him. He took to his bed, sick, and had a procession of diseases. The closing one was scarlet fever, and he came out of it stone deaf. Within a year or two speech departed, of course. But some years later he was taught to talk, after a fashion—one couldn't always make out what it was he was trying to say. Of course he could not modulate his voice, since he couldn't hear himself talk. When he supposed he was talking low and confidentially, you could hear him in Illinois.

Four years ago (1902) I was invited by the University of Missouri to come out there and receive the honorary degree of LL.D. I took that opportunity to spend a week in Hannibal—a city now, a village in my day. It had been fifty-five years since Tom Nash and I had had that adventure. When I was at the railway station ready to leave Hannibal, there was a great crowd of citizens there. I saw Tom Nash approaching me across a vacant space, and I walked toward him, for I recognized him at once. He was old and white-headed, but the boy of fifteen was still visible in him. He came up to me, made a trumpet of his hands at my ear, nodded his head toward the citizens, and said, confidentially— in a yell like a fog horn—"Same damned fools, Sam."

From Susy's Biography

Papa was about twenty years old when he went on the Mississippi as a pilot. Just before he started on his tripp Grandma Clemens asked him to promise her on the Bible not to touch intoxicating liquors or swear, and he said "Yes, mother, I will," and he kept that promise seven years when Grandma released him from it.

UNDER THE INSPIRING INFLUENCE OF that remark, what a garden of forgotten reforms rises upon my sight.

New York, Tuesday, February 13, 1906
Susy's biography continued.—Cadet of Temperance.—First meeting of Mr. Clemens and Miss Langdon.—Miss Langdon an invalid.—Doctor Newton.

I recall several of them without much difficulty. In Hannibal, when I was about fifteen, I was for a short time a Cadet of Temperance, an organization which probably covered the whole United States during as much as a year—possibly even longer. It consisted in a pledge to refrain, during membership, from the use of tobacco; I mean it consisted partly in that pledge and partly in a red merino sash, but the red merino sash was the main part. The boys joined in order to be privileged to wear it— the pledge part of the matter was of no consequence. It was so small in importance that, contrasted with the sash, it was, in effect, nonexistent. The organization was weak and impermanent because there were not enough holidays to support it. We could turn out and march and show the red sashes on May Day with the Sunday schools, and on the Fourth of July with the Sunday schools, the independent fire company, and the militia company. But you can't keep a juvenile moral institution alive on two displays of its sash per year. As a private, I could not have held out beyond one procession, but I was Illustrious Grand Worthy Secretary and Royal Inside Sentinel, and had the privilege of inventing the passwords and of wearing a rosette on my sash. Under these conditions, I was enabled to remain steadfast until I had gathered the glory of two displays—May Day and the Fourth of July. Then I resigned straightway, and straightway left the lodge.

I had not smoked for three full months, and no words can adequately describe the smoke appetite that was consuming me. I had been a smoker from my ninth year—a private one during the first two years, but a public one after that—that is to say, after my father's death. I was smoking, and utterly happy, before I was thirty steps from the lodge door. I do not now know what the brand of the cigar was. It was probably not choice, or the previous smoker would not have thrown it away so soon. But I realized that it was the best cigar that was ever made. The previous smoker would have thought the same if he had been without a smoke for three months. I smoked that stub without shame. I could not do it now without shame, because now I am more refined than I was then. But I would smoke it, just the same. I know myself, and I know the human race, well enough to know that.

In those days the native cigar was so cheap that a person who could afford anything could afford cigars. Mr. Garth had a great tobacco factory, and he also had a small shop in the village for the retail sale of his products. He had one brand of cigars which even poverty itself was able to buy. He had had these in stock a good many years, and although they looked well enough on the outside, their insides had decayed to dust and would fly out like a puff of vapor when they were broken in two. This brand was very popular on account of its extreme cheapness. Mr. Garth had other brands which were cheap, and some that were bad, but the supremacy over them enjoyed by this brand was indicated by its name. It was called "Garth's damnedest." We used to trade old newspapers (exchanges) for that brand.

There was another shop in the village where the conditions were friendly to penniless boys. It was kept by a lonely and melancholy little hunchback, and we could always get a supply of cigars by fetching a bucket of water for him from the village pump, whether he needed water or not. One day we found him asleep in his chair—a custom of his—and we waited patiently for him to wake up, which was a custom of ours. But he slept so long, this time, that at last our patience was exhausted and we tried to wake him—but he was dead. I remember the shock of it yet.

In my early manhood, and in middle life, I used to vex myself with reforms, every now and then. And I never had occasion to regret these divergencies, for, whether the resulting deprivations were long or short, the rewarding pleasure which I got out of the vice when I returned to it always paid me for all that it cost. However, I feel sure that I have written about these experiments in the book called Following the Equator. By and by I will look and see. Meantime, I will drop the subject and go back to Susy's sketch of me:

From Susy's Biography

After papa had been a pilot on the Mississippi for a time, Uncle Orion Clemens, his brother, was appointed Secretary of the State of Nevada, and papa went with him out to Nevada to be his secretary. Afterwards he became interested in mining in California; then he reported for a newspaper and was on several newspapers. Then he was sent to the Sandwich Islands. After that he came back to America and his friends wanted him to lecture so he lectured. Then he went abroad on the Quaker City, and on board that ship he became equainted with Uncle Charlie (Mr. C. J. Langdon, of Elmira, New York). Papa and Uncle Charlie soon became friends, and when they returned from their journey Grandpa Langdon, Uncle Charlie's father, told Uncle Charlie to invite Mr. Clemens to dine with them at the St. Nicholas Hotel, in New York. Papa accepted the invitation and went to dine at the St. Nicholas with Grandpa and there he met mamma (Olivia Lewis Langdon) first. But they did not meet again until the next August, because papa went away to California, and there wrote "The Inocense Abroad."

I will remark here that Susy is not quite correct as to that next meeting. That first meeting was on the 27th of December, 1867, and the next one was at the house of Mrs. Berry, five days later. Miss Langdon had gone there to help Mrs. Berry receive New Year guests. I went there at ten in the morning to pay a New Year call. I had thirty-four calls on my list, and this was the first one. I continued it during thirteen hours, and put the other thirty-three off till next year.

From Susy's Biography

Mamma was the daughter of Mr. Jervis Langdon, (I don't know whether Grandpa had a middle name or not) and Mrs. Olivia Lewis Langdon, of Elmira, New York. She had one brother and one sister, Uncle Charlie (Charles J. Langdon) and Aunt Susie (Susan Langdon Crane). Mamma loved Grandpa more than any one else in the world. He was her idol and she his; I think mamma's love for grandpa must have very much resembled my love for mamma. Grandpa was a great and good man and we all think of him with respect and love. Mamma was an invalid when she was young, and had to give up study a long time.

She became an invalid at sixteen, through a partial paralysis caused by falling on the ice, and she was never strong again while her life lasted. After that fall she was not able to leave her bed during two years, nor was she able to lie in any position except upon her back. All the great physicians were brought to Elmira, one after another, during that time, but there was no helpful result. In those days both worlds were well acquainted with the name of Doctor Newton, a man who was regarded in both worlds as a quack. He moved through the land in state; in magnificence, like a portent; like a circus. Notice of his coming was spread upon the dead walls in vast colored posters, along with his formidable portrait, several weeks beforehand.

One day Andrew Langdon, a relative of the Langdon family, came to the house and said: "You have tried everybody else; now try Doctor Newton, the quack. He is downtown at the Rathburn House, practicing upon the well-to-do at war prices and upon the poor for nothing. I saw him wave his hands over Jake Brown's head and take his crutches away from him and send him about his business as good as new. I saw him do the like with some other cripples. They may have been 'temporaries' instituted for advertising purposes, and not genuine. But Jake is genuine. Send for Newton."

Newton came. He found the young girl upon her back. Over her was suspended a tackle from the ceiling. It had been there a long time, but unused. It was put there in the hope that by its steady motion she might be lifted to a sitting posture, at intervals, for rest. But it proved a failure. Any attempt to raise her brought nausea and exhaustion, and had to be relinquished. Newton opened the windows—long darkened—and delivered a short fervent prayer; then he put an arm behind her shoulders and said, "Now we will sit up, my child."

The family were alarmed and tried to stop him, but he was not disturbed, and raised her up. She sat several minutes, without nausea or discomfort. Then Newton said, "Now we will walk a few steps, my child." He took her out of bed and supported her while she walked several steps; then he said: "I have reached the limit of my art. She is not cured. It is not likely that she will ever be cured. She will never be able to walk far, but after a little daily practice she will be able to walk one or two hundred yards, and she can depend on being able to do that for the rest of her life."

His charge was fifteen hundred dollars, and it was easily worth a hundred thousand. For from the day that she was eighteen until she was fifty-six she was always able to walk a couple of hundred yards without stopping to rest; and more than once I saw her walk a quarter of a mile without serious fatigue.

Newton was mobbed in Dublin, in London, and in other places. He was rather frequently mobbed in Europe and in America, but never by the grateful Langdons and Clemenses. I met Newton once, in after years, and asked him what his secret was. He said he didn't know, but thought perhaps some subtle form of electricity proceeded from his body and wrought the cures.

New York, Wednesday, February 14, 1906
About the accident which prolonged Mr. Clemens's visit at the Langdons'.

From Susy's Biography

Soon papa came back East and papa and mamma were married.

It sounds easy and swift and unobstructed, but that was not the way of it. It did not happen in that smooth and comfortable way. There was a deal of courtship. There were three or four proposals of marriage and just as many declinations. I was roving far and wide on the lecture beat, but I managed to arrive in Elrnira every now and then and renew the siege. Once I dug an invitation out of Charley Langdon to come and stay a week. It was a pleasant week, but it had to come to an end. I was not able to invent any way to get the invitation enlarged. No schemes that I could contrive seemed likely to deceive. They did not even deceive me, and when a person cannot deceive himself the chances are against his being able to deceive other people. But at last help and good fortune came, and from a most unexpected quarter. It was one of those cases so frequent in the past centuries, so infrequent in our day—a case where the hand of Providence is in it.

I was ready to leave for New York. A democrat wagon stood outside the main gate with my trunk in it, and Barney, the coachman, in the front seat with the reins in his hand. It was eight or nine in the evening, and dark. I bade good-by to the grouped family on the front porch, and Charley and I went out and climbed into the wagon. We took our places back of the coachman on the remaining seat, which was aft toward the end of the wagon, and was only a temporary arrangement for our accommodation, and was not fastened in its place; a fact which—most fortunately for me, we were not aware of. Charley was smoking. Barney touched up the horse with the whip. He made a sudden spring forward. Charley and I went over the stern of the wagon backward. In the darkness the red bud of fire on the end of his cigar described a curve through the air which I can see yet. This was the only visible thing in all that gloomy scenery. I struck exactly on the top of my head and stood up that way for a moment, then crumbled down to the earth unconscious. It was a very good unconsciousness for a person who had not rehearsed the part. It was a cobblestone gutter, and they had been repairing it. My head struck in a dish formed by the conjunction of four cobblestones. That depression was half full of fresh new sand, and this made a competent cushion. My head did not touch any of those cobblestones. I got not a bruise. I was not even jolted. Nothing was the matter with me at all. Charley was considerably battered, but in his solicitude for me he was substantially unaware of it. The whole family swarmed out, Theodore Crane in the van with a flask of brandy. He poured enough of it between my lips to strangle me and make me bark, but it did not abate my unconsciousness. I was taking care of that myself. It was very pleasant to hear the pitying remarks trickling around over me. That was one of the happiest half dozen moments of my life. There was nothing to mar it—except that I had escaped damage. I was afraid that this would be discovered sooner or later, and would shorten my visit. I was such a dead weight that it required the combined strength of Barney and Mr. Langdon, Theodore and Charley, to lug me into the house, but it was accomplished. I was there. I recognized that this was victory. I was there. I was safe to be an incumbrance for an indefinite length of time—but for a length of time, at any rate, and a Providence was in it. They set me up in an armchair in the parlor and sent for the family physician. Poor old creature, it was wrong to rout him out, but it was business, and I was too unconscious to protest. Mrs. Crane—dear soul, she was in this house three days ago, gray and beautiful, and as sympathetic as ever—Mrs. Crane brought a bottle of some kind of liquid fire whose function was to reduce contusions. But I knew that mine would deride it and scoff at it. She poured this on my head and pawed it around with her hand, stroking and massaging, the fierce stuff dribbling down my backbone and marking its way, inch by inch, with the sensation of a forest fire. But I was satisfied. When she was getting worn out, her husband, Theodore, suggested that she take a rest and let Livy carry on the assuaging for a while. That was very pleasant. I should have been obliged to recover presently if it hadn't been for that. But under Livy's manipulations—if they had continued—I should probably be unconscious to this day. It was very delightful, those manipulations. So delightful, so comforting, so enchanting, that they even soothed the fire out of that fiendish successor to Perry Davis's "Pain-Killer."

Then that old family doctor arrived and went at the matter in an educated and practical way—that is to say, he started a search expedition for contusions and humps and bumps, and announced that there were none. He said that if I would go to bed and forget my adventure I would be all right in the morning—which was not so. I was not all right in the morning. I didn't intend to be all right, and I was far from being all right. But I said I only needed rest and I didn't need that doctor any more.

I got a good three days' extension out of that adventure, and it helped a good deal. It pushed my suit forward several steps. A subsequent visit completed the matter, and we became engaged conditionally; the condition being that the parents should consent.

In a private talk Mr. Langdon called my attention to something I had already noticed—which was that I was an almost entirely unknown person; that no one around about knew me except Charley, and he was too young to be a reliable judge of men; that I was from the other side of the continent, and that only those people out there would be able to furnish me a character, in case I had one—so he asked me for references. I furnished them, and he said we would now suspend our industries and I could go away and wait until he could write to those people and get answers.

In due course answers came. I was sent for and we had another private conference. I had referred him to six prominent men, among them two clergymen (these were all San Franciscans), and he himself had written to a bank cashier who had in earlier years been a Sunday-school superintendent in Elmira and well known to Mr. Langdon. The results were not promising. All those men were frank to a fault. They not only spoke in disapproval of me, but they were quite unnecessarily and exaggeratedly enthusiastic about it. One clergyman (Stebbins) and that ex-Sunday-school superintendent (I wish I could recall his name) added to their black testimony the conviction that I would fill a drunkard's grave. It was just one of those usual long-distance prophecies. There being no time limit, there is no telling how long you may have to wait. I have waited until now, and the fulfillment seems as far away as ever.

The reading of the letters being finished, there was a good deal of a pause, and it consisted largely of sadness and solemnity. I couldn't think of anything to say. Mr. Langdon was apparently in the same condition.

MARK TWAIN

Finally he raised his handsome head, fixed his clear and candid eye upon me, and said: "What kind of people are these? Haven't you a friend in the world?"

I said, "Apparently not."

Then he said: "I'll be your friend, myself. Take the girl. I know you better than they do."

Thus dramatically and happily was my fate settled. Afterward, hearing me talking lovingly, admiringly, and fervently of Joe Goodman, he asked me where Goodman lived. I told him out on the Pacific coast. He said: "Why, he seems to be a friend of yours! Is he?"

I said, "Indeed he is; the best one I ever had."

"Why, then," he said, "what could you have been thinking of? Why didn't you refer me to him?"

I said: "Because he would have lied just as straightforwardly on the other side. The others gave me all the vices; Goodman would have given me all the virtues. You wanted unprejudiced testimony, of course. I knew you wouldn't get it from Goodman. I did believe you would get it from those others, and possibly you did. But it was certainly less complimentary than I was expecting."

The date of our engagement was February 4, 1869. The engagement ring was plain, and of heavy gold. That date was engraved inside of it. A year later I took it from her finger and prepared it to do service as a wedding ring by having the wedding date added and engraved inside of it—February 2, 1870. It was never again removed from her finger for even a moment.

In Italy, a year and eight months ago, when death had restored her vanished youth to her sweet face and she lay fair and beautiful and looking as she had looked when she was girl and bride, they were going to take that ring from her finger to keep for the children. But I prevented that sacrilege. It is buried with her.

In the beginning of our engagement the proofs of my first book, The Innocents Abroad, began to arrive, and she read them with me. She also edited them. She was my faithful, judicious, and painstaking editor from that day forth until within three or four months of her death—a stretch of more than a third of a century.

New York, Thursday, February 15, 1906

Susy's biography continued.—Death of Mr. Langdon.—Birth of Langdon Clemens.

Papa wrote mamma a great many beautiful love letters when he was engaged to mamma, but mamma says I am too young to see them yet; I asked papa what I should do for I didn't (know) how I could write a Biography of him without his love letters, papa said that I could write mamma's opinion of them, and that would do just as well. So I'll do as papa says, and mamma says she thinks they are the loveliest love letters that ever were written, she says that Hawthorne's love letters to Mrs. Hawthorne are far inferior to these. Mamma (and papa) were going to board first in Buffalo and grandpa said he would find them a good boarding-house. But he afterwards told mamma that he had bought a pretty house for them, and had it all beautifully furnished, he had also hired a young coachman, Patrick McAleer, and had bought a horse for them, which all would be ready waiting for them, when they should arive in Buffalo; but he wanted to keep it a secret from "Youth," as grandpa called papa. What a delightful surprise it was! Grandpa went down to Buffalo with mamma and papa. And when they drove up to the house, papa said he thought the landlord of such a boarding-house must charge a great deal to those who wanted to live there. And when the secret was told papa was delighted beyond all degree. Mamma has told me the story many times, and I asked her what papa said when grandpa told him that the delightful boarding-house was his home, mamma answered that he was rather embariesed and so delighted he didn't know what to say. About six months after papa and mamma were married grandpa died; it was a terrible blow on mamma, and papa told Aunt Sue he thought Livy would never smile again, she was so broken hearted. Mamma couldn't have had a greater sorrow than that of dear grandpa's death, or any that could equal it exept the death of papa. Mamma helped take care of grandpa during his illness and she couldn't give up hope till the end had realy come.[1]

Surely nothing is so astonishing, so unaccountable, as a woman's endurance. Mrs. Clemens and I went down to Elmira about the 1st of June to help in the nursing of Mr. Langdon. Mrs. Clemens, her sister (Susy Crane), and I did all the nursing both day and night, during two months until the end. Two months of scorching, stifling heat. How much of the nursing did I do? My main watch was from midnight till

---

1. August 6, 1870.—S. L. C.

four in the morning—nearly four hours. My other watch was a midday watch, and I think it was only three hours. The two sisters divided the remaining seventeen hours of the twenty-four between them, and each of them tried generously and persistently to swindle the other out of a part of her watch. The "on" watch could not be depended upon to call the "off" watch—excepting when I was the "on" watch.

I went to bed early every night, and tried to get sleep enough by midnight to fit me for my work, but it was always a failure. I went on watch sleepy and remained miserably sleepy and wretched straight along through the four hours. I can still see myself sitting by that bed in the melancholy stillness of the sweltering night, mechanically waving a palm-leaf fan over the drawn white face of the patient; I can still recall my noddings, my fleeting unconsciousnesses, when the fan would come to a standstill in my hand and I would wake up with a start and a hideous shock. I can recall all the torture of my efforts to keep awake; I can recall the sense of the indolent march of time, and how the hands of the tall clock seemed not to move at all, but to stand still. Through the long vigil there was nothing to do but softly wave the fan—and the gentleness and monotony of the movement itself helped to make me sleepy. The malady was cancer of the stomach, and not curable. There were no medicines to give. It was a case of slow and steady perishing. At long intervals, the foam of champagne was administered to the patient, but no other nourishment, so far as I can remember.

A bird of a breed not of my acquaintance used to begin a sad and wearisome and monotonous piping in the shrubbery near the window a full hour before the dawn, every morning. He had no company; he conducted this torture all alone, and added it to my stock. He never stopped for a moment. I have experienced few things that were more maddening than that bird's lamentings. During all that dreary siege I began to watch for the dawn long before it came; and I watched for it like the duplicate, I think, of the lonely castaway on an island in the sea, who watches the horizon for ships and rescue. When the first faint gray showed through the window blinds I felt as no doubt that castaway feels when the dim threads of the looked-for ship appear against the sky.

I was well and strong, but I was a man and afflicted with a man's infirmity—lack of endurance. But neither of those young women was well nor strong: still, I never found either of them sleepy or unalert when I came on watch; yet, as I have said, they divided seventeen hours of watching between them in every twenty-four. It is a marvelous thing. It filled me with wonder and admiration; also with shame, for my dull incompetency. Of course the physicians begged those daughters to permit the employment of professional nurses, but they would not consent. The mere mention of such a thing grieved them so that the matter was soon dropped, and not again referred to.

All through her life Mrs. Clemens was physically feeble, but her spirit was never weak. She lived upon it all her life, and it was as effective as bodily strength could have been. When our children were little she nursed them through long nights of sickness, as she had nursed her father. I have seen her sit up and hold a sick child upon her knees and croon to it and sway it monotonously to and fro to comfort it, a whole night long, without complaint or respite. But I could not keep awake ten minutes at a time. My whole duty was to put wood on the fire. I did it ten or twelve times during the night, but had to be called every time, and was always asleep again before I finished the operation, or immediately afterward.

No, there is nothing comparable to the endurance of a woman. In military life she would tire out any army of men, either in camp or on the march. I still remember with admiration that woman who got into the overland stage-coach somewhere on the plains, when my brother and I crossed the continent in the summer of 1861, and who sat bolt upright and cheerful, stage after stage, and showed no wear and tear. In those days, the one event of the day, in Carson City, was the arrival of the overland coach. All the town was usually on hand to enjoy the event. The men would climb down out of the coach doubled up with cramps, hardly able to walk; their bodies worn, their spirits worn, their nerves raw, their tempers at a devilish point; but the women stepped out smiling and apparently unfatigued.

From Susy's Biography

After grandpapa's death mamma and papa went back to Buffalo; and three months afterward dear little Langdon was born. Mamma named him Langdon after grandpapa, he was a wonderfully beautiful little boy, but very, very delicate. He had wonderful blue eyes, but such a blue that mamma has never been able to describe them to me so that I could see them clearly in my mind's eye. His delicate health was a constant anxiety to mamma, and he was so good and sweet that that must have troubled her too, as I know it did.

Susy's biography mentions little Langdon.—The change of residence from Buffalo to Hartford.—Mr. Clemens tells of the sale of his Buffalo paper.

From Susy's Biography

While Langdon was a little baby he used to carry a pencil in his little hand, that was his great plaything; I believe he was very seldom seen without one in his hand. When he was in Aunt Susy's arms and would want to go to mamma he would hold out his hands to her with the backs of his hands out toward her instead of with his palmes out. (About a year and five months) after Langdon was born I was born, and my chief occupation then was to cry, so I must have added greatly to mamma's care. Soon after little Langdon was born (a year) papa and mamma moved to Hartford to live. Their house in Bufalo reminded them too much of dear grandpapa, so they moved to Hartford soon after he died.

Soon after little Langdon was born a friend of mamma's came to visit her (Emma Nigh)[1] and she was taken with the typhoid fever, while visiting mamma. At length she became so delirious, and so hard to take care of that mamma had to send to some of her friends in Elmira to come and help take care of her. Aunt Clara came, (Miss Clara L. Spaulding). She is no relation of ours but we call her Aunt Clara because she is such a great friend of mamma's. She came and helped mamma take care of Emma Nigh, but in spite of all the good care that she received, she grew worse and died.

Susy is right. Our year and a half in Buffalo had so saturated us with horrors and distress that we became restless and wanted to change, either to a place with pleasanter associations or with none at all. In accordance with the hard terms of that fearful law—the year of mourning—which deprives the mourner of the society and comradeship of his race when he most needs it, we shut ourselves up in the house and became recluses, visiting no one and receiving visits from no one. There was one exception—a single exception. David Gray—poet, and editor of the principal newspaper—was our intimate friend, through his intimacy and mine with John Hay. David had a

---

1. Nye.

young wife and a young baby. The Grays and the Clemenses visited back and forth frequently, and this was all the solace the Clemenses had in their captivity.

When we could endure imprisonment no longer, Mrs. Clemens sold the house and I sold my one-third interest in the newspaper, and we went to Hartford to live. I have some little business sense now, acquired through hard experience and at great expense; but I had none in those days. I had bought Mr. Kinney's share of that newspaper (I think the name was Kinney) at his price—which was twenty-five thousand dollars. Later I found that all that I had bought of real value was the Associated Press privilege. I think we did not make a very large use of that privilege. It runs in my mind that about every night the Associated Press would offer us five thousand words at the usual rate, and that we compromised on five hundred. Still, that privilege was worth fifteen thousand dollars, and was easily salable at that price. I sold my whole share in the paper—including that solitary asset—for fifteen thousand dollars. Kinney (if that was his name) was so delighted at his smartness in selling a property to me for twenty-five thousand that was not worth three-fourths of the money, that he was not able to keep his joy to himself, but talked it around pretty freely and made himself very happy over it. I could have explained to him that what he mistook for his smartness was a poor and driveling kind of thing. If there had been a triumph, if there had been a mental exhibition of a majestic sort, it was not his smartness; it was my stupidity; the credit was all due to me. He was a brisk and ambitious and self-appreciative young fellow, and he left straightway for New York and Wall Street, with his head full of sordid and splendid dreams—dreams of the "get rich quick" order; dreams to be realized through the dreamer's smartness and the other party's stupidity. Kinney had no place in Wall Street. He quickly lost the money he had gouged out of it.

Tuesday, February 20, 1906

About Rear-Admiral Wilkes.—And meeting Mr. Anson Burlingame in Honolulu.

Mrs. Mary Wilkes Dead.

Florence, Italy, Feb. 19.—Mrs. Mary Wilkes, widow of Rear-Admiral Wilkes, U. S. N., is dead, aged eighty-five.

It is death notices like this that enable me to realize in some sort how long I have lived. They drive away the haze from my life's road and give me glimpses of the beginning of it—glimpses of things which seem incredibly remote.

When I was a boy of ten, in that village on the Mississippi River which at that time was so incalculably far from any place and is now so near to all places, the name of Wilkes, the explorer, was in everybody's mouth, just as Roosevelt's is today. What a noise it made, and how wonderful the glory! How far away and how silent it is now! And the glory has faded to tradition. Wilkes had discovered a new world and was another Columbus. That world afterward turned mainly to ice and snow. But it was not all ice and snow—and in our late day we are rediscovering it, and the world's interest in it has revived. Wilkes was a marvel in another way, for he had gone wandering about the globe in his ships and had looked with his own eyes upon its furthest corners, its dreamlands—names and places which existed rather as shadows and rumors than as realities. But everybody visits those places now, in outings and summer excursions, and no fame is to be gotten out of it.

One of the last visits I made in Florence—this was two years ago—was to Mrs. Wilkes. She had sent and asked me to come, and it seemed a chapter out of the romantic and the impossible that I should be looking upon the gentle face of the sharer in that long-forgotten glory. We talked of the common things of the day, but my mind was not present. It was wandering among the snowstorms and the ice floes and the fogs and mysteries of the antarctic with this patriarchal lady's young husband. Nothing remarkable was said; nothing remarkable happened. Yet a visit has seldom impressed me so much as did this one.

HERE IS A PLEASANT AND welcome letter, which plunges me back into the antiquities again:

KNOLLWOOD, WESTFIELD, NEW JERSEY.
February 17, 1906

MY DEAR MR. CLEMENS:

I should like to tell you how much I thank you for an article which you wrote once, long ago, (1870 or '71) about my grandfather, Anson Burlingame.

In looking over the interesting family papers and letters, which have come into my possession this winter, nothing has impressed me more deeply than your tribute. I have read it again and again. I found it pasted into a scrapbook and apparently it was cut from a newspaper. It is signed with your name.

It seems to bring before one more clearly, than anything I have been told or read, my grandfather's personality and achievements. . .

Family traditions grow less and less in the telling. Young children are so impatient of anecdotes, and when they grow old enough to understand their value, frequent repetitions, as well as newer interests and associations, seem to have dulled, not the memory, but the spontaneity and joy of telling about the old days—so unless there is something written and preserved, how much is lost to children of the good deeds of their fathers.

Perhaps it will give you a little pleasure to know that after all these years, the words you wrote about "a good man, and a very, very great man" have fallen into the heart of one to whom his fame is very near and precious. You say "Mr. Burlingame's short history—for he was only forty-seven—reads like a fairy-tale. Its successes, its surprises, its happy situations occur all along, and each new episode is always an improvement upon the one which went before it." That seems to have been very true and it is interesting to hear, although it has the sad ring of Destiny. But how shall I ever thank you for words like these? "He was a true man, a just man, a generous man, in all his ways and by all his instincts a noble man—a man of great brain, a broad, and deep and mighty thinker. He was a great man, a very, very great man. He was imperially endowed by nature, he was faithfully befriended by circumstances, and he wrought gallantly always in whatever station he found himself." How indeed shall I thank you for these words or tell you how deeply they have touched me, and how truly I shall endeavor to teach them to my children.

That your fame may be as sacred as this, is my earnest, grateful wish, not wholly the inevitable, imperishable fame that is laid down for you, but the sweet and precious fame, to your family and friends forever, of the fair attributes you ascribe to my grandfather, which could never have been discerned by one who was not like him in spirit.

With the hope some time of knowing you,

Yours sincerely,

JEAN BURLINGAME BEATTY

(Mrs. Robert Chetwood Beatty)

This carries me back forty years, to my first meeting with that wise and just and humane and charming man and great citizen and diplomat, Anson Burlingame. It was in Honolulu. He had arrived in his ship, on his way out on his great mission to China, and I had the honor and profit of his society daily and constantly during many days. He was a handsome and stately and courtly and graceful creature, in the prime of his perfect manhood, and it was a contenting pleasure to look at him. His outlook upon the world and its affairs was as wide as the horizon, and his speech was of a dignity and eloquence proper to it. It dealt in no commonplaces, for he had no commonplace thoughts. He was a kindly man, and most lovable. He was not a petty politician, but a great and magnanimous statesman. He did not serve his country alone, but China as well. He held the balances even. He wrought for justice and humanity. All his ways were clean; all his motives were high and fine.

He had beautiful eyes; deep eyes; speaking eyes; eyes that were dreamy, in repose; eyes that could beam and persuade like a lover's; eyes that could blast when his temper was up, I judge. Preston S. Brooks, the congressional bully, found this out in his day, no doubt. Brooks had bullied everybody, insulted everybody, challenged everybody, cowed everybody, and was cock of the walk in Washington. But when he challenged the new young Congressman from the West he found a prompt and ardent man at last. Burlingame chose rifles at short range, and Brooks apologized and retired from his bullyship with the laughter of the nation ringing in his ears.

When Mr. Burlingame arrived at Honolulu I had been confined to my room a couple of weeks—by night to my bed, by day to a splint-bottom chair, deep-sunk like a basket. There was another chair, but I preferred this one, because my malady was saddle boils.

When the boatload of skeletons arrived after forty-three days in an open boat on ten days' provisions—survivors of the clipper Hornet, which had perished by fire several thousand miles away—it was necessary for me to interview them for the Sacramento Union, a journal which I had been commissioned to represent in the Sandwich Islands for a matter of five or six months. Mr. Burlingame put me on a cot and had me carried to the hospital, and during several hours he questioned the skeletons and I set down the answers in my note-book. It took me all night to write out my narrative of the Hornet disaster, and—but I will go no further with the subject now. I have already told the rest in some book of mine.

Mr. Burlingame gave me some advice, one day, which I have never forgotten, and which I have lived by for forty years. He said, in substance:

"Avoid inferiors. Seek your comradeships among your superiors in intellect and character; always climb."

Mr. Burlingame's son—now editor of Scribner's Magazine these many years and soon to reach the foothills that lie near the frontiers of age—was with him there in Honolulu; a handsome boy of nineteen, and overflowing with animation, activity, energy, and the pure joy of being alive. He attended balls and fandangos and hula hulas every night—anybody's, brown, half white, white—and he could dance all night and be as fresh as ever the next afternoon. One day he delighted me with a joke which I afterward used in a lecture in San Francisco, and from there it traveled all around in the newspapers. He said, "If a man compel thee to go with him a mile, go with him Twain."

When it was new, it seemed exceedingly happy and bright, but it has been emptied upon me upward of several million times since—never by a witty and engaging lad like Burlingame, but always by chuckle-heads of base degree, who did it with offensive eagerness and with the conviction that they were the first in the field. And so it has finally lost its sparkle and bravery, and is become to me a seedy and repulsive tramp whose proper place is in the hospital for the decayed, the friendless, and the forlorn.

New York, Wednesday, February 21, 1906
Mr. Langdon just escapes being a railway magnate.

But I am wandering far from Susy's Biography. I remember that I was about to explain a remark which I had been making about Susy's grandfather Langdon having just barely escaped once the good luck—or the bad luck—of becoming a great railway magnate. The incident has interest for me for more than one reason. Its details came to my

MARK TWAIN

knowledge in a chance way in a conversation which I had with my father-in-law when I was arranging a contract with my publisher for Roughing It, my second book. I told him the publisher had arrived from Hartford, and would come to the house in the afternoon to discuss the contract and complete it with the signatures. I said I was going to require half the profits over the essential costs of manufacture. He asked if that arrangement would be perfectly fair to both parties, and said it was neither good business nor good morals to make contracts which gave to one side the advantage. I said that the terms which I was proposing were fair to both parties. Then Mr. Langdon after a musing silence said, with something like a reminiscent sorrow in his tone, "When you and the publisher shall have gotten the contract framed to suit you both and no doubts about it are left in your minds, sign it—sign it: to-day, don't wait till tomorrow."

It transpired that he had acquired this wisdom, which he was giving me gratis, at considerable expense. He had acquired it twenty years earlier, or thereabouts, at the Astor House in New York, where he and a dozen other rising and able business men were gathered together to secure a certain railroad which promised to be a good property by and by, if properly developed and wisely managed. This was the Lehigh Valley Railroad. There were a number of conflicting interests to be reconciled before the deal could be consummated. The men labored over these things the whole afternoon, in a private parlor of that hotel. They dined, then reassembled and continued their labors until after two in the morning. Then they shook hands all around in great joy and enthusiasm, for they had achieved success and had drawn a contract in the rough which was ready for the signatures. The signing was about to begin; one of the men sat at the table with his pen poised over the fateful document, when somebody said: "Oh, we are tired to death. There is no use in continuing this torture any longer. Everything's satisfactory. Let's sign in the morning." All assented, and that pen was laid aside.

Mr. Langdon said: "We got five or ten minutes' additional sleep that night by that postponement, but it cost us several millions apiece, and it was a fancy price to pay. If we had paid out of our existing means, and the price had been a single million apiece, we should have had to sit up, for there wasn't a man among us who could have met the obligation completely. The contract was never signed. We had traded a Bank of England for ten minutes' extra sleep—a very small sleep, an apparently unimportant sleep, but it has kept us tired ever since. When you've got your contract right, this afternoon, sign it."

I followed that advice. It was thirty-five years ago, but it has kept me tired ever since.

New York, Thursday, February 22, 1906
Susy's remarks about her grandfather Langdon.—Mr. Clemens tells about Mr. Atwater, Mr. David Gray, and about meeting David Gray, Jr., at a dinner recently.

I have wandered far from Susy's chat about her grandfather, but that is no matter. In this autobiography it is my purpose to wander whenever I please and come back when I get ready. I have now come back, and we will set down what Susy has to say about her grandfather.

From Susy's Biography

I mentioned that mamma and papa couldn't stay in their house in Buffalo because it reminded them so much of grandpapa. Mamma received a letter from Aunt Susy in which Aunt Susy says a good deal about grandpapa, and the letter showed so clearly how much every one that knew grandpapa loved and respected him, that mamma let me take it to copy what is in it about grandpapa, and mamma thought it would fit in nicely here.

Quarry Farm,

April 16, '85
Livy dear, are you not reminded by to-day's report of General Grant of father? You remember how as Judge Smith and others whom father had chosen as executors were going out of the room, he said "Gentlemen I shall live to bury you all"—smiled, and was cheerful. At that time he had far less strength than General Grant seems to have, but that same wonderful courage to battle with the foe. All along there has been much to remind me of father—of his quiet patience— in General Grant. There certainly is a marked likeness in the souls of the two men. Watching, day by day, the reports from the Nation's sick room brings to mind so vividly the days of that summer of 1870. And yet they seem so far away.

I seemed as a child, compared with now, both in years and experience. The best and the hardest of life have been since then to me, and I know this is so in your life. All before seems dreamy. I sepose this was because our lives had to be all readjusted to go on without that great power in them. Father was quietly such a power in so many lives beside ours, Livy dear—not in kind or degree the same to any one but oh, a power!

The evening of the last company, I was so struck with the fact that Mr. Atwater stood quietly before father's portrait a long time and turning to me said, "We shall never see his like again," with a tremble and a choking in his voice—this after fifteen years, and from a business friend. And some stranger, a week ago, spoke of his habit of giving, as so remarkable, he having heard of father's generosity. . .

I remember Mr. Atwater very well. There was nothing citified about him or his ways. He was in middle age, and had lived in the country all his life. He had the farmer look, the farmer gait; he wore the farmer clothes, and also the farmer goatee, a decoration which had been universal when I was a boy. But was now become extinct in some of the Western towns and in all of the Eastern towns and cities. He was transparently a good and sincere and honest man. He was a humble helper of Mr. Langdon, and had been in his employ many years. His rôle was general utility. If Mr. Langdon's sawmills needed unscientific but plain common-sense inspection, Atwater was sent on that service. If Mr. Langdon's timber rafts got into trouble on account of a falling river or a rising one, Atwater was sent to look after the matter. Atwater went on modest errands to Mr. Langdon's coal mines; also to examine and report upon Mr. Langdon's interests in the budding coal-oil fields of Pennsylvania. Mr. Atwater was always busy, always moving, always useful in humble ways, always religious, and always ungrammatical, except when he had just finished talking and had used up what he had in stock of that kind of grammar. He was effective—that is, he was effective if there was plenty of time. But he was constitutionally slow, and as he had to discuss all his matters with whomsoever came along, it sometimes happened that the occasion for his services had gone by before he got them in. Mr. Langdon never would discharge Atwater, though young Charley Langdon suggested that course now and then. Young Charley could not abide Atwater, because of his provoking dilatoriness and of his comfortable contentment in it. But I loved Atwater. Atwater was a treasure to me. When he would arrive from one of his inspection journeys and sit at the table, at noon, and tell the family all about the campaign in delicious detail, leaving out not a single inane, inconsequential, and colorless incident of it, I heard it gratefully; I enjoyed Mr. Langdon's placid patience with it; the family's despondency and despair; and more than all these pleasures together, the vindictiveness in young Charley's eyes and the volcanic disturbances going on inside of him which I could not see, but which I knew were there.

I am dwelling upon Atwater just for love. I have nothing important to say about Atwater—in fact, only one thing to say about him at all. And even that one thing I could leave unmentioned if I wanted to—but I don't want to. It has been a pleasant memory to me for a whole generation. It lets in a fleeting ray of light upon Livy's gentle and calm and equable spirit. Although she could feel strongly and utter her feelings strongly, none but a person familiar with her and with all her moods would ever be able to tell by her language that that language was violent. Young Charley had many and many a time tried to lodge a seed of unkindness against Atwater in Livy's heart, but she was as steadfast in her fidelity as was her father, and Charley's efforts always failed. Many and many a time he brought to her a charge against Atwater which he believed would bring the longed-for bitter word, and at last he scored a success—for "all things come to him who waits."

I was away at the time, but Charley could not wait for me to get back. He was too glad, too eager. He sat down at once and wrote to me while his triumph was fresh and his happiness hot and contenting. He told me how he had laid the whole exasperating matter before Livy and then had asked her, "Now what do you say?" And she said, "Damn Atwater."

Charley knew that there was no need to explain this to me. He knew I would perfectly understand. He knew that I would know that he was not quoting, but was translating. He knew that I would know that his translation was exact, was perfect, that it conveyed the precise length, breadth, weight, meaning, and force of the words which Livy had really used. He knew that I would know that the phrase which she really uttered was, "I disapprove of Atwater."

He was quite right. In her mouth that word "disapprove" was as blighting and withering and devastating as another person's damn.

One or two days ago I was talking about our sorrowful and pathetic brief sojourn in Buffalo, where we became hermits, and could have no human comradeship except that of young David Gray and his young wife and their baby boy. It seems an age ago. Last night I was at a large dinner party at Norman Hapgood's palace uptown, and a very long and very slender gentleman was introduced to me—a gentleman with a fine, alert, and intellectual face, with a becoming gold pince-nez on his nose and clothed in an evening costume which was perfect from the broad spread of immaculate bosom to the rosetted slippers on his feet. His gait, his bows, and his intonations were those of an English gentleman, and I took him for an earl. I said I had not understood his name, and asked him what it was. He said "David Gray." The effect was startling. His very father stood before me, as I had known him in Buffalo thirty-six years ago. This apparition called up pleasant times in the beer mills of Buffalo with David Gray and John Hay when this David Gray was in his cradle, a beloved and troublesome possession. And this contact kept me in Buffalo during the next hour, and made it difficult for me to keep up my end of the conversation at my extremity of the dinner table. The text of my reveries was: "What was he born for? What was his father born for? What was I born for? What is anybody born for?"

His father was a poet, but was doomed to grind out his living in a most uncongenial occupation—the editing of a daily political newspaper. He was a singing bird in a menagerie of monkeys, macaws, and hyenas. His life was wasted. He had come from Scotland when he was five years old; he had come saturated to the bones with Presbyterianism of the bluest, the most uncompromising and most unlovely shade. At thirty-three, when I was comrading with him, his Presbyterianism was all gone and he had become a frank rationalist and pronounced unbeliever. After a few years news came to me in Hartford that he had had a sunstroke. By and by the news came that his brain was affected, as a result. After another considerable interval I heard, through Ned House, who had been visiting him, that he was no longer able to competently write either politics or poetry, and was living quite privately and teaching a daily Bible class of young people, and was interested in nothing else. His unbelief had passed away; his early Presbyterianism had taken its place.

This was true. Some time after this I telegraphed and asked him to meet me at the railway station. He came, and I had a few minutes' talk with him—this for the last time. The same sweet spirit of the earlier days looked out of his deep eyes. He was the same David I had known before—great, and fine, and blemishless in character, a creature to adore.

Not long afterward he was crushed and burned up in a railway disaster, at night—and I probably thought then, as I was thinking now, through the gay laughter-and-chatter fog of that dinner table: "What was he born for? What was the use of it?" These tiresome and monotonous repetitions of the human life—where is their value? Susy asked that question when she was a little child. There was nobody then who could answer it; there is nobody yet.

When Mr. Langdon died, on the 6th of August, 1870, I found myself suddenly introduced into what was to me a quite new rôle—that of business man, temporarily.

Friday, February 23, 1906

Mr. Clemens tells how he became a business man.

During the previous year or year and a half, Mr. Langdon had suffered some severe losses through a relative, an annex of the family by marriage, who had paved Memphis, Tennessee, with the wooden pavement so popular in that day. He had done this as Mr. Langdon's agent. Well managed, the contract would have yielded a sufficient profit, but through mismanagement it had merely yielded a large loss. With Mr. Langdon alive, this loss was not a matter of consequence and could not cripple the business. But with Mr. Langdon's brain and hand and credit and high character removed, it was another matter. He was a dealer in anthracite coal. He sold this coal over a stretch of country extending as far as Chicago, and he had important branches of his business in a number of cities. His agents were usually considerably in debt to him, and he was correspondingly in debt to the owners of the mines. His death left three young men in charge of the business—young Charley Langdon, Theodore Crane, and Mr. Slee. He had recently made them partners in the business, by gift. But they were unknown. The business world knew J. Langdon, a name that was a power, but these three young men were ciphers without a unit. Slee turned out afterward to be a very able man and a most capable and persuasive negotiator, but at the time that I speak of his qualities were quite unknown. Mr. Langdon had trained him, and he was well equipped for his headship of the little firm. Theodore Crane was competent in his line—that of head clerk and superintendent of the subordinate clerks. No better man could have been found for that place; but his capacities were limited to that position. He was good and upright and indestructibly honest and honorable, but he had neither desire nor ambition to be anything above chief clerk. He was much too timid for larger work or larger responsibilities. Young Charley was twenty-one, and not any older than his age—that is to say, he was a boy.

A careful statement of Mr. Langdon's affairs showed that the assets were worth eight hundred thousand dollars, and that against them was merely the ordinary obligations of the business. Bills aggregating perhaps three hundred thousand dollars—possibly four hundred thousand—would have to be paid; half in about a month, the other half in about two months. The collections to meet these obligations would come in further along. With Mr. Langdon alive, these debts could be no embarrassment. He could go to the bank in the town, or in New York, and borrow the money without any trouble, but these boys couldn't do that. They could get one hundred and fifty thousand dollars cash, at once, but that was all. It was Mr. Langdon's life insurance. It was paid promptly, but it could not go far—that is it could not go far enough. It did not fall short much—in fact, only fifty thousand dollars, but where to get the fifty thousand dollars was a puzzle. They wrote to Mr. Henry W. Sage, of Ithaca, an old and warm friend and former business partner of Mr. Langdon, and begged him to come to Elmira and give them advice and help. He replied that he would come. Then, to my consternation, the young firm appointed me to do the negotiating with him. It was like asking me to calculate an eclipse. I had no idea of how to begin nor what to say. But they brought the big balance sheet to the house and sat down with me in the library and explained, and explained, and explained, until at last I did get a fairly clear idea of what I must say to Mr. Sage.

When Mr. Sage came he and I went to the library to examine that balance sheet, and the firm waited and trembled in some other part of the house. When I got through explaining the situation to Mr. Sage I got struck by lightning again—that is to say, he furnished me a fresh astonishment. He was a man with a straight mouth and a wonderfully firm jaw. He was the kind of man who puts his whole mind on a thing and keeps that kind of a mouth shut and locked all the way through, while the other man states the case. On this occasion I should have been grateful for some slight indication from him, during my long explanation, which might indicate that I was making at least some kind of an impression upon him, favorable or unfavorable. But he kept my heart on the strain all the way through, and I never could catch any hint of what was passing through his mind. But at the finish he spoke out with that robust decision which was a part of his character and said:

"Mr. Clemens, you've got as clear a business head on your shoulders as I have come in contact with for years. What are you an author for? You ought to be a business man."

I knew better, but it was not diplomatic to say so, and I didn't. Then he said:

"All you boys need is my note for fifty thousand dollars, at three months, handed in at the bank, and with that support you will not need the money. If it shall be necessary to extend the note, tell Mr. Arnot it will be extended. The business is all right. Go ahead with it and have no fears. It is my opinion that this note will come back to me without your having extracted a dollar from it, at the end of the three months."

It happened just as he had said. Old Mr. Arnot, the Scotch banker, a very rich and very careful man and life-long friend of Mr. Langdon, watched the young firm and advised it out of his rich store of commercial wisdom, and at the end of the three months the firm was an established and growing concern, and the note was sent back to Mr. Sage without our having needed to extract anything from it. It was a small piece of paper, insignificant in its dimensions, insignificant in the sum which it represented, but formidable was its influence, and formidable was its power, because of the man who stood behind it.

The Sages and the Twichells were very intimate. One or two years later, Mr. Sage came to Hartford on a visit to Joe, and as soon as he had gone away Twichell rushed over to our house, eager to tell me something; something which had astonished him, and which he believed would astonish me. He said:

"Why, Mark, you know, Mr. Sage, one of the best business men in America, says that you have quite extraordinary business talents."

Again I didn't deny it. I would not have had that superstition dissipated for anything. It supplied a long-felt want. We are always more anxious to be distinguished for a talent which we do not possess than to be praised for the fifteen which we do possess.

Monday, February 26, 1906
Susy comes to New York with her mother and father.—Aunt Clara visits them at the Everett House.—Aunt Clara's ill luck with horses.— The omnibus incident in Germany.—Aunt Clara now ill at Hoffman

House, result of horseback accident thirty years ago.—Mr. Clemens takes Susy to see General Grant.—Mr. Clement's account of his talk with General Grant.—Mr. Clemens gives his first reading in New York—also tells about one in Boston.—Memorial to Mr. Longfellow, and one in Washington.

From Susy's Biography

Papa made arrangements to read at Vassar College the 1st of May, and I went with him. We went by way of New York City. Mamma went with us to New York and stayed two days to do some shopping. We started Tuesday, at 1/2 past two o'clock in the afternoon, and reached New York about 1/4 past six. Papa went right up to General Grants from the station and mamma and I went to the Everett House. Aunt Clara came to supper with us up in our room.

THIS IS THE SAME AUNT Clara who has already been mentioned several times. She had been my wife's playmate and schoolmate from the earliest times, and she was about my wife's age, or two or three years younger—mentally, morally, spiritually, and in all ways, a superior and lovable personality.

Persons who think there is no such thing as luck—good or bad—are entitled to their opinion. Clara Spaulding had the average human being's luck in all things save one; she was subject to ill luck with horses. It pursued her like a disease. Every now and then a horse threw her. Every now and then carriage horses ran away with her. At intervals omnibus horses ran away with her. Usually there was but one person hurt, and she was selected for that function. In Germany once our little family started from the inn (in Worms, I think it was) to go to the station. The vehicle of transportation was a great long omnibus drawn by a battery of four great horses. Every seat in the bus was occupied, and the aggregate of us amounted to a good two dozen persons, possibly one or two more. I said playfully to Clara Spaulding: "I think you ought to walk to the station. It isn't right for you to imperil the lives of such a crowd of inoffensive people as this." When we had gone a quarter of a mile and were briskly approaching a stone bridge which had no protecting railings, the battery broke and began to run. Outside we saw the long reins dragging along the ground and a young peasant racing after them and occasionally making a grab for them. Presently he achieved success, and none too soon, for the bus had already entered upon the bridge when he stopped the team. The two dozen lives were saved. Nobody offered to take up a collection, but I suggested to our friend and excursion comrade—American consul at a German city— that we get out and tip that young peasant. The consul said, with an enthusiasm native to his character: "Stay right where you are. Leave me to attend to that. His fine deed shall not go unrewarded." He jumped out and arranged the matter, and we continued our journey. Afterward I asked him what he gave the peasant, so that I could pay my half. He told me, and I paid it. It is twenty-eight years ago, yet from that day to this, although I have passed through some stringent seasons, I have never seriously felt or regretted that outlay. It was twenty-three cents.

Clara Spaulding, now Mrs. John B. Stanchfield, is in New York at present, and I went to the Hoffman House yesterday to see her, but it was as I was expecting: she is too ill to see any but physicians and nurses. This illness has its source in a horseback accident which fell to her share thirty years ago and which resulted in broken bones of the foot and ankle. The broken bones were badly set and she always walked with a limp afterward. Some months ago the foot and ankle began to pain her unendurably and it was decided that she must come to New York and have the bones rebroken and reset. I saw her in the private hospital about three weeks after that operation, and the verdict was that the operation was successful. This turned out to be a mistake. She came to New York a month or six weeks ago, and another rebreaking and resetting was accomplished. A week ago, when I called, she was able to hobble about the room by help of crutches, and she was very happy in the conviction that now she was going to have no more trouble. But it appears that this dreadful surgery-work must be done over once more. But she is not fitted for it. The pain is reducing her strength, and I was told that it has been for the past three days necessary to exclude her from contact with all but physicians and nurses.

From Susy's Biography

We and Aunt Clara were going to the theatre right after supper, and we expected papa to take us there and to come home as early as he could. But we got through dinner and he didn't come, and didn't come, and mamma got more perplexed and worried, but at last we thought we would have to go without him. So we put on our things and started

MARK TWAIN

down stairs but before we'd goten half down we met papa coming up with a great bunch of roses in his hand. He explained that the reason he was so late was that his watch stopped and he didn't notice and kept thinking it an hour earlier than it really was. The roses he carried were some Col. Fred Grant sent to mamma. We went to the theatre and enjoyed "Adonis" (word illegible) acted very much. We reached home about 1/2 past eleven o'clock and went right to bed. Wednesday morning we got up rather late and had breakfast about 1/2 past nine o'clock. After breakfast mamma went on shopping and papa and I went to see papa's agent about some business matters. After papa had gotten through talking to Cousin Charlie (Webster), papa's agent, we went to get a friend of papa's, Major Pond, to go and see a Dog Show with us. Then we went to see the dogs with Major Pond and we had a delightful time seeing so many dogs together; when we got through seeing the dogs papa thought he would go and see General Grant and I went with him—this was April 29, 1885. Papa went up into General Grant's room and he took me with him, I felt greatly honored and delighted when papa took me into General Grant's room and let me see the General and Col. Grant, for General Grant is a man I shall be glad all my life that I have seen. Papa and General Grant had a long talk together and papa has written an account of his talk and visit with General Grant for me to put into this biography.

Susy has inserted in this place that account of mine—as follows:

April 29, 1885

I called on General Grant and took Susy with me. The General was looking and feeling far better than he had looked or felt for some months. He had ventured to work again on his book that morning—the first time he had done any work for perhaps a month. This morning's work was his first attempt at dictating, and it was a thorough success, to his great delight. He had always said that it would be impossible for him to dictate anything, but I had said that he was noted for clearness of statement, and as a narrative was simply a statement of consecutive facts, he was consequently peculiarly qualified and equipped for dictation. This turned out to be true. For he had dictated two hours that morning to a shorthand writer, had never hesitated for words, had not repeated himself, and the manuscript when finished needed no revision. The two hours' work was an account of Appomattox—and this was such an extremely important feature that his book would necessarily have been severely lame without it. Therefore I had taken a shorthand writer there before, to see if I could not get him to write at least a few lines about Appomattox.[1] But he was at that time not well enough to undertake it. I was aware that of all the hundred versions of Appomattox, not one was really correct. Therefore I was extremely anxious that he should leave behind him the truth. His throat was not distressing him, and his voice was much better and stronger than usual. He was so delighted to have gotten Appomattox accomplished once more in his life—to have gotten the matter off his mind—that he was as talkative as his old self. He received Susy very pleasantly, and then fell to talking about certain matters which he hoped to be able to dictate next day; and he said in substance that, among other things, he wanted to settle once for all a question that had been bandied about from mouth to mouth and from newspaper to newspaper. That question was: "With whom originated the idea of the march to the sea? Was it Grant's, or was it Sherman's idea?" Whether I or some one else (being anxious to get the important fact settled) asked him with whom the idea originated, I don't remember. But I remember his answer. I shall always remember his answer. General Grant said:

"NEITHER OF US ORIGINATED THE idea of Sherman's march to the sea. The enemy did it."

He went on to say that the enemy, however, necessarily originated a great many of the plans that the general on the opposite side gets the credit for; at the same time that the enemy is doing that, he is laying open other moves which the opposing general sees and takes advantage of. In this case, Sherman had a plan all thought out, of course. He meant to destroy the two remaining railroads in that part of the country, and that would have finished up that region. But General Hood did not play the military part that he was expected to play. On the contrary, General Hood made a dive at Chattanooga. This left the march to the sea open to Sherman, and so after sending part of his army to defend and hold what he had acquired in the Chattanooga region, he was perfectly free to proceed, with the rest of it, through Georgia. He saw the opportunity, and he would not have been fit for his place if he had not seized it.

---

1. I was his publisher, I was putting his Personal Memoirs to press at the time.—S. L. C.

"He wrote me" (the General is speaking) "what his plan was, and I sent him word to go ahead. My staff were opposed to the movement." (I think the General said they tried to persuade him to stop Sherman. The chief of his staff, the General said, even went so far as to go to Washington without the General's knowledge and get the ear of the authorities, and he succeeded in arousing their fears to such an extent that they telegraphed General Grant to stop Sherman.)

Then General Grant said, "Out of deference to the government, I telegraphed Sherman and stopped him twenty-four hours; and then, considering that that was deference enough to the government, I telegraphed him to go ahead again."

I have not tried to give the General's language, but only the general idea of what he said. The thing that mainly struck me was his terse remark that the enemy originated the idea of the march to the sea. It struck me because it was so suggestive of the General's epigrammatic fashion—saying a great deal in a single crisp sentence. (This is my account, and signed Mark Twain.)

AFTER PAPA AND GENERAL GRANT had had their talk, we went back to the hotel where mamma was, and papa told mamma all about his interview with General Grant. Mamma and I had a nice quiet afternoon together.

THAT PAIR OF DEVOTED COMRADES were always shutting themselves up together when there was opportunity to have what Susy called "a cozy time." From Susy's nursery days to the end of her life, she and her mother were close friends, intimate friends, passionate adorers of each other. Susy's was a beautiful mind, and it made her an interesting comrade. And with the fine mind she had a heart like her mother's. Susy never had an interest or an occupation which she was not glad to put aside for that something which was in all cases more precious to her—a visit with her mother.

Susy died at the right time, the fortunate time of life, the happy age—twenty-four years. At twenty-four, such a girl has seen the best of life—life as a happy dream. After that age the risks begin; responsibility comes, and with it the cares, the sorrows, and the inevitable tragedy. For her mother's sake, I would have brought her back from the grave if I could, but not for my own.

Then papa went to read in public; there were a great many authors that read, that Thursday afternoon, beside papa; I would have liked to have gone and heard papa read, but papa said he was going to read in Vassar just what he was planning to read in New York, so I stayed at home with mamma.

I think that that was the first exploitation of a new and devilish invention—the thing called an Authors' Reading. This witch's Sabbath took place in a theater, and began at two in the afternoon. There were nine readers on the list, and I believe I was the only one who was qualified by experience to go at the matter in a sane way. I knew, by my old acquaintanceship with the multiplication table, that nine times ten are ninety, and that consequently the average of time allowed to each of these readers should be restricted to ten minutes. There would be an introducer, and he wouldn't understand his business—this disastrous fact could be counted upon as a certainty. The introducer would be ignorant, windy, eloquent, and willing to hear himself talk. With nine introductions to make, added to his own opening speech—well, I could not go on with these harrowing calculations; I foresaw that there was trouble on hand. I had asked for the sixth place in the list. When the curtain went up and I saw that our half circle of minstrels were all on hand, I made a change in my plan. I judged that in asking for sixth place I had done all that was necessary to establish a fictitious reputation for modesty, and that there could be nothing gained by pushing this reputation to the limit; it had done its work and it was time, now, to leave well enough alone, and do better. So I asked to be moved up to third place, and my prayer was granted.

The performance began at a quarter past two, and I, number three in a list of ten (if we include the introducer), was not called to the bat until a quarter after three. My reading was ten minutes long. When I had selected it originally, it was twelve minutes long, and it had taken me a good hour to find ways of reducing it by two minutes without damaging it. I was through in ten minutes. Then I retired to my seat to enjoy the agonies of the audience. I did enjoy them for an hour or two; then all the cruelty in my nature was exhausted and my native humanity came to the front again. By half past five a third of the house was asleep; another third were dying; and the rest were dead. I got out the back way and went home.

During several years, after that, the Authors' Readings continued. Every now and then we assembled in Boston, New York, Philadelphia, Baltimore, Washington, and scourged the people. It was found impossible to teach the persons who managed these orgies any sense. Also it was found impossible to teach the readers any sense. Once I went to Boston to help in one of these revels which had been instigated in the interest of a memorial to Mr. Longfellow. Howells was always a member of these traveling afflictions, and I was never able to teach him to rehearse his proposed reading by the help of a watch and cut it down to a proper length. He couldn't seem to learn it. He was a bright man in all other ways, but whenever he came to select a reading for one of these carousals his intellect decayed and fell to ruin. I arrived at his house in Cambridge the night before the Longfellow Memorial occasion, and I probably asked him to show me his selection. At any rate, he showed it to me—and I wish I may never attempt the truth again if it wasn't seven thousand words. I made him set his eye on his watch and keep game while I should read a paragraph of it. This experiment proved that it would take me an hour and ten minutes to read the whole of it, and I said, "And mind you, this is not allowing anything for such interruptions as applause—for the reason that after the first twelve minutes there wouldn't be any."

He had a time of it to find something short enough, and he kept saying that he never would find a short enough selection that would be good enough—that is to say, he never would be able to find one that would stand exposure before an audience.

I said: "It's no matter. Better that than a long one—because the audience could stand a bad short one, but couldn't stand a good long one."

We got it arranged at last. We got him down to fifteen minutes, perhaps. But he and Doctor Holmes and Aldrich and I had the only short readings that day out of the most formidable accumulation of authors that had ever thus far been placed in position before the enemy—a battery of sixteen. I think that that was the occasion when we had sixteen. It was in the afternoon, and the place was packed, and the air would have been very bad, only there wasn't any. I can see that mass of people yet, opening and closing their mouths like fishes gasping for breath. It was intolerable.

That graceful and competent speaker, Professor Norton, opened the game with a very handsome speech, but it was a good twenty minutes long. And a good ten minutes of it, I think, were devoted to the introduction of Dr. Oliver Wendell Holmes, who hadn't any more need of an introduction than the Milky Way. Then Doctor Holmes recited—as only Doctor Holmes could recite it—"The Last Leaf," and the house rose as one individual and went mad with worshiping delight. And the house stormed along, and stormed along, and got another poem out of the Doctor as an encore; it stormed again and got a third one—though the storm was not so violent this time as had been the previous outbreaks. By this time Doctor Holmes had, himself, lost a part of his mind, and he actually went on reciting poem after poem until silence had taken the place of encores and he had to do the last encore by himself.

I had learned, by this time, to stipulate for third place on the program. The performance began at two o'clock. My train for Hartford would leave at four o'clock. I would need fifteen minutes for transit to the station. I needed ten minutes for my reading. I did my reading in the ten minutes; I fled at once from the theater, and I came very near not catching that train. I was told afterward that by the time reader number eight stepped forward and trained his gun on the house, the audience were drifting out of the place in groups, shoals, blocks, and avalanches, and that about that time the siege was raised and the conflict given up, with six or seven readers still to hear from.

At the reading in Washington in the spring of '88 there was a crowd of readers. They all came overloaded, as usual. Thomas Nelson Page read forty minutes by the watch, and he was no further down than the middle of the list. We were all due at the White House at half past nine. The President and Mrs. Cleveland were present, and at half past ten they had to go away—the President to attend to some official business which had been arranged to be considered after our White House reception, it being supposed by Mr. Cleveland, who was inexperienced in Authors' Readings, that our reception at the White House would be over by half past eleven, whereas if he had known as much about Authors' Readings as he knew about other-kinds of statesmanship, he would have known that we were not likely to get through before time for early breakfast.

Monday, March 5, 1906
Mrs. Clemens's warning to Mr. Clemens when he attends the Cleveland reception at the White House.—Describes the Paris house in which they lived in 1893—also room in Villa Viviani—also dining-

room in house at Riverdale.—Tells how Mr. Clemens was "dusted off" after the various dinners—and the card system of signals.—Letter from Mr. Gilder regarding Mr. Cleveland's sixty-ninth birthday.— Mason.

I was always heedless. I was born heedless, and therefore I was constantly, and quite unconsciously, committing breaches of the minor proprieties, which brought upon me humiliations which ought to have humiliated me, but didn't, because I didn't know anything had happened. But Livy knew; and so the humiliations fell to her share, poor child, who had not earned them and did not deserve them. She always said I was the most difficult child she had. She was very sensitive about me. It distressed her to see me do heedless things which could bring me under criticism, and so she was always watchful and alert to protect me from the kind of transgressions which I have been speaking of.

When I was leaving Hartford for Washington, upon the occasion referred to, she said: "I have written a small warning and put it in a pocket of your dress vest. When you are dressing to go to the Authors' Reception at the White House you will naturally put your fingers in your vest pockets, according to your custom, and you will find that little note there. Read it carefully and do as it tells you. I cannot be with you, and so I delegate my sentry duties to this little note. If I should give you the warning by word of mouth, now, it would pass from your head and be forgotten in a few minutes."

It was President Cleveland's first term. I had never seen his wife— the young, the beautiful, the good-hearted, the sympathetic, the fascinating. Sure enough, just as I had finished dressing to go to the White House I found that little note, which I had long ago forgotten. It was a grave little note, a serious little note, like its writer, but it made me laugh. Livy's gentle gravities often produced that effect upon me, where the expert humorist's best joke would have failed, for I do not laugh easily.

When we reached the White House and I was shaking hands with the President, he started to say something, but I interrupted him and said, "If Your Excellency will excuse me, I will come back in a moment; but now I have a very important matter to attend to, and it must be attended to at once." I turned to Mrs. Cleveland, the young, the beautiful, the fascinating, and gave her my card, on which I had written "He did not"—and I asked her to sign her name below those words.

She said: "He did not? He did not what?"

"Oh," I said, "never mind. We cannot stop to discuss that now. This is urgent. Won't you please sign your name?" (I handed her a fountain pen.)

"Why," she said, "I cannot commit myself in that way. Who is it that didn't?—and what is it that he didn't?"

"Oh," I said, "time is flying, flying, flying! Won't you take me out of my distress and sign your name to it? It's all right. I give you my word it's all right."

She looked nonplused, but hesitatingly and mechanically she took the pen and said: "I will sign it. I will take the risk. But you must tell me all about it, right afterward, so that you can be arrested before you get out of the house in case there should be anything criminal about this."

Then she signed; and I handed her Mrs. Clemens's note, which was very brief, very simple, and to the point. It said, "Don't wear your arctics in the White House." It made her shout; and at my request she summoned a messenger and we sent that card at once to the mail on its way to Mrs. Clemens in Hartford.

During 1893 and '94 we were living in Paris, the first half of the time at the Hotel Brighton, in the rue de Rivoli, the other half in a charming mansion in the rue de l'Université, on the other side of the Seine, which, by good luck, we had gotten hold of through another man's ill luck. This was Pomeroy, the artist. Illness in his family had made it necessary for him to go to the Riviera. He was paying thirty-six hundred dollars a year for the house, but allowed us to have it at twenty-six hundred. It was a lovely house; large, rambling, quaint, charmingly furnished and decorated; built upon no particular plan; delightfully rambling, uncertain, and full of surprises. You were always getting lost in it, and finding nooks and corners and rooms which you didn't know were there and whose presence you had not suspected before. It was built by a rich French artist; and he had also furnished it and decorated it himself. The studio was coziness itself. We used it as drawing-room, sitting-room, living-room, dancing-room—we used it for everything. We couldn't get enough of it. It is odd that it should have been so cozy, for it was forty feet long, forty feet high, and thirty feet wide, with a vast fireplace on each side in the middle, and a musicians' gallery at one end. But we had, before this, found out that under the proper conditions spaciousness and coziness do go together most affectionately and congruously. We had found it out a year or two earlier, when we were living in the Villa Viviani three miles outside the walls of Florence. That house had a room in it which was forty feet square and forty feet high, and at first we couldn't endure it. We called it the Mammoth Cave; we called it the skating-rink; we called it the Great Sahara; we called it all sorts of names intended to convey our disrespect. We had to pass through it to get from one end of the house to the other, but we passed straight through and did not loiter—and yet before long, and without our knowing how it happened, we found ourselves infesting that vast place day and night, and preferring it to any other part of the house.

Four or five years ago, when we took a house on the banks of the Hudson, at Riverdale, we drifted from room to room on our tour of inspection, always with a growing doubt as to whether we wanted that house or not. But at last when we arrived in a dining-room that was sixty feet long, thirty feet wide, and had two great fireplaces in it, that settled it.

But I have wandered. What I was proposing to talk about was quite another matter—to wit: In that pleasant Paris house Mrs. Clemens gathered little dinner companies together once or twice a week, and it goes without saying that in these circumstances my defects had a large chance for display. Always, always without fail, as soon as the guests were out of the house, I saw that I had been miscarrying again. Mrs. Clemens explained to me the various things which I had been doing and which should have been left undone. The children had a name for this performance. They called it "dusting off papa."

At last I had an inspiration. It is astonishing that it had not occurred to me earlier. I said: "Why, livy, you know that dusting me off after these dinners is not the wise way. You could dust me off after every dinner for a year and I should always be just as competent to do the forbidden thing at each succeeding dinner as if you had not said a word, because in the meantime I have forgotten all these instructions. I think the correct way is for you to dust me off immediately before the guests arrive, and then I can keep some of it in my head and things will go better."

She recognized that that was wisdom and that it was a very good idea. Then we set to work to arrange a system of signals to be delivered by her to me during dinner; signals which would indicate definitely which particular crime I was now engaged in, so that I could change to another. The children got a screen arranged so that they could be behind it during the dinner and listen for the signals and entertain themselves with them. The system of signals was very simple, but it was very effective. If Mrs. Clemens happened to be so busy, at any time, talking with her elbow neighbor that she overlooked something that I was doing, she was sure to get a low-voiced hint from behind that screen in these words:

"Blue card, mamma"; or, "Red card, mamma"—"Green card, mamma"—so that I was under double and triple guard. What the mother didn't notice the children detected for her.

As I say, the signals were quite simple, but very effective. At a hint from behind the screen, Livy would look down the table and say, in a voice full of interest, if not of counterfeited apprehension, "What did you do with the blue card that was on the dressing table—"

That was enough. I knew what was happening—that I was talking the lady on my right to death and never paying any attention to the one on my left. The blue card meant "Let the lady on your right have a reprieve; destroy the one on your left"; so I would at once go to talking vigorously to the lady on my left. It wouldn't be long till there would be another hint, followed by a remark from Mrs. Clemens which had in it an apparently casual reference to a red card, which meant, "Oh, are you going to sit there all the evening and never say anything? Do wake up and talk." So I woke up and drowned the table with talk. We had a number of cards, of different colors, each meaning a definite thing, each calling attention to some crime or other in my common list; and that system was exceedingly useful. It was entirely successful. It was like Buck Fanshaw's riot. It broke up the riot before it got a chance to begin. It headed off crime after crime all through the dinner, and I always came out at the end successful, triumphant, with large praises owing to me, and I got them on the spot.

It is a far call back over the accumulation of years to that night in the White House when Mrs. Cleveland signed the card. Many things have happened since then. The Cleveland family have been born since then. Ruth, the first-born, whom I never knew, but with whom I corresponded when she was a baby, lived only a few years.

To-day comes this letter, and it brings back the Clevelands, and the past, and my lost little correspondent.

March 3, 1906
EDITORIAL DEPARTMENT,
THE CENTURY MAGAZINE,
UNION SQUARE, NEW YORK.

MY DEAR MR. CLEMENS:

President Finley and I are collecting letters to Ex-President Cleveland from his friends, appropriate to his 69th birthday.

If the plan appeals to you, will you kindly send a sealed greeting under cover to me at the above address, and I will send it, and the other letters, South to him in time for him to get them, all together, on the 18th of the present month.

Yours sincerely,
R. W. GILDER
MR. SAMUEL L. CLEMENS

When the little Ruth was about a year or a year and a half old, Mason, an old and valued friend of mine, was consul-general at Frankfort-on-the-Main. I had known him well in 1867, '68, and '69, in America, and I and mine had spent a good deal of time with him and his family in Frankfort in 1892-93. He was a thoroughly competent, diligent, and conscientious official. Indeed, he possessed these qualities in so large a degree that among American consuls he might fairly be said to be monumental, for at that time our consular service was largely—and I think I may say mainly—in the hands of ignorant, vulgar, and incapable men who had been political heelers in America, and had been taken care of by transference to consulates, where they could be supported at the government's expense instead of being transferred to the poorhouse, which would have been cheaper and more patriotic. Mason, in '78, had been consul-general in Frankfort several years—four, I think. He had come from Marseilles with a great record. He had been consul there during thirteen years, and one part of his record was heroic. There had been a desolating cholera epidemic, and Mason was the only representative of any foreign country who stayed at his post and saw it through. And during that time he not only represented his own country, but he represented all the other countries in Christendom and did their work, and did it well and was praised for it in words of no uncertain sound. This great record of Mason's had saved him from official decapitation straight along while Republican Presidents occupied the chair, but now it was occupied by a Democrat. Mr. Cleveland was not seated in it—he was not yet inaugurated—before he was deluged with applications from Democratic politicians desiring the appointment of a thousand or so politically useful Democrats to Mason's place. A year or two later Mason wrote me and asked me if I couldn't do something to save him from destruction.

Tuesday, March 6, 1906

Mr. Clemens makes Baby Ruth intercede in behalf of Mr. Mason, and he is retained in his place.—Mr. Clemens's letter to ex-President Cleveland.—Mr. Cleveland as sheriff, in Buffalo.—As Mayor, he vetoes ordinance of railway corporation.—Mr. Clemens and Mr. Cable visit Governor Cleveland at Capitol, Albany.—Mr. Clemens sits on the bells and summons sixteen clerks.

I was very anxious to keep him in his place, but at first I could not think of any way to help him, for I was a mugwump. We, the mugwumps, a little company made up of the unenslaved of both parties, the very best men to be found in the two great parties—that was our idea of it— voted sixty thousand strong for Mr. Cleveland in New York and elected him. Our principles were high and very definite. We were not a party; we had no candidates; we had no axes to grind. Our vote laid upon the man we cast it for no obligation of any kind. By our rule we could not ask for office; we could not accept office. When voting, it was our duty to vote for the best man, regardless of his party name. We had no other creed. Vote for the best man—that was creed enough.

Such being my situation, I was puzzled to know how to try to help Mason and at the same time save my mugwump purity undefiled. It was a delicate place. But presently, out of the ruck of confusions in my mind, rose a sane thought, clear and bright—to wit: since it was a mugwump's duty to do his best to put the best man in office, necessarily it must be a mugwump's duty to keep the best man in when he was already there. My course was easy now. It might not be quite delicate for a mugwump to approach the President directly, but I could approach him indirectly, with all delicacy, since in that case not even courtesy would require him to take notice of an application which no one could prove had ever reached him.

Yes, it was easy and simple sailing now. I could lay the matter before Ruth, in her cradle, and wait for results. I wrote the little child, and said to her all that I have just been saying about mugwump principles and the limitations which they put upon me. I explained that it would not be proper for me to apply to her father in Mr. Mason's behalf, but I detailed to her Mr. Mason's high and honorable record and suggested that she take the matter in her own hands and do a patriotic work, which I felt some delicacy about venturing upon myself. I asked her to forget that her father was only President of the United States, and her subject and servant: I asked her not to put her application in the form of a command, but to modify this, and give it the fictitious and pleasanter form of a mere request—that it would be no harm to let him gratify himself with the superstition that he was independent and could do as he pleased in the matter. I begged her to put stress, and plenty of it, upon the proposition that to keep Mason in his place would be a benefaction to the nation; to enlarge upon that, and keep still about all other considerations.

In due time I received a letter from the President, written with his own hand, signed by his own hand, acknowledging Ruth's intervention and thanking me for enabling him to save to the country the services of so good and well tried a servant as Mason, and thanking me, also, for the detailed fullness of Mason's record, which could leave no doubt in anyone's mind that Mason was in his right place and ought to be kept there.

In the beginning of Mr. Cleveland's second term a very strong effort to displace Mason was made, and Mason wrote me again. He was not hoping that we would succeed this time, because the assault upon his place was well organized, determined, and exceedingly powerful, but he hoped I would try again and see what I could do. I was not disturbed. It seemed to me that he did not know Mr. Cleveland or he would not be disturbed himself. I believed I knew Mr. Cleveland, and that he was not the man to budge an inch from his duty in any circumstances, and that he was a Gibraltar against whose solid bulk a whole Atlantic of assaulting politicians would dash itself in vain.

I wrote Ruth Cleveland once more. Mason remained in his place and I think he would have remained in it without Ruth's intercession. There have been other Presidents since, but Mason's record has protected him, and the many and powerful efforts to dislodge him have all failed. Also, he has been complimented with promotions. He was promoted from consul-general in Frankfort to consul-general at Berlin, our highest consular post in Germany. A year ago he was promoted another step— to the consul-generalship in Paris, and he holds that place yet.

Ruth, the child, remained not long on earth to help make it beautiful and to bless the home of her parents. But, little creature as she was, she did high service for her country, as I have shown, and it is right that this should be recorded and remembered.

In accordance with the suggestion made in Gilder's letter (as copied in yesterday's talk) I have written the following note to ex-President Cleveland:

> Honored Sir:—
>
> Your patriotic virtues have won for you the homage of half the nation and the enmity of the other half. This places your character as a citizen upon a summit as high as Washington's. The verdict is unanimous and unassailable. The votes of both sides are necessary in cases like these, and the votes of the one side are quite as valuable as are the votes of the other. Where the votes are all in a man's favor the verdict is against him. It is sand, and history will wash it away. But the verdict for you is rock, and will stand.
>
> S. L. Clemens
As of date March 18, 1906

When Mr. Cleveland was a member of a very strong and prosperous firm of lawyers, in Buffalo, just before the 'seventies, he was elected to the mayoralty. Presently a formidably rich and powerful railway corporation worked an ordinance through the city government whose purpose was to take possession of a certain section of the city inhabited altogether by the poor, the helpless, and the inconsequential, and drive those people out. Mr. Cleveland vetoed the ordinance. The other members of his law firm were indignant and also terrified. To them the thing which he had done meant disaster to their business. They waited upon him and begged him to reconsider his action. He declined to do it. They insisted. He still declined. He said that his official position imposed upon him a duty which he could not honorably avoid; therefore he should be loyal to it; that the helpless situation of these inconsequential citizens made it his duty to stand by them and be their friend, since they had no other; that he was sorry if this conduct of his must bring disaster upon the firm, but that he had no choice; his duty was plain, and he would stick to the position which he had taken. They intimated that this would lose him his place in the firm. He said he did not wish to be a damage to the co-partnership, therefore they could remove his name from it, and without any hard feeling on his part.

During the time that we were living in Buffalo in '70 and '71, Mr. Cleveland was sheriff, but I never happened to make his acquaintance, or even see him. In fact, I suppose I was not even aware of his existence. Fourteen years later, he was become the greatest man in the state. I was not living in the state at the time. He was Governor, and was about to step into the post of President of the United States. At that time I was on the public highway in company with another bandit, George W. Cable. We were robbing the public with readings from our works during four months—and in the course of time we went to Albany to levy tribute, and I said, "We ought to go and pay our respects to the Governor."

So Cable and I went to that majestic Capitol building and stated our errand. We were shown into the Governor's private office, and I saw Mr. Cleveland for the first time. We three stood chatting together. I was born lazy, and I comforted myself by turning the corner of a table into a sort of seat. Presently the Governor said: "Mr. Clemens, I was a fellow citizen of yours in Buffalo a good many months, a good while ago, and during those months you burst suddenly into a mighty fame, out of a previous long-continued and no doubt proper obscurity—but I was a nobody, and you wouldn't notice me nor have anything to do with me. But now that I have become somebody, you have changed your style, and you come here to shake hands with me and be sociable. How do you explain this kind of conduct?"

"Oh," I said, "it is very simple. Your Excellency. In Buffalo you were nothing but a sheriff. I was in society. I couldn't afford to associate with sheriffs. But you are a Governor, now, and you are on your way to the Presidency. It is a great difference, and it makes you worth while."

There appeared to be about sixteen doors to that spacious room. From each door a young man now emerged, and the sixteen lined up and moved forward and stood in front of the Governor with an aspect of respectful expectancy in their attitude. No one spoke for a moment. Then the Governor said: "You are dismissed, gentlemen. Your services are not required. Mr. Clemens is sitting on the bells."

There was a cluster of sixteen bell-buttons on the corner of the table against which I had been lounging,

Susy's biography.—Susy and her father escort Mrs. Clemens to train, then go over Brooklyn Bridge.—On the way to Vassar they discuss German profanity.—Mr. Clemens tells of the sweet and profane German nurse.—The arrival at Vassar and the dreary reception—told by Susy—the reading, etc. Mr. Clemens's opinion of girls.—He is to talk to the Barnard girls this afternoon.

FROM SUSY'S BIOGRAPHY

The next day mamma planned to take the four-o'clock car back to Hartford. We rose quite early that morning and went to the Vienna Bakery and took breakfast there. From there we went to a German bookstore and bought some German books for Clara's birthday.

Then mamma and I went to do some shopping and papa went to see General Grant. After we had finnished doing our shopping we went home to the hotel together. When we entered our rooms in the hotel we saw on the table a vase full of exquisett red roses. Mamma who is very fond of flowers exclaimed "Oh I wonder who could have sent them." We both looked at the card in the midst of the roses and saw that it was written on in papa's handwriting, it was written in German. "Liebes Geshchenk on die Mamma." (I am sure I didn't say "on"—that is Susy's spelling, not mine.—S. L. C.) Mamma was delighted. Papa came home and gave mamma her ticket; and after visiting a while with her went to see Major Pond and mamma and I sat down to our lunch. After lunch most of our time was taken up with packing, and at about three o'clock we went to escort mamma to the train. We got on board the train with her and stayed with her about five minutes and then we said good-bye to her and the train started for Hartford. It was the first time I had ever beene away from home without mamma in my life, although I was 13 yrs. old. Papa and I drove back to the hotel and got Major Pond and then went to see the Brooklyn Bridge we went across it to Brooklyn on the cars and then walked back across it from Brooklyn to New York. We enjoyed looking at the beautiful scenery and we could see the bridge moove under the intense heat of the sun. We had a perfectly delightful time, but were pretty tired when we got back to the hotel.

The next morning we rose early, took our breakfast and took an early train to Poughkeepsie. We had a very pleasant journey to

Poughkeepsie. The Hudson was magnificent—shrouded with beautiful mist. When we arrived at Poughkeepsie it was raining quite hard; which fact greatly dissapointed me because I very much wanted to see the outside of the buildings of Vasser College and as it rained that would be impossible. It was quite a long drive from the station to Vasser College and papa and I had a nice long time to discuss and laugh over German profanity. One of the German phrases papa particularly enjoys is "O heilige maria Mutter Jesus!" Jean has a German nurse, and this was one of her phrases, there was a time when Jean exclaimed "Ach Gott!" to every trifle, but when mamma found it out she was shocked and instantly put a stop to it.

It brings that pretty little German creature vividly before me—a sweet and innocent and plump little creature, with peachy cheeks; a clear-souled little maiden and without offense, notwithstanding her profanities, and she was loaded to the eyebrows with them. She was a mere child. She was not fifteen yet. She was just from Germany, and knew no English. She was always scattering her profanities around, and they were such a satisfaction to me that I never dreamed of such a thing as modifying her. For my own sake, I had no disposition to tell on her. Indeed, I took pains to keep her from being found out. I told her to confine her religious expressions to the children's quarters, and urged her to remember that Mrs. Clemens was prejudiced against pieties on week days. To the children, the little maid's profanities sounded natural and proper and right because they had been used to that kind of talk in Germany, and they attached no evil importance to it. It grieves me that I have forgotten those vigorous remarks. I long hoarded them in my memory as a treasure. But I remember one of them still, because I heard it so many times. The trial of that little creature's life was the children's hair. She would tug and strain with her comb, accompanying her work with her misplaced pieties. And when finally she was through with her triple job she always fired up and exploded her thanks toward the sky, where they belonged, in this form: "Gott sei Dank! Ich bin schon fertig mit'm Gott verdammtes Haar!" (I believe I am not quite brave enough to translate it.)

From Susy's Biography

We at length reached Vasser College and she looked very finely, her buildings and her grounds being very beautiful. We went to the front doore and rang the bell. The young girl who came to the doore wished to know who we wanted to see. Evidently we were not expected. Papa told her who we wanted to see and she showed us to the parlor. We waited, no one came; and waited, no one came, still no one came. It was beginning to seem pretty awkard, "Oh well this is a pretty piece of business," papa exclaimed. At length we heard footsteps coming down the long corridor and Miss C, (the lady who had invited papa) came into the room. She greeted papa very pleasantly and they had a nice little chatt together. Soon the lady principal also entered and she was very pleasant and agreable. She showed us to our rooms and said she would send for us when dinner was ready. We went into our rooms, but we had nothing to do for half an hour exept to watch the rain drops as they fell upon the window panes. At last we were called to dinner, and I went down without papa as he never eats anything in the middle of the day. I sat at the table with the lady principal and enjoyed very much seing all the young girls trooping into the dining-room. After dinner I went around the College with the young ladies and papa stayed in his room and smoked. When it was supper time papa went down and ate supper with us and we had a very delightful supper. After supper the young ladies went to their rooms to dress for the evening. Papa went to his room and I went with the lady principal. At length the guests began to arive, but papa still remained in his room until called for. Papa read in the chapell. It was the first time I had ever heard him read in my life—that is in public. When he came out on the stage I remember the people behind me exclaimed "Oh how queer he is! Isn't he funny!" I thought papa was very funny, although I did not think him queer. He read "A Trying Situation" and "The Golden Arm," a ghost story that he heard down South when he was a little boy. "The Golden Arm" papa had told me before, but he had startled me so that I did not much wish to hear it again. But I had resolved this time to be prepared and not to let myself be startled, but still papa did, and very very much; he startled the whole roomful of people and they jumped as one man. The other story was also very funny and interesting and I enjoyed the evening inexpressibly much. After papa had finished reading we all went down to the collation in the dining-room, and after that there was dancing and singing. Then the guests went away and papa and I went to bed. The next morning we rose early, took an early train for Hartford and reached Hartford at 1/2 past 2 o'clock. We were very glad to get back.

MARK TWAIN

How charitably she treats that ghastly experience! It is a dear and lovely disposition, and a most valuable one, that can brush away indignities and discourtesies and seek and find the pleasanter features of an experience. Susy had that disposition, and it was one of the jewels of her character that had come to her straight from her mother. It is a feature that was left out of me at birth. And at seventy I have not yet acquired it. I did not go to Vassar College professionally, but as a guest—as a guest, and gratis. Aunt Clara (Mrs. Stanchfield) was a graduate of Vassar and it was to please her that I inflicted that journey upon Susy and myself. The invitation had come to me from both the lady mentioned by Susy and the president of the college—a sour old saint who has probably been gathered to his fathers long ago; and I hope they enjoy him; I hope they enjoy his society. I think I can get along without it, in either end of the next world.

We arrived at the college in that soaking rain, and Susy has described, with just a suggestion of dissatisfaction, the sort of reception we got. Susy had to sit in her damp clothes half an hour while we waited in the parlor; then she was taken to a fireless room and left to wait there again, as she has stated. I do not remember that president's name, and I am sorry. He did not put in an appearance until it was time for me to step upon the platform in front of that great garden of young and lovely blossoms. He caught up with me and advanced upon the platform with me and was going to introduce me. I said in substance, "You have allowed me to get along without your help thus far, and if you will retire from the platform I will try to do the rest without it." I did not see him any more, but I detest his memory.

Of course my resentment did not extend to the students, and so I had an unforgettable good time talking to them. And I think they had a good time, too, for they responded as one man, to use Susy's unimprovable phrase.

Girls are charming creatures. I shall have to be twice seventy years old before I change my mind as to that. I am to talk to a crowd of them this afternoon, students of Barnard College (the sex's annex to Columbia University), and I think I shall have just as pleasant a time with those lassies as I had with the Vassar girls twenty-one years ago.

Thursday, March 8, 1906
Letter from brother of Captain Tonkray.—Mr. Clemens replied that original of "Huckleberry Finn" was Tom Blankenship.—Tom's father

Town Drunkard.—Describes Tom's character.—Death of Injun Joe.—Storm which came that night.—Incident of the Episcopal sextons and their reforms.—Mr. Dawson's school in Hannibal.—Arch Fuqua's great gift.

For thirty years, I have received an average of a dozen letters a year from strangers who remember me, or whose fathers remember me as boy and young man. But these letters are almost always disappointing. I have not known these strangers nor their fathers. I have not heard of the names they mention; the reminiscences to which they call my attention have had no part in my experience; all of which means that these strangers have been mistaking me for somebody else. But at last I have the refreshment, this morning, of a letter from a man who deals in names that were familiar to me in my boyhood. The writer incloses a newspaper clipping which has been wandering through the press for four or five weeks, and he wants to know if his brother, Captain Tonkray, was really the original of "Huckleberry Finn."

"Huckleberry Finn" Dead

Original of Mark Twain's Famous Character Had Led Quiet Life in Idaho

(By Direct Wire to the Times.)

Wallace, (Idaho), Feb. 2.—(Exclusive dispatch.) Capt. A. O. Tonkray, commonly known as "Huckleberry Finn," said to be the original of Mark Twain's famous character, was found dead in his room at Murray this morning from heart failure.

Capt. Tonkray, a native of Hannibal, Mo., was 65 years old. In early life, he ran on steamboats on the Mississippi and the Missouri rivers, in frequent contact with Samuel L. Clemens, and tradition has it "Mark Twain" later used Tonkray as his model for "Huckleberry Finn." He came to Murray in 1884 and had been living a quiet life since.

I have replied that "Huckleberry Finn" was Tom Blankenship. As this writer evidently knew the Hannibal of the 'forties, he will easily recall Tom Blankenship. Tom's father was at one time Town Drunkard, an exceedingly well-defined and unofficial office of those days. He succeeded General—(I forget the General's name)[1] and for a time he was sole and only incumbent of the office; but afterward Jimmy Finn proved competency and disputed the place with him, so we had two town drunkards at one time—and it made as much trouble in that village as Christendom experienced in the fourteenth century, when there were two Popes at the same time.

In Huckleberry Finn I have drawn Tom Blankenship exactly as he was. He was ignorant, unwashed, insufficiently fed; but he had as good a heart as ever any boy had. His liberties were totally unrestricted. He was the only really independent person—boy or man—in the community, and by consequence he was tranquilly and continuously happy, and was envied by all the rest of us. We liked him; we enjoyed his society. And as his society was forbidden us by our parents, the prohibition trebled and quadrupled its value, and therefore we sought and got more of his society than of any other boy's. I heard, four years ago, that he was justice of the peace in a remote village in Montana, and was a good citizen and greatly respected.

During Jimmy Finn's term he was not exclusive; he was not finical; he was not hypercritical; he was largely and handsomely democratic— and slept in the deserted tanyard with the hogs. My father tried to reform him once, but did not succeed. My father was not a professional reformer. In him the spirit of reform was spasmodic. It only broke out now and then, with considerable intervals between. Once he tried to reform Injun Joe. That also was a failure. It was a failure, and we boys were glad. For Injun Joe, drunk, was interesting and a benefaction to us, but Injun Joe, sober, was a dreary spectacle. We watched my father's experiments upon him with a good deal of anxiety, but it came out all right and we were satisfied. Injun Joe got drunk oftener than before, and became intolerably interesting.

I think that in Tom Sawyer I starved Injun Joe to death in the cave. But that may have been to meet the exigencies of romantic literature. I can't remember now whether the real Injun Joe died in the cave or out of it, but I do remember that the news of his death reached me at a most

---

1. Gaines.

unhappy time—that is to say, just at bedtime on a summer night, when a prodigious storm of thunder and lightning accompanied by a deluging rain that turned the streets and lanes into rivers caused me to repent and resolve to lead a better life. I can remember those awful thunder-bursts and the white glare of the lightning yet, and the wild lashing of the rain against the windowpanes. By my teachings I perfectly well knew what all that wild rumpus was for—Satan had come to get Injun Joe, I had no shadow of doubt about it. It was the proper thing when a person like Injun Joe was required in the under world, and I should have thought it strange and unaccountable if Satan had come for him in a less spectacular way. With every glare of lightning I shriveled and shrank together in mortal terror, and in the interval of black darkness that followed I poured out my lamentings over my lost condition, and my supplications for just one more chance, with an energy and feeling and sincerity quite foreign to my nature.

But in the morning I saw that it was a false alarm and concluded to resume business at the old stand and wait for another reminder.

The axiom says, "History repeats itself." A week or two ago my nephew, by marriage, Edward Loomis, dined with us, along with his wife, my niece (née Julie Langdon). He is vice-president of the Delaware and Lackawanna Railway system. The duties of his office used to carry him frequently to Elmira, New York; the exigencies of his courtship carried him there still oftener, and so in the course of time he came to know a good many of the citizens of that place. At dinner he mentioned a circumstance which flashed me back over about sixty years and landed me in that little bedroom on that tempestuous night. He said Mr. Buckly was sexton of the Episcopal church in Elmira, and had been for many years the competent superintendent of all the church's worldly affairs, and was regarded by the whole congregation as a stay, a blessing, a priceless treasure. But he had a couple of defects—not large defects, but they seemed large when flung against the background of his profoundly religious character: he drank a good deal, and he could outswear a brakeman. A movement arose to persuade him to lay aside these vices, and after consulting with his pal, who occupied the same position as himself in the other Episcopal church, and whose defects were duplicates of his own and had inspired regret in the congregation whom he was serving, they concluded to try for reform—not wholesale, but half at a time. They took the liquor pledge and waited for results. During nine days the results were entirely satisfactory, and they were recipients of many compliments and much congratulation. Then on New Year's Eve they had business a mile and a half out of town, just beyond the New York State line. Everything went well with them that evening in the barroom of the inn—but at last the celebration of the occasion by those villagers came to be of a burdensome nature. It was a bitter cold night and the multitudinous hot toddies that were circulating began, by and by, to exert a powerful influence upon the new prohibitionists. At last Buckly's friend remarked, "Buckly, does it occur to you that we are outside the diocese?" That ended reform No. 1.

Then they took a chance in reform No. 2. For a while that one prospered and they got much applause.

One morning this stepnephew of mine, Loomis, met Buckly on the street and said: "You have made a gallant struggle against those defects of yours. I am aware that you failed on No. 1, but I am also aware that you are having better luck with No. 2."

"Yes," Buckly said, "No. 2 is all right and sound up to date, and we are full of hope."

Loomis said: "Buckly, of course you have your troubles like other people, but they never show on the outside. I have never seen you when you were not cheerful. Are you always cheerful? Really always cheerful?"

"Well no," he said. "No, I can't say that I am always cheerful, but—Well, you know that kind of a night that comes; you wake up way in the night and the whole world is sunk in gloom and there are storms and earthquakes and all sorts of disasters in the air threatening and you get cold and chill; and when that happens to me I recognize how sinful I am and it goes all clear to my heart and wrings it and I have such terrors and terrors—oh, they are indescribable, those terrors that assail and thrill me, and I slip out of bed and get on my knees and pray and pray and pray and promise that I will be good, etc. And then, you know, in the morning the sun shines out so lovely and the birds sing and the whole world is so beautiful, and—b' god! I rally!"

Now I will quote a brief paragraph from this letter which I have received from Mr. Tonkray. He says:

You no doubt are at a loss to know who I am. I will tell you. In my younger days I was a resident of Hannibal, Mo., and you and I were schoolmates attending Mr. Dawson's school along with Sam and Will Bowen and Andy Fuqua and others whose names I have forgotten. I was then about the smallest boy in school, for my age, and they called me little Aleck Tonkray for short.

I DON'T REMEMBER ALECK TONKRAY, but I knew those other people as well as I knew the town drunkards. I remember Dawson's schoolhouse perfectly. If I wanted to describe it I could save myself the trouble by conveying the description of it to these pages from Tom Sawyer. I can remember the drowsy and inviting summer sounds that used to float in through the open windows from that distant boy-Paradise, Cardiff Hill, and mingle with the murmurs of the studying pupils and make them the more dreary by the contrast. I remember Andy Fuqua, the oldest pupil—a man of twenty-five. I remember the youngest pupil, Nannie Owsley, a child of seven. I remember George RoBards, eighteen or twenty years old, the only pupil who studied Latin. I remember vaguely the rest of the twenty-five boys and girls. I remember Mr. Dawson very well. I remember his boy, Theodore, who was as good as he could be. In fact he was inordinately good, extravagantly good, offensively good, detestably good—and he had pop-eyes—and I would have drowned him if I had had a chance. In that school we were all about on an equality, and, so far as I remember, the passion of envy had no place in our hearts, except in the case of Arch Fuqua—the other one's brother. Of course we all went barefoot in the summertime. Arch Fuqua was about my own age—ten or eleven. In the winter we could stand him, because he wore shoes then, and his great gift was hidden from our sight and we were enabled to forget it. But in the summertime he was a bitterness to us. He was our envy, for he could double back his big toe and let it fly and you could hear it snap thirty yards. There was not another boy in the school that could approach this feat. He had not a rival as regards a physical distinction—except in Theodore Eddy, who could work his ears like a horse. But he was no real rival, because you couldn't hear him work his ears; so all the advantage lay with Arch Fuqua.

Friday, March 9, 1906
Mr. Clemens tells of several of his schoolmates in Mr. Dawson's Hannibal school: George RoBards and Mary Moss; John RoBards, who traveled far; John Garth and Helen Kercheval.—Mr. Kercheval's slave woman and his apprentice saved Mr. Clemens from drowning in Bear Creek.—Meredith, who became a guerrilla chief in Civil War.— Will and Sam Bowen, Mississippi pilots—died of yellow fever.

I am talking of a time sixty years ago and upward. I remember the names of some of those schoolmates, and, by fitful glimpses, even their faces rise before me for a moment—only just long enough to be recognized; then they vanish. I catch glimpses of George RoBards, the Latin pupil—slender, pale, studious, bending over his book and absorbed in it, his long straight black hair hanging down below his jaws like a pair of curtains on the sides of his face. I can see him give his head a toss and flirt one of the curtains back around his head—to get it out of his way, apparently; really to show off. In that day it was a great thing among the boys to have hair of so flexible a sort that it could he flung back in that way, with a flirt of the head. George RoBards was the envy of us all. For there was no hair among us that was so competent for this exhibition as his. My hair was a dense ruck of short curls, and so was my brother Henry's. We tried all kinds of devices to get these crooks straightened out so that they would flirt, but we never succeeded. Sometimes, by soaking our heads and then combing and brushing our hair down tight and flat to our skulls, we could get it straight, temporarily, and this gave us a comforting moment of joy. But the first time we gave it a flirt it all shriveled into curls again and our happiness was gone.

George was a fine young fellow in all ways. He and Mary Moss were sweethearts and pledged to eternal constancy, from a time when they were merely children. But Mr. Lakenan arrived now and became a resident. He took an important position in the little town at once, and maintained it. He brought with him a distinguished reputation as a lawyer. He was educated, cultured; he was grave even to austerity; he was dignified in his conversation and deportment. He was a rather oldish bachelor—as bachelor oldishness was estimated in that day. He was a rising man. He was contemplated with considerable awe by the community, and as a catch he stood at the top of the market. That blooming and beautiful thing, Mary Moss, attracted his favor. He laid siege to her and won. Everybody said she accepted him to please her parents, not herself. They were married. And everybody again, testifying, said he continued her schooling all by himself, proposing to educate her up to standard and make her a meet companion for him. These things may have been true. They may not have been true. But they were interesting. That is the main requirement in a village like that. George went away, presently, to some far-off region and there he died—of a broken heart, everybody said. That could be true, for he had good cause. He would go far before he would find another Mary Moss.

How long ago that little tragedy happened! None but the white heads know about it now. Lakenan is dead these many years, but Mary still lives, and is still beautiful, although she has grandchildren. I saw her and one of her married daughters when I went out to Missouri four years ago to receive an honorary LL.D. from Missouri University.

John RoBards was the little brother of George, a wee chap with silky golden curtains to his face which dangled to his shoulders and below, and could be flung back ravishingly. When he was twelve years old he crossed the plains with his father amid the rush of the gold seekers of '49; and I remember the departure of the cavalcade when it spurred westward. We were all there to see and to envy. And I can still see that proud little chap sailing by on a great horse, with his long locks streaming out behind. We were all on hand to gaze and envy when he returned, two years later, in unimaginable glory—for he had traveled. None of us had ever been forty miles from home. But he had crossed the continent. He had been in the gold mines, that fairyland of our imagination. And he had done a still more wonderful thing. He had been in ships—in ships on the actual ocean; in ships on three actual oceans. For he had sailed down the Pacific and round the Horn among icebergs and through snowstorms and wild wintry gales, and had sailed on and turned the corner and flown northward in the trades and up through the blistering equatorial waters—and there in his brown face were the proofs of what he had been through. We would have sold our souls to Satan for the privilege of trading places with him.

I saw him when I was out on that Missouri trip four years ago. He was old then—though not quite so old as I—and the burden of life was upon him. He said his granddaughter, twelve years old, had read my books and would like to see me. It was a pathetic time, for she was a prisoner in her room and marked for death. And John knew that she was passing swiftly away. Twelve years old—just her grandfather's age when he rode away on that great journey. In her I seemed to see that boy again. It was as if he had come back out of that remote past and was present before me in his golden youth. Her malady was heart disease, and her brief life came to a close a few days later.

Another of those schoolboys was John Garth. And one of the prettiest of the schoolgirls was Helen Kercheval. They grew up and married. He became a prosperous banker and a prominent and valued citizen; and a few years ago he died, rich and honored. He died. It is what I have to say about so many of those boys and girls. The widow still lives, and there are grandchildren, I saw John's tomb when I made that Missouri visit.

Mr. Kercheval had an apprentice in the early days when I was nine years old, and he had also a slave woman who had many merits. But I can't feel either very kindly or forgivingly toward either that good apprentice boy or that good slave woman, for they saved my life. One day when I was playing on a loose log which I supposed was attached to a raft—but it wasn't—it tilted me into Bear Creek. And when I had been under water twice and was coming up to make the third and fatal descent, my fingers appeared above the water and that slave woman seized them and pulled me out. Within a week I was in again, and that apprentice had to come along just at the wrong time, and he plunged in and dived, pawed around on the bottom and found me, and dragged me out, emptied the water out of me, and I was saved again. I was drowned seven times after that before I learned to swim—once in Bear Creek and six times in the Mississippi. I do not now know who the people were who interfered with the intentions of a Providence wiser than themselves, but I hold a grudge against them yet.

Another schoolmate was John Meredith, a boy of a quite uncommonly sweet and gentle disposition. He grew up, and when the Civil War broke out he became a sort of guerrilla chief on the Confederate side, and I was told that in his raids upon Union families in the country parts of Monroe County—in earlier times the friends and familiars of his father—he was remorseless in his devastations and sheddings of blood. It seems almost incredible that this could have been that gentle comrade of my school days; yet it can be true, for Robespierre when he was young was like that. John has been in his grave many and many a year.

Will Bowen was another schoolmate, and so was his brother, Sam, who was his junior by a couple of years. Before the Civil War broke out both became St. Louis and New Orleans pilots. While Sam was still very young he had a curious adventure. He fell in love with a girl of sixteen, only child of a very wealthy German brewer. He wanted to marry her, but he and she both thought that the papa would not only not consent, but would shut his door against Sam. The old man was not so disposed, but they were not aware of that. He had his eye upon them, and it was not a hostile eye. That indiscreet young couple got to living together surreptitiously. Before long the old man died. When the will was examined it was found that he had left the whole of his wealth to Mrs. Samuel A. Bowen. Then the poor things made another mistake. They rushed down to the French suburb, Carondelet, and got a magistrate to marry them and date the marriage back a few months. The old brewer had some nieces and nephews and cousins, and different kinds of assets of that sort, and they traced out the fraud and proved it and got the property. This left Sam with a girl wife on his hands and the necessity of earning a living for her at the pilot wheel. After a few years Sam and another pilot were bringing a boat up from New Orleans when the yellow fever broke out among the few passengers and the crew. Both pilots were stricken with it and there was nobody to take their place at the wheel. The boat was landed at the head of Island 82 to wait for succor. Death came swiftly to both pilots—and there they lie buried, unless the river has cut the graves away and washed the bones into the stream, a thing which has probably happened long ago.

Monday, March 12, 1906

Mr. Clemens comments on the killing of six hundred Moros—men, women and children—in a crater bowl near Jolo in the Philippines—our troops commanded by General Wood.—Contrasts this "battle" with various other details of our military history.—The newspapers' attitude toward the announcements.—The President's message of congratulation.

We will stop talking about my schoolmates of sixty years ago, for the present, and return to them later. They strongly interest me, and I am not going to leave them alone permanently. Strong as that interest is, it is for the moment pushed out of the way by an incident of to-day, which is still stronger. This incident burst upon the world last Friday in an official cablegram from the commander of our forces in the Philippines to our government at Washington. The substance of it was as follows:

A tribe of Moros, dark-skinned savages, had fortified themselves in the bowl of an extinct crater not many miles from Jolo; and as they were hostiles, and bitter against us because we have been trying for eight years to take their liberties away from them, their presence in that position was a menace. Our commander, Gen. Leonard Wood, ordered a reconnaissance. It was found that the Moros numbered six hundred, counting women and children; that their crater bowl was in the summit of a peak or mountain twenty-two hundred feet above sea level, and very difficult of access for Christian troops and artillery. Then General Wood ordered a surprise, and went along himself to see the order carried out. Our troops climbed the heights by devious and difficult trails, and even took some artillery with them. The kind of artillery is not specified, but in one place it was hoisted up a sharp acclivity by tackle a distance of some three hundred feet. Arrived at the rim of the crater, the battle began. Our soldiers numbered five hundred and forty. They were assisted by auxiliaries consisting of a detachment of native constabulary in our pay—their numbers not given—and by a naval detachment, whose numbers are not stated. But apparently the contending parties were about equal as to number—six hundred men on our side, on the edge of the bowl; six hundred men, women, and children in the bottom of the bowl. Depth of the bowl, 50 feet.

General Wood's order was, "Kill or capture the six hundred."

The battle began—it is officially called by that name—our forces firing down into the crater with their artillery and their deadly small arms of precision; the savages furiously returning the fire, probably with brickbats—though this is merely a surmise of mine, as the weapons used by the savages are not nominated in the cablegram. Heretofore the Moros have used knives and clubs mainly; also ineffectual trade-muskets when they had any.

The official report stated that the battle was fought with prodigious energy on both sides during a day and a half, and that it ended with a complete victory for the American arms. The completeness of the victory is established by this fact: that of the six hundred Moros not one was left alive. The brilliancy of the victory is established by this other fact, to wit: that of our six hundred heroes only fifteen lost their lives.

General Wood was present and looking on. His order had been, "Kill or capture those savages." Apparently our little army considered that the "or" left them authorized to kill or capture according to taste, and that their taste had remained what it has been for eight years, in our army out there—the taste of Christian butchers.

The official report quite properly extolled and magnified the "heroism" and "gallantry" of our troops, lamented the loss of the fifteen who perished, and elaborated the wounds of thirty-two of our men who suffered injury, and even minutely and faithfully described the nature of the wounds, in the interest of future historians of the United States. It mentioned that a private had one of his elbows scraped by a missile, and the private's name was mentioned. Another private had the end of his nose scraped by a missile. His name was also mentioned—by cable, at one dollar and fifty cents a word.

Next day's news confirmed the previous day's report and named our fifteen killed and thirty-two wounded again, and once more described the wounds and gilded them with the right adjectives.

Let us now consider two or three details of our military history. In one of the great battles of the Civil War 10 per cent of the forces engaged on the two sides were killed and wounded. At Waterloo, where four hundred thousand men were present on the two sides, fifty thousand fell, killed and wounded, in five hours, leaving three hundred and fifty thousand sound and all right for further adventures. Eight years ago, when the pathetic comedy called the Cuban War was played, we summoned two hundred and fifty thousand men. We fought a number of showy battles, and when the war was over we had lost two hundred and sixty-eight men out of our two hundred and fifty thousand, in killed and wounded in the field, and just fourteen times as many by the gallantry of the army doctors in the hospitals and camps. We did not exterminate the Spaniards—far from it. In each engagement we left an average of 2 per cent of the enemy killed or crippled on the field.

Contrast these things with the great statistics which have arrived from that Moro crater! There, with six hundred engaged on each side, we lost fifteen men killed outright, and we had thirty-two wounded—counting that nose and that elbow. The enemy numbered six hundred—including women and children—and we abolished them utterly, leaving not even a baby alive to cry for its dead mother. This is incomparably the greatest victory that was ever achieved by the Christian soldiers of the United States.

Now then, how has it been received? The splendid news appeared with splendid display heads in every newspaper in this city of four million and thirteen thousand inhabitants, on Friday morning. But there was not a single reference to it in the editorial columns of any one of those newspapers. The news appeared again in all the evening papers of Friday, and again those papers were editorially silent upon our vast achievement. Next day's additional statistics and particulars appeared in all the morning papers, and still without a line of editorial rejoicing or a mention of the matter in any way. These additions appeared in the evening papers of that same day (Saturday) and again without a word of comment. In the columns devoted to correspondence, in the morning and evening papers of Friday and Saturday, nobody said a word about the "battle." Ordinarily those columns are teeming with the passions of the citizen; he lets no incident go by, whether it be large or small, without pouring out his praise or blame, his joy or his indignation, about the matter in the correspondence column. But, as I have said, during those two days he was as silent as the editors themselves. So far as I can find out, there was only one person among our eighty millions who allowed himself the privilege of a public remark on this great occasion— that was the President of the United States. All day Friday he was as studiously silent as the rest. But on Saturday he recognized that his duty required him to say something, and he took his pen and performed that duty. If I know President Roosevelt—and I am sure I do—this utterance cost him more pain and shame than any other that ever issued from his pen or his mouth. I am far from blaming him. If I had been in his place my official duty would have compelled me to say what he said. It was a convention, an old tradition, and he had to be loyal to it. There was no help for it. This is what he said:

WASHINGTON, March 10.
WOOD, MANILA:
   I congratulate you and the officers and men of your command upon the brilliant feat of arms wherein you and they so well upheld the honor of the American flag.
                                   (Signed) THEODORE ROOSEVELT

His whole utterance is merely a convention. Not a word of what he said came out of his heart. He knew perfectly well that to pen six hundred helpless and weaponless savages in a hole like rats in a trap and massacre them in detail during a stretch of a day and a half, from a safe position on the heights above, was no brilliant feat of arms—and would not have been a brilliant feat of arms even if Christian America, represented by its salaried soldiers, had shot them down with bibles and the Golden Rule instead of bullets. He knew perfectly well that our uniformed assassins had not upheld the honor of the American flag, but had done as they have been doing continuously for eight years in the Philippines—that is to say, they had dishonored it.
   The next day, Sunday—which was yesterday—the cable brought us additional news—still more splendid news—still more honor for the

flag. The first display head shouts this information at us in stentorian capitals: "WOMEN SLAIN IN MORO SLAUGHTER."

"Slaughter" is a good word. Certainly there is not a better one in the Unabridged Dictionary for this occasion.

The next display line says:

"With Children They Mixed in Mob in Crater, and All Died Together."

They were mere naked savages, and yet there is a sort of pathos about it when that word children falls under your eye, for it always brings before us our perfectest symbol of innocence and helplessness; and by help of its deathless eloquence color, creed, and nationality vanish away and we see only that they are children—merely children. And if they are frightened and crying and in trouble, our pity goes out to them by natural impulse. We see a picture. We see the small forms. We see the terrified faces. We see the tears. We see the small hands clinging in supplication to the mother; but we do not see those children that we are speaking about. We see in their places the little creatures whom we know and love.

The next heading blazes with American and Christian glory like to the sun in the zenith:

"Death List is Now 900."

I was never so enthusiastically proud of the flag till now!

The next heading explains how safely our daring soldiers were located. It says:

"Impossible to Tell Sexes Apart in Fierce Battle on Top of Mount Dajo."

The naked savages were so far away, down in the bottom of that trap, that our soldiers could not tell the breasts of a woman from the rudimentary paps of a man—so far away that they couldn't tell a toddling little child from a black six-footer. This was by all odds the least dangerous battle that Christian soldiers of any nationality were ever engaged in.

The next heading says:

"Fighting for Four Days."

So our men were at it four days instead of a day and a half. It was a long and happy picnic with nothing to do but sit in comfort and fire the Golden Rule into those people down there and imagine letters to write home to the admiring families, and pile glory upon glory. Those savages fighting for their liberties had the four days, too, but it must have been a sorrowful time for them. Every day they saw two hundred and twenty-five of their number slain, and this provided them grief and mourning for the night—and doubtless without even the relief and consolation of knowing that in the meantime they had slain four of their enemies and wounded some more on the elbow and the nose.

The closing heading says:

"Lieutenant Johnson Blown from Parapet by Exploding Artillery Gallantly Leading Charge."

Lieutenant Johnson had pervaded the cablegrams from the first. He and his wound have sparkled around through them like the serpentine thread of fire that goes excursioning through the black crisp fabric of a fragment of burnt paper. It reminds one of Gillette's comedy farce of a few years ago. "Too Much Johnson." Apparently Johnson was the only wounded man on our side whose wound was worth anything as an advertisement. It has made a great deal more noise in the world than has any similar event since "Humpty Dumpty" fell off the wall and got injured. The official dispatches do not know which to admire most, Johnson's adorable wound or the nine hundred murders. The ecstasies flowing from army headquarters on the other side of the globe to the White House, at one dollar and a half a word, have set fire to similar ecstasies in the President's breast. It appears that the immortally wounded was a Rough Rider under Lieutenant-Colonel Theodore Roosevelt at San Juan Hill—that twin of Waterloo—when the colonel of the regiment, the present Major-General Dr. Leonard Wood, went to the rear to bring up the pills and missed the fight. The President has a warm place in his heart for anybody who was present at that bloody collision of military solar systems, and so he lost no time in cabling to the wounded hero, "How are you?" And got a cable answer, "Fine, thanks." This is historical. This will go down to posterity.

Johnson was wounded in the shoulder with a slug. The slug was in a shell—for the account says the damage was caused by an exploding shell which blew Johnson off the rim. The people down in the hole had no artillery; therefore it was our artillery that blew Johnson off the rim. And so it is now a matter of historical record that the only officer of ours who acquired a wound of advertising dimensions got it at our hands, and not the enemies'. It seems more than probable that if we had placed our soldiers out of the way of our own weapons, we should have come out of the most extraordinary battle in all history without a scratch.

Wednesday, March 14, 1906

Moro slaughter continued.—Luncheon for Geo. Harvey.—Opinions of the guests as to Moro fight.—Cable from General Wood explaining and apologizing.—What became of the wounded?—President Roosevelt's joy over the splendid achievement.—McKinley's joy over capture of Aguinaldo.

The ominous paralysis continues. There has been a slight sprinkle—an exceedingly slight sprinkle—in the correspondence columns, of angry rebukes of the President for calling this cowardly massacre a "brilliant feat of arms" and for praising our butchers for "holding up the honor of the flag" in that singular way; but there is hardly a ghost of a whisper about the feat of arms in the editorial columns of the papers.

I hope that this silence will continue. It is about as eloquent and as damaging and effective as the most indignant words could be, I think. When a man is sleeping in a noise, his sleep goes placidly on; but if the noise stops, the stillness wakes him. This silence has continued five days now. Surely it must be waking the drowsy nation. Surely the nation must be wondering what it means. A five-day silence following a world-astonishing event has not happened on this planet since the daily newspaper was invented.

At a luncheon party of men convened yesterday to God-speed George Harvey, who is leaving today for a vacation in Europe, all the talk was about the brilliant feat of arms; and no one had anything to say about it that either the President or Major-General Dr. Wood or the damaged Johnson would regard as complimentary, or as proper comment to put into our histories. Harvey said he believed that the shock and shame of this episode would eat down deeper and deeper into the hearts of the nation and fester there and produce results. He believed it would destroy the Republican party and President Roosevelt. I cannot believe that the prediction will come true, for the reason that prophecies which promise valuable things, desirable things, good things, worthy things, never come true. Prophecies of this kind are like wars fought in a good cause—they are so rare that they don't count.

Day before yesterday the cable note from the happy General Doctor Wood was still all glorious. There was still proud mention and elaboration of what was called the "desperate hand-to-hand fight," Doctor Wood not seeming to suspect that he was giving himself away, as the phrase goes—since if there was any very desperate hand-to-hand fighting it would necessarily happen that nine hundred hand-to-hand fighters, if really desperate, would surely be able to kill more than fifteen of our men before their last man and woman and child perished.

Very well, there was a new note in the dispatches yesterday afternoon—just a faint suggestion that Doctor Wood was getting ready to lower his tone and begin to apologize and explain. He announces that he assumes full responsibility for the fight. It indicates that he is aware that there is a lurking disposition here amid all this silence to blame somebody. He says there was "no wanton destruction of women and children in the fight, though many of them were killed by force of necessity because the Moros used them as shields in the hand-to-hand fighting."

This explanation is better than none; indeed, it is considerably better than none. Yet if there was so much hand-to-hand fighting there must have arrived a time, toward the end of the four days' butchery, when only one native was left alive. We had six hundred men present; we had lost only fifteen; why did the six hundred kill that remaining man—or woman, or child?

Doctor Wood will find that explaining things is not in his line. He will find that where a man has the proper spirit in him and the proper force at his command, it is easier to massacre nine hundred unarmed animals than it is to explain why he made it so remorselessly complete. Next he furnishes us this sudden burst of unconscious humor, which shows that he ought to edit his reports before he cables them:

"Many of the Moros feigned death and butchered the American hospital men who were relieving the wounded."

We have the curious spectacle of hospital men going around trying to relieve the wounded savages—for what reason? The savages were all massacred. The plain intention was to massacre them all and leave none alive. Then where was the use in furnishing mere temporary relief to a person who was presently to be exterminated? The dispatches call this battue a "battle." In what way was it a battle? It has no resemblance to a battle. In a battle there are always as many as five wounded men to one killed outright. When this so-called battle was over, there were certainly not fewer than two hundred wounded savages lying on the field. What became of them? Since not one savage was left alive!

The inference seems plain. We cleaned up our four days' work and made it complete by butchering those helpless people.

The President's joy over this achievement brings to mind an earlier presidential ecstasy. When the news came, in 1901, that Colonel Funston had penetrated to the refuge of the patriot, Aguinaldo, in the mountains, and had captured him by the use of these arts, to wit: by forgery, by lies, by disguising his military marauders in the uniform of the enemy, by pretending to be friends of Aguinaldo's and by disarming suspicion by cordially shaking hands with Aguinaldo's officers and in that moment shooting them down—when the cablegram announcing this "brilliant feat of arms" reached the White House, the newspapers said that that meekest and mildest and gentlest of men, President McKinley, could not control his joy and gratitude, but was obliged to express it in motions resembling a dance.

Monday, March 5, 1906
(Dictated March 15th)

Mr. Clemens talks to the West Side Young Men's Christian Association in the Majestic Theater.—Patrick's funeral.—Luncheon next day at the Hartford Club.—Mr. Clemens meets eleven of his old friends.—They tell many stories.—Mr. Twichell's story on board the "Kanawha," about Richard Croker's father.—The Mary Ann story!—Decoration Day and the fiery major and Mr. Twichell's interrupted prayer.

Yesterday, in the afternoon, I talked to the West Side Young Men's Christian Association in the Majestic Theater. The audience was to have been restricted to the membership, or at least to the membership's sex, but I had asked for a couple of stage boxes and had invited friends of mine of both sexes to occupy them. There was trouble out at the doors and I became afraid that these friends would not get in. My secretary volunteered to go out and see if she could find them and rescue them from the crowd. She was a pretty small person for such a service, but maybe her lack of dimensions was in her favor, rather than against it. She plowed her way through the incoming masculine wave and arrived outside, where she captured the friends, and also had an adventure. Just as the police were closing the doors of the theater and announcing to the crowd that the place was full and no more could be admitted, a flushed and excited man crowded his way to the door and got as much as his nose in, but there the officer closed the door and the man was outside. He and my secretary were for the moment the center of attention—she because of her solitariness in that sea of masculinity, and he because he had been defeated before folks, a thing which we all enjoy, even when we are West Side Young Christians and ought to let on that we don't. The man looked down at my secretary—anybody can do that without standing on a chair—and he began pathetically—I say began pathetically; the pathos of his manner and his words was confined to his beginning. He began on my secretary, then shifted to the crowd for a finish. He said, "I have been a member of this West Side Young Men's Christian Association in good standing for seven years, and have always done the best I could, yet never once got any reward." He paused half an instant, shot a bitter glance at the closed door, and added, with deep feeling, "It's just my God damned luck."

I think it damaged my speech for my secretary. The speech was well enough—certainly better than the report of it in the papers—but in spite of her compliments, I knew there was nothing in it so good as what she had heard outside; and by the delight which she exhibited in that outsider's eloquence I knew that she knew it.

I will insert here a passage from the newspaper report, because it refers to Patrick.

Definition of a Gentleman

Mark Twain went on to speak of the man who left $10,000 to disseminate his definition of a gentleman. He denied that he had ever defined one, but said if he did he would include the mercifulness, fidelity, and justice the Scripture read at the meeting spoke of. He produced a letter from William Dean Howells, and said:

"He writes he is just sixty-nine, but I have known him longer than that. 'I was born to be afraid of dying, not of getting old,' he says. Well, I'm the other way. It's terrible getting old. You gradually lose your faculties and fascinations and become troublesome. People try to make you think you are not. But I know I'm troublesome.

"Then he says no part of life is so enjoyable as the eighth decade. That's true. I've just turned it, and I enjoy it very much. 'If old men were not so ridiculous'—Why didn't he speak for himself? 'But,' he goes on, 'they are ridiculous, and they are ugly.' I never saw a letter with so many errors in it. Ugly! I was never ugly in my life! Forty years ago I was not so good-looking. A looking glass then lasted me three months. Now I can wear it out in two days.

"'You've been up in Hartford burying poor old Patrick. I suppose he was old, too,' says Mr. Howells. No, he was not old. Patrick came to us thirty-six years ago—a brisk, lithe young Irishman. He was as beautiful in his graces as he was in his spirit, and he was as honest a man as ever lived. For twenty-five years he was our coachman, and if I were going to describe a gentleman in detail I would describe Patrick.

"At my own request I was his pallbearer with our old gardener. He drove me and my bride so long ago. As the little children came along he drove them, too. He was all the world to them, and for all in my house he had the same feelings of honor, honesty, and affection.

"He was sixty years old, ten years younger than I. Howells suggests he was old. He was not old. He had the same gracious and winning ways to the end. Patrick was a gentleman, and to him I would apply the lines:

"'So may I be courteous to men, faithful to friends,
True to my God, a fragrance in the path I trod.'"

AT THE FUNERAL I SAW Patrick's family. I had seen no member of it for a good many years. The children were men and women. When I had seen them last they were little creatures. So far as I could remember I had not seen them since as little chaps they joined with ours, and with the children of the neighbors, in celebrating Christmas Eve around a Christmas tree in our house, on which occasion Patrick came down the chimney (apparently) disguised as Saint Nicholas, and performed the part to the admiration of the little and the big alike.

John, our old gardener, was a fellow pallbearer with me. The rest were Irish coachmen and laborers—old friends of Patrick. The cathedral was half filled with people.

I spent the night at Twichell's house, that night, and at noon next day at the Hartford Club I met, at a luncheon, eleven of my oldest friends—Charley Clarke, editor of the Courant; Judge Hammersley of the Supreme Court; Colonel Cheney; Sam Dunham; Twichell; Rev. Dr. Parker; Charles E. Perkins; Archie Welsh. A deal of pretty jolly reminiscing was done, interspersed with mournings over beloved members of the old comradeship whose names have long ago been carved upon their gravestones.

Several things were told on Twichell illustrative of his wide catholicity of feeling and conduct, and I was able to furnish something in this line myself. Three or four years ago, when Sir Thomas Upton came over here to race for the America cup, I was invited to go with Mr. Rogers and a half a dozen other worldlings in Mr. Rogers's yacht, the Kanawha, to see the race. Mr. Rogers is fond of Twichell and wanted to invite him to go also, but was afraid to do it because he thought Twichell would be uncomfortable among those worldings. I said I didn't think that would be the case. I said Twichell was chaplain in a fighting brigade all through the Civil War, and was necessarily familiar with about all the different kinds of worldlings that could be started; so Mr. Rogers told me—though with many misgivings—to invite him, and that he would do his best to see that the worldlings should modify their worldliness and pay proper respect and deference to Twichell's cloth.

When Twichell and I arrived at the pier at eight in the morning, the launch was waiting for us. All the others were on board. The yacht was anchored out there, ready to sail. Twichell and I went aboard and ascended to the little drawing-room on the upper deck. The door stood open, and as we approached we heard hilarious laughter and talk proceeding from that place, and I recognized that the worldlings were having a worldly good time. But as Twichell appeared in the door all that hilarity ceased as suddenly as if it had been shut off with an electric button, and the gay faces of the worldlings at once put on a most proper and impressive solemnity. The last word we had heard from these people was the name of Richard Croker, the celebrated Tammany leader, all-round blatherskite and chief pillager of the municipal till. Twichell shook hands all around and broke out with: "I heard you mention Richard Croker. I knew his father very well indeed. He was head teamster in our brigade in the Civil War—the Sickles brigade—a fine man—as fine a man as a person would want to know. He was always splashed over with mud, of course, but that didn't matter. The man inside the muddy clothes was a whole man; and he was educated, he was highly educated. He was a man who had read a great deal. And he was a Greek scholar; not a mere surface scholar, but a real one; used to read aloud from his Greek Testament, and when he hadn't it handy he could recite from it from memory, and he did it well and with spirit. Presently I was delighted to see that every now and then he would come over of a Sunday morning and sit under the trees in our camp with our boys and listen to my ministrations. I couldn't refrain from introducing myself to him—that is, I couldn't refrain from speaking to him about this, and I said: 'Mr. Croker, I want to tell you what a pleasure it is to see you come and sit with my boys and listen to me. For I know what it must cost you to do this, and I want to express my admiration for a man who can put aside his religious prejudices and manifest the breadth and tolerance that you have manifested.' He flushed, and said with eloquent emphasis, 'Mr. Twichell, do you take me for a God damned papist?'"

Mr. Rogers said to me, aside, "This relieves me from my burden of uneasiness."

Twichell, with his big heart, his wide sympathies, and his limitless benignities and charities and generosities, is the kind of person that people of all ages and both sexes fly to for consolation and help in time of trouble. He is always being levied upon by this kind of persons. Years ago—many years ago—a soft-headed young donkey who had been reared under Mr. Twichell's spiritual ministrations sought a private interview—a very private interview—with him, and said:

"Mr. Twichell, I wish you would give me some advice. It is a very important matter with me. It lies near my heart and I want to proceed wisely. Now it is like this: I have been down to the Bermudas on the first vacation I have ever had in my life, and there I met a most charming young lady, native of that place, and I fell in love with her, Mr. Twichell. I fell in love with her, oh so deeply! Well, I can't describe it, Mr. Twichell. I can't describe it. I have never had such feelings before, and they just consume me; they burn me up. When I got back here I found I couldn't think of anybody but that girl. I wanted to write to her, but I was afraid. I was afraid. It seemed too bold. I ought to have taken advice, perhaps—but really I was not myself. I had to write—I couldn't help it. So I wrote to her. I wrote to her as guardedly as my feelings would allow—but I had the sense all the time that I was too bold—I was too bold—she wouldn't like it. I—Well, sometimes I would almost think maybe she would answer; but then there would come a colder wave and I would say, 'No, I shall never hear from her— she will be offended.' But at last, Mr. Twichell, a letter has come. I don't know how to contain myself. I want to write again, but I may spoil it—I may spoil it—and I want your advice. Tell me if I had better venture. Now here she has written—here is her letter, Mr. Twichell. She says this: she says—she says—'You say in your letter you wish it could be your privilege to see me half your time. How would you like it to see me all the time?' What do you think of that, Mr. Twichell? How does that strike you? Do you think she is not offended? Do you think that that indicates a sort of a shadowy leaning toward me? Do you think it, Mr. Twichell? Could you say that?"

MARK TWAIN

"Well," Twichell said, "I would not like to be too sanguine. I would not like to commit myself too far. I would not like to put hopes into your mind which could fail of fruition, but, on the whole—on the whole—daring is a good thing in these cases. Sometimes daring—a bold front—will accomplish things that timidity would fail to accomplish. I think I would write her—guardedly of course—but write her."

"Oh, Mr. Twichell, oh, you don't know how happy you do make me! I'll write her right away. But I'll be guarded. I'll be careful—careful."

Twichell read the rest of the letter—saw that this girl was just simply throwing herself at this young fellow's head and was going to capture him by fair means or foul, but capture him. But he sent the young fellow away to write the guarded letter.

In due time he came with the girl's second letter and said: "Mr. Twichell, will you read that? Now read that. How does that strike you? Is she kind of leaning my way? I wish you could say so, Mr. Twichell. You see there, what she says. She says—'You offer to send me a present of a ring—' I did it, Mr. Twichell! I declare it was a bold thing—but—but—I couldn't help it. I did that intrepid thing—and that is what she says: 'You offer to send me a ring. But my father is going to take a little vacation excursion in the New England states and he is going to let me go with him. If you should send the ring here it might get lost. We shall be in Hartford a day or two. Won't it be safer to wait till then and you put it on my finger yourself?'

"What do you think of that, Mr. Twichell? How does it strike you? Is she leaning? Is she leaning?"

"Well," Twichell said, "I don't know about that. I must not be intemperate. I must not say things too strongly, for I might be making a mistake. But I think—I think—on the whole I think she is leaning—I do—I think she is leaning—"

"Oh, Mr. Twichell, it does my heart so much good to hear you say that! Mr. Twichell, if there was anything I could do to show my gratitude for those words—well, you see the condition I am in—and to have you say that—"

Twichell said: "Now wait a minute—now let's not make any mistake here. Don't you know that this is a most serious position? It can have the most serious results upon two lives. You know there is such a thing as a mere passing fancy that sets a person's soul on fire for the moment. That person thinks it is love, and that it is permanent love—that it is real love. Then he finds out, by and by, that it was but a momentary insane passion—and then perhaps he has committed himself for life, and he wishes he was out of that predicament. Now let us make sure of this thing. I believe that if you try, and conduct yourself wisely and cautiously—I don't feel sure, but I believe that if you conduct yourself wisely and cautiously you can beguile that girl into marrying you."

"Oh, Mr. Twichell, I can't express—"

"Well, never mind expressing anything. What I am coming at is this: let us make sure of our position. If this is real love, go ahead! If it is nothing but a passing fancy, drop it right here, for both your sakes. Now tell me, is it real love? If it is real love how do you arrive at that conclusion? Have you some way of proving to your entire satisfaction that this is real, genuine, lasting, permanent love?"

"Mr. Twichell, I can tell you this. You can just judge for yourself. From the time that I was a baby in the cradle up, Mr. Twichell, I have had to sleep close to my mother, with a door open between, because I have always been subject to the most horrible nightmares, and when they break out my mother has to come running from her bed and appease me and comfort me and pacify me. Now then, Mr. Twichell, from the cradle up, whenever I got hit with those nightmare convulsions I have always sung out, 'Mamma, Mamma, Mamma.' Now I sing out, 'Mary Ann, Mary Ann, Mary Ann.'"

So they were married. They moved to the West and we know nothing more about the romance.

Fifteen or twenty years ago, Decoration Day happened to be more like the Fourth of July for temperature than like the 30th of May. Twichell was orator of the day. He pelted his great crowd of old Civil War soldiers for an hour in the biggest church in Hartford, while they mourned and sweltered. Then they marched forth and joined the procession of other old soldiers and tramped through clouds of dust to the cemetery and began to distribute the flags and the flowers—a tiny flag and a small basket of flowers to each military grave. This industry went on and on and on, everybody breathing dust—for there was nothing else to breathe; everybody streaming with perspiration; everybody tired and wishing it was over. At last there was but one basket of flowers left, only one grave still undecorated. A fiery little major, whose patience was all gone, was shouting:

"Corporal Henry Jones, Company C, Fourteenth Connecticut Infantry—"

No response. Nobody seemed to know where that corporal was buried.

The major raised his note a degree or two higher:

"Corporal Henry Jones, Company C, Fourteenth Connecticut Infantry. Doesn't anybody know where that man is buried?"

No response. Once, twice, three times, he shrieked again, with his temper ever rising higher and higher:

"Corporal Henry Jones, Company C, Fourteenth Connecticut Infantry. Doesn't anybody know where that man is buried?"

No response. Then he slammed the basket of flowers on the ground and said to Twichell, "Proceed with the finish."

The crowd massed themselves together around Twichell with uncovered heads, the silence and solemnity interrupted only by subdued sneezings, for these people were buried in the dim cloud of dust. After a pause Twichell began an impressive prayer, making it brief to meet the exigencies of the occasion. In the middle of it he made a pause. The drummer thought he was through, and let fly a rub-a-dub-dub—and the little major stormed out, "Stop that drum!" Twichell tried again. He got almost to the last word safely, when somebody trod on a dog and the dog let out a howl of anguish that could be heard beyond the frontier. The major said, "God damn that dog!"—and Twichell said, "Amen."

Friday, March 16, 1906

Schoolmates of sixty years ago: Mary Miller, one of Mr. Clemens's first sweethearts—Artimisia Briggs, another—Mary Lacy, another—Jimmie McDaniel, to whom Mr. Clemens told his first humorous story.—Mr. Richmond, Sunday-school teacher, afterwards owner of Tom Sawyer's cave, which is now being ground into cement.—Hickman, the showy young captain.—Reuel Gridley, and the sack of flour incident.—The Levin Jew boys called Twenty-two.—George Butler, nephew of Ben Butler.—The incident of getting into bed with Will Bowen to catch the measles, and the successful and nearly fatal case which resulted.

We will return to those school children of sixty years ago. I recall Mary Miller. She was not my first sweetheart, but I think she was the first one that furnished me a broken heart. I fell in love with her when she was eighteen and I nine—but she scorned me, and I recognized that this was a cold world. I had not noticed that temperature before. I believe I was as miserable as a grown man could be. But I think that this sorrow did not remain with me long. As I remember it, I soon transferred my worship to Artimisia Briggs, who was a year older than Mary Miller. When I revealed my passion to her she did not scoff at it. She did not make fun of it. She was very kind and gentle about it. But she was also firm, and said she did not want to be pestered by children.

And there was Mary Lacy. She was a schoolmate. But she also was out of my class because of her advanced age. She was pretty wild and determined and independent. She was ungovernable, and was considered incorrigible. But that was all a mistake. She married, and at once settled down and became in all ways a model matron and was as highly respected as any matron in the town. Four years ago she was still living, and had been married fifty years.

Jimmie McDaniel was another schoolmate. His age and mine about tallied. His father kept the candy shop and he was the most envied little chap in the town—after Tom Blankenship—for, although we never saw him eating candy, we supposed that it was, nevertheless, his ordinary diet. He pretended that he never ate it, didn't care for it because there was nothing forbidden about it—there was plenty of it and he could have as much of it as he wanted. Still, there was circumstantial evidence that suggested that he only scorned candy in public to show off, for he had the worst teeth in town. He was the first human being to whom I ever told a humorous story, so far as I can remember. This was about Jim Wolfe and the cats; and I gave him that tale the morning after that memorable episode. I thought he would laugh his remaining teeth out. I had never been so proud and happy before, and I have seldom been so proud and happy since. I saw him four years ago when I was out there. He was working in a cigar-making shop. He wore an apron that came down to his knees and a beard that came nearly half as far, and yet it was not difficult for me to recognize him. He had been married fifty-four years. He had many children and grandchildren and great-grandchildren, and also even posterity, they all said—thousands—yet the boy to whom I had told the cat story when we were fourteen years old was still present in that cheerful little old man.

Artimisia Briggs got married not long after refusing me. She married Richmond, the stone mason, who was my Methodist Sunday-school teacher in the earliest days, and he had one distinction which I envied him: He was a very kindly and considerate Sunday-school teacher, and patient and compassionate, so he was the favorite teacher with us little chaps. In that school they had slender oblong pasteboard blue tickets, each with a verse from the Testament printed on it, and you could get a blue ticket by reciting two verses. By reciting five verses you could get three blue tickets, and you could trade these at the bookcase and borrow a book for a week. I was under Mr. Richmond's spiritual care every now and then for two or three years, and he was never hard upon me. I always recited the same five verses every Sunday. He was always satisfied with the performance. He never seemed to notice that these were the same five foolish virgins that he had been hearing about every Sunday for months. I always got my tickets and exchanged them for a book. They were pretty dreary books, for there was not a bad boy in the entire bookcase. They were all good boys and good girls and drearily uninteresting, but they were better society than none, and I was glad to have their company and disapprove of it.

Twenty years ago Mr. Richmond had become possessed of Tom Sawyer's cave in the hills three miles from town, and had made a tourist resort of it. In 1849, when the gold-seekers were streaming through our little town of Hannibal, many of our grown men got the gold fever, and I think that all the boys had it. On the Saturday holidays in summertime we used to borrow skiffs whose owners were not present and go down the river three miles to the cave hollow, and there we staked out claims and pretended to dig gold, panning out half a dollar a day at first; two or three times as much, later, and by and by whole fortunes, as our imaginations became inured to the work. Stupid and un-prophetic lads! We were doing this in play and never suspecting. Why, that cave hollow and all the adjacent hills were made of gold!— but we did not know it. We took it for dirt. We left its rich secret in its own peaceful possession and grew up in poverty and went wandering about the world struggling for bread—and this because we had not the gift of prophecy. That region was all dirt and rocks to us, yet all it needed was to be ground up and scientifically handled and it was gold. That is to say, the whole region was a cement mine—and they make the finest kind of Portland cement there now, five thousand barrels a day, with a plant that cost $2,000,000.

Several months ago a telegram came to me from there saying that Tom Sawyer's cave was now being ground into cement. Would I like to say anything about it in public? But I had nothing to say. I was sorry we lost our cement mine, but it was not worth while to talk about it at this late day, and, to take it all around, it was a painful subject, anyway. There are seven miles of Tom Sawyer's cave—that is to say, the lofty ridge which conceals that cave stretches down the bank of the Mississippi seven miles to the town of Saverton.

For a little while Reuel Gridley attended that school of ours. He was an elderly pupil; he was perhaps twenty-two or twenty-three years old. Then came the Mexican War and he volunteered. A company of infantry was raised in our town and Mr. Hickman, a tall, straight, handsome athlete of twenty-five, was made captain of it and had a sword by his side and a broad yellow stripe down the leg of his gray uniform pants. And when that company marched back and forth through the streets in its smart uniform—which it did several times a day for drill—its evolutions were attended by all the boys whenever the school hours permitted. I can see that marching company yet, and I can almost feel again the consuming desire that I had to join it. But they had no use for boys of twelve and thirteen, and before I had a chance in another war the desire to kill people to whom I had not been introduced had passed away.

I saw the splendid Hickman in his old age. He seemed about the oldest man I had ever seen—an amazing and melancholy contrast with the showy young captain I had seen preparing his warriors for carnage so many, many years before. Hickman is dead—it is the old story. As Susy said, "What is it all for?"

Reuel Gridley went away to the wars and we heard of him no more for fifteen or sixteen years. Then one day in Carson City, while I was having a difficulty with an editor on the sidewalk—an editor better built for war than I was—I heard a voice say: "Give him the best you've got, Sam. I'm at your back." It was Reuel Gridley. He said he had not recognized me by my face, but by my drawling style of speech.

He went down to the Reese River mines about that time and presently he lost an election bet in his mining camp, and by the terms of it he was obliged to buy a fifty-pound sack of self-rising flour and carry it through the town, preceded by music, and deliver it to the winner of the bet. Of course the whole camp was present and full of fluid and enthusiasm. The winner of the bet put up the sack at auction for the benefit of the United States Sanitary Fund, and sold it. The purchaser put it up for the Fund and sold it. The excitement grew and grew. The sack was sold over and over again for the benefit of the Fund. The news

MARK TWAIN

of it came to Virginia City by telegraph. It produced great enthusiasm, and Reuel Gridley was begged by telegraph to bring the sack and have an auction in Virginia City. He brought it. An open barouche was provided, also a brass band. The sack was sold over and over again at Gold Hill, then was brought up to Virginia City toward night and sold—and sold again, netting twenty or thirty thousand dollars for the Sanitary Fund. Gridley carried it across California, selling it at various towns. He sold it for large sums in Sacramento and in San Francisco. He brought it East, sold it in New York and in various other cities, finally carried it out to a great fair at St. Louis, went on selling it, finally made it up into small cakes and sold those at a dollar apiece. First and last, the sack of flour which had originally cost five dollars, perhaps, netted more than two hundred thousand dollars for the Sanitary Fund. Reuel Gridley has been dead these many, many years—it is the old story.

In that school were the first Jews I had ever seen. It took me a good while to get over the awe of it. To my fancy they were clothed invisibly in the damp and cobwebby mold of antiquity. They carried me back to Egypt, and in imagination I moved among the Pharaohs and all the shadowy celebrities of that remote age. The name of the boys was Levin. We had a collective name for them which was the only really large and handsome witticism that was ever born on those premises. We called them Twenty-two—and even when the joke was old and had been worn threadbare we always followed it with the explanation, to make sure that it would be understood, "Twice Levin—twenty-two."

There were other boys whose names remain with me. Irving Ayres—but no matter; he's dead.

George Butler, whom I remember as a child of seven wearing a blue leather belt with a brass buckle, and hated and envied by all the boys on account of it. He was a nephew of General Ben Butler and fought gallantly at Ball's Bluff and in several other actions of the Civil War. He is dead, long and long ago.

Will Bowen (dead long ago), Ed Stevens (dead long ago) and John Briggs were special mates of mine. John is still living.

In 1845, when I was ten years old, there was an epidemic of measles in the town and it made a most alarming slaughter among the little people. There was a funeral almost daily, and the mothers of the town were nearly demented with fright. My mother was greatly troubled. She worried over Pamela and Henry and me, and took constant and extraordinary pains to keep us from coming into contact with the contagion. But upon reflection I believed that her judgment was at fault. It seemed to me that I could improve upon it if left to my own devices. I cannot remember now whether I was frightened about the measles or not, but I clearly remember that I grew very tired of the suspense I suffered on account of being continually under the threat of death. I remember that I got so weary of it and so anxious to have the matter settled one way or the other, and promptly, that this anxiety spoiled my days and my nights. I had no pleasure in them. I made up my mind to end this suspense and settle this matter one way or the other and be done with it. Will Bowen was dangerously ill with the measles and I thought I would go down there and catch them. I entered the house by the front way and slipped along through rooms and halls, keeping sharp watch against discovery, and at last I reached Will's bedroom in the rear of the house on the second floor and got into it uncaptured. But that was as far as my victory reached. His mother caught me there a moment later and snatched me out of the house and gave me a most competent scolding and drove me away. She was so scared that she could hardly get her words out, and her face was white. I saw that I must manage better next time, and I did. I hung about the lane at the rear of the house and watched through cracks in the fence until I was convinced that the conditions were favorable. Then I slipped through the back yard and up the back way and got into the room and into the bed with Will Bowen without being observed. I don't know how long I was in the bed. I only remember that Will Bowen, as society, had no value for me, for he was too sick to even notice that I was there. When I heard his mother coming I covered up my head, but that device was a failure. It was dead summertime—the cover was nothing more than a limp blanket or sheet, and anybody could see that there were two of us under it. It didn't remain two very long. Mrs. Bowen snatched me out of that bed and conducted me home herself, with a grip on my collar which she never loosened until she delivered me into my mother's hands along with her opinion of that kind of a boy.

It was a good case of measles that resulted. It brought me within a shade of death's door. It brought me to where I no longer felt any interest in anything, but, on the contrary, felt a total absence of interest—which was most placid and tranquil and sweet and delightful and enchanting. I have never enjoyed anything in my life any more than I enjoyed dying that time. I was, in effect, dying. The word had been passed and the family notified to assemble around the bed and see me off. I knew them all. There was no doubtfulness in my vision. They were all crying, but that did not affect me. I took but the vaguest interest in it, and that merely because I was the center of all this emotional attention and was gratified by it and felt complimented. When Doctor Cunningham had made up his mind that nothing more could be done for me he put bags of hot ashes all over me. He put them on my breast, on my wrists, on my ankles; and so, very much to his astonishment—and doubtless to my regret—he dragged me back into this world and set me going again.

Wednesday, March 21, 1906

Mental telegraphy.—Letter from Mr. Jock Brown.—Search for Dr. John Brown's letters a failure.—Mr. Twichell and his wife, Harmony, have an adventure in Scotland.—Mr. Twichell's picture of a military execution.—Letter relating to foundation of the Players' Club.—The mismanagement which caused Mr. Clemens to be expelled from the club.—He is now an honorary member.

Certainly mental telegraphy is an industry which is always silently at work—oftener than otherwise, perhaps, when we are not suspecting that it is affecting our thought. A few weeks ago when I was dictating something about Dr. John Brown of Edinburgh and our pleasant relations with him during six weeks there, and his pleasant relations with our little child, Susy, he had not been in my mind for a good while—a year, perhaps—but he has often been in my mind since, and his name has been frequently upon my lips and as frequently falling from the point of my pen. About a fortnight ago I began to plan an article about him and about Marjorie Fleming, whose first biographer he was, and yesterday I began the article. To-day comes a letter from his son Jock, from whom I had not previously heard for a good many years. He has been engaged in collecting his father's letters for publication. This labor would naturally bring me into his mind with some frequency, and I judge that his mind telegraphed his thoughts to me across the Atlantic. I imagine that we get most of our thoughts out of somebody else's head, by mental telegraphy—and not always out of heads of acquaintances, but, in the majority of cases, out of the heads of strangers; strangers far removed—Chinamen, Hindus, and all manner of remote foreigners whose language we should not be able to understand, but whose thoughts we can read without difficulty.

DEAR MR. CLEMENS:

I hope you remember me, Jock, son of Dr. John Brown.
At my father's death I handed to Dr. J. T. Brown all the
letters I had to my father, as he intended to write his
life, being his cousin and life-long friend. He did write a
memoir, published after his death in 1901, but he made
no use of the letters and it was little more than a critique
of his writings. If you care to see it I shall send it. Among
the letters which I got back in 1902 were some from you
and Mrs. Clemens. I have now got a large number of letters
written by my father between 1830 and 1882 and intend
publishing a selection in order to give the public an idea
of the man he was. This I think they will do. Miss E. T.
MacLaren is to add the necessary notes. I now write to
ask you if you have letters from him and if you will let
me see them and use them. I enclose letters from yourself
and Mrs. Clemens which I should like to use, 15 sheets
typewritten. Though I did not write as I should to you on
the death of Mrs. Clemens, I was very sorry to hear of it
through the papers, and as I now read these letters, she rises
before me, gentle and lovable as I knew her. I do hope you
will let me use her letter, it is most beautiful, I also hope
you will let me use yours. . .

I am

Yours very sincerely,
JOHN BROWN

We have searched for Doctor John's letters, but without success.
I do not understand this. There ought to be a good many, and none
should be missing, for Mrs. Clemens held Doctor John in such love
and reverence that his letters were sacred things in her eyes and she
preserved them and took watchful care of them. During our ten years'
absence in Europe many letters and like memorials became scattered
and lost, but I think it unlikely that Doctor John's have suffered this fate.
I think we shall find them yet.

These thoughts about Jock bring back to me the Edinburgh of thirty-three years ago, and the thought of Edinburgh brings to my mind one of Rev. Joe Twichell's adventures. A quarter of a century ago Twichell and Harmony, his wife, visited Europe for the first time, and made a stay of a day or two in Edinburgh. They were devotees of Scott, and they devoted that day or two to ransacking Edinburgh for things and places made sacred by contact with the Magician of the North. Toward midnight, on the second night, they were returning to their lodgings on foot; a dismal and steady rain was falling, and by consequence they had George Street all to themselves. Presently the rainfall became so heavy that they took refuge from it in a deep doorway, and there in the black darkness they discussed with satisfaction all the achievements of the day. Then Joe said:

"It has been hard work, and a heavy strain on the strength, but we have our reward. There isn't a thing connected with Scott in Edinburgh that we haven't seen or touched—not one. I mean the things a stranger could have access to. There is one we haven't seen, but it's not accessible—a private collection of relics and memorials of Scott of great interest, but I do not know where it is. I can't get on the track of it. I wish we could, but we can't. We've got to give the idea up. It would be a grand thing to have a sight of that collection, Harmony."

A voice out of the darkness said, "Come upstairs and I will show it to you."

And the voice was as good as its word. The voice belonged to the gentleman who owned the collection. He took Joe and Harmony upstairs, fed them and refreshed them; and while they examined the collection he chatted and explained. When they left at two in the morning they realized that they had had the star time of their trip.

Joe has always been on hand when anything was going to happen—except once. He got delayed in some vexatious and unaccountable way, or he would have been blown up at Petersburg when the mined defenses of that place were flung heavenward in the Civil War.

When I was in Hartford the other day he told me about another of his long string of providential opportunities. I think he thinks Providence is always looking out for him when interesting things are going to happen. This was the execution of some deserters during the Civil War. When we read about such things in history we always have the same picture—blindfolded men kneeling with their heads bowed; a file of stern and alert soldiers fronting them with their muskets ready; an austere officer in uniform standing apart who gives sharp terse orders: "Make ready. Take aim. Fire." There is a belch of flame and smoke, the victims fall forward, expiring, the file shoulders arms, wheels, marches erect and stiff-legged off the field, and the incident is closed.

Joe's picture is different. And I suspect that it is the true one—the common one. In this picture the deserters requested that they might be allowed to stand, not kneel; that they might not be blindfolded, but permitted to look the firing file in the eye. These requests were granted. The men stood erect and soldierly; they kept their color, they did not blench; their eyes were steady. But these things could not be said of any other of the persons present. A general of brigade sat upon his horse, white-faced—white as a corpse. The officer commanding the squad was white-faced—white as a corpse. The firing file were white-faced and their forms wobbled so that the wobble was transmitted to their muskets when they took aim. The officer of the squad could not command his voice, and his tone was weak and poor, not brisk and stern. When the file had done its deadly work it did not march away martially erect and stiff-legged. It wobbled.

This picture commends itself to me as being the truest one that any one has yet furnished of a military execution.

In searching for Doctor Brown's letters—a failure—we have made a find which we were not expecting. Evidently it marks the foundation of the Players' Club, and so it has value for me.

DALY'S THEATRE,

NEW YORK, Jan. 2, 1888.
Mr. Augustin Daly will be very much pleased to have
Mr. S. L. Clemens meet Mr. Booth, Mr. Barrett and
Mr. Palmer and a few friends at lunch on Friday next, January
6th (at one o'clock in Delmonico's) to discuss the formation of
a new club which it is thought will claim your interest.

R.S.V.P.

All the founders, I think, were present at that luncheon—among them Booth, Barrett, Palmer, General Sherman, Bispham, Aldrich, and the rest. I do not recall the other names. I think Laurence Hutton states in one of his books that the club's name—The Players'—had been already selected and accepted before this luncheon took place, but I take that to be a mistake. I remember that several names were proposed, discussed, and abandoned at the luncheon; that finally Thomas Bailey Aldrich suggested that compact and simple name, The Players'; and that even that happy title was not immediately accepted. However, the discussion was very brief. The objections to it were easily routed and driven from the field, and the vote in its favor was unanimous.

I lost my interest in the club three years ago—for cause—but it has lately returned to me, to my great satisfaction. Mr. Booth's bequest was a great and generous one—but he left two. The other one was not much of a benefaction. It was a relative of his who needed a support. As secretary he governed the club and its board of managers like an autocrat from the beginning until three or four months ago, when he retired from his position superannuated. From the beginning, I left my dues and costs to be paid by my business agent in Hartford—Mr. Whitmore. He attended to all business of mine. I interested myself in none of it. When we went to Europe in '91 I left a written order in the secretary's office continuing Whitmore in his function of paymaster of my club dues. Nothing happened until a year had gone by. Then a bill for dues reached me in Europe. I returned it to the secretary and reminded him of my order, which had not been changed. Then for a couple of years the bills went to Whitmore, after which a bill came to me in Europe. I returned it with the previous remarks repeated. But about every two years the sending of bills to me would be resumed. I sent them back with the usual remarks. Twice the bills were accompanied by offensive letters from the secretary. These I answered profanely. At last we came home, in 1901. No bills came to me for a year. Then we took a residence at Riverdale-on-the-Hudson, and straightway came a Players' bill for dues. I was aweary, aweary, and I put it in the waste basket. Ten days later the bill came again, and with it a shadowy threat. I waste-basketed it. After another ten days the bill came once more, and this time the threat was in a concreted condition. It said very peremptorily that if the bill were not paid within a week I would be expelled from the club and posted as a delinquent. This went the way of its predecessors, into the waste basket. On the named day I was posted as expelled.

Robert Reid, David Munro, and other special friends in the club were astonished and put themselves in communication with me to find out what this strange thing meant. I explained to them. They wanted me to state the case to the management and require a reconsideration of the decree of expulsion, but I had to decline that proposition. And therefore things remained as they were until a few months ago, when the ancient secretary retired from the autocracy. The boys thought that my return to the club would be plain and simple sailing now, but I thought differently. I was no longer a member. I could not become a member without consenting to be voted for by the board, like any other candidate, and I would not do that. The management had expelled me upon the mere statement of a clerk that I was a delinquent. They had not asked me to testify in my defense. They might properly argue from that that I had not all of a sudden become a rascal, and that I might be able to explain the situation if asked. The board's whole proceeding had been like all the board's proceedings from the beginning—arbitrary, insolent, stupid. That board's proper place, from the beginning, was the idiot asylum. I could not allow myself to be voted for again, because from my view of the matter I had never lawfully and legitimately ceased to be a member. However, a way fair and honorable to all concerned was easily found to bridge the separating crack. I was made an honorary member, and I have been glad to resume business at the old stand.

Friday, March 22, 1906

Susy's biography.—Langdon's illness and death.—Susy tells of interesting men whom her father met in England and Scotland—Dr. John Brown, Mr. Charles Kingsley. Mr. Henry M. Stanley, Sir Thomas Hardy, Mr. Henry Irving, Robert Browning, Sir Charles Dilke, Charles Reade, William Black, Lord Houghton, Frank Buckland, Tom Hughes, Anthony Trollope, Tom Hood, Doctor Macdonald, and Harrison Ainsworth.— Mr. Clemens tells of meeting Lewis Carroll—of luncheon at Lord Houghton's.—Letters from Mr. and Mrs. Clemens to Doctor Brown.— Mr. Clemens's regret that he did not take Mrs. Clemens for a last visit to Doctor Brown.

From Susy's Biography

I stopped in the middle of mamma's early history to tell about our tripp to Vassar because I was afraid I would forget about it, now I will go on where I left off. Some time after Miss Emma Nigh died papa took mamma and little Langdon to Elmira for the summer. When in Elmira Langdon began to fail but I think mamma did not know just what was the matter with him.

I was the cause of the child's illness. His mother trusted him to my care and I took him for a long drive in an open barouche for an airing. It was a raw, cold morning, but he was well wrapped about with furs and, in the hands of a careful person, no harm would have come to him. But I soon dropped into a reverie and forgot all about my charge. The furs fell away and exposed his bare legs. By and by the coachman noticed this, and I arranged the wraps again, but it was too late. The child was almost frozen. I hurried home with him, I was aghast at what I had done, and I feared the consequences. I have always felt shame for that treacherous morning's work and have not allowed myself to think of it when I could help it. I doubt if I had the courage to make confession at that time. I think it most likely that I have never confessed until now.

From Susy's Biography

At last it was time for papa to return to Hartford, and Langdon was real sick at that time, but still mamma decided to go with him, thinking the journey might do him good. But after they reached Hartford he became very sick, and his trouble prooved to be diptheeria. He died about a week after mamma and papa reached Hartford. He was burried by the side of grandpa at Elmira, New York. (Susy rests there with them.—S. L. C.) After that, mamma became very very ill, so ill that there seemed great danger of death, but with a great deal of good care she recovered. Some months afterward mamma and papa (and Susy, who was perhaps fourteen or fifteen months old at the time.—S. L. C.) went to Europe and stayed for a time in Scotland and England. In Scotland mamma and papa became very well equanted with Dr. John Brown, the author of "Rab and His Friends," and he met, but was not so well equanted with, Mr. Charles Kingsley, Mr. Henry M. Stanley, Sir Thomas Hardy grandson of the Captain Hardy to whom Nellson said "Kiss me Hardy," when dying on shipboard, Mr. Henry Irving, Robert Browning, Sir Charles Dilke, Mr. Charles Reade, Mr. William Black, Lord Houghton, Frank Buckland, Mr. Tom Hughes, Anthony Trollope, Tom Hood, son of the poet—and mamma and papa were quite well equanted with Dr. Macdonald and family, and papa met Harison Ainsworth.

I remember all these men very well indeed, except the last one. I do not recall Ainsworth. By my count, Susy mentions fourteen men. They are all dead except Sir Charles Dilke and Mr. Tom Hughes.

We met a great many other interesting people, among them Lewis Carroll, author of the immortal Alice—but he was only interesting to look at, for he was the stillest and shyest full-grown man I have ever met except "Uncle Remus." Doctor Macdonald and several other lively talkers were present, and the talk went briskly on for a couple of hours, but Carroll sat still all the while except that now and then he answered a question. His answers were brief. I do not remember that he elaborated any of them.

At a dinner at Smalley's we met Herbert Spencer. At a large luncheon party at Lord Houghton's we met Sir Arthur Helps, who was a celebrity of worldwide fame at the time, but is quite forgotten now. Lord Elcho, a large, vigorous man, sat at some distance down the table. He was talking earnestly about Godalming. It was a deep and flowing and unarticulated rumble, but I got the Godalming pretty clearly every time it broke free of the rumble, and as all the strength was on the first end of the word it startled me every time, because it sounded so like swearing. In the middle of the luncheon Lady Houghton rose, remarked to the guests on her right and on her left in a matter-of-fact way, "Excuse me, I have an engagement," and without further ceremony she went off to meet it. This would have been doubtful etiquette in America. Lord Houghton told a number of delightful stories. He told them in French, and I lost nothing of them but the nubs.

I will insert here one or two of the letters referred to by Jock Brown in the letter which I received from him a day or two ago, and which we copied into yesterday's record:

June 22, 1876

DEAR DOCTOR BROWN:

Indeed I was a happy woman to see the familiar handwriting. I do hope that we shall not have to go so long again without a word from you. I wish you could come over to us for a season; it seems as if it would do you good, you and yours would be so very welcome.

We are now where we were two years ago, on the farm on the top of a high hill where my sister spends her summers. The children are grown fat and hearty, feeding chickens and ducks twice a day, and are keenly alive to all the farm interests. Mr. J. T. Fields was with us with his wife a short time ago, and you may be sure we talked most affectionately of you. We do so earnestly desire that you may continue to improve in health; do let us know of

your welfare as often as possible. Love to your sister. Kind
regards to your son please.

As ever affectionately your friend,
Livy L. Clemens

Dear Doctor Brown:

We had grown so very anxious about you that it was a
great pleasure to see the dear, familiar handwriting again,
but the contents of the letter did make us inexpressibly
sad. We have talked so much since about your coming to
see us. Would not the change do you good? Could you not
trust yourself with us? We would do everything to make you
comfortable, and happy that we could, and you have so many
admirers in America that would be so happy and proud to
welcome you. Is it not possible for you to come? Perhaps the
entire change would give you a new and healthier lease of life.

Our children are both well and happy; I wish that you could
see them. Susie is very motherly to the little one. Mr. Clemens
is hard at work on a new book now. He has a new book of
sketches recently out, which he is going to send you in a few
days; most of the sketches are old, but some few are new.

Oh Doctor Brown how can you speak of your life as
a wasted one? What you have written has alone done
an immense amount of good, and I know for I speak from
experience that one must get good every time they meet and
chat with you. I receive good every time I even think of you.
Can a life that produces such an effect on others be a wasted
life? I feel that while you live the world is sweeter and better.
You ask if Clara is "queer and wistful and commanding,"
like your Susie. We think she is more queer, (more quaint)
perhaps more commanding, but not nearly so wistful in her
ways as "your Susie." . . . I must leave a place for Mr. C. Do
you think about coming to us. Give my love to your sister
and your son. Affectionately,

Livy L. CLemens

Dear Doctor,

If you and your son Jock only would run over here! What
a welcome we would give you! and besides, you would forget

cares and the troubles that come of them. To forget pain is to be painless; to forget care is to be rid of it; to go abroad is to accomplish both. Do try the prescription!

Always with love,

SAML. L. CLEMENS

P.S. Livy, you haven't signed your letter. Don't forget that. S. L. C.

P.P.S. I hope you will excuse Mr. Clemens's P.S. to me; it is characteristic for him to put it right on the letter. Livy L. C.

(S. L. C. to Dr. Brown's Son, Jock.)

HARTFORD, June 1, 1882.

MY DEAR MR. BROWN:

I was three thousand miles from home, at breakfast in New Orleans, when the damp morning paper revealed the sorrowful news among the cable dispatches. There was no place in America, however remote, or however rich or poor or high or humble, where words of mourning for your honoured father were not uttered that morning, for his works had made him known and loved all over the land. To Mrs. Clemens and me, the loss is a personal one, and our grief the grief which one feels for one who was peculiarly near and dear. Mrs. Clemens has never ceased to express regret that we came away from England the last time without going to see him, and often we have since projected a voyage across the Atlantic for the sole purpose of taking him by the hand and looking into his kind eyes once more before he should be called to his rest.

We both thank you greatly for the Edinburgh papers which you sent. My wife and I join in affectionate remembrances and greetings to yourself and your aunt, and in the sincere tender of our sympathies. Faithfully yours,

S. L. CLEMENS

P.S. Our Susy is still "Megalopis." He gave her that name.

Can you spare us a photograph of your father? We have none but the one taken in group with ourselves.

IT WAS MY FAULT THAT she never saw Doctor John in life again. How many crimes I committed against that gentle and patient and forgiving spirit! I always told her that if she died first, the rest of my life would be made up of self-reproaches for the tears I had made her shed. And she always replied that if I should pass from life first, she would never have to reproach herself with having loved me the less devotedly or the less constantly because of those tears. We had this conversation again, and for the thousandth time, when the night of death was closing about her—though we did not suspect that.

In the letter last quoted above, I say, "Mrs. Clemens has never ceased to express regret that we came away from England the last time without going to see him." I think that that was intended to convey the impression that she was a party concerned in our leaving England without going to see him. It is not so. She urged me, she begged me, she implored me to take her to Edinburgh to see Doctor John—but I was in one of my devil moods, and I would not do it. I would not do it because I should have been obliged to continue the courier in service until we got back to Liverpool. It seemed to me that I had endured him as long as I could. I wanted to get aboard ship and be done with him. How childish it all seems now! And how brutal—that I could not be moved to confer upon my wife a precious and lasting joy because it would cause me a small inconvenience. I have known few meaner men than I am. By good fortune this feature of my nature does not often get to the surface, and so I doubt if any member of my family except my wife ever suspected how much of that feature there was in me. I suppose it never failed to arrive at the surface when there was opportunity, but it was as I have said—the opportunities have been so infrequent that this worst detail of my character has never been known to any but two persons—Mrs. Clemens, who suffered from it, and I, who suffer from the remembrance of the tears it caused her.

Friday, March 23, 1906

Some curious letter superscriptions which have come to Mr. Clemens.—Our inefficient postal system under Postmaster-General Key.—Reminiscences of Mrs. Harriet Beecher Stowe.—Story of Rev. Charlie Stowe's little boy.

A good many years ago Mrs. Clemens used to keep as curiosities some of the odd and strange superscriptions that decorated letters that came to me from strangers in out-of-the-way corners of the earth. One of these superscriptions was the work of Dr. John Brown, and the letter must have been the first one he wrote me after we came home from Europe in August or September, '74. Evidently the Doctor was guessing at our address from memory, for he made an amusing mess of it. The superscription was as follows:

> Mr. S. L. Clemens.
> (Mark Twain),
> Hartford, N. Y.
> Near Boston, U. S. A.

Now then comes a fact which is almost incredible, to wit: the New York Post Office, which did not contain a single salaried idiot who could not have stated promptly who the letter was for and to what town it should go, actually sent that letter to a wee little hamlet hidden away in the remotenesses of the vast State of New York—for what reason? Because that lost and never previously heard-of hamlet was named Hartford. The letter was returned to the New York Post Office from that hamlet. It was returned innocent of the suggestion, "Try Hartford, Connecticut," although the hamlet's postmaster knew quite well that that was the Hartford the writer of the letter was seeking. Then the New York Post Office opened the envelope, got Doctor John's address out of it, then inclosed it in a fresh envelope and sent it back to Edinburgh. Doctor John then got my address from Menzies, the publisher, and sent the letter to me again. He also inclosed the former envelope—the one that had had the adventures—and his anger at our postal system was like the fury of an angel. He came the nearest to being bitter and offensive than ever he came in his life, I suppose. He said that in Great Britain it was the postal department's boast that by no ingenuity could a man so disguise and conceal a Smith or a Jones or a Robinson in a letter address that the department couldn't find that man, whereas—then he let fly at our system, which was apparently designed to defeat a letter's attempts to get to its destination when humanly possible.

Doctor John was right about our department—at that time. But that time did not last long. I think Postmaster-General Key was in office then. He was a new broom, and he did some astonishing sweeping for a while. He made some cast-iron rules which worked great havoc with the nation's correspondence. It did not occur to him—rational things seldom occurred to him—that there were several millions of people among us who seldom wrote letters; who were utterly ignorant of postal rules, and who were quite sure to make blunders in writing letter addresses whenever blunders were possible, and that it was the government's business to do the very best it could by the letters of these innocents and help them get to their destinations, instead of inventing ways to block the road. Key suddenly issued some boiler-iron rules—one of them was that a letter must go to the place named on the envelope, and the effort to find its man must stop there. He must not be searched for. If he wasn't at the place indicated the letter must be returned to the sender. In the case of Doctor John's letter the Post Office had a wide discretion—not so very wide, either. It must go to a Hartford. That Hartford must be near Boston; it must also be in the State of New York. It went to the Hartford that was farthest from Boston, but it filled the requirement of being in the State of New York—and it got defeated.

Another rule instituted by Key was that letter superscriptions could not end with "Philadelphia"—or "Chicago," or "San Francisco," or "Boston," or "New York," but, in every case, must add the state, or go to the Dead Letter Office. Also, you could not say "New York, N. Y.," you must add the word City to the first "New York" or the letter must go to the Dead Letter Office.

During the first thirty days of the dominion of this singular rule sixteen hundred thousand tons of letters, more or less, went to the Dead Letter Office from the New York Post Office alone. The Dead Letter Office could not contain them and they had to be stacked up outside the building. There was not room outside the building inside the city, so they were formed into a rampart around the city; and if they had had it there during the Civil War we should not have had so much trouble and uneasiness about an invasion of Washington by the Confederate armies. They could neither have climbed over or under that breastwork nor bored nor blasted through it. Mr. Key was soon brought to a more rational frame of mind.

Then a letter arrived for me inclosed in a fresh envelope. It was from a village priest in Bohemia or Galicia, and was boldly addressed:

Mark Twain

Somewhere.

It had traveled over several European countries; it had met with hospitality and with every possible assistance during its wide journey; it was ringed all over, on both sides, with a chain-mail mesh of postmarks—there were nineteen of them altogether. And one of them was a New York postmark. The postal hospitalities had ceased at New York—within three hours and a half of my home. There the letter had been opened, the priest's address ascertained, and the letter had then been returned to him, as in the case of Dr. John Brown.

Among Mrs. Clemens's collection of odd addresses was one on a letter from Australia, worded thus:

Mark Twain

God Knows Where.

That superscription was noted by newspapers[1] here and there and yonder while it was on its travels, and doubtless suggested another odd superscription invented by some stranger in a far-off land—and this was the wording of it:

Mark Twain,

Somewhere,

(Try Satan)

That stranger's trust was not misplaced. Satan courteously sent it along.

This morning's mail brings another of these novelties. It comes from France—from a young English girl—and is addressed:

---

1. This letter was originally mailed in New York by Brander Matthews and Francis Wilson.

MARK TWAIN,
C/O PRESIDENT ROOSEVELT,
THE WHITE HOUSE,
WASHINGTON,
AMERICA, U. S. A.

It was not delayed, but came straight along bearing the Washington postmark of yesterday.

In a diary which Mrs. Clemens kept for a little while, a great many years ago, I find various mentions of Mrs. Harriet Beecher Stowe, who was a near neighbor of ours in Hartford, with no fences between. And in those days she made as much use of our grounds as of her own, in pleasant weather. Her mind had decayed and she was a pathetic figure. She wandered about all the day long in the care of a muscular Irishwoman. Among the colonists of our neighborhood the doors always stood open in pleasant weather. Mrs. Stowe entered them at her own free will, and as she was always softly slippered and generally full of animal spirits, she was able to deal in surprises, and she liked to do it. She would slip up behind a person who was deep in dreams and musings and fetch a war whoop that would jump that person out of his clothes. And she had other moods. Sometimes we would hear gentle music in the drawing-room and would find her there at the piano singing ancient and melancholy songs with infinitely touching effect.

Her husband, old Professor Stowe, was a picturesque figure. He wore a broad slouch hat. He was a large man, and solemn. His beard was white and thick and hung far down on his breast. His nose was enlarged and broken up by a disease which made it look like a cauliflower. The first time our little Susy ever saw him she encountered him on the street near our house and came flying wide-eyed to her mother and said, "Santa Claus has got loose."

Monday, March 26, 1906

Mr. Clemens comments on newspaper clipping.—Tells Mr. Howells the scheme of this autobiography.—Tells the newspaper account of girl who tried to commit suicide.—Newspapers in remote villages and in great cities contrasted.—Remarks about Capt. E. L. Marsh and Dick Higham.—Higbie's letter, and "Herald" letter to Higbie.

Baby Advice in a Car
Old Man Got It, Five-Year-Old Gave It,
Mother Said, "Shut Up"

A benevolent-looking old man clung to a strap in a crowded Broadway car bound uptown Saturday afternoon. In a corner seat in front of him huddled a weak-looking little woman who clasped a baby to her breast. Beside her sat another child, a girl perhaps five years old, who seemed to be attracted by the old man's kindly face, for she gazed at him and the baby with her bright, intelligent eyes opened wide. He smiled at her interest and said to her:

"My! What a nice baby! Just such a one as I was looking for, I am going to take it."

"You can't," declared the little girl, quickly. "She's my sister."

"What! Won't you give her to me?"

"No, I won't."

"But," he insisted, and there was real wistfulness in his tones, "I haven't a baby in my home."

"Then write to God. He'll send you one," said the child confidently,

The old man laughed. So did the other passengers. But the mother evidently scented blasphemy.

"Tillie," said she, "shut up and behave yourself!"

That is a scrap which I have cut from this morning's Times. It is very prettily done, charmingly done; done with admirable ease and grace—with the ease and grace that are born of feeling and sympathy, as well as of practice with the pen. Every now and then a newspaper reporter astonishes me with felicities like this. I was a newspaper reporter myself forty-four years ago, and during three subsequent years—but as I remember it I and my comrades never had time to cast our things in a fine literary mold. That scrap will be just as touching and just as beautiful three hundred years hence as it is now.

I intend that this autobiography shall become a model for all future autobiographies when it is published, after my death, and I also intend that it shall be read and admired a good many centuries because of its form and method—a form and method whereby the past and the present are constantly brought face to face, resulting in contrasts which newly fire up the interest all along like contact of flint with steel. Moreover, this autobiography of mine does not select from my life its showy episodes, but deals merely in the common experiences which go to make up the life of the average human being, and the narrative must interest the average human being because these episodes are of a sort which he is familiar with in his own life, and in which he sees his own life reflected and set down in print. The usual, conventional autobiographer seems to particularly hunt out those occasions in his career when he came into contact with celebrated persons, whereas his contacts with the uncelebrated were just as interesting to him, and would be to his reader, and were vastly more numerous than his collisions with the famous.

Howells was here yesterday afternoon, and I told him the whole scheme of this autobiography and its apparently systemless system— only apparently systemless, for it is not that. It is a deliberate system, and the law of the system is that I shall talk about the matter which for the moment interests me, and cast it aside and talk about something else the moment its interest for me is exhausted. It is a system which follows no charted course and is not going to follow any such course. It is a system which is a complete and purposed jumble—a course which begins nowhere, follows no specified route, and can never reach an end while I am alive, for the reason that it it I should talk to the stenographer two hours a day for a hundred years, I should still never be able to set down a tenth part of the things which have interested me in my lifetime. I told Howells that this autobiography of mine would live a couple of thousand years without any effort and would then take a fresh start and live the rest of the time.

He said he believed it would, and asked me if I meant to make a library of it.

I said that that was my design, but that if I should live long enough the set of volumes could not be contained merely in a city, it would require a state, and that there would not be any multi-billionaire alive, perhaps, at any time during its existence who would be able to buy a full set, except on the installment plan.

Howells applauded, and was full of praises and indorsement, which was wise in him and judicious. If he had manifested a different spirit I would have thrown him out of the window. I like criticism, but it must be my way.

Day before yesterday there was another of those happy literary efforts of the reporters, and I meant to cut it out and insert it to be read with a sad pleasure in future centuries, but I forgot and threw the paper away. It was a brief narrative, but well stated. A poor little starved girl of sixteen, clothed in a single garment, in midwinter (albeit properly speaking this is spring), was brought in her pendent rags before a magistrate by a policeman, and the charge against her was that she had been found trying to commit suicide. The judge asked her why she was moved to that crime, and she told him, in a low voice broken by sobs, that her life had become a burden which she could no longer bear; that she worked sixteen hours a day in a sweat shop; that the meager wage she earned had to go toward the family support; that her parents were never able to give her any clothes or enough to eat; that she had worn this same ruined garment as long back as she could remember; that her poor companions were her envy because often they had a penny to spend for some pretty trifle for themselves; that she could not remember when she had had a penny for such a purpose. The court, the policemen, and the other spectators cried with her—a sufficient proof that she told her pitiful tale convincingly and well. And the fact that I also was moved by it, at second hand, is proof that that reporter delivered it from his heart through his pen, and did his work well.

In the remote parts of the country the weekly village newspaper remains the same curious production it was when I was a boy, sixty years ago, on the banks of the Mississippi. The metropolitan daily of the great city tells us every day about the movements of Lieutenant-General So-and-so and Rear-Admiral So-and-so, and what the Vanderbilts are doing. These great dailies keep us informed of Mr. Carnegie's movements and sayings; they tell us what President Roosevelt said yesterday and what he is going to do to-day. They tell us what the children of his family have been saying, just as the princelings of Europe are daily quoted—and we notice that the remarks of the Roosevelt children are distinctly princely in that the things they say are rather notably not worth while.

Now the court circular of the remote village newspaper has always dealt, during these sixty years, with the comings and goings and sayings of its local princelings. They have told us during all those years, and they still tell us, what the principal grocery man is doing and how he has bought a new stock; they tell us that relatives are visiting the ice-cream man, that Miss Smith has arrived to spend a week with the Joneses, and so on, and so on. And all that record is just as intensely interesting to the villagers as is the record I have just been speaking of, of the doings and sayings of the colossally conspicuous personages of the United States. This shows that human nature is all alike; it shows that we like to know what the big people are doing, so that we can envy them. It shows that the big personage of a village bears the same proportion to the little people of the village that the President of the United States bears to the nation. It shows that conspicuousness is the only thing necessary in a person to command our interest and, in a larger or smaller sense, our worship. We recognize that there are no trivial occurrences in life if we get the right focus on them. In a village they are just as prodigious as they are when the subject is a personage of national importance.

The Swangos

(From The Hazel Green (Ky.) Herald.)

Dr. Bill Swango is able to be in the saddle again.

Aunt Rhod Swango visited Joseph Catron and wife Sunday.

Mrs. Shiloh Swango attended the auction at Maytown Saturday.

W. W. Swango has a nice bunch of cattle ready for the Mount Sterling market.

James Murphy bought ten head of cattle from W. W. Swango last week.

Mrs. John Swango of Montgomery County visited Shiloh Swango and family last week.

Mrs. Sarah Ellen Swango, wife of Wash, the noted turkey trader of Valeria, was the guest of Mrs. Ben Murphy Saturday and Sunday.

Now that is a very genuine and sincere and honest account of what the Swangos have been doing lately in the interior of Kentucky. We see at a glance what a large place that Swango tribe hold in the admiration and worship of the villagers of Hazel Green, Kentucky. In this account, change Swango to Vanderbilt; then change it to Carnegie; next time change it to Rockefeller; next time change it to the President; next time to the Mayor of New York.

Capt. E. L. Marsh
Former Elmiran Who Died at Des Moines, Iowa, Recently

Captain E. L. Marsh, aged sixty-four years, died at Des Moines, Iowa, a week ago Friday—February 23—after a long illness. The deceased was born in Enfield, Tompkins county, N. Y., in 1842, later came to Elmira to live with his parents and in 1857 left Elmira to locate in Iowa, where he has lived the greater part of the time since, the only exception being brief times of residence in the south and east. He enlisted in Company D, of the Second Iowa at Des Moines, and was elected a captain in that regiment. He served throughout the war with marked courage and efficiency. After the war Captain Marsh went to New Orleans, where he remained during most of the reconstruction period and then went to New York, where he engaged in paving business for several years. He went back to Des Moines in 1877 and resided there during the almost thirty years since. He engaged in the real estate business there with great success. He was married in 1873 and is survived by his wife and two children. Captain Marsh was a member of the Loyal Legion, Commandery of Iowa, and was senior vice commander of the order for Iowa. He was a member of the G. A. R., also, and a member of the Congregational church. Captain Marsh was the son of Mr. and Mrs. Sheppard Marsh, and Mrs. Marsh was twin sister of the late Mrs. Jervis Langdon of this city. Captain Marsh was a very dear and close friend of his cousin, General Charles J. Langdon, of Elmira.

This clipping from a Des Moines, Iowa, newspaper arrives this morning. Ed Marsh was a cousin of my wife, and I remember him very well. He was present at our wedding thirty-six years ago, and was a handsome young bachelor. Aside from my interest in him as a cousin of my young bride, he had another interest for me in the fact that in his company of the Second Iowa Infantry was Dick Higham. Five years before the war, Dick, a good-natured, simple-minded, winning lad of seventeen, was an apprentice in my brother's small printing-office in Keokuk, Iowa. He had an old musket and he used to parade up and down with it in the office, and he said he would rather be a soldier than anything else. The rest of us laughed at him and said he was nothing but a disguised girl, and that if he were confronted by the enemy he would drop his gun and run.

But we were not good prophets. By and by when President Lincoln called for volunteers Dick joined the Second Iowa Infantry, about the time that I was thrown out of my employment as Mississippi River pilot and was preparing to become an imitation soldier on the Confederate side in Rails County, Missouri. The Second Iowa was moved down to the neighborhood of St. Louis and went into camp there. In some way or other it disgraced itself—and if I remember rightly the punishment decreed was that it should never unfurl its flag again until it won the privilege by gallantry in battle. When General Grant, by and by— February, '62—was ordering the charge upon Fort Donelson, the Second Iowa begged for the privilege of leading the assault, and got it. Ed Marsh's company, with Dick in it serving as a private soldier, moved up the hill and through and over the felled trees and other obstructions in the forefront of the charge, and Dick fell with a bullet through the center of his forehead—thus manfully wiping from the slate the chaffing prophecy of five or six years before. Also, what was left of the Second Iowa finished that charge victorious, with its colors flying and never more to be furled in disgrace.

Ed Marsh's sister also was at our wedding. She and her brother bore for each other an almost idolatrous love, and this endured until about a year ago. About the time of our marriage that sister married a blatherskite by the name of Talmage Brown. He was a smart man and intemperately religious. Through his smartness he acquired a large fortune, and in his will, made shortly before his death, he appointed Ed Marsh as one of the executors. The estate was worth a million dollars or more, but its affairs were in a very confused condition. Ed Marsh and the other one or two executors performed their duty faithfully, and without remuneration. It took them years to straighten out the estate's affairs, but they accomplished it. During the succeeding years all went pleasantly. But at last, about a year ago, some relatives of the late Talmage Brown persuaded the widow to bring suit against Ed Marsh and his fellow executors for a large sum of money which it was pretended they had either stolen or had wasted by mismanagement. That severed the devoted relationship which had existed between the brother and sister throughout their lives. The mere bringing of the suit broke Ed Marsh's heart, for he was a thoroughly honorable man and could not bear even the breath of suspicion. He took to his bed and the case went to court. He had no word of blame for his sister, and said that no one was to blame but the Browns. They had poisoned her mind. The case was heard in court. Then the judge threw it out with many indignant comments. But the news of the rehabilitation reached

Marsh too late to save him. He did not rally. He has been losing ground gradually for the past two months, and now at last the end has come.

This morning arrives a letter from my ancient silver-mining comrade, Calvin H. Higbie, a man whom I have not seen nor had communication with for forty-four years. Higbie figures in a chapter of mine in Roughing It, where the tale is told of how we discovered a rich blind lead in the Wide West Mine in Aurora—or, as we called that region then, Esmeralda-—and how, instead of making our ownership of that exceedingly rich property permanent by doing ten days' work on it, as required by the mining laws, he went off on a wild-goose chase to hunt for the mysterious cement mine; and how I went off nine miles to Walker River to nurse Captain John Nye through a violent case of spasmodic rheumatism or blind staggers, or some malady of the kind; and how Cal and I came wandering back into Esmeralda one night just in time to be too late to save our fortune from the jumpers.[1]

I will insert here this letter, and as it will not see the light until Higbie and I are in our graves, I shall allow myself the privilege of copying his punctuation and his spelling, for to me they are a part of the man. He is as honest as the day is long. He is utterly simple-minded and straightforward, and his spelling and his punctuation are as simple and honest as he is himself. He makes no apology for them, and no apology is needed. They plainly state that he is not educated, and they as plainly state that he makes no pretense to being educated.

GREENVILLE, PLUMAS CO., CALIFORNIA
March 15–1906,
SAML. L. CLEMENS.
NEW YORK CITY, N. Y.

MY DEAR SIR—

Two or three parties have ben after me to write up my recolections of Our associations in Nevada, in the early 60's and have come to the conclusion to do so, and have ben jocting down incidents that came to mind, for several years. What I am in dout is, the date you came to Aurora, Nevada- allso, the first trip you made over thee Sieras to California, after coming to Nev. allso as near as possable

---

1. Roughing It is dedicated to Higbie.

date, you tended sick man, on, or near Walker River, when our mine was jumped, dont think for a moment that I intend to steal any of your Thunder, but onely to mention some instances that you failed to mention, in any of your articles, Books &c. that I ever saw. I intend to submit the articles to you so that you can see if anything is objectionabl, if so to erase, same, & add anything in its place you saw fit.

I was burned out a few years since, and all old data, went up in smoke, is the reason I ask for above dates, have ben sick more or less for 2 or 3 years, unable to earn anything to speak of, & the finances are getting pretty low, and I will admit that it is mainly for the purpose of Earning a little money, that my first attempt at writing will be made- and I should be so pleased to have your candid opinion, of its merits, and what in your wisdom in such matters, would be its value for publication. I enclose a coppy of Herald in answer to enquiry I made, if such an article was desired.

Hoping to hear from you as soon as convenient, I remain with great respect,

Yours &c
C. H. HIGBIE

(Copy.)

NEW YORK, Mar. 6-'06
C. H. HIGBIE,
GREENVILLE- CAL.

DRSIR

I should be glad indeed to receive your account of your experiences with Mark Twain, if they are as interesting as I should imagine they would be the Herald would be quite willing to pay you verry well for them, of course, it would be impassible for me to set a price on the matter until I had an opertunity of examining it. if you will kindly send it on, with the privilege of our authenticating it through Mr. Clemens, I shall be more than pleased, to give you a quick decision and make you an offer as it seems worth to us. however, if you have any particular sum in mind which you think should be the price I would suggest that you communicate with me to that effect.

Yours truly
New York Herald,
By GEO. R. MINER
Sunday Editor.

I have written Higbie and asked him to let me do his literary trading for him. He can shovel sand better than I can—as will appear in the next chapter—but I can beat him all to pieces in the art of fleecing a publisher.

Tuesday, March 27, 1906

Higbie's spelling.—Mr. Clemens's scheme for getting Higbie a job at the Pioneer.—In 1863 Mr. Clemens goes to Virginia City to be sole reporter on "Territorial Enterprise."—Mr. Clemens tries his scheme for finding employment for the unemployed, on a young St. Louis reporter, with great success. Also worked the scheme for his nephew, Mr. Samuel E. Moffett.

I have allowed Higbie to assist the Herald man's spelling and make it harmonize with his own. He has done it well and liberally and without prejudice.

To my mind he has improved it, for I have had an aversion to good spelling for sixty years and more, merely for the reason that when I was a boy there was not a thing I could do creditably except spell according to the book. It was a poor and mean distinction, and I early learned to disenjoy it. I suppose that this is because the ability to spell correctly is a talent, not an acquirement. There is some dignity about an acquirement, because it is a product of your own labor. It is wages earned, whereas to be able to do a thing merely by the grace of God, and not by your own effort, transfers the distinction to our heavenly home—where possibly it is a matter of pride and satisfaction, but it leaves you naked and bankrupt.

Higbie was the first person to profit by my great and infallible scheme for finding work for the unemployed. I have tried that scheme, now and then, for forty-four years. So far as I am aware it has always succeeded, and it is one of my high prides that I invented it, and that in basing it upon what I conceived to be a fact of human nature I estimated that fact of human nature accurately.

Higbie and I were living in a cotton-domestic lean-to at the base of a mountain. It was very cramped quarters, with barely room for us and the stove—wretched quarters, indeed, for every now and then, between eight in the morning and eight in the evening, the thermometer would make an excursion of fifty degrees. We had a silver-mining claim under the edge of a hill half a mile away, in partnership with Bob Howland and Horatio Phillips, and we used to go there every morning, carrying with us our luncheon, and remain all day picking and blasting in our shaft, hoping, despairing, hoping again, and gradually but surely running out of funds. At last, when we were clear out and still had struck nothing, we saw that we must find some other way of earning a living. I secured a place in a near-by quartz mill to screen sand with a long-handled shovel. I hate a long-handled shovel. I never could learn to swing it properly. As often as any other way the sand didn't reach the screen at all, but went over my head and down my back, inside of my clothes. It was the most detestable work I have ever engaged in, but it paid ten dollars a week and board—and the board was worth while, because it consisted not only of bacon, beans, coffee, bread, and molasses, but we had stewed dried apples every day in the week just the same as if it were Sunday. But this palatial life, this gross and luxurious life, had to come to an end, and there were two sufficient reasons for it. On my side, I could not endure the heavy labor; and on the company's side, they did not feel justified in paying me to shovel sand down my back; so I was discharged just at the moment that I was going to resign.

If Higbie had taken that job all would have been well and everybody satisfied, for his great frame would have been competent. He was muscled like a giant. He could handle a long-handled shovel like an emperor, and he could work patiently and contentedly twelve hours on a stretch without ever hastening his pulse or his breath. Meantime, he had found nothing to do, and was somewhat discouraged. He said, with an outburst of pathetic longing, "If I could only get a job at the Pioneer!"

I said, "What kind of a job do you want at the Pioneer?"

He said, "Why, laborer. They get five dollars a day."

I said, "If that's all you want I can arrange it for you."

Higbie was astonished. He said, "Do you mean to say that you know the foreman there and could get me a job and yet have never said anything about it?"

"No," I said, "I don't know the foreman."

"Well," he said, "who is it you know? How is it you can get me the job?"

"Why," I said, "that's perfectly simple. If you will do as I tell you to do, and don't try to improve on my instructions, you shall have the job before night."

He said, eagerly, "I'll obey the instructions, I don't care what they are."

"Well," I said, "go there and say that you want work as a laborer; that you are tired of being idle; that you are not used to being idle, and can't stand it; that you just merely want the refreshment of work and require nothing in return."

He said, "Nothing?"

I said, "That's it—nothing."

"No wages at all?"

"No, no wages at all."

"Not even board?"

"No, not even board. You are to work for nothing. Make them understand that—that you are perfectly willing to work for nothing. When they look at that figure of yours that foreman will understand that he has drawn a prize. You'll get the job."

Higbie said, indignantly, "Yes, a hell of a job."

I said: "You said you were going to do it, and now you are already criticizing. You have said you would obey my instructions. You are always as good as your word. Clear out, now, and get the job."

He said he would.

I was pretty anxious to know what was going to happen—more anxious than I would have wanted him to find out. I preferred to seem entirely confident of the strength of my scheme, and I made good show of that confidence. But really I was very anxious. Yet I believed that I knew enough of human nature to know that a man like Higbie would not be flung out of that place without reflection when he was offering those muscles of his for nothing. The hours dragged along and he didn't return. I began to feel better and better. I began to accumulate confidence. At sundown he did at last arrive and I had the joy of knowing that my invention had been a fine inspiration and was successful.

He said the foreman was so astonished at first that he didn't know how to take hold of the proposition, but that he soon recovered and was evidently very glad that he was able to accommodate Higbie and furnish him the refreshment he was pining for.

Higbie said, "How long is this to go on?"

I said: "The terms are that you are to stay right there; do your work just as if you were getting the going wages for it. You are never to make any complaint; you are never to indicate that you would like to have wages or board. This will go on one, two, three, four, five, six days, according to the make of that foreman. Some foremen would break down under the strain in a couple of days. There are others who would last a week. It would be difficult to find one who could stand out a whole fortnight without getting ashamed of himself and offering you wages. Now let's suppose that this is a fortnight foreman. In that case you will not be there a fortnight. Because the men will spread it around that the very ablest laborer in this camp is so fond of work that he is willing and glad to do it without pay. You will be regarded as the latest curiosity. Men will come from the other mills to have a look at you. You could charge admission and get it, but you mustn't do that. Stick to your colors. When the foremen of the other mills cast their eyes upon this bulk of yours and perceive that you are worth two ordinary men they'll offer you half a man's wages. You are not to accept until you report to your foreman. Give him an opportunity to offer you the same. If he doesn't do it, then you are free to take up with that other man's offer. Higbie, you'll be foreman of a mine or a mill inside of three weeks, and at the best wages going."

It turned out just so—and after that I led an easy life, with nothing to do, for it did not occur to me to take my own medicine. I didn't want a job as long as Higbie had one. One was enough for so small a family—and so during many succeeding weeks I was a gentleman of leisure, with books and newspapers to read and stewed dried apples every day for dinner the same as Sunday, and I wanted no better career than this in this life. Higbie supported me handsomely, never once complained of it, never once suggested that I go out and try for a job at no wages and keep myself.

That would be in 1862. I parted from Higbie about the end of '62—or possibly it could have been the beginning of '63—and went to Virginia City, for I had been invited to come there and take William H. Wright's place as sole reporter on the Territorial Enterprise and do Wright's work for three months while he crossed the plains to Iowa to visit his family. However, I have told all about this in Roughing It.

I have never seen Higbie since, in all these forty-four years.

Shortly after my marriage, in 1870, I received a letter from a young man in St. Louis who was possibly a distant relative of mine—I don't remember now about that—but his letter said that he was anxious and ambitious to become a journalist—and would I send him a letter of introduction to some St. Louis newspaper and make an effort to get him a place as a reporter? It was the first time I had had an opportunity to make a new trial of my great scheme. I wrote him and said I would get him a place on any newspaper in St. Louis; he could choose the one he preferred, but he must promise me to faithfully follow out the instructions which I should give him. He replied that he would follow out those instructions to the letter and with enthusiasm. His letter was overflowing with gratitude—premature gratitude. He asked for the instructions. I sent them. I said he must not use a letter of introduction from me or from anyone else. He must go to the newspaper of his choice and say that he was idle, and weary of being idle, and wanted work—that he was pining for work, longing for work—that he didn't care for wages, didn't want wages, but would support himself; he wanted work, nothing but work, and not work of a particular kind, but any kind of work they would give him to do. He would sweep out the editorial rooms; he would keep the inkstands full, and the mucilage bottles; he would run errands; he would make himself useful in every way he could.

I suspected that my scheme would not work with everybody—that some people would scorn to labor for nothing and would think it matter for self-contempt; also that many persons would think me a fool to suggest such a project; also that many persons would not have character enough to go into the scheme in a determined way and test it. I was interested to know what kind of a candidate this one was, but of course I had to wait some time to find out. I had told him he must never ask for wages; he must never be beguiled into making that mistake; that sooner or later an offer of wages would come from somewhere, and in that case he must go straight to his employer and give him the opportunity to offer him the like wages, in which case he must stay where he was—that as long as he was in anybody's employ he must never ask for an advance of wages; that would always come from somewhere else if he proved his worthiness.

The scheme worked again. That young fellow chose his paper, and during the first few days he did the sweeping out and other humble work, and kept his mouth shut. After that the staff began to take notice of him. They saw that they could employ him in lots of ways that saved time and effort for them at no expense. They found that he was alert and willing. They began presently to widen his usefulness. Then he ventured to risk another detail of my instructions; I had told him not to be in a hurry about it, but to make his popularity secure first. He took up that detail now. When he was on his road between office and home, and when he was out on errands, he kept his eyes open, and whenever he saw anything that could be useful in the local columns he wrote it out, then went over it and abolished adjectives, went over it again and extinguished other surplusages, and finally when he got it boiled down to the plain facts with the ruffles and other embroideries all gone, he laid it on the city editor's desk. He scored several successes, and saw his stuff go into the paper unpruned. Presently the city editor when short of help sent him out on an assignment. He did his best with it, and with good results. This happened with more and more frequency. It brought him into contact with all the reporters of all the newspapers. He made friends with them and presently one of them told him of a berth that was vacant, and that he could get it and the wages too. He said he must see his own employers first about it. In strict accordance with my instructions he carried the offer to his own employers, and the thing happened which was to be expected. They said they could pay that wage as well as any other newspaper—stay where he was.

This young man wrote me two or three times a year and he always had something freshly encouraging to report about my scheme. Now and then he would be offered a raise by another newspaper. He carried the news to his own paper; his own paper stood the raise every time and he remained there. Finally he got an offer which his employers could not meet and then they parted. This offer was a salary of three thousand a year, to be managing editor on a daily in a Southern city of considerable importance, and it was a large wage for that day and region. He held that post three years. After that I never heard of him any more.

About 1886 my nephew, Samuel E. Moffett, a youth in the twenties, lost his inherited property and found himself obliged to hunt for something to do by way of making a living. He was an extraordinary young fellow in several ways. A nervous malady had early unfitted him for attending school in any regular way, and he had come up without a school education—but this was no great harm for him, for he had a prodigious memory and a powerful thirst for knowledge. At twelve years he had picked up, through reading and listening, a large and varied treasury of knowledge, and I remember one exhibition of it which was very offensive to me. He was visiting in our house and I was trying to build a game out of historical facts drawn from all the ages. I had put in a good deal of labor on this game, and it was hard labor, for the facts were not in my head. I had to dig them painfully out of the books. The boy looked over my work, found that my facts were not accurate and the game, as it stood, not usable. Then he sat down and built the whole game out of his memory. To me it was a wonderful performance, and I was deeply offended.

As I have said, he wrote me from San Francisco in his early twenties, and said he wanted to become a journalist, and would I send him some letters of introduction to the newspaper editors of that city? I wrote back and put him strictly under those same old instructions. I sent him no letter of introduction and forbade him to use one furnished by anybody else. He followed the instructions strictly. He went to work in the Examiner, a property of William R. Hearst. He cleaned out the editorial rooms and carried on the customary drudgeries required by my scheme. In a little while he was on the editorial staff at a good salary. After two or three years the salary was raised to a very good figure indeed. After another year or two he handed in his resignation—for in the meantime he had married and was living in Oakland, or one of those suburbs, and did not like the travel to and fro between the newspaper and his home in the late hours of the night and the morning. Then he was told to stay in Oakland, write his editorials there and send them over, and the large salary was continued. By and by he was brought to New York to serve on Mr. Hearst's New York paper, and when he finally resigned from that employment he had been in Mr. Hearst's employ sixteen years without a break. Then he became an editorial writer on the New York World with the privilege of living out of town and sending his matter in. His wage was eight thousand dollars a year. A couple of years ago Collier's Weekly offered him an easy berth and one which was particularly desirable in his case, since it would deal mainly with historical matters, past and present—and that was an industry which he liked. The salary was to be ten thousand dollars. He came to me for advice, and I told him to accept, which he did. When Mr. Pulitzer found that he was gone from the World he was not pleased with his managing editor for letting him go, but his managing editor was not to blame. He didn't know that Moffett was going until he received his resignation. Pulitzer offered Moffett a billet for twenty years, this term to be secured in such a way that it could not be endangered by Pulitzer's death, and to this offer was added the extraordinary proposition that Moffett could name his own salary. But of course Moffett remains with Collier, his agreement with Collier's having been already arrived at satisfactorily to both parties.

Wednesday, March 28, 1906

Orion Clemens's personality.—His adventure at the house of Doctor Meredith.—Death of Mr. Clemens's father, just after having been made county judge.

My brother's experience was another conspicuous example of my scheme's efficiency. I will talk about that by and by. But for the moment my interest suddenly centers itself upon his personality, moved thereto by this passing mention of him—and so I will drop other matters and sketch that personality. It is a very curious one. In all my seventy years I have not met the twin of it.

Orion Clemens was born in Jamestown, Fentress County, Tennessee, in 1825. He was the family's first-born and antedated me ten years. Between him and me came a sister, Margaret, who died, aged nine, in 1839 in that village of Florida, Missouri, where I was born; and Pamela, mother of Samuel E. Moffett, who was an invalid all her life and died in the neighborhood of New York a year ago, aged about seventy-five. Also there was a brother, Benjamin, who died in 1842, aged ten.

Orion's boyhood was spent in that wee little log hamlet of Jamestown up there among the knobs—so called—of East Tennessee, among a very sparse population of primitives who were as ignorant of the outside world and as unconscious of it as the other wild animals were that inhabited the forest around. The family migrated to Florida, Missouri, then moved to Hannibal, Missouri, when Orion was ten years old. When he was fifteen or sixteen he was sent to St. Louis and there he learned the printer's trade. One of his characteristics was eagerness. He woke with an eagerness about some matter or other every morning; it consumed him all day; it perished in the night and he was on fire with a fresh new interest next morning before he could get his clothes on. He exploited in this way three hundred and sixty-five red-hot new eagernesses every year of his life—until he died sitting at a table with a pen in his hand, in the early morning, jotting down the conflagration for that day and preparing to enjoy the fire and smoke of it until night should extinguish it. He was then seventy-two years old. But I am forgetting another characteristic, a very pronounced one. That was his deep glooms, his despondencies, his despairs; these had their place in each and every day along with the eagernesses. Thus his day was divided—no, not divided, mottled—from sunrise to midnight with alternating brilliant sunshine and black cloud. Every day he was the most joyous and hopeful man that ever was, I think, and also every day he was the most miserable man that ever was.

While he was in his apprenticeship in St. Louis he got well acquainted with Edward Bates, who was afterward in Mr. Lincoln's first Cabinet. Bates was a very fine man, an honorable and upright man, and a distinguished lawyer. He patiently allowed Orion to bring to him each new project; he discussed it with him and extinguished it by argument and irresistible logic—at first. But after a few weeks he found that this labor was not necessary; that he could leave the new project alone and it would extinguish itself the same night. Orion thought he would like to become a lawyer. Mr. Bates encouraged him, and he studied law nearly a week, then of course laid it aside to try something new. He wanted to become an orator. Mr. Bates gave him lessons. Mr. Bates walked the floor reading from an English book aloud and rapidly turning the English into French, and he recommended this exercise to Orion. But as Orion knew no French, he took up that study and wrought at it with enthusiasm two or three days; then gave it up. During his apprenticeship in St. Louis he joined a number of churches, one after another, and taught in the Sunday-schools—changing his Sunday-school every time he changed his religion. He was correspondingly erratic in his politics—Whig to-day, Democrat next week, and anything fresh that he could find in the political market the week after. I may remark here that throughout his long life he was always trading religions and enjoying the change of scenery. I will also remark that his sincerity was never doubted; his truthfulness was never doubted; and in matters of business and money his honesty was never questioned. Notwithstanding his forever-recurring caprices and changes, his principles were high, always high, and absolutely unshakable. He was the strangest compound that ever got mixed in a human mold. Such a person as that is given to acting upon impulse and without reflection; that was Orion's way. Everything he did he did with conviction and enthusiasm and with a vainglorious pride in the thing he was doing—and no matter what that thing was, whether good, bad, or indifferent, he repented of it every time in sackcloth and ashes before twenty-four hours had sped. Pessimists are born, not made. Optimists are born, not made. But I think he was the only person I have ever known in whom pessimism and optimism were lodged in exactly equal proportions. Except in the matter of grounded principle, he was as unstable as water. You could dash his spirits with a single word; you could raise them into the sky again with another one. You could break his heart with a word of disapproval; you could make him as happy as an angel with a word of approval. And there was no occasion to put any sense or any vestige of mentality of any kind into these miracles; anything you might say would answer.

He had another conspicuous characteristic, and it was the father of those which I have just spoken of. This was an intense lust for approval. He was so eager to be approved, so girlishly anxious to be approved by anybody and everybody, without discrimination, that he was commonly ready to forsake his notions, opinions, and convictions at a moment's notice in order to get the approval of any person who disagreed with them. I wish to be understood as reserving his fundamental principles all the time. He never forsook those to please anybody. Born and reared among slaves and slaveholders, he was yet an abolitionist from his boyhood to his death. He was always truthful; he was always sincere; he was always honest and honorable. But in light matters—matters of small consequence, like religion and politics and such things—he never acquired a conviction that could survive a disapproving remark from a cat.

He was always dreaming; he was a dreamer from birth, and this characteristic got him into trouble now and then. Once when he was twenty-three or twenty-four years old, and was become a journeyman, he conceived the romantic idea of coming to Hannibal without giving us notice, in order that he might furnish to the family a pleasant surprise. If he had given notice, he would have been informed that we had changed our residence and that that gruff old bass-voiced sailorman, Doctor Meredith, our family physician, was living in the house which we had formerly occupied and that Orion's former room in that house was now occupied by Doctor Meredith's two ripe old-maid sisters. Orion arrived at Hannibal per steamboat in the middle of the night, and started with his customary eagerness on his excursion, his mind all on fire with his romantic project and building and enjoying his surprise in advance. He was always enjoying things in advance; it was the make of him. He never could wait for the event, but he must build it out of dream-stuff and enjoy it beforehand—consequently sometimes when the event happened he saw that it was not as good as the one he had invented in his imagination, and so he had lost profit by not keeping the imaginary one and letting the reality go.

When he arrived at the house he went around to the back door and slipped off his boots and crept upstairs and arrived at the room of those old maids without having wakened any sleepers. He undressed in the dark and got into bed and snuggled up against somebody. He was a little surprised, but not much, for he thought it was our brother Ben. It was winter, and the bed was comfortable, and the supposed Ben added to the comfort—and so he was dropping off to sleep very well satisfied with his progress so far and full of happy dreams of what was going to happen in the morning. But something else was going to happen sooner than that, and it happened now. The old maid that was being crowded squirmed and struggled and presently came to a half waking condition and protested against the crowding. That voice paralyzed Orion. He couldn't move a limb; he couldn't get his breath; and the crowded one began to paw around, found Orion's new whiskers, and screamed, "Why, it's a man!" This removed the paralysis, and Orion was out of the bed and clawing around in the dark for his clothes in a fraction of a second. Both maids began to scream, so Orion did not wait to get his whole outfit. He started with such parts of it as he could grab. He flew to the head of the stairs and started down, and he was paralyzed again at that point, because he saw the faint yellow flame of a candle soaring up the stairs from below and he judged that Doctor Meredith was behind it, and he was. He had no clothes on to speak of, but no matter, he was well enough fixed for an occasion like this, because he had a butcher knife in his hand. Orion shouted to him, and this saved his life, for the doctor recognized his voice. Then, in those deep sea-going bass tones of his that I used to admire so much when I was a little boy, he explained to Orion the change that had been made, told him where to find the Clemens family, and closed with some quite unnecessary advice about posting himself before he undertook another adventure like that—advice which Orion probably never needed again as long as he lived.

When my father died, in 1847, the disaster happened—as is the customary way with such things—just at the very moment when our fortunes had changed and we were about to be comfortable once more, after several years of grinding poverty and privation which had been inflicted upon us by the dishonest act of one Ira Stout, to whom my father had lent several thousand dollars—a fortune in those days and in that region. My father had just been elected clerk of the Surrogate Court. This modest prosperity was not only quite sufficient for us and for our ambitions, but he was so esteemed—held in such high regard and honor throughout the county—that his occupancy of that dignified office would, in the opinion of everybody, be his possession as long as he might live. He went to Palmyra, the county-seat, to be sworn in, about the end of February. In returning home, horseback, twelve miles, a storm of sleet and rain assailed him and he arrived at the house in a half-frozen condition. Pleurisy followed and he died on the 24th of March.

Thus our splendid new fortune was snatched from us and we were in the depths of poverty again. It is the way such things are accustomed to happen.

The Clemens family was penniless again. Orion came to the rescue.

Thursday, March 29, 1906

Mr. Clemens as apprentice to Mr. Ament.—Wilhelm H's dinner, and the potato incident.—The printing of Rev. Alexander Campbell's sermon.—Incident of dropping watermelon on Henry's head.—Orion buys Hannibal "Journal," which is a failure—then he goes to Muscatine, Iowa, and marries.—Mr. Clemens starts out alone to see the world—visits St. Louis, New York, Philadelphia, Washington, then goes to Muscatine and works in Orion's office—finds fifty-dollar bill—thinks of going to explore the Amazon and collect coca—gets Horace Bixby to train him as pilot—starts with Orion for Nevada when Orion is made Secretary to Territory of Nevada.

But I am in error. Orion did not come to Hannibal until two or three years after my father's death. He remained in St. Louis. He was a journeyman printer and earning wages. Out of his wage he supported my mother and my brother Henry, who was two years younger than I. My sister Pamela helped in this support by taking piano pupils. Thus we got along, but it was pretty hard sledding. I was not one of the burdens, because I was taken from school at once upon my father's death and placed in the office of the Hannibal Courier, as printer's apprentice, and Mr. Ament, the editor and proprietor of the paper, allowed me the usual emolument of the office of apprentice—that is to say, board and clothes, but no money. The clothes consisted of two suits a year, but one of the suits always failed to materialize and the other suit was not purchased so long as Mr. Ament's old clothes held out. I was only about half as big as Ament, consequently his shirts gave me the uncomfortable sense of living in a circus tent, and I had to turn up his pants to my ears to make them short enough.

There were two other apprentices. One was Wales McCormick, seventeen or eighteen years old, and a giant. When he was in Ament's clothes they fitted him as the candle mold fits the candle—thus he was generally in a suffocated condition, particularly in the summertime. He was a reckless, hilarious, admirable creature; he had no principles and was delightful company. At first we three apprentices had to feed in the kitchen with the old slave cook and her very handsome and bright and well-behaved young mulatto daughter. For his own amusement—for he was not generally laboring for other people's amusement—Wales was constantly and persistently and loudly and elaborately making love to that mulatto girl and distressing the life out of her and worrying the old mother to death. She would say, "Now, Marse Wales, Marse Wales, can't you behave yourself?" With encouragement like that, Wales would naturally renew his attentions and emphasize them. It was killingly funny to Ralph and me. And, to speak truly, the old mother's distress about it was merely a pretense. She quite well understood that by the customs of slaveholding communities it was Wales's right to make love to that girl if he wanted to. But the girl's distress was very real. She had a refined nature, and she took all Wales's extravagant love-making in earnest.

We got but little variety in the way of food at that kitchen table, and there wasn't enough of it, anyway. So we apprentices used to keep alive by arts of our own—that is to say, we crept into the cellar nearly every night, by a private entrance which we had discovered, and we robbed the cellar of potatoes and onions and such things, and carried them downtown to the printing-office, where we slept on pallets on the floor, and cooked them at the stove and had very good times. Wales had a secret of cooking a potato which was noble and wonderful and all his own. Since Wales's day I have seen a potato cooked in that way only once. It was when Wilhelm II, Emperor of Germany, commanded my presence at a private feed toward the end of the year 1891. And when that potato appeared on the table it surprised me out of my discretion and made me commit the unforgivable sin, before I could get a grip on my discretion again—that is to say, I made a joyful exclamation of welcome over the potato, addressing my remark to the Emperor at my side without waiting for him to take the first innings. I think he honestly tried to pretend that he was not shocked and outraged, but he plainly was; and so were the other half-dozen grandees who were present. They were all petrified, and nobody could have said a word if he had tried. The ghastly silence endured for as much as half a minute, and would have lasted until now, of course, if the Emperor hadn't broken it himself, for no one else there would have ventured that. It was at half past six in the evening, and the frost did not get out of the atmosphere entirely until close upon midnight, when it did finally melt away—or wash away—under generous floods of beer.

As I have indicated, Mr. Ament's economies were of a pretty close and rigid kind. By and by, when we apprentices were promoted from the basement to the ground floor and allowed to sit at the family table, along with the one journeyman, Pet MacMurray, the economies continued. Mrs. Ament was a bride. She had attained to that distinction very recently, after waiting a good part of a lifetime for it, and she was the right woman in the right place, according to the Amentian idea, for she did not trust the sugar bowl to us, but sweetened our coffee herself. That is, she went through the motions. She didn't really sweeten it. She seemed to put one heaping teaspoonful of brown sugar into each cup, but, according to Wales, that was a deceit. He said she dipped the spoon in the coffee first to make the sugar stick, and then scooped the sugar out of the bowl with the spoon upside down, so that the effect to the eye was a heaped-up spoon, whereas the sugar on it was nothing but a layer. This all seems perfectly true to me, and yet that thing would be so difficult to perform that I suppose it really didn't happen, but was one of Wales's lies.

I have said that Wales was reckless, and he was. It was the recklessness of ever-bubbling and indestructible good spirits flowing from the joy of youth. I think there wasn't anything that that vast boy wouldn't do to procure five minutes' entertainment for himself. One never knew where he would break out next. Among his shining characteristics was the most limitless and adorable irreverence. There didn't seem to be anything serious in life for him; there didn't seem to be anything that he revered.

Once the celebrated founder of the at that time new and widespread sect called Campbellites arrived in our village from Kentucky, and it made a prodigious excitement. The farmers and their families drove or tramped into the village from miles around to get a sight of the illustrious Alexander Campbell and to have a chance to hear him preach. When he preached in a church many had to be disappointed, for there was no church that would begin to hold all the applicants; so in order to accommodate all, he preached in the open air in the public square, and that was the first time in my life that I had realized what a mighty population this planet contains when you get them all together.

He preached a sermon on one of these occasions which he had written especially for that occasion. All the Campbellites wanted it printed, so that they could save it and read it over and over again, and get it by heart. So they drummed up sixteen dollars, which was a large sum then, and for this great sum Mr. Ament contracted to print five hundred copies of that sermon and put them in yellow paper covers. It was a sixteen-page duodecimo pamphlet, and it was a great event in our office. As we regarded it, it was a book, and it promoted us to the dignity of book printers. Moreover, no such mass of actual money as sixteen dollars, in one bunch, had ever entered that office on any previous occasion. People didn't pay for their paper and for their advertising in money; they paid in dry-goods, sugar, coffee, hickory wood, oak wood, turnips, pumpkins, onions, watermelons—and it was very seldom indeed that a man paid in money, and when that happened we thought there was something the matter with him.

We set up the great book in pages—eight pages to a form—and by help of a printer's manual we managed to get the pages in their apparently crazy but really sane places on the imposing-stone. We printed that form on a Thursday. Then we set up the remaining eight pages, locked them into a form, and struck a proof. Wales read the proof, and presently was aghast, for he had struck a snag. And it was a bad time to strike a snag, because it was Saturday; it was approaching noon; Saturday afternoon was our holiday, and we wanted to get away and go fishing. At such a time as this Wales struck that snag and showed us what had happened. He had left out a couple of words in a thin-spaced page of solid matter and there wasn't another break-line for two or three pages ahead. What in the world was to be done? Overrun all those pages in order to get in the two missing words? Apparently there was no other way. It would take an hour to do it. Then a revise must be sent to the great minister; we must wait for him to read the revise; if he encountered any errors we must correct them. It looked as if we might lose half the afternoon before we could get away. Then

Wales had one of his brilliant ideas. In the line in which the "out" had been made occurred the name Jesus Christ. Wales reduced it in the French way to J. C. It made room for the missing words, but it took 99 per cent of the solemnity out of a particularly solemn sentence. We sent off the revise and waited. We were not intending to wait long. In the circumstances we meant to get out and go fishing before that revise should get back, but we were not speedy enough. Presently that great Alexander Campbell appeared at the far end of that sixty-foot room, and his countenance cast a gloom over the whole place. He strode down to our end and what he said was brief, but it was very stern, and it was to the point. He read Wales a lecture. He said, "So long as you live, don't you ever diminish the Saviour's name again. Put it all in." He repeated this admonition a couple of times to emphasize it, then he went away.

In that day the common swearers of the region had a way of their own of emphasizing the Saviour's name when they were using it profanely, and this fact intruded itself into Wales's incorrigible mind. It offered him an opportunity for a momentary entertainment which seemed to him to be more precious and more valuable than even fishing and swimming could afford. So he imposed upon himself the long and weary and dreary task of overrunning all those three pages in order to improve upon his former work and incidentally and thoughtfully improve upon the great preacher's admonition. He enlarged the offending J. C. into Jesus H. Christ. Wales knew that that would make prodigious trouble, and it did. But it was not in him to resist it. He had to succumb to the law of his make. I don't remember what his punishment was, but he was not the person to care for that. He had already collected his dividend.

It was during my first year's apprenticeship in the Courier office that I did a thing which I have been trying to regret for fifty-five years. It was a summer afternoon and just the kind of weather that a boy prizes for river excursions and other frolics, but I was a prisoner. The others were all gone holidaying. I was alone and sad. I had committed a crime of some sort and this was the punishment. I must lose my holiday, and spend the afternoon in solitude besides. I had the printing-office all to myself, there in the third story. I had one comfort, and it was a generous one while it lasted. It was the half of a long and broad watermelon, fresh and red and ripe. I gouged it out with a knife, and I found accommodation for the whole of it in my person—though it did crowd me until the juice ran out of my ears. There remained then the shell, the hollow shell. It was big enough to do duty as a cradle. I didn't want to waste it, and I couldn't think of anything to do with it which could afford entertainment. I was sitting at the open window which looked out upon the sidewalk of the main street three stories below, when it occurred to me to drop it on somebody's head. I doubted the judiciousness of this, and I had some compunctions about it, too, because so much of the resulting entertainment would fall to my share and so little to the other person. But I thought I would chance it. I watched out of the window for the right person to come along—the safe person—but he didn't come. Every time there was a candidate he or she turned out to be an unsafe one, and I had to restrain myself. But at last I saw the right one coming. It was my brother Henry. He was the best boy in the whole region. He never did harm to anybody, he never offended anybody. He was exasperatingly good. He had an overflowing abundance of goodness—but not enough to save him this time. I watched his approach with eager interest. He came strolling along, dreaming his pleasant summer dream and not doubting but that Providence had him in His care. If he had known where I was he would have had less confidence in that superstition. As he approached his form became more and more foreshortened. When he was almost under me he was so foreshortened that nothing of him was visible from my high place except the end of his nose and his alternately approaching feet. Then I poised the watermelon, calculated my distance, and let it go, hollow side down. The accuracy of that gunnery was beyond admiration. He had about six steps to make when I let that canoe go, and it was lovely to see those two bodies gradually closing in on each other. If he had had seven steps to make, or five steps to make, my gunnery would have been a failure. But he had exactly the right number to make, and that shell smashed down right on the top of his head and drove him into the earth up to the chin, the chunks of that broken melon flying in every direction like a spray. I wanted to go down there and condole with him, but it would not have been safe. He would have suspected me at once. I expected him to suspect me, anyway, but as he said nothing about this adventure for two or three days—I was watching him in the meantime in order to keep out of danger—I was deceived into believing that this time he didn't suspect me. It was a mistake. He was only waiting for a sure opportunity. Then he landed a cobblestone on the side of my head which raised a bump there so large that I had to wear two hats for a time. I carried this crime to my mother, for I was always anxious to get

Henry into trouble with her and could never succeed. I thought that I had a sure case this time when she should come to see that murderous bump. I showed it to her, but she said it was no matter. She didn't need to inquire into the circumstances. She knew I had deserved it, and the best way would be for me to accept it as a valuable lesson, and thereby get profit out of it.

About 1849 or 1850 Orion severed his connection with the printing-house in St. Louis and came up to Hannibal and bought a weekly paper called the Hannibal Journal, together with its plant and its good-will, for the sum of five hundred dollars cash. He borrowed the cash, at ten per cent interest, from an old farmer named Johnson who lived five miles out of town. Then he reduced the subscription price of the paper from two dollars to one dollar. He reduced the rates for advertising in about the same proportion, and thus he created one absolute and unassailable certainty—to wit: that the business would never pay him a single cent of profit. He took me out of the Courier office and engaged my services in his own at three dollars and a half a week, which was an extravagant wage, but Orion was always generous, always liberal with everybody except himself. It cost him nothing in my case, for he never was able to pay me a single penny as long as I was with him. By the end of the first year he found he must make some economies. The office rent was cheap, but it was not cheap enough. He could not afford to pay rent of any kind, so he moved the whole plant into the house we lived in, and it cramped the dwelling-place cruelly. He kept that paper alive during four years, but I have at this time no idea how he accomplished it. Toward the end of each year he had to turn out and scrape and scratch for the fifty dollars of interest due Mr. Johnson, and that fifty dollars was about the only cash he ever received or paid out, I suppose, while he was proprietor of that newspaper, except for ink and printing-paper. The paper was a dead failure. It had to be that from the start. Finally he handed it over to Mr. Johnson, and went up to Muscatine, Iowa, and acquired a small interest in a weekly newspaper there. It was not a sort of property to marry on—but no matter. He came across a winning and pretty girl who lived in Quincy, Illinois, a few miles below Keokuk, and they became engaged. He was always falling in love with girls, but by some accident or other he had never gone so far as engagement before. And now he achieved nothing but misfortune by it, because he straightway fell in love with a Keokuk girl—at least he imagined that he was in love with her, whereas I think she did the imagining for him. The first thing he knew he was engaged to her; and he was in a great quandary. He didn't know whether to marry the Keokuk one or the Quincy one, or whether to try to marry both of them and suit every one concerned. But the Keokuk girl soon settled that for him. She was a master spirit and she ordered him to write the Quincy girl and break off that match, which he did. Then he married the Keokuk girl and they began a struggle for life which turned out to be a difficult enterprise, and very unpromising.

To gain a living in Muscatine was plainly impossible, so Orion and his new wife went to Keokuk to live, for she wanted to be near her relatives. He bought a little bit of a job-printing plant—on credit, of course—and at once put prices down to where not even the apprentices could get a living out of it, and this sort of thing went on.

I had not joined the Muscatine migration. Just before that happened (which I think was in 1853) I disappeared one night and fled to St. Louis. There I worked in the composing-room of the Evening News for a time, and then started on my travels to see the world. The world was New York City, and there was a little World's Fair there. It had just been opened where the great reservoir afterward was, and where the sumptuous public library is now being built—Fifth Avenue and 42d Street. I arrived in New York with two or three dollars in pocket change and a ten-dollar bank bill concealed in the lining of my coat. I got work at villainous wages in the establishment of John A. Gray & Green in Cliff Street, and I found board in a sufficiently villainous mechanics' boarding-house in Duane Street. The firm paid my wages in wildcat money at its face value, and my week's wage merely sufficed to pay board and lodging. By and by I went to Philadelphia and worked there some months as a "sub" on the Inquirer and the Public Ledger. Finally I made a flying trip to Washington to see the sights there, and in 1854 I went back to the Mississippi Valley, sitting upright in the smoking-car two or three days and nights. When I reached St. Louis I was exhausted. I went to bed on board a steamboat that was bound for Muscatine. I fell asleep at once, with my clothes on, and didn't wake again for thirty-six hours.

I worked in that little job office in Keokuk as much as two years, I should say, without ever collecting a cent of wages, for Orion was never able to pay anything—but Dick Higham and I had good times. I don't know what Dick got, but it was probably only uncashable promises.

One day in the midwinter of 1856 or 1857—I think it was 1856—I was coming along the main street of Keokuk in the middle of the forenoon. It was bitter weather—so bitter that that street was deserted, almost. A light dry snow was blowing here and there on the ground and on the pavement, swirling this way and that way and making all sorts of beautiful figures, but very chilly to look at. The wind blew a piece of paper past me and it lodged against a wall of a house. Something about the look of it attracted my attention and I gathered it in. It was a fifty-dollar bill, the only one I had ever seen, and the largest assemblage of money I had ever seen in one spot. I advertised it in the papers and suffered more than a thousand dollars' worth of solicitude and fear and distress during the next few days lest the owner should see the advertisement and come and take my fortune away. As many as four days went by without an applicant; then I could endure this kind of misery no longer.

I felt sure that another four could not go by in this safe and secure way. I felt that I must take that money out of danger. So I bought a ticket for Cincinnati and went to that city. I worked there several months in the printing-office of Wrightson & Company. I had been reading Lieutenant Herndon's account of his explorations of the Amazon and had been mightily attracted by what he said of coca. I made up my mind that I would go to the head-waters of the Amazon and collect coca and trade in it and make a fortune. I left for New Orleans in the steamer Paul Jones with this great idea filling my mind. One of the pilots of that boat was Horace Bixby. Little by little I got acquainted with him, and pretty soon I was doing a lot of steering for him in his daylight watches. When I got to New Orleans I inquired about ships leaving for Pará and discovered that there weren't any, and learned that there probably wouldn't be any during that century. It had not occurred to me to inquire about these particulars before leaving Cincinnati, so there I was. I couldn't get to the Amazon. I had no friends in New Orleans and no money to speak of. I went to Horace Bixby and asked him to make a pilot out of me. He said he would do it for five hundred dollars, one hundred dollars cash in advance. So I steered for him up to St. Louis, borrowed the money from my brother-in-law, and closed the bargain. I had acquired this brother-in-law several years before. This was Mr. William A. Moffett, a merchant, a Virginian—a fine man in every way. He had married my sister Pamela, and the Samuel E. Moffett of whom I have been speaking was their son. Within eighteen months I was become a competent pilot, and I served that office until the Mississippi River traffic was brought to a standstill by the breaking out of the Civil War.

Meantime Orion had been sweating along with his little job office in Keokuk, and he and his wife were living with his wife's family—ostensibly as boarders, but it is not likely that Orion was ever able to pay the board. On account of charging nothing for the work done in his job office, he had almost nothing to do there. He was never able to get it through his head that work done on a profitless basis deteriorates and is presently not worth anything, and that customers are obliged to go where they can get better work, even if they must pay better prices for it. He had plenty of time, and he took up Blackstone again. He also put up a sign which offered his services to the public as a lawyer. He never got a case, in those days, nor even an applicant, although he was quite willing to transact law business for nothing and furnish the stationery himself. He was always liberal that way.

Presently he moved to a wee little hamlet called Alexandria, two or three miles down the river, and he put up that sign there. He got no bites. He was by this time very hard aground. But by this time I was beginning to earn a wage of two hundred and fifty dollars a month as pilot, and so I supported him thenceforth until 1861, when his ancient friend, Edward Bates, then a member of Mr. Lincoln's first Cabinet, got him the place of Secretary of the new Territory of Nevada, and Orion and I cleared for that country in the overland stagecoach, I paying the fares, which were pretty heavy, and carrying with me what money I had been able to save—this was eight hundred dollars, I should say—and it was all in silver coin and a good deal of a nuisance because of its weight. And we had another nuisance, which was an Unabridged Dictionary. It weighed about a thousand pounds, and was a ruinous expense, because the stagecoach company charged for extra baggage by the ounce. We could have kept a family for a time on what that dictionary cost in the way of extra freight—and it wasn't a good dictionary, anyway—didn't have any modern words in it—only had obsolete ones that they used to use when Noah Webster was a child.

Friday, March 30, 1906

Mr. Clemens's interview with Tchaykoffsky.—Presides at a meeting of the association formed in interest of the adult blind.—His first meeting with Helen Keller.—Helen Keller's letter, which Mr. Clemens read at this meeting.

I will drop Orion for the present and return and pick him up by and by. For the moment I am more interested in the matters of to-day than I am in Orion's adventures and mine of forty-five years ago.

Three days ago a neighbor brought the celebrated Russian revolutionist, Tchaykoffsky, to call upon me. He is grizzled, and shows age—as to exteriors—but he has a Vesuvius, inside, which is a strong and active volcano yet. He is so full of belief in the ultimate and almost immediate triumph of the revolution and the destruction of the fiendish autocracy, that he almost made me believe and hope with him. He has come over here expecting to arouse a conflagration of noble sympathy in our vast nation of eighty millions of happy and enthusiastic freemen. But honesty obliged me to pour some cold water down his crater. I told him what I believed to be true: that our Christianity which we have always been so proud of—not to say so vain of—is now nothing but a shell, a sham, a hypocrisy; that we have lost our ancient sympathy with oppressed peoples struggling for life and liberty; that when we are not coldly indifferent to such things we sneer at them, and that the sneer is about the only expression the newspapers and the nation deal in with regard to such things; that his mass meetings would not be attended by people entitled to call themselves representative Americans, even if they may call themselves Americans at all; that his audiences will be composed of foreigners who have suffered so recently that they have not yet had time to become Americanized and their hearts turned to stone in their breasts; that these audiences will be drawn from the ranks of the poor, not those of the rich; that they will give and give freely, but they will give from their poverty and the money result will not be large. I said that when our windy and flamboyant President conceived the idea, a year ago, of advertising himself to the world as the new Angel of Peace, and set himself the task of bringing about the peace between Russia and Japan and had the misfortune to accomplish his misbegotten purpose, no one in all this nation except Doctor Seaman and myself uttered a public protest against this folly of follies. That at that time I believed that that fatal peace had postponed the Russian nation's imminent liberation from its age-long chains indefinitely—probably for centuries; that I believed at that time that Roosevelt had given the Russian revolution its death-blow, and that I am of that opinion yet.

I will mention here, in parenthesis, that I came across Doctor Seaman last night for the first time in my life, and found that his opinion also remains to-day as he expressed it at the time that that infamous peace was consummated.

Tchaykoffsky said that my talk depressed him profoundly, and that he hoped I was wrong.

I said I hoped the same.

He said, "Why, from this very nation of yours came a mighty contribution only two or three months ago, and it made us all glad in Russia. You raised two millions of dollars in a breath—in a moment, as it were—and sent that contribution, that most noble and generous contribution, to suffering Russia. Does not that modify your opinion?"

"No," I said, "it doesn't. That money came not from Americans, it came from Jews; much of it from rich Jews, but the most of it from Russian and Polish Jews on the East Side—that is to say, it came from the very poor. The Jew has always been benevolent. Suffering can always move a Jew's heart and tax his pocket to the limit. He will be at your mass meetings. But if you find any Americans there put them in a glass case and exhibit them. It will be worthy fifty cents a head to go and look at that show and try to believe in it."

He asked me to come to last night's meeting and speak, but I had another engagement and could not do it. Then he asked me to write a line or two which could be read at the meeting, and I did that cheerfully.

(From The New York Times.)

Arms to Free Russia, Tchaykoffsky's Appeal

Revolutionist Speaks to Cheering Audience of 3,000

Says the Battle is Near

Mark Twain Writes That He Hopes Czars and Grand Dukes Will Soon Become Scarce

"Tovarishzy!"

When Nicholas Tchaykoffsky, hailed by his countrymen here as the father of the revolutionary movement in Russia, spoke this word last night in Grand Central Palace 3,000 men and women rose to their feet, waved their hats, and cheered madly for three minutes. The word means "Comrades!" It is the watchword of the revolutionists. The spirit of revolution possessed the mass meeting called to greet the Russian patriot now visiting New York.

Fight is what he wants, and arms to fight with. He told the audience so last night and, by their cheers, they promised to do their part in supplying the sinews of war.

Mark Twain could not attend because he had already accepted an invitation to another meeting, but he sent this letter:

DEAR MR. TCHAYKOFFSKY:

I thank you for the honor of the invitation, but I am not able to accept it because Thursday evening I shall be presiding at a meeting whose object is to find remunerative work for certain classes of our blind who would gladly support themselves if they had the opportunity.

My sympathies are with the Russian revolution, of course. It goes without saying. I hope it will succeed, and now that I have talked with you I take heart to believe it will. Government by falsified promises, by lies, by treachery, and by the butcher knife, for the aggrandizement of a single family of drones and its idle and vicious kin has been borne quite long enough in Russia, I should think. And it is to be hoped that the roused nation, now rising in its strength, will presently put an end to it and set up the republic in its place. Some of us, even the white-headed, may live to see the blessed day when czars and grand dukes will be as scarce there as I trust they are in heaven.

Most sincerely yours,
MARK TWAIN

Mr. Tchaykoffsky made an impassioned appeal for help to inaugurate a real revolution and overturn the Czar and all his allies.

THE ENGAGEMENT WHICH I SPOKE of to Tchaykoffsky was to act as chairman at the first meeting of the association which was formed five months ago in the interest of the adult blind. Joseph H. Choate and I had a very good time there, and I came away with the conviction that that excellent enterprise is going to flourish, and will bear abundant fruit. The State of New York contains six thousand listed blind persons and also a thousand or so who have not been searched out and listed. There are between three and four hundred blind children. The state confines its benevolence to these. It confers upon them a book education. It teaches them to read and write. It feeds them and shelters them. And of course it pauperizes them, because it furnishes them no way of earning a living for themselves. The state's conduct toward the adult blind—and this conduct is imitated by the legislatures of most of the other states—is purely infamous. Outside of the blind asylums the adult blind person has a hard time. He lives merely by the charity of the compassionate, when he has no relatives able to support him—and now and then, as a benevolence, the state stretches out its charitable hand and lifts him over to Blackwell's Island and submerges him among that multitudinous population of thieves and prostitutes.

But in Massachusetts, in Pennsylvania, and in two or three other states, associations like this new one we have formed have been at work for some years, supported entirely by private subscriptions, and the benefits conferred and the work accomplished are so fine and great that their official reports read like a fairy-tale. It seems almost proven that there are not so very many things accomplishable by persons gifted with sight which a blind person cannot learn to do and do as well as that other person.

Helen Keller was to have been present last night, but she is ill in bed and has been ill in bed during several weeks, through overwork in the interest of the blind, the deaf, and the dumb. I need not go into any particulars about Helen Keller. She is fellow to Caesar, Alexander, Napoleon, Homer, Shakespeare, and the rest of the immortals. She will be as famous a thousand years from now as she is to-day.

I remember the first time I ever had the privilege of seeing her. She was fourteen years old then. She was to be at Laurence Hutton's house on a Sunday afternoon, and twelve or fifteen men and women had been invited to come and see her. Henry Rogers and I went together. The company had all assembled and had been waiting awhile. The wonderful child arrived now, with her about equally wonderful teacher, Miss Sullivan. The girl began to deliver happy exclamations, in her broken speech. Without touching anything, and without seeing anything, of course, and without hearing anything, she seemed to quite well recognize the character of her surroundings. She said, "Oh the books, the books, so many, many books. How lovely!"

The guests were brought one after another and introduced to her. As she shook hands with each she took her hand away and laid her fingers lightly against Miss Sullivan's lips, who spoke against them the person's name. When a name was difficult, Miss Sullivan not only spoke it against Helen's fingers, but spelled it upon Helen's hand with her own fingers—stenographically, apparently, for the swiftness of the operation was suggestive of that.

Mr. Howells seated himself by Helen on the sofa and she put her fingers against his lips and he told her a story of considerable length, and you could see each detail of it pass into her mind and strike fire there and throw the flash of it into her face. Then I told her a long story, which she interrupted all along and in the right places, with cackles, chuckles, and care-free bursts of laughter. Then Miss Sullivan put one of Helen's hands against her lips and spoke against it the question, "What is Mr. Clemens distinguished for?" Helen answered, in her crippled speech, "For his humor." I spoke up modestly and said, "And for his wisdom." Helen said the same words instantly—"And for his wisdom." I suppose it was a case of mental telegraphy, since there was no way for her to know what it was I had said.

After a couple of hours spent very pleasantly, some one asked if Helen would remember the feel of the hands of the company after this considerable interval of time, and be able to discriminate the hands and name the possessors of them. Miss Sullivan said, "Oh, she will have no difficulty about that." So the company filed past, shook hands in turn, and with each handshake Helen greeted the owner of the hand pleasantly and spoke the name that belonged to it without hesitation, until she encountered Mr. Rogers, toward the end of the procession. She shook hands with him, then paused, and a reflecting expression came into her face. Then she said: "I am glad to meet you now. I have not met you before." Miss Sullivan told her she was mistaken; this gentleman was introduced to her when she first arrived in the room. But Helen was not affected by that. She said no, she never had met this gentleman before. Then Mr. Rogers said that perhaps the confusion might be explained by the fact that he had his glove on when he was introduced to Helen. Of course that explained the matter.

This was not in the afternoon, as I have misstated. It was in the forenoon, and by and by the assemblage proceeded to the dining-room and sat down to luncheon. I had to go away before it was over, and as I passed by Helen I patted her lightly on the head and passed on. Miss Sullivan called to me and said: "Stop, Mr. Clemens. Helen is distressed because she did not recognize your hand. Won't you come back and do that again?" I went back and patted her lightly on the head, and she said at once, "Oh, it's Mr. Clemens."

Perhaps some one can explain this miracle, but I have never been able to do it. Could she feel the wrinkles in my hand through her hair? Some one else must answer this. I am not competent.

As I have said, Helen was not able to leave her sick-bed, but she wrote a letter, two or three days ago, to be read at the meeting, and Miss Holt, the secretary, sent it to me by a messenger at mid-afternoon yesterday. It was lucky for me that she didn't reserve it and send it to me on the platform last night, for in that case I could not have gotten through with it. I read it to the house without a break in my voice, and also without even a tremor in it that could be noticed, I think. But it was because I had read it aloud to Miss Lyon at mid-afternoon, and I knew the dangerous places and how to be prepared for them. I told the house in the beginning that I had this letter and that I would read it at the end of the evening's activities. By and by when the end had arrived and Mr. Choate had spoken, I introduced the letter with a few words. I said that if I knew anything about literature, here was a fine and great and noble sample of it; that this letter was simple, direct, unadorned, unaffected, unpretentious, and was moving and beautiful and eloquent; that no fellow to it had ever issued from any girl's lips since Joan of Arc, that immortal child of seventeen, stood alone and friendless in her chains, five centuries ago, and confronted her judges—the concentrated learning and intellect of France—and fenced with them week by week and day by day, answering them out of her great heart and her untaught but marvelous mind, and always defeating them, always camping on the field and master of it as each day's sun went down. I said I believed that this letter, written by a young woman who has been stone deaf, dumb, and blind ever since she was eighteen months old, and who is one of the most widely and thoroughly educated women in the world, would pass into our literature as a classic and remain so. I will insert the letter here.

WRENTHAM, MASS., March 27, 1906

MY DEAR MR. CLEMENS:

It is a great disappointment to me not to be with you and the other friends who have joined their strength to uplift the blind. The meeting in New York will be the greatest occasion in the movement which has so long engaged my heart: and I regret keenly not to be present and feel the inspiration of living contact with such an assembly of wit, wisdom and philanthropy. I should be happy if I could have spelled into my hand the words as they fall from your lips, and receive, even as it is uttered, the eloquence of our newest Ambassador to the blind. We have not had such advocates before. My disappointment is softened by the thought that never at any meeting was the right word so sure to be spoken. But, superfluous as all other appeal must seem after you and Mr. Choate have spoken, nevertheless, as I am a woman, I cannot be silent, and I ask you to read this letter, knowing that it will be lifted to eloquence by your kindly voice.

To know what the blind man needs, you who can see must imagine what it would be not to see, and you can imagine it more vividly if you remember that before your journey's end you may have to go the dark way yourself. Try to realize what blindness means to those whose joyous activity is stricken to inaction.

It is to live long, long days, and life is made up of days. It is to live immured, baffled, impotent, all God's world shut out. It is to sit helpless, defrauded, while your spirit strains and tugs at its fetters, and your shoulders ache for the burden they are denied, the rightful burden of labor.

The seeing man goes about his business confident and self-dependent. He does his share of the work of the world in mine, in quarry, in factory, in counting-room, asking of others no boon, save the opportunity to do a man's part and to receive the laborer's guerdon. In an instant accident blinds him. The day is blotted out. Night envelops all the visible world. The feet which once bore him to his task with firm and confident stride stumble and halt and fear the forward step. He is forced to a new habit of idleness, which like a canker consumes the mind and destroys its beautiful faculties. Memory confronts him with his lighted past. Amid the tangible ruins of his life as it promised to be he gropes his pitiful way. You have met him on your busy thoroughfares with faltering feet and outstretched hands, patiently "dredging" the universal dark, holding out for sale his petty wares, or his cap for your pennies; and this was a Man with ambitions and capabilities.

It is because we know that these ambitions and capabilities can be fulfilled, that we are working to improve the condition of the adult blind. You cannot bring back the light to the vacant eyes; but you can give a helping hand to the sightless along their dark pilgrimage. You can teach them new skill. For work they once did with the aid of their eyes you can substitute work that they can do with their hands. They ask only opportunity, and opportunity is a torch in darkness. They crave no charity, no pension, but the satisfaction that comes from lucrative toil, and this satisfaction is the right of every human being.

At your meeting New York will speak its word for the blind, and when New York speaks, the world listens. The true message of New York is not the commercial ticking of busy telegraphs, but the mightier utterances of such gatherings as yours. Of late our periodicals have been filled with depressing revelations of great social evils. Querulous critics have pointed to every flaw in our civic structure. We have listened long enough to the pessimists. You once told me you were a pessimist, Mr. Clemens, but great men are usually mistaken about themselves. You are an optimist. If you were not, you would not preside at the meeting. For it is an answer to pessimism. It proclaims that the heart and the wisdom of a great city are devoted to the good of mankind, that in this busiest city in the world no cry of distress goes up but receives a compassionate and generous answer. Rejoice that the cause of the blind has been heard in New York; for the day after, it shall be heard round the world.

Yours sincerely,
HELEN KELLER

Monday, April 2, 1906
Government of new Territory of Nevada.—Governor Nye and the practical jokers.—Mr. Clemens begins journalistic life on Virginia City "Enterprise"—reports legislative sessions.—He and Orion prosper.—Orion builds $12,000 house.—Governor Nye turns Territory of Nevada into a state.

Present Postmaster at Washington to be Made Collector at
Niagara—Platt Not Consulted.

(Special to The New York Times.)

Washington, March 31.—President Roosevelt surprised the capital
this afternoon by announcing that he would appoint Benjamin F.
Barnes as Postmaster of Washington, to succeed John A. Merritt of
New York. Mr. Merritt, who for several years has been Postmaster here,
has been chosen for Collector of the Port of Niagara, succeeding the
late Major James Low.

Mr. Barnes is at present assistant secretary to the President. Only
a short time ago he figured extensively in the newspapers for having
ordered the forcible ejection from the White House of Mrs. Minor
Morris, a Washington woman who had called to see the President.
What attracted attention to the case was not the ejection itself, but the
violence with which it was performed.

Mrs. Morris, who had been talking to Barnes in an ordinary
conversational tone, and with no indications of excitement, so far as
the spectators observed, was seized by two policemen and dragged by
the arms out of the building and across the asphalt walk in front of the
White House, a distance corresponding to that of two ordinary city
blocks. During a part of the journey a negro carried her by the feet. Her
dress was torn and trampled.

She was locked up on a charge of disorderly conduct, and when it
was learned that she would be released on that charge a policeman, a
relative of Barnes's, was sent to the House of Detention to prefer a charge
of insanity against her so that she would have to be held. She was held
accordingly until two physicians had examined her and pronounced her
sane. He was denounced by Mrs. Morris, by various newspapers, and by
Mr. Tillman in the Senate.

The appointment of Barnes to be Postmaster so soon after
this incident has created endless talk here. It is taken to be the
President's way of expressing confidence in Barnes and repaying him

for the pain he suffered as a result of the newspaper criticisms of his course.

ORION CLEMENS AGAIN. TO CONTINUE.

The government of the new Territory of Nevada was an interesting menagerie. Governor Nye was an old and seasoned politician from New York—politician, not statesman. He had white hair. He was in fine physical condition. He had a winningly friendly face and deep lustrous brown eyes that could talk as a native language the tongue of every feeling, every passion, every emotion. His eyes could outtalk his tongue, and this is saying a good deal, for he was a very remarkable talker, both in private and on the stump. He was a shrewd man. He generally saw through surfaces and perceived what might be going on inside without being suspected of having an eye on the matter.

When grown-up persons indulge in practical jokes, the fact gauges them. They have lived narrow, obscure, and ignorant lives, and at full manhood they still retain and cherish a job lot of leftover standards and ideals that would have been discarded with their boyhood if they had then moved out into the world and a broader life. There were many practical jokers in the new Territory. I do not take pleasure in exposing this fact, for I liked those people; but what I am saying is true. I wish I could say a kindlier thing about them instead. If I could say they were burglars, or hatrack thieves, or something like that, that wouldn't be utterly uncomplimentary. I would prefer it, but I can't say those things. They would not be true. These people were practical jokers, and I will not try to disguise it. In other respects they were plenty good enough people; honest people; reputable and likable. They played practical jokes upon each other with success, and got the admiration and applause and also the envy of the rest of the community. Naturally they were eager to try their arts on big game, and that was what the Governor was. But they were not able to score. They made several efforts, but the Governor defeated these efforts without any trouble and went on smiling his pleasant smile as if nothing had happened. Finally the joker chiefs of Carson City and Virginia City conspired together to see if their combined talent couldn't win a victory, for the jokers were getting into a very uncomfortable place. The people were laughing at them, instead of at their proposed victim. They banded themselves together to the number of ten and invited the Governor to what was a most extraordinary attention in those days—pickled-oyster stew and champagne—luxuries very seldom seen in that region, and existing rather as fabrics of the imagination than as facts.

The Governor took me with him. He said, disparagingly: "It's a poor invention. It doesn't deceive. Their idea is to get me drunk and leave me under the table, and from their standpoint this will be very funny. But they don't know me. I am familiar with champagne and have no prejudices against it."

The fate of the joke was not decided until two o'clock in the morning. At that hour the Governor was serene, genial, comfortable, contented, happy, and sober, although he was so full that he couldn't laugh without shedding champagne tears. Also, at that hour the last joker joined his comrades under the table, drunk to the last perfection. The Governor remarked: "This is a dry place, Sam. Let's go and get something to drink and go to bed."

The Governor's official menagerie had been drawn from the humblest ranks of his constituents at home—harmless good fellows who had helped in his campaigns, and now they had their reward in petty salaries payable in greenbacks that were worth next to nothing. Those boys had a hard time to make both ends meet. Orion's salary was eighteen hundred dollars a year, and he couldn't even support his dictionary on it. But the Irishwoman who had come out on the Governor's staff charged the menagerie only ten dollars a week apiece for board and lodging. Orion and I were of her boarders and lodgers; and so, on these cheap terms the silver I had brought from home held out very well.

At first I roamed about the country seeking silver, but at the end of '62 or the beginning of '63 when I came up from Aurora to begin a journalistic life on the Virginia City Enterprise, I was presently sent down to Carson City to report the legislative session. Orion was soon very popular with the members of the legislature, because they found that whereas they couldn't usually trust each other, nor anybody else, they could trust him. He easily held the belt for honesty in that country, but it didn't do him any good in a pecuniary way, because he had no talent for either persuading or scaring legislators. But I was differently situated. I was there every day in the legislature to distribute compliment and censure with evenly balanced justice and spread the same over half a page of the Enterprise every morning; consequently I was an influence. I got the legislature to pass a law requiring every corporation doing business in the territory to record its charter in full, without skipping a word, in a record to be kept by the Secretary of the Territory—my brother. All the charters were framed in exactly the same words. For this record service he was authorized to charge forty cents a folio of one hundred words for making the record; five dollars for furnishing a certificate of each record, and so on. Everybody had a toll-road franchise, but no toll road. But the franchise had to be recorded and paid for. Everybody was a mining corporation, and had to have himself recorded and pay for it. Very well, we prospered. The record service paid an average of one thousand dollars a month, in gold.

Governor Nye was often absent from the Territory. He liked to run down to San Francisco every little while and enjoy a rest from Territorial civilization. Nobody complained, for he was prodigiously popular. He had been a stage-driver in his early days in New York or New England, and had acquired the habit of remembering names and faces, and of making himself agreeable to his passengers. As a politician this had been valuable to him, and he kept his arts in good condition by practice. By the time he had been Governor a year he had shaken hands with every human being in the Territory of Nevada, and after that he always knew these people instantly at sight and could call them by name. The whole population, of 20,000 persons, were his personal friends, and he could do anything he chose to do and count upon their being contented with it. Whenever he was absent from the Territory—which was generally—Orion served his office in his place, as Acting Governor, a title which was soon and easily shortened to "Governor." Mrs. Governor Clemens enjoyed being a Governor's wife. No one on this planet ever enjoyed a distinction more than she enjoyed that one. Her delight in being the head of society was so frank that it disarmed criticism, and even envy. Being the Governor's wife and head of society, she looked for a proper kind of house to live in—a house commensurate with these dignities—and she easily persuaded Orion to build that house. Orion could be persuaded to do anything. He built and furnished the house at a cost of twelve thousand dollars, and there was no other house in that capital that could approach this property for style and cost.

When Governor Nye's four-year term was drawing to a close, the mystery of why he had ever consented to leave the great State of New York and help inhabit that sage-brush desert was solved. He had gone out there in order to become a United States Senator. All that was now necessary was to turn the Territory into a State. He did it without any difficulty. That patch of sand and that sparse population were not well fitted for the heavy burden of a State government, but no matter, the people were willing to have the change, and so the Governor's game was made.

Orion's game was made, too, apparently, for he was as popular because of his honesty as the Governor was for more substantial reasons. But at the critical moment the inborn capriciousness of his character rose up without warning, and disaster followed.

Wednesday, April 4, 1906

The Morris case again.—Scope of this autobiography, a mirror.—More about Nast sale; laurels for Mr. Clemens.—Clippings in regard to Woman's University Club reception; Mr. Clemens comments on them.—Vassar benefit at Hudson Theater; Mr. Clemens meets many old friends.

MRS. MORRIS CASE IN SENATE

NOMINATION OF BARNES OPENS WAY FOR AN INQUIRY

(Special to The New York Times.)

WASHINGTON, April 3.—Criticism of the appointment of Mr. Roosevelt's Assistant Secretary, B. F. Barnes, to be Postmaster of Washington continues. It now seems likely that the appointment may have a hard time in passing the Senate. Barnes's action in having Mrs. Minor Morris put out of the White House is the chief ground of opposition. The Senate Committee on Post Offices and Post Roads has determined to investigate Barnes's action in the Morris case, and eye witnesses of the affair have been summoned to appear before the committee to-morrow and tell what they saw. This is the same investigation which Mr. Tillman requested and which the Senate refused to grant. It now comes as the result of the President's action in appointing Barnes Postmaster. The witnesses who are to appear before the committee were not asked to testify in the investigation which the President made when he decided that Barnes's course was justified.

There was much speculation to-day as to who Mr. Barnes's successor as Assistant Secretary would be. The Evening Star to-night devotes a column and a half to suggestions on the subject, saying that the leading candidates are John L. McGrew, a clerk in the White House offices; Warren Young, Chief Executive Clerk; M. C. Latta, the President's personal stenographer; James J. Corbett of New York, Robert Fitzsimmons, Augustus Ruhlin, and James J. Jeffries.

The article is illustrated with two pictures of Corbett and Fitzsimmons.

THAT IS NEAT, AND CAUSES me much gentle delight. The point of that whole matter lies in the last four names that are mentioned in it. These four men are prize-fighters—the most celebrated ones now living.

Is the incident now closed? Again we cannot tell. The smell of it may linger in American history a thousand years yet.

This autobiography of mine differs from other autobiographies—differs from all other autobiographies, except Benvenuto's, perhaps. The conventional biography of all the ages is an open window. The autobiographer sits there and examines and discusses the people that go by—not all of them, but the notorious ones, the famous ones; those that wear fine uniforms, and crowns when it is not raining; and very great poets and great statesmen—illustrious people with whom he has had the high privilege of coming in contact. He likes to toss a wave of recognition to these with his hand as they go by, and he likes to notice that the others are seeing him do this, and admiring. He likes to let on that in discussing these occasional people that wear the good clothes he is only interested in interesting his reader and is in a measure unconscious of himself.

But this autobiography of mine is not that kind of an autobiography. This autobiography of mine is a mirror, and I am looking at myself in it all the time. Incidentally I notice the people that pass along at my back—I get glimpses of them in the mirror—and whenever they say or do anything that can help advertise me and flatter me and raise me in my own estimation, I set these things down in my autobiography. I rejoice when a king or a duke comes my way and makes himself useful to this autobiography, but they are rare customers, with wide intervals between. I can use them with good effect as lighthouses and monuments along my way, but for real business I depend upon the common herd.

Here is some more about the Nast sale:

MARK TWAIN

30 CENTS FOR MCCURDY POEM.
OTHER LITERARY CURIOSITIES FROM THE NAST
COLLECTION AT AUCTION.

The sale of autograph letters, wash drawings, pencil and pen and ink sketches, the property of the late Thomas Nast, the cartoonist, was continued yesterday by the Merwin-Clayton Company.

Five letters from Theodore Roosevelt as Police Commissioner, colonel of the Rough Riders, Governor, and President, to Mr. Nast, thanking him for sketches and expressing warm friendship for the cartoonist, brought prices ranging from $1.50 to $2.25.

Richard A. McCurdy's autograph letter and original autograph poem addressed to Nast, with a typewritten copy of the poem, brought 30 cents the lot.

The following letter written by Gen. Philip H. Sheridan to Nast was bid in at $12.25 by J. H. Manning, a son of the late Daniel Manning:

May 12, 1875.

DEAR NAST:

"It is true. I will be married on the 30th of June coming unless there is a slip between the cup and the lip, which is scarcely possible. I will not have any wedding for many reasons, among them the recent death of my father.

"I am very happy, but wish the d—d thing was over.

Yours truly,
SHERIDAN

"P. S. and M. I.—I send the inclosed for your oldest. Please send me yours to be kept for mine.

"P. H. S."

A letter written by Lincoln, and which was laid over a piece of white silk bearing a faded red stain, sold for $38. The attached certificate stated that the silk was from the dress of Laura Keene, worn on the night of Lincoln's assassination, and that the stain was made by his blood.

Gen. W. T. Sherman's letter to Nast, dated March 9, 1879, indorsing a testimonial of the cartoonist's services to the army and navy, sold for $6.

A scrapbook containing sketches of Lincoln, Sumner, Greeley, Walt Whitman, and many water-color sketches, brought $75.

A sketch of William M. Tweed and his companion, Hunt, under arrest, brought $21. Two companion Christmas sketches by Nast, representing a child telephoning to Santa Claus, brought $43 each. A sketch of Gen. Grant was bid in for $36. A sketch of the "G. O. P." elephant brought $28. A sketch representing the Saviour, full face, with nimbus, brought $65.

An autograph photograph of Theodore Roosevelt, dated 1884, was bid in at $5.

It is a great satisfaction to me to notice that I am still ahead— ahead of Roosevelt, ahead of Sherman, ahead of Sheridan, even ahead of Lincoln. These are fine laurels, but they will not last. A time is coming when some of them will wither. A day will come when a mere scratch of Mr. Lincoln's pen will outsell a whole basketful of my letters. A time will come when a scratch of the pens of those immortal soldiers, Sherman and Sheridan, will outsell a thousand scratches of mine, and so I shall enjoy my supremacy now, while I may. I shall read that clipping over forty or fifty times, now, while it is new and true, and let the desolating future take care of itself.

Day before yesterday all Vassar, ancient and modern, packed itself into the Hudson Theater, and I was there. The occasion was a benefit arranged by Vassar and its friends to raise money to aid poor students of that college in getting through the college course. I was not aware that I was to be a feature of the show, and was distressed and most uncomfortably inflamed with blushes when I found it out. Really the distress and the blushes were manufactured, for at bottom I was glad. I held a reception on that stage for an hour or two, and all Vassar, ancient and modern, shook hands with me. Some of the moderns were too beautiful for words, and I was very friendly with those. I was so hoping somebody would want to kiss me for my mother, but I didn't dare to suggest it myself. Presently, however, when it happened, I did what I could to make it contagious, and succeeded. This required art, but I had it in stock. I seemed to take the old and the new as they came, without discrimination, but I averaged the percentage to my advantage, and without anybody's suspecting, I think.

Among that host I met again as many as half a dozen pretty old girls whom I had met in their bloom at Vassar that time that Susy and I visited the college so long ago. Yesterday at the University Club, almost all the five hundred were of the young and lovely, untouched by care, unfaded by age. There were girls there from Smith, Wellesley, Radcliffe, Vassar, and Barnard, together with a sprinkling of college girls from the South, from the Middle West and the Pacific coast.

I delivered a moral sermon to the Barnard girls at Columbia University a few weeks ago, and now it was like being among old friends. There were dozens of Barnard girls there, scores of them, and I had already shaken hands with them at Barnard. As I have said, the reporter heard many things there yesterday, but there were several which he didn't hear. One sweet creature wanted to whisper in my ear, and I was nothing loath. She raised her dainty form on tiptoe, lifting herself with a grip of her velvet hands on my shoulders, and put her lips to my ear and said, "How do you like being the belle of New York?" It was so true, and so gratifying, that it crimsoned me with blushes, and I could make no reply. The reporter lost that.

Two girls, one from Maine, the other from Ohio, were grandchildren of fellow-passengers who sailed with me in the Quaker City in the Innocents Abroad excursion thirty-nine years ago.

Thursday, April 5, 1906

Ellen Terry's farewell banquet, on fiftieth anniversary.—Mr. Clement's cablegram.—Mr. Clemens has fine new idea for a play; Mr. Hammond Trumbull squelches it.—Orion Clemens is defeated as Secretary of State.—At Mr. Camp's suggestion Mr. Clemens speculates unfortunately.—Mr. Camp offers to buy Tennessee land for $200,000.— Orion refuses.—Mr. Clemens just discovers that he still owns one thousand acres of the Tennessee land.—Orion comes East, gets position on Hartford "Evening Post."—After various business ventures he returns to Keokuk and tries raising chickens.

The other day I furnished a sentiment in response to a man's request— to wit:

"The noblest work of God?" Man.

"Who found it out?" Man.

I thought it was very good, and smart, but the other person didn't. . .

Ellen Terry has been a queen of the English stage for fifty years, and will retire from it on the 28th of this month, which will be the fiftieth anniversary. She will retire in due form at a great banquet in

London, and cablegrams meet for the occasion will flow in upon the banqueters from old friends of hers in America and other formerly distant regions of the earth—there are no distant regions now. The American cablegrams are being collected by a committee in New York, and by request I have furnished mine. To do these things by cable, at twenty-five cents a word, is the modern way and the only way. They could go by post at no expense, but it wouldn't be good form. (Privately I will remark that they do go by mail—dated to suit the requirements.)

Cablegram to Ellen Terry, London.

Age has not withered, nor custom staled, the admiration and affection I have felt for you so many many years. I lay them at your honored feet with the strength and freshness of their youth upon them undiminished.

MARK TWAIN

She is a lovely character, as was also Sir Henry Irving, who lately departed this life. I first knew them thirty-four years ago in London, and thenceforth held them in high esteem and affection.

ORION CLEMENS RESUMED

There were several candidates for all the offices in the gift of the new State of Nevada save two—United States Senator (Governor Nye) and Secretary of State (Orion Clemens). Nye was certain to get a Senatorship, and Orion was so sure to get the Secretaryship that no one but him was named for that office. But he was hit with one of his spasms of virtue on the very day that the Republican party was to make its nominations in the convention. Orion refused to go near the convention. He was urged, but all persuasions failed. He said his presence there would be an unfair and improper influence, and that if he was to be nominated the compliment must come to him as a free and unspotted gift. This attitude would have settled his case for him without further effort, but he had another spasm of virtue on the same day, and that made it absolutely sure. It had been his habit for a great many years to change his religion with his shirt, and his ideas about temperance at the same time. He would be a teetotaler for a while and the champion of the cause; then he would change to the other side for a time. On nomination day he suddenly changed from a friendly attitude toward whisky—which was the popular attitude—to uncompromising teetotalism, and went absolutely dry. His friends besought and implored, but all in vain. He could not be persuaded to cross the threshold of a saloon. The paper next morning contained the list of chosen nominees. His name was not in it. He had not received a vote.

His rich income ceased when the State government came into power. He was without an occupation. Something had to be done. He put up his sign as attorney at law, but he got no clients. It was strange. It was difficult to account for. I cannot account for it—but if I were going to guess at a solution I should guess that by the make of him he would examine both sides of a case so diligently and so conscientiously that when he got through with his argument neither he nor a jury would know which side he was on. I think that his client would find out his make in laying his case before him, and would take warning and withdraw it in time to save himself from probable disaster.

I had taken up my residence in San Francisco about a year before the time I have just been speaking of. One day I got a tip from Mr. Camp, a bold man who was always making big fortunes in ingenious speculations and losing them again in the course of six months by other speculative ingenuities. Camp told me to buy some shares in the Hale and Norcross. I bought fifty shares at three hundred dollars a share. I bought on a margin, and put up 20 per cent. It exhausted my funds. I wrote Orion and offered him half, and asked him to send his share of the money. I waited and waited. He wrote and said he was going to attend to it. The stock went along up pretty briskly. It went higher and higher. It reached a thousand dollars a share. It climbed to two thousand, then to three thousand; then to twice that figure. The money did not come, but I was not disturbed. By and by that stock took a turn and began to gallop down. Then I wrote urgently. Orion answered that he had sent the money long ago—said he had sent it to the Occidental Hotel. I inquired for it. They said it was not there. To cut a long story short, that stock went on down until it fell below the price I had paid for it. Then it began to eat up the margin, and when at last I got out I was very badly crippled.

When it was too late, I found out what had become of Orion's money. Any other human being would have sent a check, but he sent gold. The hotel clerk put it in the safe and never thought of it again, and there it reposed all this time, enjoying its fatal work, no doubt. Another man might have thought to tell me that the money was not in a letter, but was in an express package, but it never occurred to Orion to do that.

Later, Mr. Camp gave me another chance. He agreed to buy our Tennessee land for two hundred thousand dollars, pay a part of the amount in cash and give long notes for the rest. His scheme was to import foreigners from grape-growing and wine-making districts in Europe, settle them on the land, and turn it into a wine-growing country. He knew what Mr. Longworth thought of those Tennessee grapes, and was satisfied. I sent the contracts and things to Orion for his signature, he being one of the three heirs. But they arrived at a bad time—in a doubly bad time, in fact. The temperance virtue was temporarily upon him in strong force, and he wrote and said that he would not be a party to debauching the country with wine. Also he said how could he know whether Mr. Camp was going to deal fairly and honestly with those poor people from Europe or not?—and so, without waiting to find out, he quashed the whole trade, and there it fell, never to be brought to life again. The land, from being suddenly worth two hundred thousand dollars, became as suddenly worth what it was before—nothing, and taxes to pay. I had paid the taxes and the other expenses for some years, but I dropped the Tennessee land there, and have never taken any interest in it since, pecuniarily or otherwise, until yesterday.

I had supposed, until yesterday, that Orion had frittered away the last acre, and indeed that was his impression. But a gentleman arrived yesterday from Tennessee and brought a map showing that by a correction of the ancient surveys we still own a thousand acres, in a coal district, out of the hundred thousand acres which my father left us when he died in 1847. The gentleman brought a proposition; also he brought a reputable and well-to-do citizen of New York. The proposition was that the Tennesseean gentleman should sell that land; that the New York gentleman should pay all the expenses and fight all the lawsuits, in case any should turn up, and that of such profit as might eventuate the Tennesseean gentleman should take a third, the New Yorker a third, and Sam Moffett and his sister (Mrs. Charles L. Webster), and I—who are the surviving heirs—the remaining third.

This time I hope we shall get rid of the Tennessee land for good and all and never hear of it again. It was created under a misapprehension; my father loaded himself up with it under a misapprehension; he unloaded it on to us under a misapprehension, and I should like to get rid of the accumulated misapprehensions and what is left of the land as soon as possible.

I came East in January, 1867. Orion remained in Carson City perhaps a year longer. Then he sold his twelve-thousand-dollar house and its furniture for thirty-five hundred in greenbacks at about 30 per cent discount. He and his wife took first-class passage in the steamer for New York. In New York they stopped at an expensive hotel; explored the city in an expensive way; then fled to Keokuk, and arrived there about as nearly penniless as they were when they had migrated thence in July, '61. About 1871 or '72 they came to New York. They were obliged to go somewhere. Orion had been trying to make a living in the law ever since he had arrived from the Pacific coast, but he had secured only two cases. Those he was to try free of charge—but the possible result will never be known, because the parties settled the case out of court without his help.

I had bought my mother a house in Keokuk. I was giving her a stated sum monthly, and Orion another stated sum. They all lived together in the house.

But, as I say, they came East and Orion got a job as proofreader on the New York Evening Post at ten dollars a week. They took a single small room, and in it they cooked, and lived on that money. By and by Orion came to Hartford and wanted me to get him a place as reporter on a Hartford paper. Here was a chance to try my scheme again, and I did it. I made him go to the Hartford Evening Post, without any letter of introduction, and propose to scrub and sweep and do all sorts of things for nothing, on the plea that he didn't need money, but only needed work, and that was what he was pining for. Within six weeks he was on the editorial staff of that paper at twenty dollars a week, and he was worth the money. He was presently called for by some other paper at better wages, but I made him go to the Post people and tell them about it. They stood the raise and kept him. It was the pleasantest berth he had ever had in his life. It was an easy berth. He was in every way comfortable. But ill luck came. It was bound to come.

A new Republican daily was to be started in Rutland, Vermont, by a stock company of well-to-do politicians, and they offered Orion the chief editorship at three thousand a year. He was eager to accept. His wife was equally eager—no, twice as eager, three times as eager. My beseechings and reasonings went for nothing. I said:

"You are as weak as water. Those people will find it out right away. They will easily see that you have no backbone; that they can deal with you as they would deal with a slave. You may last six months, but not longer. Then they will not dismiss you as they would dismiss a gentleman: they will fling you out as they would fling out an intruding tramp."

It happened just so. Then Orion and his wife migrated to that persecuted and unoffending Keokuk once more. Orion wrote from there that he was not resuming the law; that he thought that what his health needed was the open air, in some sort of outdoor occupation; that his old father-in-law had a strip of ground on the river border a mile above Keokuk with some sort of a house on it, and his idea was to buy that place and start a chicken farm and provide Keokuk with chickens and eggs, and perhaps butter—but I don't know whether you can raise butter on a chicken farm or not. He said the place could be had for three thousand dollars cash, and I sent the money. Orion began to raise chickens, and he made a detailed monthly report to me, whereby it appeared that he was able to work off his chickens on the Keokuk people at a dollar and a quarter a pair. But it also appeared that it cost a dollar and sixty cents to raise the pair. This did not seem to discourage Orion, and so I let it go. Meantime he was borrowing a hundred dollars per month of me regularly, month by month. Now to show Orion's stern and rigid business ways—and he really prided himself on his large business capacities—the moment he received the advance of a hundred dollars at the beginning of each month, he sent me his note for the amount, and with it he sent, out of that money, three months' interest on the hundred dollars at 6 per cent per annum, these notes being always for three months. I did not keep them, of course. They were of no value to anybody.

As I say, he always sent a detailed statement of the month's profit and loss on the chickens—at least the month's loss on the chickens—and this detailed statement included the various items of expense—corn for the chickens, a bonnet for the wife, boots for himself, and so on; even car fares, and the weekly contribution of ten cents to help out the missionaries who were trying to damn the Chinese after a plan not satisfactory to those people. But at last when among those details I found twenty-five dollars for pew rent I struck. I told him to change his religion and sell the pew.

Mr. Clemens's present house unsatisfactory because of no sunshine.—
Mr. Clemens meets Etta in Washington Square. Recalls ballroom in
Virginia City forty-four years ago.—Orion resumed; he invents wood-
sawing machine; invents steam canal boat.—Orion's autobiography.—
His death.

This house is No. 21 Fifth Avenue, and stands on the corner of Ninth
Street within a couple of hundred yards of Washington Square. It was
built fifty or sixty years ago by Renwick, the architect of the Roman
Catholic Cathedral. It is large, and every story has good and spacious
rooms, but not enough sunshine.

Yesterday I went down to Washington Square, turned out to the
left to look at a house that stands on the corner of the Square and
University Place. Presently I stepped over to the corner of the Square
to take a general look at the frontage of the house. While crossing the
street I met a woman, and was conscious that she recognized me, and it
seemed to me that there was something in her face that was familiar to
me. I had the instinct that she would turn and follow me and speak to
me, and the instinct was right. She was a fat little woman, with a gentle
and kindly but aged and homely face, and she had white hair, and was
neatly but poorly dressed. She said:

"Aren't you Mr. Clemens?"

"Yes," I said, "I am."

She said, "Where is your brother Orion?"

"Dead," I said.

"Where is his wife?"

"Dead," I said; and added, "I seem to know you, but I cannot place
you."

She said, "Do you remember Etta Booth?"

I had known only one Etta Booth in my lifetime, and that Etta
rose before me in an instant, and vividly. It was almost as if she stood
alongside of this fat little antiquated dame in the bloom and diffidence
and sweetness of her thirteen years, her hair in plaited tails down
her back and her fiery-red frock stopping short at her knees. Indeed
I remembered Etta very well. And immediately another vision rose
before me, with that child in the center of it and accenting its sober
tint like a torch with her red frock. But it was not a quiet vision; not
a reposeful one. The scene was a great ballroom in some ramshackle

building in Gold Hill or Virginia City, Nevada. There were two or three hundred stalwart men present and dancing with cordial energy. And in the midst of the turmoil Etta's crimson frock was swirling and flashing; and she was the only dancer of her sex on the floor. Her mother, large, fleshy, pleasant, and smiling, sat on a bench against the wall in lonely and honored state and watched the festivities in placid contentment. She and Etta were the only persons of their sex in the ballroom. Half of the men represented ladies, and they had a handkerchief tied around the left arm so that they could be told from the men. I did not dance with Etta, for I was a lady myself. I wore a revolver in my belt, and so did all the other ladies—likewise the gentlemen. It was a dismal old barn of a place, and was lighted from end to end by tallow-candle chandeliers made of barrel hoops suspended from the ceiling, and the grease dripped all over us. That was in the beginning of the winter of 1862. It has taken forty-four years for Etta to cross my orbit again.

I asked after her father.

"Dead," she said.

I asked after her mother.

"Dead," she said.

Another question brought out the fact that she had long been married, but had no children. We shook hands and parted. She walked three or four steps, then turned and came back, and her eyes filled, and she said:

"I am a stranger here, and far from my friends—in fact I have hardly any friends left. Nearly all of them are dead. I must tell my news to you. I must tell it to somebody. I can't bear it by myself, while it is so new. The doctor has just told me that my husband can live only a very little while, and I was not dreaming it was so bad as this."

Orion Resumed

I think the poultry experiment lasted only a year, possibly two years. It had then cost me six thousand dollars. It is my impression that Orion was not able to give the farm away, and that his father-in-law took it back as a kindly act of self-sacrifice.

Orion returned to the law business, and I suppose he remained in that harness off and on for the succeeding quarter of a century, but so far as my knowledge goes he was only a lawyer in name, and had no clients.

My mother died in her eighty-eighth year, in the summer of 1890. She had saved some money, and she left it to me, because it had come from me. I gave it to Orion and he said, with thanks, that I had supported him long enough and now he was going to relieve me of that burden and would also hope to pay back some of that expense, and maybe the whole of it. Accordingly, he proceeded to use up that money in building a considerable addition to the house, with the idea of taking boarders and getting rich. We need not dwell upon this venture. It was another of his failures. His wife tried hard to make the scheme succeed, and if anybody could have made it succeed she would have done it. She was a good woman and was greatly liked. Her vanity was pretty large and inconvenient, but she had a practical side, too, and she would have made that boarding-house lucrative if circumstances had not been against her.

Orion had other projects for recouping me, but as they always required capital I stayed out of them, but they did not materialize. Once he wanted to start a newspaper. It was a ghastly idea, and I squelched it with a promptness that was almost rude. Then he invented a wood-sawing machine and patched it together himself, and he really sawed wood with it. It was ingenious; it was capable; and it would have made a comfortable little fortune for him; but just at the wrong time Providence interfered again. Orion applied for a patent and found that the same machine had already been patented and had gone into business and was thriving.

Presently the State of New York offered a fifty-thousand-dollar prize for a practical method of navigating the Erie Canal with steam canal boats. Orion worked at that thing two or three years, invented and completed a method, and was once more ready to reach out and seize upon imminent wealth, when somebody pointed out a defect. His steam canal boat could not be used in the wintertime; and in the summertime the commotion its wheels would make in the water would wash away the State of New York on both sides.

Innumerable were Orion's projects for acquiring the means to pay off his debt to me. These projects extended straight through the succeeding thirty years, but in every case they failed. During all those thirty years Orion's well-established honesty kept him in offices of trust where other people's money had to be taken care of, but where no salary was paid. He was treasurer of all the benevolent institutions; he took care of the money and other property of widows and orphans; he never lost a cent for anybody, and never made one for himself. Every time he changed his religion the church of his new faith was glad to get him; made him treasurer at once, and at once he stopped the graft and the leaks in that church. He exhibited a facility in changing his political complexion that was a marvel to the whole community. Once this curious thing happened, and he wrote me all about it himself.

One morning he was a Republican, and upon invitation he agreed to make a campaign speech at the Republican mass meeting that night. He prepared the speech. After luncheon he became a Democrat and agreed to write a score of exciting mottoes to be painted upon the transparencies which the Democrats would carry in their torchlight procession that night. He wrote these shouting Democratic mottoes during the afternoon, and they occupied so much of his time that it was night before he had a chance to change his politics again; so he actually made a rousing Republican campaign speech in the open air while his Democratic transparencies passed by in front of him, to the joy of every witness present.

He was a most strange creature—but in spite of his eccentricities he was beloved, all his life, in whatsoever community he lived. And he was also held in high esteem, for at bottom he was a sterling man.

About twenty-five years ago—along there somewhere—I wrote and suggested to Orion that he write an autobiography. I asked him to try to tell the straight truth in it; to refrain from exhibiting himself in creditable attitudes exclusively, and to honorably set down all the incidents of his life which he had found interesting to him, including those which were burned into his memory because he was ashamed of them. I said that this had never been done, and that if he could do it his autobiography would be a most valuable piece of literature. I said I was offering him a job which I could not duplicate in my own case, but I would cherish the hope that he might succeed with it. I recognize now that I was trying to saddle upon him an impossibility. I have been dictating this autobiography of mine daily for three months; I have thought of fifteen hundred or two thousand incidents in my life which I am ashamed of, but I have not gotten one of them to consent to go on paper yet. I think that that stock will still be complete and unimpaired when I finish this autobiography, if I ever finish it. I believe that if I should put in all those incidents I would be sure to strike them out when I came to revise this book.

While we were living in Vienna in 1898 a cablegram came from

Keokuk announcing Orion's death. He was seventy-two years old. He had gone down to the kitchen in the early hours of a bitter December morning; he had built the fire, and then sat down at a table to write something, and there he died, with the pencil in his hand and resting against the paper in the middle of an unfinished word—an indication that his release from the captivity of a long and troubled and pathetic and unprofitable life was swift and painless.

Monday, April 9, 1906

Letter from French girl inclosing cable about "Huck Finn."—The Juggernaut Club.—Letter from librarian of Brooklyn Public Library in regard to "Huckleberry Finn" and "Tom Sawyer."—Mr. Clemens's reply.—The deluge of reporters trying to discover contents of that letter.

This morning's mail brings me from France a letter from a French friend of mine, inclosing this New York cablegram:

Mark Twain Interdit

New York, 27 mars. (Par dépêche de notre correspondant particulier.)—Les directeurs de la bibliothèque de Brooklyn ont mis les deux derniers livres de Mark Twain à l'index pour les enfants au-dessous de quinze ans, les considérant comme malsains.

Le célèbre humoriste a écrit a des fonctionnaires une lettre pleine d'esprit et de sarcasme. Ces messieurs se refusent à la publier, sous le prétexte qu'ils n'ont pas l'autorisation de l'auteur de le faire.

The letter is from a French girl who lives at St. Dié, in Joan of Arc's region. I have never seen this French girl, but she wrote me about five years ago and since then we have exchanged friendly letters three or four times a year. She closes her letter with this paragraph:

Something in a newspaper that I read this morning has surprised me very much. I have cut it out because, often, these informations are forged and, if this is the case, the slip of paper will be my excuse. Please, allow me to smile, my dear unseen Friend! I cannot imagine for a minute that you have been very sorry about it.—In France, such a measure would have for immediate result to make every one in the country buy these books, and I—for one,—am going to get them as soon as I go through Paris, perfectly sure that I'll find them as wholesome as all you have written. I know your pen well. I know it has never been dipped in anything but clean, clear ink.

I MUST GO BACK NOW to that French cablegram. Its information is not exactly correct, but it is near enough. Huck Finn and Tom Sawyer are not recent books. Tom is more than thirty years old. The other book has been in existence twenty-one years. When Huck appeared, twenty-one years ago, the public library of Concord, Massachusetts, flung him out indignantly, partly because he was a liar and partly because after deep meditation and careful deliberation he made up his mind on a difficult point, and said that if he'd got to betray Jim or go to hell, he would go to hell—which was profanity, and those Concord purists couldn't stand it.

After this disaster, Huck was left in peace for sixteen or seventeen years. Then the public library of Denver flung him out. He had no similar trouble until four or five months ago—that is to say, last November. At that time I received the following letter:

SHEEPSHEAD BAY BRANCH
BROOKLYN PUBLIC LIBRARY
1657 SHORE ROAD
BROOKLYN-NEW YORK, Nov. 19th, '05

DEAR SIR:

I happened to be present the other day at a meeting of the children's librarians of the Brooklyn Public Library. In the course of the meeting it was stated that copies of "Tom Sawyer" and "Huckleberry Finn" were to be found in some of the children's rooms of the system. The Sup't of the Children's Dep't—a conscientious and enthusiastic young woman—was greatly shocked to hear this, and at once ordered that they be transferred to the adults' department. Upon this I shamefacedly confessed to having read "Huckleberry Finn" aloud to my defenseless blind people, without regard to their age, color, or previous condition of servitude. I also reminded them of Brander Matthews's opinion of the book, and stated the fact that I knew it almost at heart, having got more pleasure from it than from any book I have ever read, and reading is the greatest pleasure I have in life. My warm defense elicited some further discussion and criticism, from which I gathered that the prevailing opinion of Huck was that he was a deceitful boy who said "sweat" when he should have said "perspiration." The upshot of the matter was that there is to be further consideration of these books at a meeting early in January which I am especially invited to attend. Seeing you the other night at the performance of "Peter Pan" the thought came to me that you (who know Huck as well as I—you can't know him better or love him more—) might be willing to give me a word or two to say in witness of his good character though he "warn't no more quality than a mud cat."

I would ask as a favor that you regard this communication as confidential, whether you find time to reply to it or not; for I am loath for obvious reasons to bring the institution from which I draw my salary into ridicule, contempt or reproach.

Yours very respectfully,
Asa Don Dickinson
(In charge Department for the Blind
and Sheepshead Bay Branch, Brooklyn Public Library.)

That was a very private letter. I didn't know the author of it, but I thought I perceived that he was a safe man and that I could venture to write a pretty private letter in return and trust that he would not allow its dreadful contents to leak out and get into the newspapers. I wrote him on the 21st:

21 Fifth Avenue,
November 21, 1905

Dear Sir:

I am greatly troubled by what you say. I wrote Tom Sawyer and Huck Finn for adults exclusively, and it always distresses me when I find that boys and girls have been allowed access to them. The mind that becomes soiled in youth can never again be washed clean; I know this by my own experience, and to this day I cherish an unappeasable bitterness against the unfaithful guardians of my young life, who not only permitted but compelled me to read an unexpurgated Bible through before I was 15 years old. None can do that and ever draw a clean sweet breath again this side of the grave. Ask that young lady—she will tell you so.

Most honestly do I wish I could say a softening word or two in defence of Huck's character, since you wish it, but really in my opinion it is no better than those of Solomon, David, Satan, and the rest of the sacred brotherhood.

If there is an unexpurgated in the Children's Department, won't you please help that young woman remove Huck and Tom from that questionable companionship? Sincerely yours,

(Signed) S. L. CLEMENS

I shall not show your letter to anyone—it is safe with me.
A couple of days later I received this handsome rejoinder in return:

SHEEPSHEAD BAY BRANCH
BROOKLYN PUBLIC LIBRARY
1657 SHORE ROAD
BROOKLYN-NEW YORK, Nov. 23rd, '05

DEAR SIR:

Your letter rec'd. I am surprised to hear that you think Huck and Tom would have an unwholesome effect on boys and girls. But relieved to hear that you would not place them in the same category with many of the scriptural reprobates. I know of one boy who made the acquaintance of Huck in 1884, at the age of eight, and who has known him intimately ever since, and I can assure you he is not an atom the worse for the 20 years' companionship. On the contrary he will always feel grateful to Huck's father—I don't mean Pop—for the many hours spent with him and Jim, when sickness and sorrow were forgotten.

Huckleberry Finn was the first book I selected to read to my blind (for selfish reasons I am afraid), and the amount of innocent enjoyment it gave them, has never been equalled by anything I have since read.

Thanking you for the almost unhoped for courtesy of your reply, I am

Yours very respectfully,
ASA DON DICKINSON

MARK TWAIN

Four months drifted tranquilly by. Then there was music! There came a freshet of newspaper reporters and they besieged my secretary all day. Of course I was in bed. I am always in bed. She barred the stairs against them. They were bound to see me, if only for a moment, but none of them got by her guard. They said a report had sprung up that I had written a letter some months before to the Brooklyn Public Library; that according to that report the letter was pungent and valuable, and they wanted a copy of it. They said the head officials of the Brooklyn Library declared that they had never seen the letter and that they had never heard of it until the reporters came and asked for it. I judged by this that my man—who was not in the head library, but in a branch of it—was keeping his secret all right, and I believed he could be trusted to continue to keep that secret, for his own sake as well as mine. That letter would be a bombshell for me if it got out—but it would hoist him, too. So I feel pretty confident that for his own sake, if for no other, he would protect me.

My secretary had a hard day of it, but I had a most enjoyable one. She never allowed any reporter to get an idea of the nature of the letter; she smoothed all those young fellows down and sent them away empty.

They renewed the assault next day, but I told her to never mind—human nature would win the victory for us. There would be an earthquake somewhere, or a municipal upheaval here, or a threat of war in Europe—something would be sure to happen in the way of a big excitement that would call the boys away from No. 21 Fifth Avenue for twenty-four hours, and that would answer every purpose; they wouldn't think of that letter again, and we should have peace.

I knew the reporters would get on the right track very soon, so I wrote Mr. Dickinson and warned him to keep his mouth hermetically sealed. I told him to be wise and wary. His answer bears date March 28th.

> BAY RIDGE BRANCH
> BROOKLYN PUBLIC LIBRARY
> 73D STREET AND SECOND AVENUE
> BROOKLYN-NEW YORK, Mar. 28, '06

DEAR MR. CLEMENS:

Your letter of the 26th inst. rec'd this moment. As I have now been transferred to the above address, it has been a long time reaching me.

I have tried to be wary and wise and am very grateful to you for your reticence. The poor old B. P. L. has achieved some very undesirable notoriety. I thought my head was coming off when I heard from my chief on the telephone night before last. But yesterday he began to be amused, I think, at the teapot tempest.

Last night I reached home at 11.30 and found a Herald man sitting on the steps, leaning his head against the door post. He had been there since 7.30 and said he would cheerfully sit there till morning if I would give him the least hint of the letter's contents. But I was wise and wary.

At the January meeting it was decided not to place Huck and Tom in the Children's rooms along with "Little Nellie's Silver Mine" and "Dotty Dimple at Home." But the books have not been "restricted" in any sense whatever. They are placed on open shelves among the adult fiction, and any child is free to read adult fiction if he chooses.

I am looking forward with great eagerness to seeing and hearing you to-morrow night at the Waldorf. As I have a wild scheme for a national library for the blind, they have been generous enough to place a couple of boxes at my disposal. The "young lady" whom you mentioned in your letter—the Sup't of the Children's Dep't—and several other B. P. L.'s, I hope will be present.

I am very sorry to have caused you so much annoyance through reporters, but be sure that I have said nothing nor will say anything to them about the contents of that letter. And please don't you tell on me!

Yours very respectfully,
ASA DON DICKINSON

I saw him at the Waldorf the next night, where Choate and I made our public appeal in behalf of the blind, and found him to be a very pleasant and safe and satisfactory man.

Now that I have heard from France, I think the incident is closed—for it had its brief run in England, two or three weeks ago, and in Germany also. When people let Huck Finn alone he goes peacefully along, damaging a few children here and there and yonder, but there will be plenty of children in heaven without those, so it is no great matter. It is only when well-meaning people expose him that he gets his real chance to do harm. Temporarily, then, he spreads havoc all around in the nurseries and no doubt does prodigious harm while he has his chance. By and by, let us hope, people that really have the best interests of the rising generation at heart will become wise and not stir Huck up.

Tuesday, April 10, 1906

Child's letter about "Huckleberry Finn" being flung out of Concord Library.—Ambassador White's autobiography.—Mr. Clemens's version of the Fiske-Cornell episode.—Another example of his great scheme for finding employment for the unemployed.—This client wins the Fiske lawsuit.

When Huck Finn was flung out of the Concord Public Library twenty-one years ago, a number of letters of sympathy and indignation reached me—mainly from children, I am obliged to admit—and I kept some of them so that I might reread them now and then and apply them as a salve to my soreness. I have overhauled those ancient letters this morning and among them I find one from a little girl who resents that library's treatment of Huck and then goes innocently along and gives me something more of a dig than even the library had done. She says:

I AM ELEVEN YEARS OLD, and I live on a farm near Rockville, Maryland. Once this winter we had a boy to work for us named John. We lent him "Huck Finn" to read, and one night he let his clothes out of the window and left in the night. The last we heard from him he was out in Ohio; and father says if we had lent him "Tom Sawyer" to read he would not have stopped on this side of the ocean.

BLESS HER GENTLE HEART, SHE was trying to cheer me up, and her effort is entitled to the praise which the country journalist conferred upon the Essex band after he had praised the whole Fourth of July celebration in detail, and had exhausted his stock of compliments. But he was obliged to lay something in the nature of a complimentary egg, and with a final heroic effort he brought forth this, "The Essex band done the best they could."

I have been reading another chapter or two in Ambassador White's autobiography, and I find the book charming, particularly where he talks about me. I find any book charming that talks about me. I am expecting this one of mine to do something in that line, and it is my purpose that it shall not lose sight of that subject long at a time. Mr. White was the first president of Cornell University, and he gives the university's side of the Willard Fiske trouble. I stopped at that point. I didn't read his version, for I want to give another version first, and as this version may conflict with his, I wish to set it down now before its complexion shall have a chance to undergo a change by coming in contact with his version.

This brings me back to another example of my great scheme for finding work for the unemployed. The famous Fiske-Cornell episode of a quarter of a century ago grew up in this way. About fifty years ago, when Willard Fiske was a poor and untaught and friendless boy of thirteen, he and Bayard Taylor took steerage passage in a sailing ship and crossed the ocean. They found their way to Iceland, and Willard Fiske remained there a year or two. He acquired the Norse languages and perfected himself in them. He also became an expert scholar in the literature of those languages. By and by he returned to America, and while still a very young man and hardly of age, he got a place as instructor in that kind of learning in the infant Cornell University. This seat of learning was at Ithaca, New York, and Mr. McGraw was a citizen of that little town. He had made a fortune in the electric telegraph, and it was his purpose to leave a large part of it to the university. He had a lovely young daughter, and she and young Fiske fell in love with each other. They were aware of this; the girl's parents were aware of it; the university was aware of it; Ithaca was aware of it. All these parties expected Fiske to propose, but he didn't do it. There was no way to account for it, and so all the parties, including the girl, went on from month to month and year to year in a condition of suppressed surprise, waiting for the mystery to solve itself. Which it still didn't do. At last Mr. McGraw died, and the fact developed that he had left no will. Therefore the daughter was sole heir. However, she knew what her father's intention had been, so she turned over to the university a good part of the fortune and thus made the intention good.

The years drifted along and the relations between Fiske and Miss McGraw remained the same. But there was no proposal. Fiske had a quite definite reason for not proposing. It was that he was very poor and the girl very rich, and he was not willing to seem to marry her for her money. This was good morals, good principle, good sentiment—but it was not business. Things remained just in this way for years and years, and the devotion of the couple to each other went along unimpaired by time. At last, when they were well stricken in years, and when Miss McGraw had developed pulmonary consumption, she invited Fiske and Charles Dudley Warner and his wife to make a trip up the Nile with her in the old-fashioned dahabiyeh, a trip which occupied a matter of three months. Miss McGraw had already been on the other side of the ocean several months, and she had been buying all sorts of beautiful things—pictures, sculpture, costly rugs, and so on—wherewith to adorn a little palace which she was building in Ithaca.

At last there on board the dahabiyeh a sorrowful time came—for Miss McGraw's malady was making great progress and it was manifest that she could not live long. Then she came out frankly and said she wanted to marry Fiske so that she could leave her fortune to him. Fiske wanted to marry her, but his ideas remained unimpaired in his heart and head and he was not willing to accept the fortune. The Warners wrought with him. They used their best persuasions. He was as anxious for the marriage as was Miss McGraw, but he wouldn't accept the fortune. At last he was persuaded to a modification of the terms. He was willing to accept the little palace and its furnishings and three hundred thousand dollars; he would accept nothing more. The marriage took place. Mrs. Fiske made a will, and in the will she left the palace and its furnishings and three hundred thousand dollars to her husband, Willard Fisk. She left the residue of the fortune to Cornell University.

By and by Fiske arrived at an understanding of the fact that he had not acted wisely. The income of three hundred thousand dollars was wholly inadequate. He could not live in the Ithaca house on any such income as that. He did not try to live in it. There it stood, with all those beautiful things in it which Miss McGraw had gathered in her travels in Europe, and Fiske lived elsewhere—lived most comfortably elsewhere—lived where three hundred thousand dollars was really a fortune, and he was entirely satisfied. He lived in Italy. He was as dear and sweet a soul as I have ever known. His was a character which won friends for him, and whoso became his friend remained so, ever afterward.

Now followed this curious circumstance. Cornell had received by Mrs. Fiske's will a noble addition to its endowment—two million dollars, if I remember rightly. No doubt Cornell University was satisfied. But the university's lawyers, picking and searching around through Mrs. Fiske's will, found a defect in it which neither Mrs. Fiske nor Charley Warner, who drew the will, suspected was there. It was something about "residue." It was the opinion of those lawyers that the university might claim the little palace and its rich equipment, and make the claim good in a court of law.

The claim was put forward. Fiske and Warner were outraged by this insolence, this greed. Both knew that it was the desire of the dying wife that her husband should live in that house and have the sacred companionship of those things which had been selected by her own hands for its adornment. Both knew that but for Fiske's stubborn resistance he would have had not only the house, but a great sum of money besides, and now that the university proposed to take the house away from Fiske—well, it was time for the worm to turn. The worm turned. Fiske was the worm. Fiske resisted the university's claim and the university brought suit.

Now then, I must go back to a point antedating the bringing of this suit three or four years. One day in Hartford a young fellow called and wanted to see me. I think he said he was from Canada. He said he had a strong desire, an irresistible desire, to become a lawyer, and he thought that if he could get some work to do that would support him, he could meantime use his off hours, if he had any, in studying Blackstone. He thought he could be a journalist. He thought he could at least become a good reporter, and his idea was to get me to use my influence with the Hartford newspaper people to the end that he might get the sort of chance he was after.

I said: "Certainly, I will get you a berth in any newspaper in the town. Choose your own paper."

He was very grateful. These clients of mine always are, until they learn the conditions. I furnished him the conditions in the same old way. He considered a moment and then said:

"How simple that is; how sure it is; how certain it is; how actually infallible it is, human nature being constructed as it is—how is it that that has not been thought of before?" Then he added, as he went out of the door, "I choose the Courant, and I will have the job before night."

About three months afterward he came out to report progress. He had moved along so briskly, from sweeper-out, up through the several grades, that he was now on the editorial staff, and was very happy, particularly as staff work allowed him a good deal of off time for the study of the law, and the law was where his high ambition lay.

I come back now to that Fiske lawsuit. We had gone to Elmira one summer to spend the summer, as usual, at Quarry Farm, and we were visiting Mrs. Clemens's family down in the town for a while. A young man called and said he would like to see me. I went to the library and saw him there. It was the young man of whom I have been talking, but as I had not seen him for three or four years I did not at first recall him. He said that while he was on the Courant he saved all the money he could, and studied the law diligently in his off hours—that now, recently, he had given up journalism and was going to make a break into the law; that he had canvassed the field and had decided that he would become office assistant to David B. Hill of Elmira, New York—that is to say, he had decided to do this, evidently without requiring Mr. Hill to state whether he wanted it so or not. Hill was a very distinguished lawyer and a big politician, a man of vast importance and influence—and he is still that to-day, in his old age. The application was made and Hill said promptly that he didn't need anybody's assistance. But young Bacon said he didn't want any pay, he only wanted a chance to work; he could support himself. He would do anything that could be of any assistance to Mr. Hill, even to sweeping out the office; that he wanted to work, and he wanted to be near a man like Hill because he was determined to become a lawyer. Well, as he was not expensive and showed a determination that pleased Hill, Hill gave him office room. Very well, the usual thing happened, the thing that always happens. Little by little Bacon got to beguiling out of Hill things to do, and presently Hill was furnishing him the things to do without any beguilement.

"Now then," Bacon said, "Mr. Clemens, I've got a chance—I've got a chance." Professor Willard Fiske brought his case to Mr. Hill. Mr. Hill examined it carefully and declined to take it. He said Fiske had no case, and therefore he did not wish to take it merely to lose it. Fiske insisted, and presently Hill said: "Well, here's this young fellow here in my office. If he wants to take your case, all right; I will advise him and help him to the best of my ability without charge"; and he asked if Fiske was willing to put the case into Bacon's hands. Fiske did it.

Then young Bacon had this happy idea. There being nothing for Fiske in the apparent conditions, he went to the university charter to see what he might find there. He found a very pleasant thing there; to use a phrase of the day, he struck oil in that charter. He brought the charter to Mr. Hill and showed him this large fact: that Cornell University was not privileged to accept or to acquire any property if, at the time, it already possessed property worth three millions of dollars. Cornell University possessed property worth more than that at the time that Mrs. Fiske made her will, and it still possessed that amount.

Hill said, "Well, Bacon, the case is yours—that is to say, well, Bacon, the case is Fiske's. It is the university, now, that has no show."

Bacon won the case. It was his first case. He charged Fiske a hundred thousand dollars for his services. Fiske handed him the check, and his thanks therewith.

I didn't see Bacon again for some years—I don't know how many—and then he told me that that first lawsuit of his was also his last one; that that first fee of his was the only one he had ever received; that he had hardly pocketed his check until he ran across a most charming young widow possessed of a great fortune and he took them both in. I think I will say nothing more about my great scheme for providing jobs for the unemployed. I think I have proven that it is a good and effective scheme.

Wednesday, April 11, 1906

Mr. Frank Fuller and his enthusiastic launching of Mr. Clemens's first New York lecture.—Results not in fortune, but in fame.—Leads to a lecture tour under direction of Redpath.—Clipping in regard to Frank Fuller, and Mr. Clemens's comments.

I am not glancing through my books to find out what I have said in them. I refrain from glancing through those books for two reasons: first—and this reason always comes first in every matter connected with my life—laziness. I am too lazy to examine the books. The other reason is—well, let it go. I had another reason, but it had slipped out of my mind while I was arranging the first one. I think it likely that in the book called Roughing It I have mentioned Frank Fuller. But I don't know, and it isn't any matter.

When Orion and I crossed the continent in the overland stagecoach in the summer of 1861, we stopped two or three days in Great Salt Lake City. I do not remember who the Governor of Utah Territory was at that time, but I remember that he was absent—which is a common habit of territorial Governors, who are nothing but politicians who go out to the outskirts of countries and suffer the privations there in order to build up States and come back as United States Senators. But the man who was acting in the Governor's place was the Secretary of the Territory, Frank Fuller—called Governor, of course, just as Orion was in the great days when he got that accident-title through Governor Nye's absences. Titles of honor and dignity once acquired in a democracy, even by accident and properly usable for only forty-eight hours, are as permanent here as eternity is in heaven. You can never take away those titles. Once a justice of the peace for a week, always "judge" afterward. Once a major of militia for a campaign on the Fourth of July, always a major. To be called colonel, purely by mistake and without intention, confers that dignity on a man for the rest of his life. We adore titles and heredities in our hearts, and ridicule them with our mouths. This is our democratic privilege.

Well, Fuller was acting Governor, and he gave us a very good time during those two or three days that we rested in Great Salt Lake City. He was an alert and energetic man; a pushing man; a man who was able to take an interest in anything that was going—and not only that, but take five times as much interest in it as it was worth, and ten times as much as anybody else could take in it—a very live man.

I was on the Pacific coast thereafter five or six years, and returned to the States by the way of the Isthmus in January, '67. In the previous year I had spent several months in the Sandwich Islands for the Sacramento Union, and had returned to San Francisco empty as to cash, but full of information—information proper for delivery from the lecture platform. My letters from the Islands had given me a large notoriety—local notoriety. It did not extend eastward more than a hundred miles or so, but it was a good notoriety to lecture on, and I made use of it on the platform in California and Nevada and amassed twelve or fifteen hundred dollars in the few nights that I labored for the instruction and amusement of my public. Fifteen hundred dollars was about half—the doorkeeper got the rest. He was an old circus man and knew how to keep door.

When I arrived in New York I found Fuller there in some kind of business. He was very hearty, very glad to see me, and wanted to show me his wife. I had not heard of a wife before; had not been aware that he had one. Well, he showed me his wife, a sweet and gentle woman with most hospitable and kindly and winning ways. Then he astonished me by showing me his daughters. Upon my word, they were large and matronly of aspect, and married—he didn't say how long. Oh, Fuller was full of surprises. If he had shown me some little children, that would have been well enough, and reasonable. But he was too young-looking a man to have grown children. Well, I couldn't fathom the mystery and I let it go. Apparently it was a case where a man was well along in life, but had a handsome gift of not showing his age on the outside.

Governor Fuller—it is what all his New York friends called him now, of course—was in the full storm of one of his enthusiasms. He had one enthusiasm per day, and it was always a storm. He said I must take the biggest hall in New York and deliver that lecture of mine on the Sandwich Islands—said that people would be wild to hear me. There was something catching about that man's prodigious energy. For a moment he almost convinced me that New York was wild to hear me. I knew better. I was well aware that New York had never heard of me, was not expecting to hear of me, and didn't want to hear of me—yet that man almost persuaded me. I protested, as soon as the fire which he had kindled in me had cooled a little, and went on protesting. It did no good. Fuller was sure that I should make fame and fortune right away without any trouble. He said leave it to him—just leave everything to him—go to the hotel and sit down and be comfortable—he would lay fame and fortune at my feet in ten days.

I was helpless. I was persuadable, but I didn't lose all of my mind, and I begged him to take a very small hall, and reduce the rates to side-show prices. No, he would not hear of that—said he would have the biggest hall in New York City. He would have the basement hall in Cooper Institute, which seated three thousand people and there was room for half as many more to stand up; and he said he would fill that place so full, at a dollar a head, that those people would smother and he could charge two dollars apiece to let them out. Oh, he was all on fire with his project. He went ahead with it.

He said it shouldn't cost me anything. I said there would be no profit. He said: "Leave that alone. If there is no profit that is my affair. If there is profit it is yours. If it is loss, I stand the loss myself, and you will never hear of it."

He hired Cooper Institute, and he began to advertise this lecture in the usual way—a small paragraph in the advertising columns of the newspapers. When this had continued about three days I had not yet heard anybody or any newspaper say anything about that lecture, and I got nervous. "Oh," he said, "it's working around underneath. You don't see it on the surface." He said, "Let it alone; now, let it work."

Very well, I allowed it to work—until about the sixth or seventh day. The lecture would be due in three or four days more—still I was not able to get down underneath, where it was working, and so I was filled with doubt and distress. I went to Fuller and said he must advertise more energetically.

He said he would. So he got a barrel of little things printed that you hang on a string—fifty in a bunch. They were for the omnibuses. You could see them swinging and dangling around in every omnibus. My anxiety forced me to haunt those omnibuses. I did nothing for one or two days but sit in buses and travel from one end of New York to the other and watch those things dangle, and wait to catch somebody pulling one loose to read it. It never happened—at least it happened only once. A man reached up and pulled one of those things loose, said to his friend, "Lecture on the Sandwich Islands by Mark Twain. Who can that be, I wonder"—and he threw it away and changed the subject.

I couldn't travel in the omnibuses any more. I was sick. I went to Fuller and said: "Fuller, there is not going to be anybody in Cooper Institute that night, but you and me. It will be a dead loss, for we shall both have free tickets. Something must be done. I am on the verge of suicide. I would commit suicide if I had the pluck and the outfit." I said, "You must paper the house, Fuller. You must issue thousands of complimentary tickets. You must do this. I shall die if I have to go before an empty house that is not acquainted with me and that has never heard of me, and that has never traveled in the bus and seen those things dangle."

"Well," he said, with his customary enthusiasm, "I'll attend to it. It shall be done. I will paper that house, and when you step on the platform you shall find yourself in the presence of the choicest audience, the most intelligent audience, that ever a man stood before in this world."

And he was as good as his word. He sent whole basketsful of complimentary tickets to every public-school teacher within a radius of thirty miles of New York—he deluged those people with complimentary tickets—and on the appointed night they all came. There wasn't room in Cooper Institute for a third of them. The lecture was to begin at half past seven. I was so anxious that I had to go to that place at seven. I couldn't keep away.

I wanted to see that vast vacant Mammoth Cave and die. But when I got near the building I found that all the streets for a quarter of a mile around were blocked with people, and traffic was stopped. I couldn't believe that those people were trying to get into Cooper Institute, and yet that was just what was happening. I found my way around to the back of the building and got in there by the stage door. And sure enough, the seats, the aisles, the great stage itself, was packed with bright-looking human beings raked in from the centers of intelligence—the schools. I had a deal of difficulty to shoulder my way through the mass of people on the stage, and when I had managed it and stood before the audience, that stage was full. There wasn't room enough left for a child.

I was happy, and I was excited beyond expression. I poured the Sandwich Islands out on to those people with a free hand, and they laughed and shouted to my entire content. For an hour and fifteen minutes I was in Paradise. From every pore I exuded a divine delight— and when we came to count up we had thirty-five dollars in the house.

Fuller was just as jubilant over it as if it had furnished the fame and the fortune of his prophecy. He was perfectly delighted, perfectly enchanted. He couldn't keep his mouth shut for several days. "Oh," he said, "the fortune didn't come in—that didn't come in—that's all right. That's coming in later. The fame is already here, Mark. Why, in a week you'll be the best-known man in the United States. This is no failure. This is a prodigious success."

That episode must have cost him four or five hundred dollars, but he never said a word about that. He was as happy, as satisfied, as proud, as delighted, as if he had laid the fabled golden egg and hatched it.

He was right about the fame. I certainly did get a working quantity of fame out of that lecture. The New York newspapers praised it. The country newspapers copied those praises. The lyceums of the country— it was right in the heyday of the old lyceum lecture system—began to call for me. I put myself in Redpath's hands, and I caught the tail end of the lecture season. I went West and lectured every night, for six or eight weeks, at a hundred dollars a night—and I now considered that the whole of the prophecy was fulfilled. I had acquired fame, and also fortune. I don't believe these details are right, but I don't care a rap. They will do just as well as the facts. What I mean to say is, that I don't know whether I made that lecturing excursion in that year or whether it was the following year. But the main thing is that I made it, and that the opportunity to make it was created by that wild Frank Fuller and his insane and immortal project.

All this was thirty-eight or thirty-nine years ago. Two or three times since then, at intervals of years, I have run across Frank Fuller for a moment—only a moment, and no more. But he was always young. Never a gray hair; never a suggestion of age about him; always enthusiastic; always happy and glad to be alive. Last fall his wife's brother was murdered in a horrible way. Apparently a robber had concealed himself in Mr. Thompson's room, and in the night had beaten him to death with a club. A couple of months ago I ran across Fuller on the street, and he was looking so very, very old, so withered, so moldy, that I could hardly recognize him. He said his wife was dying of the shock caused by the murder of her brother; that nervous prostration was carrying her off, and she could not live more than a few days—so I went with him to see her.

She was sitting upright on a sofa and was supported all about with pillows. Now and then she leaned her head for a little while on a support. Breathing was difficult for her. It touched me, for I had seen that picture so many, many times. During two or three months Mrs. Clemens sat up like that, night and day, struggling for breath. When she was made drowsy by opiates and exhaustion she rested her head a little while on a support, just as Mrs. Fuller was doing, and got naps of two minutes' or three minutes' duration.

I did not see Mrs. Fuller alive again. She passed to her rest about three days later.

A NOTE ABOUT THE AUTHOR

Mark Twain (1835–1910) was an American humorist, novelist, and lecturer. Born Samuel Langhorne Clemens, he was raised in Hannibal, Missouri, a setting which would serve as inspiration for some of his most famous works. After an apprenticeship at a local printer's shop, he worked as a typesetter and contributor for a newspaper run by his brother Orion. Before embarking on a career as a professional writer, Twain spent time as a riverboat pilot on the Mississippi and as a miner in Nevada. In 1865, inspired by a story he heard at Angels Camp, California, he published "The Celebrated Jumping Frog of Calaveras County," earning him international acclaim for his abundant wit and mastery of American English. He spent the next decade publishing works of travel literature, satirical stories and essays, and his first novel, *The Gilded Age: A Tale of Today* (1873). In 1876, he published *The Adventures of Tom Sawyer*, a novel about a mischievous young boy growing up on the banks of the Mississippi River. In 1884 he released a direct sequel, *The Adventures of Huckleberry Finn*, which follows one of Tom's friends on an epic adventure through the heart of the American South. Addressing themes of race, class, history, and politics, Twain captures the joys and sorrows of boyhood while exposing and condemning American racism. Despite his immense success as a writer and popular lecturer, Twain struggled with debt and bankruptcy toward the end of his life, but managed to repay his creditors in full by the time of his passing at age 74. Curiously, Twain's birth and death coincided with the appearance of Halley's Comet, a fitting tribute to a visionary writer whose steady sense of morality survived some of the darkest periods of American history.

A NOTE FROM THE PUBLISHER

Spanning many genres, from non-fiction essays to literature classics to children's books and lyric poetry, Mint Edition books showcase the master works of our time in a modern new package. The text is freshly typeset, is clean and easy to read, and features a new note about the author in each volume. Many books also include exclusive new introductory material. Every book boasts a striking new cover, which makes it as appropriate for collecting as it is for gift giving. Mint Edition books are only printed when a reader orders them, so natural resources are not wasted. We're proud that our books are never manufactured in excess and exist only in the exact quantity they need to be read and enjoyed. To learn more and view our library, go to minteditionbooks.com

bookfinity & MINT EDITIONS

Enjoy more of your favorite classics with Bookfinity,
a new search and discovery experience for readers.
With Bookfinity, you can discover more vintage
literature for your collection, find your Reader Type,
track books you've read or want to read,
and add reviews to your favorite books.
Visit www.bookfinity.com, and click on
Take the Quiz to get started.

Don't forget to follow us
@bookfinityofficial and @mint_editions

CPSIA information can be obtained
at www.ICGtesting.com
Printed in the USA
JSHW021152200323
39186JS00008B/438